Date Due

MAR 19 2004			
5-11-04			

BRODART Cat. No. 23 233 Printed in U.S.A.

Springer Series: FOCUS ON WOMEN

Violet Franks, Ph.D., Series Editor

Confronting the major psychological, medical, and social issues of today and tomorrow. *Focus on Women* provides a wide range of books on the changing concerns of women.

1980
THE SAFETY OF FERTILITY CONTROL
Editor-in-Chief: Louis G. Keith, M.D.; Associate Editors: Deryck R. Kent, M.D.; Gary S. Berger, M.D., and Janelle R. Brittain, M.B.A.

1980
THERAPY WITH WOMEN: A Feminist Philosophy of Treatment
Susan Sturdivant, Ph.D.

1981
SHELTERING BATTERED WOMEN: A National Study and Service Guide
Albert R. Roberts, D.S.W.

1981
WOMEN OVER FORTY: Visions and Realities (2nd ed., 1989)
Jean D. Grambs, Ed.D.

1983
THE STEREOTYPING OF WOMEN: Its Effects on Mental Health
Violet Franks, Ph.D., and Esther D. Rothblum, Ph.D., Editors

1984
THE BATTERED WOMAN SYNDROME
Lenore E. Walker, Ed.D.

1984
WOMEN THERAPISTS WORKING WITH WOMEN: New Theory and Process of Feminist Therapy
Claire M. Brody, Ph.D., Editor

1986
CAREER GUIDE FOR WOMEN SCHOLARS
Suzanna Rose, Ph.D.

1986
A MOTE IN FREUD'S EYE: From Psychoanalysis to the Psychology of Women
Hannah Lerman, Ph.D.

1987
WOMEN'S THERAPY GROUPS: Paradigms of Feminist Treatment
Claire M. Brody, Ph.D, Editor

1987
WOMEN AND DEPRESSION: A Lifespan Perspective
Ruth Formanek, Ph.D., and Anita Gurian, Ph.D., Editors

1989
TRANSITIONS IN A WOMAN'S LIFE: Major Life Events in Developmental Context
Ramona T. Mercer, Ph.D., F.A.A.N., Elizabeth G. Nichols, D.N.S., F.A.A.N., Glen C. Doyle. Ed.D., R.N.

1992
NEW DIRECTIONS IN FEMINIST PSYCHOLOGY: Practice, Theory, and Research
Joan C. Chrisler, Ph.D., and Doris Howard, Ph.D., Editors

1993
THE EMPLOYED MOTHER AND THE FAMILY CONTEXT
Judith Frankel, Ph.D., Editor

1993
WOMEN AND ANGER
Sandra P. Thomas, Ph.D., R.N., Editor

1994
TREATING ABUSE IN FAMILIES: A Feminist and Community Approach
Elaine Leeder, M.S.W., C.S.W., M.P.H., Ph.D.

1995
WOMEN AND SUICIDAL BEHAVIOR
Silvia Sara Canetto, Ph.D., and David Lester, Ph.D., Editors

Silvia Sara Canetto, PhD, is an Assistant Professor of Psychology at Colorado State University. She has doctoral degrees from the University of Padova, Italy, and Northwestern University Medical School, Chicago, and a Master of Arts degree from the Hebrew University of Jerusalem. Dr. Canetto has published on gender, aging, life-threatening behaviors, and couple/family processes.

David Lester, PhD, has doctoral degrees from Brandeis University (in psychology) and the University of Cambridge (in social and political science). He has written over 350 scholarly articles and books on suicide and is past President of the International Association for Suicide Prevention.

WOMEN AND SUICIDAL BEHAVIOR

Silvia Sara Canetto, *PhD*

David Lester, *PhD*

Editors

SPRINGER PUBLISHING COMPANY

Springer Publishing Company, Inc.
536 Broadway
New York, NY 10012

Cover design by Tom Yabut
Production Editor: Pam Lankas

95 96 97 98 99 / 5 4 3 2 1

Library of Congress Cataloging-in-Publication Data

Women and suicidal behavior / Silvia Sara Canetto, David Lester, editors.
p. cm. — (Springer series, focus on women)
Includes bibliographical references and index.
ISBN 0-8261-8630-0
1. Women—Suicidal behavior—Cross-cultural studies.
I. Canetto, Silvia Sara. II. Lester, David, 1942– . III. Series.
HV6545.9.W66 1994
362.2′8′082—dc20 94-31918
CIP

Printed in the United States of America

Contents

Part V *Pre*vention, *Inter*vention and *Post*vention

Contributors

Maude H. Alston, PhD, is an Assistant Professor of Nursing at North Carolina Agricultural and Technical State University in Greensboro, North Carolina, where she teaches psychiatric nursing. She completed her doctorate in Child Development and Family Relations at the University of North Carolina at Greensboro with a dissertation entitled, *Suicide Among Women: An Occupational Model*. Her research interests include the impact of gender, race, and age on suicidal behaviors.

Sharon Eylar Anderson, PhD, is an Associate Professor of Nursing at Florida International University. Dr. Anderson is a sociologist with a masters degree in Community Health Nursing and masters and doctoral degrees in Sociology from the University of Colorado. Her research interests include suicide among minority and elderly populations and the effects of illness on the social integration of the aged.

Brenda J. Bettridge, PhD, is a child psychologist at the Child Development Centre in Cornwall, Ontario, Canada. She earned her doctorate from the University of Montreal and her masters from the University of Oregon. Her areas of specialization include female adolescent development, the psychology of gender, and self-destructive behaviors.

William M. Butler, PhD, is a Clinical Assistant Professor of Psychology at the University of Vermont. Dr. Butler specializes in the evaluation and treatment of both sexual offenders and survivors of sexual assault. He also conducts research in the area of hostage-taking. Dr. Butler received his doctorate in Clinical Psychology from the University of Vermont.

A. Kay Clifton, PhD, MSW, teaches social psychology and social work and chairs the Department of Behavioral Sciences at the College of Mount St. Joseph in Cincinnati. She trains, researches, and writes in the areas of women's physical and mental health and their relationship with the environment.

Susan A. Eisenhandler, PhD, is an Assistant Professor of Sociology at the University of Connecticut at Waterbury. Her research and publications have focused on the social construction of identity among community-dwelling older adults. Her work explores issues of personal and social autonomy, changes in health and orientation to time, and the kinds of social relations that sustain self and identity in later life.

Olga Eizner Favreau, PhD, obtained her doctorate degree at McGill University, Montreal, Canada. She is currently Professor of Psychology at the University of Montreal. She has conducted research on psychophysics and in women's studies and has published over 30 articles, some of which have appeared in *Science* and *Scientific American*. She is a fellow of the Canadian Psychological Association.

Karen M. Fondacaro, PhD,is a Clinical Assistant Professor of Psychology at the University of Vermont. Dr. Fondacaro's clinical and research focus is in the area of interpersonal violence. She works with victims and offenders of sexual assault and other violent crimes. She also conducts research on child maltreatment and the mental health of female and male offenders.

Beth Howard-Pitney, PhD, is a Senior Research Scientist at the Stanford Center for Research in Disease Prevention. Dr. Howard-Pitney received her doctorate in Social Psychology from the University of Minnesota, Minneapolis. Recent work includes research on evaluating training programs for alcohol service workers, community-based nutrition education, and American-Indian adolescent suicide prevention. She is an author of *Restoring Balance: Community-Directed Health Promotion for American Indians and Alaska Natives*.

Farah A. Ibrahim, PhD, is a Professor of Psychology in the Counseling Program at the University of Connecticut. She received her doctorate from Pennsylvania State University and masters degrees from Edinboro State University (USA) and the University of Peshawar (Pakistan). Her research has focused on abused women, Asian-American women, identity development from a gender and cultural perspective, transcultural counseling, and human rights issues.

Howard I. Kushner, PhD, is a Professor of History (of Medicine) at San Diego State University and director of the graduate program in interdisciplinary studies. His doctorate is from Cornell University. His most recent book is *Self-Destruction in the Promised Land: A Psychocultural Biology of American Suicide*, published in paperback as *American Suicide: A Psychocultural Exploration*. In 1990, Kushner was elected a member of the International Academy for Suicide Prevention of the World Health Organization.

Teresa D. LaFromboise, PhD, Associate Professor of Education at Stanford University, received her doctorate from the University of Oklahoma in 1980. Dr. LaFromboise, a descendent of the Miami tribe, is a counseling psychologist concerned with the stress-related problems of American Indians. Her research topics include interviewing strategies in multicultural counseling and social skills interventions for bicultural competence. She also writes on American-Indian women's mental health.

Dorothy E. Lee, PhD, received her masters from Northwestern University and her doctorate from the University of Iowa. She has just retired as Professor of Sociology from Illinois State University. She has published primarily in the areas of belief systems and self destructive behaviors.

Marjorie J. Malkin, PhD, is an Associate Professor in the Department of Health Education and Recreation at Southern Illinois University, Carbondale. She has a Masters of Education and a doctorate of Education in Therapeutic Recreation from the University of Georgia, Athens. Dr. Malkin has published on leisure attitudes and cognitive evaluations of women who are depressed and suicidal.

Nancy J. Osgood, PhD, is a Professor of Gerontology and Sociology at Virginia Commonwealth University/Medical College of Virginia in Richmond, Virginia. She is the author or co-author of several books, articles, and chapters on suicide in the elderly, including *Suicide Among the Elderly in Long-Term Care Facilities* and *Suicide in Later Life*. Dr. Osgood has an interest in retirement communities, leisure and aging, and geriatric alcoholism and substance abuse.

Lois Sapsford, MSW, has a masters in Social Work from the University of Calgary, Canada. She has many years of clinical experience in the areas of family therapy, bereavement after a suicide, and child sexual abuse. She has conducted research in women's grief after a suicide in the family. Her private practice focuses on adolescent sexual abuse, grief, and child prostitution.

Judith M. Saunders, RN, DNSc, FAAN, is an Assistant Research Scientist at the City of Hope National Medical Center. Dr. Saunders has authored many articles and book chapters on suicide prevention and has published extensively on psychosocial aspects of medical illness and women's issues. She conducts research on topics such as HIV and self-care, attitudes toward suicide, psychosocial aspects of life-threatening illnesses, self-care, and ethics.

B. Joyce Stephens, PhD, is a Professor of Sociology at the State University of New York at Fredonia. She has published a book on the subculture of welfare hotels and several articles on suicidal women and on street hustlers.

Judith M. Stillion, PhD, is a Professor of Psychology and Associate Vice-Chancellor for Academic Affairs and Planning at Western Carolina University. She earned her doctorate from the University of Alabama and her masters from the University of New Mexico. She has written more than 50 articles on death and dying. Her book, *Suicide Across the Life Span: Premature Exits*, written with Eugene McDowell and Jacque May, brought a developmental dimension to the study of suicide.

Sharon M. Valente, RN, PhD, FAAN, is an Assistant Professor at the University of Southern California and a consultant at the Veterans Administration and City of Hope National Medical Center. She completed her doctorate in Psychology at the University of Southern California. She co-authored *Suicide: Assessment and Intervention*, and she has published extensively on suicide and mental health. Her research has examined suicide in psychiatric patients, attitudes toward suicide, and HIV and self-care.

Bijou Yang, PhD, is an Assistant Professor of Economics at Drexel University in Philadelphia. She earned a masters from National Taiwan University, and a doctorate from the University of Pennsylvania. She co-authored *Economic Perspectives on Suicide*, and has written extensively on social stress and the business cycle. She has also examined the impact of economic/sociological factors on suicide and homicide rates. Currently, she is working on women and employment.

Luis H. Zayas, PhD, is a psychologist and social worker on the Faculty Residency Program in Social Medicine of the Department of Family Medicine at Montefiore Medical Center, Bronx, NY. He is also a Research Associate in the Hispanic Research Center and an Adjunct Associate Professor of Psychology at Fordham University. Dr. Zayas's clinical and research interests are Hispanic family mental health, family therapy, child-rearing practices, and adolescent disorders.

James K. Zimmerman, PhD, is a clinical psychologist in practice in New York City and Westchester County, NY. He is an Assistant Professor of Psychiatry at Albert Einstein College of Medicine, Bronx, NY, and co-editor of the upcoming volume *Treatment Approaches With Suicidal Adolescents*. His interests include brief treatment, family psychotherapy, adolescent development and suicidality.

Acknowledgments

This book benefited from the assistance of a variety of people and institutions. We thank the staff at Springer, especially Mary Grace Luke, senior editor, Bob Kowkabany, editorial and production manager, and Annette Imperati, marketing director, for their support. Thanks also to our home universities, Colorado State University and Stockton State College, respectively. The interlibrary loan staff at Colorado State University was particularly helpful with obtaining materials in a timely manner. Finally, our appreciation is extended to our partners, David B. Wohl and Bijou Yang for their encouragement and support throughout the project.

Part I Introduction

1
Women and Suicidal Behavior: Issues and Dilemmas

Silvia Sara Canetto and David Lester

This book focuses on suicidal behavior in women. A concentration on women is long overdue. In most countries, women have the highest rates of suicidal behavior, even though men are more likely to die as a result of a suicidal act (Canetto & Lester, 1995). Yet, the literature on women and suicidal behavior is relatively limited, as compared to the literature on women and depression.

Two perspectives inform our approach to suicidal behavior in women. First, we examine the experiences and behavior of suicidal women *qua* women. This is in contrast to previous literature, which has tended to develop hypotheses about women's suicidal behavior on the basis of the experiences and behavior of men. Second, we include consideration of social and cultural factors, such as social class, financial resources, education, employment, social support, gender socialization, and cultural norms, again in contrast to much of the previous literature on suicidal women, which has tended to emphasize individual psychological determinants. Social and cultural factors have been made the focus of specific chapters (we have chapters on employment and suicidal behavior, as well as chapters on suicidal behavior among women from specific United States' ethnic groups). We have also integrated information about social and cultural factors in general chapters; for example, in the epidemiology chapter we cover information about Western and non-Western countries. We hope that our book will help dispel the myth that conceptual categories developed from studying suicidal behavior in White European-American men can be automatically generalized to women and people of other cultures.

WOMEN AND THE TERMINOLOGY OF SUICIDAL BEHAVIOR

Suicidologists typically call those suicidal actions in which the person survives, attempted suicides, and those in which the person dies, completed suicides. One problem with this nomenclature is that it assumes that the goal of all suicidal acts is death (Lester, 1989). We know that the outcome of a suicidal act is not a good measure of intent. Not all persons who engage in life-threatening behaviors attempt to die; conversely, not all suicidal deaths are intended. Another problem with this terminology is that it defines typical female behavior, surviving a suicidal act, as "failure," and typical male behavior, killing oneself, as "success" (Canetto, 1992). If, in fact, the majority of suicidal acts aim at improving one's life circumstances, rather than dying, it would be the people who die, usually men, who "fail" at suicide. One could introduce a reverse assumption by calling nonfatal suicidal acts successful suicides, and suicidal deaths failed suicides (Lester, 1989).

Once this conceptual transformation is made, some old research findings make sense. For example, Shneidman and Farberow (1957) described what they thought was faulty logic in the suicide notes left by people who killed themselves. These people seemed to confuse the self as experienced by the self with the self as experienced by others. For example, a statement such as, "You'll miss me when I'm gone," confuses the *me* that is remembered by others with the *I* that I am presently aware of. Prior to their death, people often act as if they will be around to witness (and enjoy) the reactions of others to their suicide. Shneidman and Farberow called this faulty logic catalogic. If one assumes that most people who engage in a suicidal act intend to communicate distress rather than kill themselves, expecting to witness the reactions of others is not illogical.

WOMEN IN SUICIDOLOGY

Suicidologists have tended to focus on suicide mortality, an infrequent and typically male phenomenon, and from that have drawn conclusions about nonfatal suicidal behavior, a more frequent and typically female phenomenon. Yet, from an epidemiological perspective, it is women's suicidal behavior that is the norm, and men's behavior that is unusual and special.

Canetto (1992) has highlighted some of the unexamined assumptions in the research on women and suicidal behaviors (for guidelines on nonsexist research, see Denmark, Russo, Frieze, & Sechzer, 1988; McHugh, Koeske, & Frieze, 1986)). She noted that women's suicidal behavior has been studied over the menstrual cycle in order to explore the possible effects of female hormonal patterns on suicidal behavior. The implication of this research is that the normal physiology of women is intrinsically pathogenic and leads to suicide. On the other hand, the role of hormones on suicidal behavior has not been studied in men. According to Canetto, elevated rates of mortality by suicide in men could have been attributed to unique male hormonal patterns, such as a deficit of estrogen or the toxic influence of testosterone. The fact that theories and research on the influence of male hormonal patterns on suicide have not developed suggests that male physiology is assumed to be nonpathogenic.

Canetto (1992) has reviewed evidence showing that several suicidologists have attributed the women's lower suicided mortality rates to their being mentally dull, passive, conforming, and suggestible. It has been theorized that women are not imaginative and intellectually complex enough to kill themselves (Durkheim, 1897/1951); that they unquestionably accept traditional and religious prohibitions against suicide (Davis, 1904); and that they passively accept the blows of life (Durkheim, 1897/1951, Neuringer & Lettieri, 1982). Men, on the other hand, presumably demonstrate imagination and initiative by killing themselves in the face of adversity. Canetto concluded that women's behaviors tend to be labeled pejoratively, even if they are associated with adaptation and survival, whereas men's behaviors are labeled positively, even when they lead to self-destruction.

DIVERSITY IN SUICIDOLOGY

The growing cultural diversity of the population living in the United States and other Western countries has led to an increasing awareness of the role that cultural, racial–ethnic, and social factors play in mental health (Homma-True, Greene, Lopez, & Trimble, 1993). Cultural values have an influence on whether, and which kind of, suicidal behavior is perceived as permissible. For example, among Asian-Americans, suicide by hanging is being replaced by suicide by firearms, concomitant with the individual's degree of assimilation into the United States' culture (McIntosh & Santos, 1985–1986).

Cultural, ethnic/racial, and social factors affect opportunities for housing, education, and employment, and thus the likelihood that a person will experience psychological distress. Furthermore, cultural, ethnic/racial, and social factors mediate the experience of the mental health system. There is evidence that diagnosis and treatment are provided based on race; for example, in the United States, overdiagnosing of schizophrenia, and the prescription of medication and restraints, are more common among people of color (Homma-True et al., 1993).

To date, our knowledge of cultural factors in suicidal behavior epidemiology, dynamics, and prevention is limited. Suicidologists have tended to focus on White, European and North-American (United States/Canadian) males. Even when cross-cultural research is conducted, much of it is from a North-American, White male perspective. Typically, North-American psychological measures are translated into the language of the other nation so as to replicate a research study first conducted on North-Americans with a different population. For example, Chiles, Ping, and Strosahl (1990) examined depression, hopelessness, and suicidal preoccupation in the United States and mainland China, based on measures developed in the United States. This North-American-centeredness of research is made worse by the tendency for researchers from other nations to gravitate to the United States for their academic training and to remain here.[1]

Finally, we would like to remind our readers that studies of suicidal behavior do not usually include simultaneous consideration of fundamental diversity dimensions, such as gender, ethnicity, social class, and sexual orientation. Due to limitations in the available data, some chapters in the present book deal with women and men as if they were homogenous groups. We hope that in the future we will be able to draw on more specific data, and thus make progress in understanding the interaction of gender, ethnicity, social class, and sexual orientation.

THE PRESENT BOOK

In the present book, we have sought to expand the concept of frameworks for understanding suicidal behavior in women. As suggested by Wicker (1985), we have adopted a variety of strategies to stimulate new insights on familiar research problems and established methodologies.

With regard to terminology, we refer to the topic of the book as *suicidal behaviors*. Suicidal behaviors are classified in terms of outcome rather than intent. The expression "nonfatal suicidal behavior" is used to refer to suicidal acts that did not result in the person's death—in lieu of the North-American "suicide attempt" and the European "parasuicide;" "fatal suicidal behavior" is reserved for those suicidal acts that resulted in death. The term "suicidal behavior," not otherwise specified, is used whenever information about outcome is not available or relevant. An advantage of this nomenclature is that it does not make assumptions about the suicidal person's intent. Not all persons who survive a suicidal act wished to live, and conversely, not all suicidal deaths are intended (see Canetto, 1992; Lester, 1989, for a discussion of suicidal behavior terminology).

In this book, women's behavior and experiences are made central to an analysis of the theoretical and empirical literature on suicidal behavior. We have encouraged contributors to develop their own theoretical frameworks, rather than simply adopting those developed for suicidal behavior in men.

We have addressed diversity issues by inviting experts on different cultural groups in the United States and Canada to examine suicidal behavior in these groups. It is clear from perusal of these chapters that the dynamics of suicidal behavior are quite different in each of the cultural groups. Furthermore, even though most chapters draw on national United States' data, we have included international data in our epidemiology chapter; in this way, the reader can get a sense of the variability in patterns of suicidal behavior in countries around the world.

We hope that our book will help you, the readers, to better understand women's suicidal behavior in all of its diversity. We also hope that a focus on the lesser-known half of the human experience, that is women's, will stimulate new insights and help you to become more effective in working with all suicidal persons.

NOTE

1. Both editors of this book are immigrants to the United States.

REFERENCES

Canetto, S. S. (1992). Gender and suicide in the elderly. *Suicide and Life-Threatening Behavior*, *22*, 80–97.

Canetto, S. S., & Lester, D. (1995). The epidemiology of women's suicidal behaviors. In S. S. Canetto & D. Lester (Eds.), *Women and suicidal behavior* (pp. 35–57). New York: Springer.

Chiles, J. A., Ping, Z. Y., & Strosahl, D. (1990). A Chinese/American cross-cultural study of depression, hopelessness, and suicidal behavior. In G. Ferrari, M. Bellini, & P. Crepet (Eds.), *Suicidal behavior and risk factors* (pp. 609–614). Bologna, Italy: Monduzzi Editore.

Davis, J. C. (1904). Suicide with some illustrative cases. *Journal of the American Medical Association*, *43*, 121–123.

Denmark, F., Russo, N. F., Frieze, I. H., & Sechzer, J. A. (1988). Guidelines for avoiding sexism in psychological research: A report of the ad hoc committee on nonsexist research. *American Psychologist*, *43*, 582–585.

Durkheim, E. (1951). *Suicide* (J. A. Spaulding & G. Simpson, Trans.). Glencoe, IL: The Free Press. (Original work published 1897)

Homma-True, R., Greene, B., Lòpez, S. R., & Trimble, J. E. (1993). Ethnocultural diversity in clinical psychology. *The Clinical Psychologist*, *46*, 50–63.

Lester, D. (1989). The study of suicide from a feminist perspective. *Crisis, 11*, 38–43.

McHugh, M. C., Koeske, R. D., & Frieze, I. H. (1986). Issues to consider in conducting nonsexist psychological research: A guide for researchers. *American Psychologist, 41*, 879–890.

McIntosh, J. L., & Santos, J. F. (1985–1986). Methods of suicide by age: Sex and race differences among the young and old. *International Journal of Aging and Human Development, 22*, 123–139.

Neuringer, C., & Lettieri, D. J. (1982). *Suicidal women*. New York: Gardner Press.

Shneidman, E. S., & Farberow, N. L. (1957). The logic of suicide. In E. S. Shneidman & N. L. Farberow (Eds.), *Clues to suicide* (pp. 31–40). New York: McGraw-Hill.

Wicker, A. W. (1985). Getting out of our conceptual ruts: Strategies for expanding conceptual frameworks. *American Psychologist, 40*, 1094–1103.

Part II Epidemiology

■ 2 Women and Suicidal Behavior: Epidemiology, Gender and Lethality in Historical Perspective[1]

Howard I. Kushner

At the 22nd Annual Meeting of the American Association for Suicidology (1989) in her keynote address entitled "Gender socialization and suicide," President Charlotte Sanborn (quoted in Harnish, 1989; Huchcroft, 1989) rehearsed the seemingly well-known datum that men were three-to-four times more likely to kill themselves than women. The reason for this, Sanborn explained, could be traced to men's socialization, which made it subsequently difficult for them to express a "softer side." Turning Henry Higgins on his head, Sanborn (1990) wondered why men couldn't be more like women? If men would act like women, their suicide mortality would decline substantially. Sanborn's view is emblematic of a persistent assumption that has informed the vast majority of suicide studies over the past two centuries. Initially formulated in the early nineteenth century, this belief was enshrined in Durkheim's (1897, 1951) definitive, *Suicide: A study in sociology*, and has remained undisputed ever since.[2]

In what follows, I argue that the assertions that women are less suicidal than men rests on contested data, whose privileging reveals a set of gendered assumptions that conflate women's biology with their behavior.[3] In so doing, I not only challenge the assumption that women are less suicidal than men, but also I suggest that we ought to rethink the presumption that the motives for suicidal behaviors may be gleaned only from the histories of those who die as a result of a suicidal act.

OFFICIAL MORTALITY STATISTICS AND WOMEN'S SUICIDAL BEHAVIOR

"Although women are more exposed to mental illness than men," wrote the leader of the French asylum movement, Etienne Esquirol (1821/1838), "suicide is less frequent among them. Observers from all nations are in agreement on that issue" (p. 584). Since the early nineteenth century, investigators (Cavan, 1928; Lester, 1988) have confirmed Esquirol's assertion, reporting that approximately three out of every four deaths by suicide in both Western Europe and North America were men.

Although contemporary data continue to report that male mortality from suicide is substantially greater than female mortality from suicide, the data also indicate that the gap between men and women has been narrowing for the past hundred years (Kramer, Pollack, Redick, & Locke, 1972: Kushner, 1985, 1989; Mathews, 1981; Stafford & Weisheit, 1988). For instance, in 1880, women accounted for 12.8% of all fatal suicides in San Diego County, California, even though they made up about one-half of the population. Consistent with national trends, the percentage of female fatal suicides grew by approximately 10% of its base per decade. Thus, by 1970 women accounted for 37.6% of all fatal suicides in San Diego County. Because they account for the population at risk, rates per 100,000 of the living population provide a more accurate indication of suicide mortality than percentages. In a century the rate had more than doubled for women from 6.7 per 100,000 to 14.4 per 100,000.

Lane's (1979) data on suicide mortality rates for white women in Philadelphia reveals a similar trend. In the 1870s the rate was 2 per 100,000. A century later, the rate reached 10.8 per 100,000—an increase of 540%. Comparing 1956–1957 rates to those of 1966–1967 in 15 industrial nations, demographer Chenais (1973) discovered that in those industrial countries with the greatest increase in suicide mortality (USA, Canada, and West Germany), "the increase is mainly among women" (p. 420) (see also Baudelot & Establet, 1984; Chenais & Vallin, 1981). Researchers studying Alberta, Canada for the period 1951 to 1977 arrived at similar conclusions (Hellon & Solomon, 1980).

But, although the differential between female and male suicide mortality has diminished, official statistics continue to report a much higher rate for men. "In all nations," writes Chenais (1973), "men suicide more than women, the rate of 'surmortalité' generally varies from two to four" (p. 420).

In an exhaustive reevaluation of Durkheim's conclusions Baudelot and Establet (1984) concluded that one social fact that has not changed is that "men kill themselves more often than women, the old more often than the young" (p. 59). In fact, no study has uncovered a greater incidence of suicide mortality for women than for men in any jurisdiction in North America or Europe.

GENDERED EXPLANATIONS

Esquirol (1838) explained that "over-excitement of their sensibilities, their flights of imagination, their exaggerated tenderness, their religious attachments, produce in them [women] illnesses opposed to suicide" (pp. 584–585). Additionally, women's "mild character and natural timidity distances them" from suicidal thoughts. Suicide was "less frequent among women," wrote French alienist Jean-Pierre Falret (1822), because of "the weakness of their physical constitution, in the sweetness of their temperament, in their natural timidity, which saves them from these murderous excesses" (pp. 17–18).

Esquirol's and Falret's explanations for women's resistance to suicide reflected widely held assumptions about the nature of women. As important, these assumptions *predated* the collection of official suicide statistics which "found" sex differences in suicide mortality.[4] In fact, as I have shown elsewhere (Kushner, 1993) both the definition of suicidal behavior and the collection of suicide mortality data were profoundly influenced by the attitudes and assumptions about women expressed by alienists like Esquirol and Falret.

Like Esquirol and Falret, other nineteenth century European and North American commentators tied the disparity between female and male suicide rates to a set of gendered distinctions that conflated physical differences with what was metaphorically feminine. "Woman," "mother," and "wife," served as a representation of a set of socially constructed behaviors attached to females that translated vaguely into an assortment of attributes that included passivity, frailty, modesty, patience, loyalty, acceptance, and self-renunciation. Social constructions (gender), as opposed to biological distinctions (sex), became the operative metaphors used to explain the alleged immunity of women to suicide.

Thus, rudimentary and incomplete statistics were proof enough for the editors of the *Annales d'hygiène* in 1829 "that women are able to bear the vicissitudes of life better than men" (quoted in Chevalier, 1984, p. 472). "There are more suicides among men than women," according to Forbes Winslow (1840), editor and founder of the British *Journal of Psychological*

Medicine, which "will not surprise those who know the energy, courage, and patience of women under misfortune; men more readily give way to despair, and to the vices consequent upon it" (p. 276).

Women proved more resistant to suicide, wrote the editor of the *Annales Médico-Psychologiques*, Alexandre Brierre de Boismont (1856), because suicide required "a degree of energy, of courage, of despair, which is not in conformity with the weak and delicate constitution of women" (p. 63). Moreover, women's heightened attachment to "family affections" and "religious principles" were, according to Brierre de Boismont, "obstacles which struggle victoriously against the idea of self-destruction" (p. 65). French alienist Louis Bertrand (1857) tied the "difference in frequency of suicide between the two sexes" (p. 75) to the fact that women were more sedentary, followed more regular practices, were more religious, more resigned to life, and better able to bear the incessant pain of life than men.

In the United States, national mortality figures were first collected in the 1850 federal census (U.S. Census, 1855), which was released in 1855. However, before any national statistics on the incidence of suicide were compiled or made public, American experts already had data from both local and state compilations, as well as from various European authorities, suggesting that men were much more likely than women to kill themselves (Cook, 1849; Hunt, 1845).

"In regard to sex," reported *The New York Times* (1861) "only about one-fourth of the whole number [of suicides] were women . . . [even] though by the last census there is an excess of females over males . . . in New York" (Section 2, p. 1). That American women seemed to kill themselves even less frequently than their European counterparts was due, according to this account, to "the greater facility of divorce" in the United States since "a large proportion of female suicides attribute their act to domestic unhappiness." "Besides," explained *The Times*, "it is a well known fact that women possess greater courage and patience under misfortune than men, and less readily give way to despair and the vices consequent upon it" (Section 2, p. 1).

This reasoning was presented throughout the century with such regularity that hardly anyone doubted the assertion in a widely republished 1881 British article (Knighton, 1881) entitled "Suicidal mania," that "religious restraints" and the possession of "a larger measure of that hope which springs eternal in the human breast," accounted for the fact that women "were less prone to commit suicide . . . than men" (p. 376). From a more secular point of view, a writer (Mulhall, 1883) in London's *The Contemporary Review* explained "that three-fourths of the cases [of suicide] are males, which shows that if the female intellect be less powerful than man's, it is at the same time better balanced, or at least more capable of standing against reverses of fortune, and facing the battle of life" (p. 907).[5]

Darwinian metaphors served to reinforce these familiar conclusions. "It is easy to understand the great male preponderance [of suicide]," wrote Henry Morselli (1882, p. 195), professor of psychological medicine at the Royal University of Turin, in 1879. "The difficulties of existence, those at least which proceed from the struggle for life, bear more heavily on man. "Woman," insisted Morselli, "only shares in these through the affections, and although she has a more impressionable nervous temperament, yet [she] possesses the faculty of resigning herself more easily to circumstances" (pp. 195–197). Morselli's views were echoed by the British psychiatrist and barrister S. A. K. Strahan (1893) *Suicide and insanity: A philosophical and sociological study*. "The comparative immunity of the female sex from self-destruction," according to Strahan, "depends in part upon the relatively less harassing part she takes in the struggle for existence; in part upon the less indulgent and vicious life she leads; and in part upon her lack of courage and natural repugnance to personal violence and disfigurement" (p. 178).

No matter what arguments were offered, the fact remained that *some* women killed themselves. Commentators explained this in two ways. First, they insisted that the motives for female and male suicides were very different. Suicide among women was portrayed as an individual emotional act and, thus inconsequential, while male suicide was seen as a barometer of national economic and social well-being. Second, building on the first assumption, because male suicide was a consequence of the stresses inherent in men's roles and responsibilities (i.e., the price of "civilization"), female suicide occurred when women *deviated* from their less-conflicted (traditional) roles.

The contrast between women's and men's motives reflected the ideology described by Welter (1966) as that "of True Womanhood, by which a woman judged herself and was judged by her husband, her neighbors, and society" (p. 230). Adherence to the virtues of "piety, purity, submissiveness and domesticity" translated into the belief that "a 'fallen woman' was a 'fallen angel,'" unworthy of the celestial company of her sex" (p. 230). Loss of purity, according to the periodical press, "brought madness or death" (pp. 230–231). And these dominant values, Welter argued, portrayed "Death Preferable to Loss of Innocence" (pp. 151–155).

Although Welter was describing American attitudes, she could have as easily turned to France for confirmation of her argument (Lieberman, 1990, 1991). Again, Esquirol's (1838) explanations were emblematic: "Women kill themselves more rarely than men," he wrote in 1821, and when they do, "more often it is [amorous] passion which impels them to this aberration" (p. 585). Back in the United States, an anonymous "Southern Physician," wrote in *The Whig Review* (1847) that "in men, real or fancied impotence is very apt to induce self-destruction—and among women, we cannot help always suspecting the dread of the consequences of secret loss of honor" (p.

142; see also Canetto, 1992–1993, for a discussion of the recent social science literature).

Three decades later Albert Rhodes (1876), an American author who lived in Paris and whose articles on "social issues" appeared regularly in American, French, and British periodicals, explained that women killed themselves for very different motives from those of men: "The woman's mode of death is usually less violent. Copious weeping relieves the woman, and often saves her, while this relief is denied to man. Besides, when the hour for the act comes, her courage is apt to fail" (p. 192). When women kill themselves, Rhodes asserted, they do so for very different motives from those of men: "Women appear to be more subject to moral influences, such as disappointed love, betrayal, desertion, jealousy, domestic trouble, and sentimental exaltation of every description." Men, on the other hand, "are rather affected by trials of a material order, such as misery, business embarrassments, losses, ungratified ambition, the abuse of alcohol, the desire to escape from justice, and so on" (p. 194).

Morselli (1882) found that men's suicides were caused by "financial embarrassments," "weariness of life," and other "egoistical motives, whilst among women, after mental diseases, there predominate passions, domestic troubles, shame and remorse" (p. 305). In contrast to men, explained Morselli, "among the causes which urge them to leave this life women always exhibit that spirit of self-denial, that delicacy of feeling and of love, which inspire all her acts" (p. 305).

Euro-American fiction reinforced this ideology. Illustrative is Hawthorne's *The Blithedale romance* (1852/1983), in which Silas Foster finally realizes that Zenobia has been spurned by her lover Hollingsworth:

> "And so you think she's drowned herself?" he cried. "What on earth should the young women do that for?" exclaimed Silas, his eyes half out of his head with mere surprise. "Why, she has more means than she can use or waste, and lacks nothing to make her comfortable, but a husband." (pp. 230–231)

Nineteenth-century European and American fiction is littered with the corpses of such women. Whether it was Zenobia; Emma in Flaubert's *Madame Bovary* (1857); Anna in Tolstoi's *Anna Karenina* (1875); or Lili Bart in Wharton's *The house of mirth* (1905), the cause was always the same: rejection after an illicit love affair that led a despairing female to the only honorable (and *predictable*) resolution—suicide. This was, of course, a literary convention, but one that gained credence from its similarity to nineteenth-century French, British, and American newspaper accounts, which invariably connected women's suicide to real and imagined loss of purity (Gates 1988; Higonnet, 1985).

If women's death by suicide could not be attributed to dishonor, it invariably was tied to women's adopting roles that nature and society had assigned to men. When women left the security of their families, explained Brierre de Boismont (1856), they substantially increased their risk of suicide. The higher rates of suicide mortality of women who "take an active part in the business of life," according to an 1883 English essay entitled "Insanity, suicide, and civilization" (Mulhall, 1883), "serve as a caution to prevent them from taking part in politics, or matters best suited for men" (p. 908). "It has been observed," wrote the American Robert N. Reeves (1897), "that as woman approaches man in her mode of life she also becomes more familiar with those abnormal conditions which have previously been peculiar to man." This presumably leads to an increase in suicide among women because "the comparative immunity of women from self-destruction in the past has depended greatly upon the relatively less harassing part she has taken in the struggle for life." As women moved "deeper into . . . vocations," such as "art, literature, finance, and even politics," they "must expect to suffer the consequences. Already," Reeves warned, "it is noticeable that feminine suicide is not entirely due to the sentimental causes of disappointed love, desertion, and jealousy, but to those trials of a more material order such as have led men to the act of self-destruction" (pp. 189–190).

By the end of the century, joining the chorus of his French and American cousins, Reginald A. Skelton (1900) summed up the view that had become commonplace:

> Though every woman has to traverse certain critical periods in her lifetime, which are dangerous both to her bodily and mental condition, yet she is exempt from many of the factors most favourable to suicide. Her affection for home and children is greater, and the religious sentiment has diminished less in woman than in man; her intellectual faculties are usually less developed, and hence also her sensibility to mental pain; inured to continual petty troubles, her patience is fortified to resist greater ones. It is without surprise, therefore, that we learn that there are four times as many men as women suicides. In the large towns, however, these factors tending to the exemption of women from suicide largely disappear. (p. 471)

Thus, Durkheim's assertion in *Suicide* (1897, 1951) that "in all the countries of the world, women commit suicide less than men" (p. 166) was based, not only on the data of his predecessors, but also on their gendered assumptions (Kushner, 1993). Durkheim too attributed what he called the relative immunity of women to suicide to the fact that women were "fundamentally traditionalist by nature, they govern their conduct by fixed beliefs and have no great intellectual needs" (p. 166). Although Durkheim insisted that his explanation for the incidence of suicide rested on social factors, throughout his study he also ascribed the low incidence of women's suicide mortality to organic influences (Besnard, 1973). For instance, Durkheim (1897/1951) suggested that "being a more instinctive creature than man, woman has only to follow her instincts to find calmness and peace" (p. 272).

Twentieth-century experts who have attempted to explain the alleged female/male disparity in the suicide morbidity rate have incorporated the assumptions of Durkheim and his predecessors. Dublin, author of the authoritative *Suicide: A sociological and statistical study* (1963), concluded that "suicide . . . may be called a masculine type of behavior." Dublin suggested that suicide by women resulted from "maladjustment." Those women who killed themselves, Dublin asserted, must have experienced a "marked increase in . . . schooling and employment. . . . Greater economic and social independence . . . played a role" (pp. 23–25). The therapeutic implications of his study were that, in order to ensure mental health, women should avoid such "masculine" activities as schooling and paid employment. Dublin concluded that "it is fortunate for mankind [sic] that the people who are least likely to lose the will to live are producing and rearing the oncoming generation" (pp. 27–28).

A leading British suicidologist, Sainsbury (1955), explained the suicide mortality differential between men and women this way: "When the biological and social roles of the two sexes are compared, the female role appears more precisely, and her biological and social functions more harmonized." Males, on the other hand, are "less restricted by social conformity" and are "encouraged" to be individualistic and "aggressive." A man is responsible "for [the] support and welfare of his family" and, as a result, "he is more subject to the stresses of mobility and change." Thus, the "male's more arduous social role" explains "the marked liability of the male" for suicide (p. 80). Such analysis states that women are happy and safe in their domestic roles, whereas men bear a heavy social burden; indeed, when a woman kills herself, it is because she has attempted to act like a man!

The American Public Health Association's study *Mental disorders/suicide* (Kramer, Pollack, Redick, & Locke, 1972) quotes the Sainsbury analysis at length and endorses it, although its authors wonder, almost as an aside, why suicide rates differ so greatly by sex "since women are exposed to some of the same factors" as men—for instance, social isolation, lack of employment, and loss of status (pp. 176–178). Davis, in an article entitled "Female labor force participation and suicide" (1981), affirms the assumptions of his predecessors that "the greater the female labor force participation . . . the greater the rate of suicide" (p. 123).

An example of similar thinking in France is found in the work of sociologists Chenais and Vallin (1981; see also Baudelot & Establet, 1984; Chenais, 1973) who attribute the increase of suicide mortality among women in industrial countries since the Second World War to their increased participation in the work force. "The influence of the economic situation on suicide," argue Chenais and Vallin, "depends very much on the manner in which individuals in difficulty find themselves inserted in society. The existence and efficacy of the levels of solidarity (which is a matter of family or other institutions) can separate the appeal of a gesture from despair" (pp. 7–8).

Thus, the dominant theories are that male suicide results from the grave stresses inherent in men's roles and responsibilities, whereas female suicide occurs when women *deviate* from their presumably less conflicted and less demanding roles and status. Those women who kill themselves after a man deserts them, do so, according to these analyses, because they can no longer fulfill their social functions as mothers and wives.

Johnson's (1979) "Durkheim revisited" is the only study that *does not* tie women's lower suicide mortality rates to their allegedly less stressful situation. Johnson agrees that "compared to men, women do not appear to have a great 'suicide problem.'" Noting that women historically "participate differently from men" in what Durkheim called "collective life," Johnson endorses the arguments of those who see women inhabiting "different social worlds" from men. She finds, however, that "married employed women have lower suicide rates than unemployed housewives," and suggests that the highest suicide mortality rates are found among those women who are the most submerged in the family (p. 145).

Johnson's (1979) reluctance to accept the sexist ideology informing so many of the explanations for the gender differential in suicide rates is well founded. Given the evidence amassed over the past two decades on women's status and experience, it can no longer be assumed that women are "naturally" or "biologically" more content than men (Tavris, 1991). Moreover, the corollary of this assumption—that the increase of suicide mortality among women is the direct result of their abandonment of traditional roles—and its logical extension—that women can avoid suicide by returning to their "natural" roles—ought to make any researcher look more carefully at the data.

NONFATAL VERSUS FATAL SUICIDAL BEHAVIORS

Almost every generalization about the incidence of suicidal behaviors in the West ultimately seeks legitimation in official statistics. The most commonly used data are compilations of coroner's reports of mortality by suicide issued by local, state, or federal agencies. How accurate are the data that inform these explanations? Is it reasonable to develop a theory of the etiology of all suicidal behaviors based on the incidence of suicide mortality?

Most contemporary studies begin with a caveat about the unreliability of suicide mortality data and then proceed to ignore their own warnings. As epidemiologist O'Carroll (1989) recently admitted, "there is an enormous body of literature that questions the validity and reliability, and thus the usefulness of suicide mortality statistics" (p. 1). Nevertheless, he insists that "there are, of course, a number of compelling reasons to use suicide mortality data. These data have been collected over many years in most countries on earth, allowing temporal and international comparisons" (p. 1). Sociologists Stafford and Weisheit (1988) second this view: "Although there are persistent doubts about the validity of suicide data (e.g., Douglas, 1967; Hooper & Guttmacher, 1979), there is no practical alternative to using them" (p. 151).

Beyond reliability is the issue of definition. In fact, there often is no relationship between a researcher's definition of suicide and the statistics employed in the discussion that follows. A case in point is Durkheim's (1897/1951) definition of suicide as "*death resulting directly or indirectly from a positive or negative act of the victim himself [sic], which he [sic] knows will produce this result*" [emphasis in original] (p. 44). Yet, Durkheim's definition was irrelevant to his own study, because all of his data on the incidence of suicide was drawn from official statistics which defined suicide in ways that were incompatible with his definition. For instance, those who sacrificed their lives for others were never listed as suicides in official statistics. And those whose deaths resulted only "indirectly" from their acts did not usually appear in the statistics either. Indeed, Durkheim must have known that officials charged with the determination of whether an act was a suicide almost always labeled those whose self-killings appeared to be informed by social alienation (socially disintegrative) as suicide, although they almost never called a socially sanctioned (integrative) death (heroism) suicide. The unquestioned assumption that suicide was an antisocial act was why Durkheim had chosen it as an indicator of social pathology in the first place. Apparently neither Durkheim nor his followers ever considered the possibility that the belief—shared by official statistics collectors and interpreters of suicide—that suicide was antisocial behavior had, *a priori*, distorted suicide mortality statistics.

Beyond the fact that official suicide mortality data are not reliable, lies the larger issue that most analyses of suicidal behavior rely on statistics that include only those who kill themselves. This bias, more than another other, has provided a statistical underpinning for the assertion that women are less suicidal than men. Researchers naturally prefer to rely on tabulated statistics that can be measured, compared, and grouped in categories (Douglas,

1976; Monk, 1975). As a result, nonfatal suicidal acts are often neglected when experts formulate their conclusions about the causes of suicidal behavior.

We can never know for certain the extent of nonfatal suicidal behavior, but most experts agree that for every fatal suicidal act there are six to eight nonfatal suicidal acts (Dublin, 1963; Hendin, 1982; Maris, 1981; Shneidman & Farberow, 1961). They indicate that women account for nonfatal suicidal behavior at a rate approximately 2.3 times greater than do men. On the other hand, men kill themselves at a rate 2.3 times greater than women (Maris, 1981; Shneidman & Farberow, 1961). If the numbers of nonfatal and fatal suicidal behaviors are added together, the rate differential between men and women collapses.

Some, mindful of this exclusion, justify it, claiming that fatal and nonfatal suicidal behaviors are distinct. Suicidologist Maris (1981), for instance, focuses on the differences in intentions, asserting that those engaging in nonfatal suicidal behavior expect to be discovered and saved, whereas those engaging in fatal suicidal behavior are less likely to place themselves in a position that allows for intervention in their actions. These differences, argues Maris, demand that nonfatal and fatal suicidal behavior be studied separately.

There are many examples that seem to support Maris' (1981) conclusion. Nevertheless, differences in intent are not *invariably* reflected in official suicide mortality statistics. A particular intention does not necessarily lead to the desired result. For instance, many persons intend to kill themselves, but, by chance, survive. Because official statistics only record results, these cases are not studied as intentional suicides.

The suicide attempt of Anna Brewster, a 32-year-old single San Diego school teacher, in January 1898, is one among many cases that exemplify the limitations of official definitions. There was little question that when Brewster took a room at the Commercial Hotel and fired a pistol at point-blank range into her temple that she expected to die. But, the outcome was different:

> Immediately afterward Miss Brewster burst from the room, holding a handkerchief to her right temple. . . . Miss Brewster pointed to a note lying on the table and said, "There are the directions, I have shot myself." To Mrs. Birdsall, who was immediately called, Miss Brewster said, "I am tired of life. I want to end it all. That's the only reason." (*San Diego Union*, January 10, 1898, 5:3)

Brewster's note was the type that experts such as Maris (1981) have identified as those left by individuals who intend to die: "It is my earnest wish that my body be taken to the morgue and dispensed of from there—

and not taken to my address. I wish the least possible expense and trouble. No funeral. No services." Both physicians who examined her "agreed that the bullet was imbedded in the brain . . . and that the chances for recovery were very dubious" (*San Diego Union*, January 10, 1898, 5:3). Nevertheless, Brewster did not die, and thus her suicide attempt was ignored by those who study such events.

Others die from complications of a botched attempt. Generally neither the coroner's report nor the death certificate will report the death as a suicide, because no matter how much the person's behavior had set up a chain of events leading to death, suicide was not the immediate cause of death. For instance, a person may not succumb to an intentional drug overdose, but die later of a cause, such as pneumonia, brought on by the attempt. This has special significance for women because they are more than twice as likely as men to employ poisons or drugs as suicidal methods (Marks & Abernathy, 1974).

Clara Dudley, a 34-year-old proprietor of "a house of ill-repute," attempted to kill herself on January 1, 1899 "by swallowing a quantity of morphine" (*San Diego Union*, January 2, 1899, 2:2). Dudley had "made previous attempts to commit suicide, having on one occasion, several months ago, inhaled gas. She was almost dead when the door of her room was burst open, and it was with the greatest of difficulty that she was brought back to life." In her latest try, reported the *San Diego Union*, Dudley lost consciousness, but according to her doctor, "she showed much improvement" (7 January 1899, 5:1). Five days later Clara Dudley died of pneumonia brought on by her suicide attempt. Both the coroner's report and her death certificate list pneumonia as the cause of death (San Diego County, California, Coroner's Reports, "Clara Dudley," January 6, 1899). Officially, her death and countless others like hers are not recorded as suicides.

Both of these scenarios, as exemplified by Brewster's and Dudley's cases, affect the reported differences in female/male suicide because women tend to survive suicidal acts more frequently than men and they also tend to die more often than men of the prolonged effects of a suicidal act (Kushner, 1989).

Additionally, official statistics do not account for unconscious intentions. Who is to say that only conscious behavior constitutes a suicide? Dorcas Antle was a 62-year-old widow who, only two months previously, had moved from Illinois to live with her son in Chula Vista, California. On April 21, 1895, Antle "took a dose of strychnine by mistake at 9 o'clock Saturday night and died in great agony 20 minutes later. She was in the habit of taking a sleeping powder upon retiring, but upon this occasion took a strychnine powder from the shelf and swallowed it" (*San Diego Union*, April 22, 1895, 5:2). The county coroner ruled that the deceased died from "strychnine poisoning; the strychnine being administered by mistake" (San Diego

County Coroner's Reports, "Dorcas Antle," 22 April 1895). The coroner's evidence rested on the deposition of Antle's son, a physician. Of course, given the paucity of available information, we cannot possibly determine whether Dorcus Antle actually made an error. Nevertheless, as a recent widow and a new arrival in California who suffered from insomnia, she fit the category of those at high risk of taking their own lives.

The case of Dorcus Antle raises another issue about the reporting of suicide mortality, especially as it relates to women. In this situation, the coroner relied on the testimony of Antle's son, a physician, to determine whether her actions were suicidal or accidental. Children (or parents or spouses), even when they are physicians, have a strong inclination to cover up a parent's death by suicide.

Finally, many deaths by suicide, especially women's, are not reported (Douglas, 1967). Coroners, physicians, and others responsible for determining whether a particular death was a suicide, are already tied to an ideology that differentiated women's motives from men's. Such preconceptions are bound to influence the collection of official statistics.

Douglas (1967) found the impulse to misrepresent women's mortality by suicide to be endemic because "the *meanings* of male suicides and of female suicides are different in Western societies" (p. 215). As we have seen, social forces outside the family, such as unemployment, are generally perceived as the cause of men's suicide, whereas strains within the family are held responsible for women's. When a woman kills herself, Douglas argues, her husband has "a much greater incentive . . . than a female in the same situation to attempt to conceal the suicidal action" (p. 215).

All this suggests that official statistics provide an unreliable guide for investigation of motive. For, even if these data presented an accurate accounting of suicide mortality (which it does not), they, nevertheless, offer an incomplete picture of intention. What we are left with is a closed loop, in which assumptions that inform judgments about whether an individual act is a suicide are presented as the reasons for the variations between female and male suicide rates.

As we have seen, experts' traditional views of women's behaviors have underlain their assumptions about the alleged maleness of suicide. Some (Chenais & Vallin, 1981; Dublin, 1963; Kramer et al., 1972; Reeves, 1897; Sainsbury, 1955; Skelton, 1900) have suggested that the way for women to guarantee their own mental health and to avoid self-destruction lies in acceptance of traditional values, particularly those of the patriarchal family. The irony here, of course, is that these same data indicate that "traditional values" have contributed to a much higher rate of nonfatal suicidal behavior by women than by men. These statistics could be used to demonstrate that women are less content with their social roles than men are with theirs. Curiously, no suicide study has ever come to that conclusion.

LETHALITY OF METHOD

If men kill themselves more often than women, the reason may be that men select more lethal methods.[6] In the United States this translates into the fact that the majority of fatal suicidal acts have employed firearms (Dublin, 1963; McIntosh & Santos, 1982; Taylor & Wicks, 1980). This is a trend that can be identified historically.

For instance, in one of the earliest statistical reports for the United States, Hunt (1845) claimed that, in 1843, 67.5% of male fatal suicides selected highly lethal methods—use of firearms, cutting their throats, or hanging themselves. On the other hand, only 36.6% of female fatal suicides employed these means. None of the women used firearms, from which Hunt concluded that women had a "horror" "of guns or pistols" (p. 232).

The *American Journal of Insanity's* (Cook, 1849) analysis of the incidence of suicide mortality in New York State for 1848 concluded "that females rarely have recourse to firearms . . . as a means of committing suicide. Hanging, drowning, and poisoning are the modes which they most frequently employ" (pp. 308–309). According to Rhodes (1876), men who killed themselves showed "a tendency toward violent methods," whereas women selected "pacific" means for suicide. "Drowning and poisoning are the favorite modes of getting rid of life in the case of women," Rhodes found, and "throat-cutting, hanging, and shooting those of the men" (pp. 192, 194).

A century later, Marks and Abernathy (1974) still found "that female attempters and completers most often use drugs-poison, whereas male completers most often use firearms" (p. 11). In San Diego County approximately one-half of all male deaths by suicide for the past 100 years have resulted from the use of firearms. National statistics reflect this same pattern (Kramer et al., 1972; Kushner, 1989).

All these studies found that suicidal women tend to choose less lethal methods, particularly poisons. For instance, Hunt (1845) found that 63% of women who died from suicide chose poisons. The percentage of women who kill themselves using firearms in San Diego County has varied, but it has remained well below the percentage who turn to poisons. At the same time, studies of the nation as a whole find (Marks & Abernathy, 1974; see also McIntosh & Santos, 1982) "an increasing proportion of women who are suiciding by firearms" (p. 15).

Percentages can be misleading. To be convincing, suicide mortality rates should be compared to rates that measure the use of firearms per 100,000 of the living population. When this is done for San Diego County, the results are striking. Over the last century, when the use of firearms by both women and men has increased, so has the rate of suicide mortality.

Should we trust data on method from the same sources that earlier in this essay I have called into question? My answer is, of course, that all official statistics are suspect. Even the coroner's reports used for reconstituted data (data derived from reevaluating coroner's reports), like mine from San Diego county, are influenced heavily by the gendered assumptions I have discussed throughout this essay. The reason for using both reconstituted and official compiled data to discuss method, rests less on their relative veracity than on the fact that, in terms of their own logic, these data (which others assume to be valid) suggest an alternative set of reasons for the differential between female and male suicide mortality. That is, the data suggest that females kill themselves less frequently than males, *not* because females' reasons are trivial compared to males', but rather because lethality is determined by cultural and social circumstance.

Statistics revealing the differences in methods chosen by female/male deaths by suicides ought to have alerted researchers that their assumptions about the "maleness" of fatal suicidal behavior rested more on socially constructed factors (like the unavailability of firearms for women) than essential emotional differences between women and men. That this generally did not occur to most researchers is further evidence for my thesis that statistics can never "speak for themselves," but rather that their meaning is always interpreted. In the case of women's and men's self-destructive behaviors, experts have constructed *a priori* theories that, in turn, have influenced their interpretation of statistics so that they have emphasized outcome (fatality) while neglecting the role that method plays in outcome.

Most psychoanalysts would insist that the method chosen for suicide reveals a great deal about both the intention and fantasies of the suicidal behavior. Those who choose "less lethal" methods may unconsciously seek intervention, or may hope to be saved at the last moment from the consequences of their acts (Alvarez, 1972). But, as Baechler (1979), Lifton (1979), and others have pointed out, *all* suicidal acts (fatal as well as nonfatal) involve a fantasy component, not the least of which may be imagining others' reactions to the suicidal act. Lifton describes this as a "quest for a future," (p. 248); while, for Baechler, suicide is a form of behavior or strategy "that seeks and finds the solution to an existential problem" (p. 11).

Moreover, we must not neglect the equally strong evidence that choices of method (as well as fantasies) are also determined by the material reality in which suicidal persons find themselves. "The relation of method," argues Hendin (1982), "cannot be understood without reference to the cultural context in which suicide occurs" (p. 144). In New York City, jumping from buildings accounts for 50% of suicides by African-Americans. "So much of the life of Harlem is lived in and on top of these tenements," writes Hendin, "that they occupy the conscious and unconscious life of their inhabitants and come to provide a tragic setting for black suicide" (p. 145).

He suggests that a similar analysis should be brought to bear on the relationship between firearms and female suicide mortality. Because firearms historically have been less available to women than poisons, the fact that women more frequently employ poisons to kill themselves has a material as well as a fantasy content.[7] "The sociocultural acceptance of guns in the United States," Hendin (1982) believes, "is related to the frequency with which they are used for suicide" (p. 145; see also Friedman, 1967; Taylor & Wicks, 1980). This connection explains why men, whose use of firearms has greater social acceptance, generally are more likely than women to resort to guns. The exception that supports this view is found in the American South. In that region, "where guns are most accepted as a part of the household and where children are often introduced to their use by their parents," Marks and Abernathy (1974) found that "firearms are used by both sexes more frequently [for suicide] than in the rest of the country" (p. 15).

In European countries, where suicide by firearms is far less frequent than in the United States, statistics indicate that males, like their American counterparts, kill themselves at about two to three times the rate of females. Moreover, throughout Europe, without exception, data shows that men choose more lethal methods than women do and men's use of firearms far exceeds that of women in every jurisdiction (Kramer, 1972; World Health Organization, 1968). Even in Denmark (Paerregaard, 1980), where firearms are forbidden, 15% of males, as compared with only 1% of females, used guns to kill themselves.

DIFFERENCES

As we have seen, suicidal behavior among men has generally been portrayed as originating from economic and social conditions, whereas suicidal behavior in women has typically been attributed to interpersonal, familial relations, or, less frequently, to women adopting male roles. Thus, experts have concluded that men's suicidal behavior, especially suicide mortality rates, can serve as a barometer of social and economic well-being, but women's suicidal behavior is a private issue requiring less public concern.

Although it would be misleading not to point out the flaws in official suicide mortality statistics, it would be foolish to assume that we ought to make no distinctions whatsoever between female and male suicidal patterns. Women are different from men. Women's history has taught us that socialization to prescribed roles has been very effective (Gilligan, 1982). Both women and men internalize social roles and gender-specific values; it would be absurd to contend that these are not manifested also in self-destructive behaviors (Canetto, 1991, 1992, 1992–1993). Value-laden as they are, the assumptions that suicide experts have projected onto women's behavior may reflect a certain level of social reality. The fact that increasing numbers of women have questioned traditional gender norms may have heightened rather than diminished the ambivalence and guilt that necessarily accompany challenges to dominant behavioral paradigms. In addition, we are only now coming to terms with the extent to which employment discrimination and harassment of women historically have contributed to this ambivalence. Thus, it is possible that some nexus exists between conforming to traditional feminine roles and low rates of fatal suicidal behavior in women (Canetto, 1991, 1992), as killing oneself is viewed as masculine. Attempting, but not "succeeding" at suicide, on the other hand, meshes with traditional expectations of women.

One of the criticisms of official statistics offered by Douglas (1967) was that husbands have more compelling reasons to hide a wife's suicide than wives have to hide a husband's. This is, according to Douglas, a woman killing herself is seen as a judgment on her husband; in contrast, when a husband kills himself, it is taken as a legitimate criticism of a particular social condition arising outside the family. What Douglas neglects to consider is the great extent to which both women and men have internalized these values, and the extent to which such internalization shapes behavior (Canetto, 1992–1993; Gordon, 1977; Mitchell, 1971; Rosenberg, 1973; Smith-Rosenberg, 1971; Smith-Rosenberg & Rosenberg, 1973; Welter, 1966).

In the Middle Ages strictures against suicide were based on the belief that a person's body was not her or his own, but God's or those above her or him in the hierarchy. Women, like serfs, have been and (as the current controversy over abortion indicates) continue to be socialized into the belief that their bodies are not theirs (Luker, 1984; Petchesky, 1984). Self-destruction must be preceded by a sense that a "self" exists. To the extent that some women have internalized those patriarchal values that have defined women's role as "selflessness," we would expect self-destruction not to be a behavior easily selected by women. Gilligan (1982) has found that when it comes to concepts of the self, women

> reveal the existence of a distinct moral language . . . which defines the moral problem as one of obligation to exercise care and avoid hurt. The inflicting of hurt is considered selfish and immoral in its reflection of unconcern, while the expression of care is seen as the fulfillment of moral responsibility. (p. 73)

Thus, one of the major restraints on women taking their lives may be their belief that they have a duty to live to care for others (Canetto, 1992). The idea that their children would be motherless may be a greater restraining influence on women than the fear by men that their children would be fatherless.[8]

Nonfatal suicidal behavior, on the other hand, has been viewed as appropriate for women, especially young women, (Canetto, 1992–1993). Because most women historically have been subsumed in the familial sphere (even when they work outside it), it has been assumed that the issues which inform their suicidal behavior revolve around familial matters. Moreover, to the extent that women have been taught that their intrinsic value can be reduced to their bodies, they may have learned to use their bodies to get what they want (Gordon, 1977). Thus, the threat to withhold their bodies (by threatening or "attempting" suicide) may be perceived by some women as a legitimate strategy to negotiate change.[9]

On the other hand, when men survive a suicidal act, they often are viewed as weak and are subject to ridicule (Canetto, 1991, 1992–1993; Kushner, 1989; Stillion, White, Edwards, & McDowell, 1989). Not only have experts assumed that men kill themselves when their careers fail or when they suffer public disgrace, such a reaction may be tacitly encouraged. To the extent that women internalize values that previously were prescribed for men, one would expect to find a growing rate of fatal suicidal behavior among women.

Of course, the difference between fatal and nonfatal suicide is not genetically programmed. Many men have engaged in nonfatal suicidal behavior to negotiate change in their relationships, and many women (most likely many more than official statistics report) have intended to kill themselves because they believed they had exhausted alternative strategies.

CONCLUSIONS

The portrayal of fatal suicidal behavior as a male behavior often tells us more about the assumptions that inform the collection of official mortality statistics than it does about the etiology of suicide. Conclusions about the epidemiology of suicidal behaviors are no more value free than the ideologies that inform them. The distortions found in official suicide statistics are not, of course, confined to sex/gender; allegations about women's suicidal behavior are symptomatic of the limitations inherent in all suicide statistics, including those on ethnicity, age, and social background.

On the other hand, these statistics are not valueless primarily because, like the values that inform them, they may sometimes reflect and reinforce social behavior. More important, we must not ignore the fact that strategies which do not necessarily result in death can be as "suicidal," in terms of intention, as those actions that result in death. If we wish to understand the etiology of suicidal behaviors, we must expand our vision beyond fatal suicidal acts. If we hope to examine suicide, insists British sociologist Taylor (1982), we "must widen the familiar question 'why do people kill themselves?' to include the broader question: 'why do so many people engage in acts of self damage which may result in death?' " (pp. 144). For Taylor, the term "suicidal" must include "any deliberate act of self damage, or potential self damage, where the individual has to await an outcome, and cannot be sure of survival" (p. 145). Perhaps Taylor throws his net too wide, but his general argument seems well taken in light of the way our emphasis on suicide mortality has distorted our view of women's suicidal behavior.

The goal of many investigations of suicide is to develop explanations for its etiology. Death is only one possible outcome of suicidal behavior. As long as studies continue to emphasize fatal suicidal behavior instead of suicidal behavior in general, we will continue to be trapped in a maze of circular reasoning in which the result of *some* self-destructive behavior is relied on to explain the causes for *all* self-destructive behavior. Certainly, if we wish to understand why similar circumstances do not always result in a suicidal act, we must examine suicidal behavior, not just outcome.

NOTES

1. Some of the material in this essay appeared in a slightly different form in my book *Self-destruction in the promised land* (Kushner, 1989). I thank Silvia Sara Canetto for her many useful comments and suggestions. All translations from the French are mine.

2. Unlike many classic texts, Durkheim's *Suicide* remains, in the words of French sociologists Baudelot and Establet (1984), "un livre vivant" (p. 9).

3. Gender is used here as the grammatical way of describing the properties associated with the distinctions of sex. As historian Scott (1986, compare to Scott, 1988, pp. 2–8 and Alcoff, 1988) has pointed out, "gender is the social organization of sexual difference (p. 1067)."

4. Among the earliest suicide statistics were those collected in Geneva beginning in 1650, but these made no distinctions between males and females (Haeberli, 1975). Although the weekly mortality rates, including suicide statistics for London were published as early as 1662, by the nineteenth century, there was still no systematic collection of suicide statistics by sex in Britain or London (Hacking, 1990). Suicide statistics for Paris were first collected during the Napoleonic era, but not until 1826 did the Administration de la justice criminelle (under the direction of le Ministère de la santé) publish them. Beginning in 1826 the data were published in the *Annales d'hygiène publique*, which recorded the incidence of suicide by age and by sex, but no distinction between nonfatal and fatal suicidal behavior (Baudelot & Establet, 1984; Chevalier, 1984).

5. That women should have been viewed as less suicidal than men is particularly puzzling given the long-held connection between suicide and insanity. For, as Showalter reminds us (Showalter, 1981, 1985), the early nineteenth-century assumption of "the predominance of women among the insane" became "a statistically verifiable phenomenon (p. 315)" during the second half of the century. Indeed, "by the end of the century," writes Showalter, "women had decisively taken the lead in

the career of psychiatric patient, a lead which they have retained ever since, and in ever-increasing numbers" (p. 316).

6. Maris (1981) defines firearms, hanging, and jumping as highly lethal; poisoning, cutting wrists, gassing, and most other methods as being of low lethality. There is, however, no necessary correlation between lethality and inflicted pain. An instantaneous death by firearms is less "painful" than slow death by strychnine.

7. A recent study (Browne, 1987) has found that female chemists are five times more likely to kill themselves than other women. This provides substance to the claim that when women have easy access to lethal methods, their rate of suicide increases.

8. This view is indirectly supported by Aveline, Baudelot, Beverraggi, and Lahlou (1984) who found that women tended to kill themselves on days when they were relatively less tied to child-care. That is, women's suicide mortality is highest on the day after the mid-weekly day off from school for French schoolchildren. Before 1972 children had Thursday off from school and women's rate increased on Friday; since then the rate for women has increased on Thursday because children are now off on Wednesday.

9. This is underlined by the fact that, according to Counts (1987), wife abuse is one of the most significant precipitants of female suicide in a number of societies, including North America. Anthropological studies (see Counts, 1987, for a review) suggest that female suicide is a culturally recognized behavior used to influence and/or take revenge against those who oppress them.

REFERENCES

American Journal of Insanity (1845–1860), *1–16*.

Alcoff, L. (1988). Cultural feminism versus post-structuralism: The identity crisis in feminist theory. *Signs: Journal of Women in Culture and Society, 13*, 404–436.

Alvarez, A. A. (1972). *The savage God: A study of suicide*. New York: Random House.

Aveline, F., Baudelot, C., Beverraggi, S., & Lahlou, S. (1984). Suicide et des rythmes sociaux. [Suicide and social rhythms]. *Economie et Statistique, 168*, 71–76.

Baechler, J. (1979). *Suicides* (B. Cooper Trans). New York: Basic Books.

Baudelot, C., & Establet, R. (1984). Suicide: L'évolution séculaire d'un fait social [Suicide and the century-long evolution of a social fact]. *Economie et Statistique, 168*, 59–70.

Baudelot, C., & Establet, R. (1986). *Durkheim et le suicide* [*Durkheim's suicide*] (2nd ed.). Paris: Presses Universitaires de France.

Bertrand, L. (1857). *Traité du suicide: Considéré dans ses rapports avec la philosophie, la théologie, la médecine, et la jurisprudence* [Treatise on suicide: Considered in light of philosophy, theology, medicine, and jurisprudence]. Paris: Baillière.

Besnard, P. (1973). Durkheim et les femmes ou *Le suicide* inachevé [Durkheim and women or attempted *Suicide*]. *Revue Française de Sociologie, 14*, 27–61.

Besnard, P. (1976). Anti- ou anté-durkheimisme? Contribution au débat sur les statistiques officielles du suicide [Against or before Durkheim? Contribution to the debate about official suicide statistics]. *Revue Française de Sociologie, 17*, 313–41.

Bigelow, L. J. (1866). The aesthetics of suicide. *The Galaxy*, 2, 471–476.

Bradford, W. (1979). *Of Plymouth plantation, 1620–1647* (S. E. Morison, Ed.). New York: Knopf. (Original work published 1647)

Brierre de Boismont, A. (1856). *Du suicide et de la folie suicide, considérés dans leurs rapports avec la statistique, la médicine, et la philosophie*. [Suicide and insane suicide, considered in their relationship with statistics, medicine, and philosophy] Paris: Baillière.

Browne, M. W. (1987, August 4). Women in chemistry: Higher suicide risk seen. *New York Times*, 21.

Canetto, S. S. (1991). Gender roles, suicide attempts, and substance abuse. *Journal of Psychology, 125*, 605–620.

Canetto, S. S. (1992). Gender and suicide in the elderly. *Suicide and Life-Threatening Behavior, 22*, 80–97.

Canetto, S. S. (1992–1993). She died for love and he for glory: Gender myths of suicidal behavior. *Omega, 26*, 1–17.

Cavan, R. S. (1928). *Suicide*. Chicago: The University of Chicago Press.

Chenais, J. C. (1973). L'évolution de la mortalité par suicide dans divers pays industrialisés [The evolution of mortality due to suicide in various industrial nations]. *Population, 28*, 419–422.

Chenais, J. C., & Vallin, J. (1981). Le suicide et la crise économique [Suicide and economic crisis]. *Population et Sociétés, 147*, 6–9.

Chevalier, L. (1984). *Classes laborieuses et classes dangereuses à Paris pendant la première moitié du XIX ième siècle* [Working and dangerous classes in Paris during the first half of the 19th century]. Paris: Hachette.

Cook, G. P. (1849). Statistics of suicide, which have occurred in the State of New York from Dec. 1st 1847 to Dec. 1, 1848. *American Journal of Insanity, 5*, 308–309.

Counts, D. A. (1987). Female suicide and wife abuse: A cross-cultural perspective. *Suicide and Life-Threatening Behavior, 17*, 194–204.

Davis, R. A. (1981). Female labor force participation, status integration and suicide, 1950–1969. *Suicide and Life Threatening Behavior, 11*, 111–123.

Douglas, J. D. (1967). *The social meanings of suicide*. Princeton: Princeton University Press.

Dublin, L. I. (1963). *Suicide: A sociological and statistical study*. New York: Ronald.

Durkheim, E. (1951). *Suicide: A study in sociology*. (J. A. Spaulding & G. Simpson, Trans.). Glencoe, IL: The Free Press. (Original work published 1897)

Esquirol, J. E. (1838). Du suicide [Suicide]. Reprinted and revised in *Des maladies mentales* (Vol. 1, pp. 526–676). Paris: Baillière. (Original work published 1821)

Falret, J. P. (1822). *De l'hypochondrie et du suicide* [*Depression and suicide*]. Paris: Croullebois.

Friedman, P. (1967). Suicide among police: A study of 93 suicides among New York City policemen, 1934–1940. In E. S. Shneidman (Ed.), *Essays in self-destruction* (pp. 414–449). New York: Science House.

Gates, B. T. (1980). Suicide and the Victorian physicians. *Journal of the History of the Behavioral Sciences, 16*, 164–174.

Gates, B. T. (1988). *Victorian suicide: Mad crimes and sad histories*. Princeton: Princeton University Press.

Gilligan, C. (1982). *In a different voice: Psychological theory and women's development*. Cambridge, MA: Harvard University Press.

Gordon, L. (1977). *Woman's body, woman's right*. New York: Penguin.

Hacking, I. (1990). *The taming of chance*. Cambridge, UK: Cambridge University Press.

Haeberli, L. (1975). Le suicide à Genève au XVIIIe siècle [Suicide in Geneva in the 18th century]. In L. Binz & S. Stelling-Michaud (Ed.), *Pour une histoire qualitative: Etudes offertes à Sven Stelling-Michaud* (pp. 115–129). Geneva: Presses Universitaires Romandes.

Harnisch, P. (1989, Summer). Suicide and gender. *NewsLink, 14*, 1,3.

Hawthorne, N. (1983). *The Blithedale romance*. New York: Penguin Books. (Original work published 1852)

Hellon, C. P., & Solomon, M. I. (1980). Suicide and age in Alberta, Canada, 1951 to 1977: The changing profile. *Archives of General Psychiatry, 37*, 508–509.

Hendin, H. (1982). *Suicide in America*. New York: Norton.

Higonnet, M. (1985). Suicide: Representations of the feminine in the Nineteenth Century. *Poetics Today, 6*, 103–118.

Hooper, K., & Guttmacher, S. (1979). Rethinking suicide: a critical epidemiology. *International Journal of Health Services, 9*, 417–438.

Huchcroft, S. (1989, Fall). What can we learn from female suicides? *NewsLink, 15*, pp. 12–13.

Hunt, E. K. (1845). Statistics of suicides in the United States. *American Journal of Insanity, 1*, 225–234.

Johnson, K. K. (1979). Durkheim revisited: Why do women kill themselves? *Suicide and Life-Threatening Behavior, 9*, 145–153.

Knighton, W. (1881). Suicidal mania. *Littel's living age, 148*, 376–381.

Kramer, M., Pollack, E. S., Redick, R. W., & Locke, B. Z. (1972). *Mental disorders/suicide*. Cambridge, MA: Harvard University Press.

Kushner, H. I. (1985). Women and suicide in historical perspective. *Signs: Journal of Women in Culture and Society, 10*, 537–552.

Kushner, H. I. (1989). *Self-destruction in the promised land: A psychocultural biology of American suicide*. New Brunswick: Rutgers University Press.

Kushner, H. I. (1993). Suicide, gender, and the fear of modernity in nineteenth-century medical and social thought. *Journal of Social History, 26*, 461–490.

Lane, R. (1979). *Violent death in the city: Suicide, accident, and murder in Nineteenth Century Philadelphia*. Cambridge, MA: Harvard University Press.

Lester, D. (1988). The suicide rates of American women. In D. Lester (Ed.), *Why women kill themselves* (pp. 25–33). Springfield, IL: Charles C. Thomas.

Lieberman, L. (1990, December). *Revising reality: The construction of suicide in Nineteenth-Century France*. Paper presented at the 105th annual meeting of the American Historical Association, New York.

Lieberman, L. J. (1991). Romanticism and the culture of suicide in Nineteenth-Century France. *Comparative Studies in Society and History, 33*, 73–85.

Lifton, R. J. (1979). *The broken connection: On death and the continuity of life*. New York: Simon and Schuster.

Luker, K. (1984). *Abortion and the politics of motherhood*. Berkeley: University of California Press.

Maris, R. (1981). *Pathways to suicide: A survey of self-destructive behavior*. Baltimore, MD: Johns Hopkins University Press.

Marks, A., & Abernathy, T. (1974). Toward a sociocultural perspective on means of self-destruction. *Suicide and Life-Threatening Behavior, 4*, 3–17.

Masaryk, T. G. (1970). *Suicide and the meaning of civilization* (W. B. Weist & R. G. Batson, Trans.). Chicago: University of Chicago Press.

Mathews, J. (1981, December 26). Darker side of sunny California, a high suicide rate under study. *The Washington Post*, A9.

McIntosh, J. L., & Santos, J. F. (1982). Changing patterns in methods of suicide by race and sex. *Suicide and Life-Threatening Behavior, 12*, 221–233.

Merllié, D. (1987). Le suicide et ses statistiques: Durkheim et sa posterité [Suicide and its statistics: Durkheim and his descendants]. *Revue Philosophique de la France et l'Étranger, 1086*, 303–25.

Mitchell, J. (1971). *The woman's estate*. New York: Pantheon Books.

Monk, M. (1975). Epidemiology. In S. Perlin (Ed.), *A handbook for the study of suicide* (pp. 185–211). New York: Oxford University Press.

Morselli, H. (1882). *Suicide: An essay on comparative moral statistics*. New York: Appleton.

Mulhall, M. G. (1883). Insanity, suicide, and civilization. *The Contemporary Review, 63*, 901–908.

New York Times. (1861, January 17). Suicides in New York City in 1860, section 2, p. 1.

O'Carroll, P. W. (1989). A consideration of the validity and reliability of suicide mortality data. *Suicide and Life-Threatening Behavior, 19*, 1–16.

Paerregaard, G. (1980). Suicide in Denmark: A statistical review for the past 150 years. *Suicide and Life-Threatening Behavior, 10*, 150–157.

Petchesky, R. P. (1984). *Abortion and women's choice: The state sexuality, and reproductive freedom*. New York: Longman.

Reeves, R. N. (1897). Suicide and the environment. *Popular Science Monthly, 51*, 186–191.

Rhodes, A. (1876). Suicide. *The Galaxy, 21*, 188–199.

Rosenberg, C. E. (1973). Sexuality, class and role in 19th-Century America. *American Quarterly, 25*, 131–154.

Sainsbury, P. (1955). *Suicide in London: An ecological study*. London: Chapman & Hall.

Sanborn, C. (1990). Gender socialization and suicide. *Suicide and Life-Threatening Behavior, 20*, 148–155.

San Diego County, California, *Coroner's Reports*. (1880–1986).

San Diego Union. (1880–1993).

Scott, J. W. (1986). Gender: A useful category of historical analysis. *American Historical Review, 91*, 1053–1075.

Scott, J. W. (1988). *Gender and the politics of history*. New York: Columbia University Press.

Shneidman, E. S., & Farberow, N. L. (1961). Statistical comparisons between attempted and committed suicides. In N. L. Farberow and E. S. Shneidman (Eds.), *The cry for help* (pp. 24–37). New York: McGraw-Hill.

Showalter, E. (1981). Victorian women and insanity. In A. Scull (Ed.), *Madhouse, mad-doctors, and madmen: The social history of psychiatry in the Victorian era* (pp. 313–331). Philadelphia: University of Pennsylvania Press.

Showalter, E. (1985). *The female malady: Women, madness, and English culture, 1830–1980*. New York: Random House.

Skelton, R. A. (1900). Statistics of suicide. *The Nineteenth Century, 48*, 465–495.

Smith-Rosenberg, C. (1971). Beauty, the beast, and the militant woman: A case study in sex roles and social stress in Jacksonian America. *American Quarterly, 23*, 562–584.

Smith-Rosenberg, C., & Rosenberg, C. E. (1973). The female animal: Medical and biological views of woman and her role in Nineteenth-Century America. *Journal of American History, 60*, 332–356.

Stafford, M. C., & Weisheit, R. A. (1988). Changing age patterns of U. S. male and female suicide rates, 1934–1983. *Suicide and Life-Threatening Behavior, 18*, 149–63.

Stillion, J. M., White, H., Edwards, P. J., & McDowell, E. E. (1989). Ageism and sexism in suicide attitudes. *Death Studies, 12*, 247–261.

Strahan, S. A. K. (1893). *Suicide and insanity: A philosophical and sociological study*. London: Swan Sonnenschein.

A Southern Physician. (1847). Suicide. *The American Whig Review, 6*, 137–145.

A Southern Physician. (1854). Suicide. *The Democratic Review, 34*, 405–417.

Tavris, C. (1991). The mismeasure of woman: Paradoxes and perspectives in the study of gender. In J. D. Goodchilds (Ed.), *Psychological perspectives on human diversity in America* (pp. 87–136). Washington, DC: American Psychological Association.

Taylor, M., & Wicks, J. (1980). The choice of weapons: A study of suicide by sex, race, and religion. *Suicide and Life-Threatening Behavior, 10*, 142–149.

Taylor, S. (1982). *Durkheim and the study of suicide*. New York: St. Martin's Press.

U. S. Census Office. (1855). 7th Census, 1850. *Mortality statistics of the seventh census of the United States, 1850*. Washington, DC: Nicholson.

Welter, B. (1966). The cult of true womanhood: 1820–1860. *American Quarterly, 18*, 151– 174.

World Health Organization. (1968). *World health statistics report*. Geneva, Switzerland: Author.

Winslow, F. (1978). *The anatomy of suicide*. Boston: Longwood Press. (Original work published 1840)

■ 3
The Epidemiology of Women's Suicidal Behavior[1]

Silvia Sara Canetto and David Lester

This chapter reviews the data on the epidemiology of suicidal behaviors in women. The first part of the chapter deals with the nature of the data, and specifically issues of data comprehensiveness, validity, and reliability. While it is generally recognized that the data on nonfatal suicidal behavior have limitations, it is often less well recognized that the data on fatal suicidal behavior may be a particularly poor measure of women's suicide mortality (Kushner, 1993; Phillips & Ruth, 1993). Keeping this in mind, the second part of this chapter critically reviews the information on rates of nonfatal and fatal suicidal behavior.

THE NATURE AND LIMITATIONS OF THE DATA ON SUICIDAL BEHAVIORS

Information on rates of nonfatal and fatal suicidal behaviors is available through local epidemiological surveys and/or official government sources. This information has a number of limitations, including variations in the data comprehensiveness, as well as variations and biases in the criteria used for the determination of suicidal behavior and mortality.

Data Comprehensiveness

Information on nonfatal suicidal behavior is available through time-limited local epidemiological surveys. No country maintains an ongoing, nationally comprehensive record of nonfatal suicidal behaviors. Thus, the information on nonfatal suicidal behavior is neither longitudinally nor geographically comprehensive.

Information on rates of fatal suicidal behavior is usually available through official government sources and local epidemiological surveys. Many countries compile official mortality statistics and report them to the World Health Organization (WHO). Official suicide mortality data, however, are not available for many nations, including most African and many Middle Eastern countries (Diekstra, 1990). Furthermore, official mortality statistics do not include information about factors such as occupation, socioeconomic status, or living arrangements. Local epidemiological studies typically cover a broader range of variables than national mortality statistics but may not be generalizable beyond the community from which the sample was drawn.

A problem common to both national and local data sources is that information about suicidal cases is not always simultaneously classified by sex, age, and ethnicity. Therefore, important comparisons across specific gender/age/ethnic sub-groups are impossible.

Data Validity and Reliability

The most serious limitations of available data result from variations in definitions of suicidal behaviors, reporting practices, and criteria used for the determination of suicidal behavior and mortality (McIntosh, 1989; O'Carroll, 1989). One major problem is the lack of standardized definitions of the main types of suicidal behaviors. For example, DeLeo and Diekstra (1990) note that some authors use "attempted suicide" and "parasuicide" as synonyms, while others view the former as "implying an intention (however vague and ambiguous) to do away with oneself, while the latter encompasses also so-called 'contraintentioned' acts, meaning that the individual uses the semantic blanket of 'suicide' with a conscious absence of any lethal intention" (pp. 178–179). This lack of standardized terminology makes it difficult to compare studies.

A second problem involves variations in reporting practices and criteria used for the determination of suicidal behaviors and mortality. As discussed above, the classification of self-destructive behaviors as suicidal is hampered by a lack of consensus over terminology. The recording of an act as suicidal may be affected by the clinician's training, beliefs about and social consequences of the suicidal behavior, the characteristics of the suicidal person (e.g., age, sex, and ethnicity) and the circumstances of the suicidal action (e.g., method used and antecedents).

A large proportion of nonfatal suicidal acts never reach the attention of the medical and psychological community. Of those which do, some never go beyond the individual private clinician and are therefore not recorded. According to studies reviewed by Jack (1992), as many as one-third of suicidal persons do not attend the hospital for treatment, and at least 10 percent are discharged from the emergency room without being admitted to the hospital.

It is well known that the classification of a death as suicide is influenced by the background of coroners and medical examiners, the cultural beliefs about and social consequences of death by suicide (e.g., burial practices and attitudes toward surviving members), and the circumstances of death (e.g., the method employed) (McIntosh, 1989; O'Carroll, 1989). For example, according to a study by Walsh, Walsh, and Whelan (1975), coroners are more likely to miss a suicide if the method of suicide is drowning, jumping, or ingesting poison.

While it is generally accepted that official statistics of death by suicide underestimate "true" prevalence, it is less well recognized that underreporting biases may affect some groups more than others. There is evidence indicating that women's suicidal deaths are particularly susceptible to underreporting and misclassification (Phillips & Ruth, 1993). First, women tend to use methods (e.g., poison) that are more likely to lead to misclassification (Phillips & Ruth, 1993; Walsh, Walsh, & Whelan, 1975). Second, because self-poisoning leaves room for at least temporary rescue, a woman's death from complications of a self-poisoning act may not be recorded as intentional (Kushner, 1985, 1993). Third, because it is generally assumed that killing oneself is a masculine activity, coroners may miss the suicidal clues in a woman's death (Canetto, 1992–1993; Kushner, 1985, 1993). Finally, because it is generally believed that women's suicidal behavior is precipitated by interpersonal problems, family members may be more likely to hide a woman's suicidal death than a man's (Douglas, 1967).

Summary and Conclusions

Given the variations in the comprehensiveness, criteria, and methods of data recording, one ought to consider the data on suicidal behaviors as conservative estimates. The possibility of systematic and unsystematic biases should also be considered. With these forewarnings, we now move to a discussion of the available epidemiological data on women's suicidal behavior.

THE EPIDEMIOLOGY OF WOMEN'S NONFATAL SUICIDAL BEHAVIOR

Nationality, Ethnicity, and Culture

Available studies indicate that in industrialized countries the majority of nonfatal suicidal acts are performed by women (see Jack, 1992; Kessler & McRae, 1983; Weissman, 1974; Wexler, Weissman, & Kasl, 1978, for reviews). For example, women outnumber men in all countries reviewed by Weissman, except India and Poland. Another exception is Sri Lanka, where women and men were found to have similar rates of nonfatal suicidal behavior (Hettiarachchi & Kodituwakku, 1989). The female to male ratio of nonfatal suicidal behavior is usually on the order of 2:1 (Weissman, 1974). In the United States, this ratio is estimated to be 3:1 (McIntosh, 1993). According to Whitehead, Johnson and Ferrence (1973), the higher rates of nonfatal suicidal behavior for females, as compared to males, may be an artifact of biased data collection, and specifically, the exclusion of data on nonfatal suicidal behavior from jails. In their London, Ontario, study, which included information from general hospitals, psychiatric hospitals, senior citizen homes, nursing homes, veteran hospitals, supervised homes, family physicians, and the county jail, female and male rates were found to be similar.

Overall rates of nonfatal suicidal behavior, however, vary considerably across localities and times of data collection. For example, according to data from a multicentre study of nonfatal suicidal behavior in selected European catchment areas during the year 1989, women had higher rates of nonfatal suicidal behavior than men in all catchment areas but one (Helsinki, Finland), with the female to male ratio ranging from 0.71:1 to 2.15:1 (Platt et al., 1992). The overall incidence of female nonfatal suicidal behavior, however, varied from a high of 595 per 100,000 in Pontoise, France, to a low of 95 in Guipuzcoa, Spain.

Within-country variations across ethnic and religious groups have been documented. For example, in Singapore, rates of suicidal behavior are highest among Indian women (344 per 100,000), followed by Chinese women (112 per 100,000), and Malay women (51 per 100,000) (Kok, 1988). Similarly, a Malay study found that Indian women committed a majority of the nonfatal suicidal acts, even though Indians represented 25 percent of the population (Maniam, 1988). Data from a five-site United States' study (Moscicki et al., 1988) indicated that Whites were more likely to have engaged in nonfatal suicidal behavior than non-Whites.

Age

According to a 1974 review of national and international studies, nonfatal suicidal behavior is most prevalent in individuals ages 20 to 30 (Weissman, 1974). More recent studies confirm historical trends. In the 1980s, nonfatal suicidal behavior was found to be most common in females under the age of 30 in Durban, South Africa (Bosch & Schlebusch, 1987), among West Indians living in Great Britain (Merrill & Owens, 1987), and among Indians living in Malaysia (Maniam, 1988). A Dutch study of suicidal persons seen by general practitioners between 1979 and 1986 reported that the majority of these suicidal individuals were 15 to 34 years of age (Diekstra & van Egmond, 1989). Finally, a multicentre European study (Platt et al., 1992) found that women's nonfatal suicidal behavior was most common among 25 to 34 year olds in 7 of 15 areas surveyed, and among 14 to 24 year olds in five other areas. In 13 of the 15 areas surveyed, the lowest rate was among women 55 years of age or older.

Social class, education, employment, and economic resources

The phenomenon of nonfatal suicidal behavior has been described as reaching epidemic proportions (Jack, 1992). According to information reviewed by Jack, five million persons in the United States were estimated to have engaged in nonfatal suicidal behavior in 1985. This phenomenon, notes Jack, is not limited to the United States; it is also found in Great Britain where the incidence of deliberate self-poisoning increased by 90 percent between 1967 and 1977.

According to Jack, the risk for nonfatal suicidal behavior is not the same for "all [individuals] without regard for class, creed, or other social category" (p. 3), for in industrialized countries, nonfatal suicidal behavior is most prevalent among working-class females. For example, there is evidence that lower socioeconomic background (Moscicki et al., 1988) and diminished educational achievement (Platt, Hawton, Kreitman, Fagg, & Foster, 1988; Petronis, Samuels, Moscicki, & Anthony, 1990) are associated with increased risk for nonfatal suicidal behavior. Furthermore, according to a study by Platt and colleagues (1988), the risk for nonfatal suicidal behavior is greater among unemployed females than among unemployed males. In fact, an Oxford study (Hawton, Fagg, & Simkin, 1988) found that between 1979 and 1982, rates of nonfatal suicidal behavior among unemployed women were 7.5 to 10.9 times higher than among employed women, and that these rates were particularly high for women unemployed for more than a year. It has also been noted that unemployment and occupational status as a housewife are predictors of repeated suicidal behavior (Hawton et al., 1988; Suleiman, Moussa, & El-Islam, 1989). Finally, it has been found that suicidal women tend to have financial problems (Kreitman & Schreiber, 1979).

Personal relationships

The evidence regarding the relationship status of suicidal women is equivocal. Perhaps this is because studies have not looked at the data on women and men separately. Due to the typical age of persons who engage in nonfatal suicidal behavior, one would expect a preponderance of single persons. According to a review of studies by Weissman (1974), suicidal persons tend to be married. Age-standardized population comparisons, however, often show an excess of divorced persons. In addition, a recent epidemiological study of five United States' communities by Petronis et al. (1990) reported that being separated or divorced was associated with increased risk for nonfatal suicidal behavior.

There is consistent evidence indicating that the relationships of persons who are suicidal are typically hostile (Richman & Rosenbaum, 1970; Rosenbaum & Richman, 1970; Wolk-Wasserman, 1986). Suicidal women who are married or in a heterosexual relationship tend to report battering (Arcel, Mantonakis, Petersson, Jemos, & Kaliteraki, 1992; Bergman & Brismar, 1991; Stephens, 1985), "physical violence sufficient to cause damage" (Kreitman & Schreiber, 1979, p. 476), psychological violence, serious emotional neglect, and/or sexual infidelity (Arcel et al., 1992; Stephens, 1985). According to a Swedish study of inpatient admissions by Bergman and Brismar (1991), battered women were eight times more likely to be hospitalized for a nonfatal suicidal act than non-battered women. It is noteworthy that these battered suicidal women rarely reported the physical abuse to the physician who treated them after their suicidal act, a finding which is consistent with other reports on battered women. This prompted the authors to recommend that caretakers always consider the possibility of on-going physical abuse in suicidal women.

Finally, several studies (e.g., Adityanjee, 1986; Arcel et al., 1992; Kok, 1988; Sefa-Dedeh & Canetto, 1992) have documented that nonfatal suicidal behavior in women is often associated with the rigid expectations and the powerlessness of being a daughter, wife, or daughter-in-law within patriarchal family systems and societies. For example, Adityanjee (1986), commenting on the high rates of nonfatal and fatal suicidal behavior among married females in India, concluded that "the ominous role of marriage in case of females as a predisposing factor for suicides and suicidal attempts is understandable in the context of the prevalent problems surrounding dowries and consequent maltreatment of brides in the extended families" (p. 67). Similarly, a study of the relationships of Greek and Danish suicidal women (Arcel et al., 1992) reported that suicidal married women were "dominated by their husbands and suffered significant restrictions in mobility and financial control" (p. 195).

Method

The choice of suicidal method is influenced by familiarity and accessibility. For example, in Ghana (Sefa-Dedeh & Canetto, 1992), India (Adityanjee, 1986: Ponnudurai, Jeyakar, & Saraswathy, 1986), Malaysia (Maniam, 1988), and Sri Lanka (Hettiarachchi & Kodituwakku, 1989), common substances used by women in acts of nonfatal suicidal behavior are household poisons. In industrialized countries, the majority of women's nonfatal suicidal acts involve medically-prescribed psychotropic drugs (Jack, 1992; Weissman, 1974). Such choice of suicidal method is not surprising, given that in these countries women are more likely than men to be prescribed and to take psychotropic drugs, especially sedative-hypnotics (Cooperstock, 1982; Fidell, 1982). As expected, the specific drugs used in each country are usually those most widely prescribed and/or available (Weissman, 1974).

Mental disorders

Theoretical approaches to nonfatal suicidal behavior have been dominated by the assumption of major psychopathology. Several studies have confirmed an association between nonfatal suicidal behavior and the diagnosis of mental disorder. For example, Moscicki et al. (1988) found that persons who had a lifetime diagnosis of mental disorder had the highest risk for nonfatal suicidal behavior. Similarly, Sorenson and Golding (1988) reported that individuals with a mental disorder diagnosis were more likely to think about killing themselves and to engage in nonfatal suicidal behavior than those without such a diagnosis. One potential confounding factor, however, is suicidal ideation being taken as an indication of mental disorder.

Jack (1992), however, has questioned the idea that individuals who engage in suicidal behavior are necessarily psychologically disturbed. He cited a study by Kreitman and Schreiber (1979) in which a majority of young suicidal females did not qualify for a major clinical psychological diagnosis, and a study by Newson-Smith and Hirsch (1979) showing that signs of mental disorder, when present, were transient in the vast majority of self-poisoners.

Information about the specific clinical conditions of suicidal women, as distinct from those of suicidal men, is unavailable since most studies do not report their findings by sex. The most common major clinical diagnosis assigned to suicidal persons is depression, accounting for 35 to 79 percent of all reported cases (Weissman, 1974). It is possible, however, that the diagnosis of depression may be given because of the suicidal behavior, rather than independently.

The second most common diagnosis associated with suicidal behaviors is substance abuse/dependence (Canetto, 1991). A recent study of five communities in the United States (Petronis et al., 1990) found that the risk for suicidal behavior was associated with cocaine use, but not with the illicit use of marijuana, sedative-hypnotics, or sympathomimetic stimulants. In another study in the United States (Gomberg, 1989), women with alcohol problems, especially those under the age of 40, were more likely to have engaged in nonfatal suicidal behavior than a control group of women with no alcohol problems. Yet, according to a study of nonfatal suicidal behavior conducted in Edinburgh, Scotland, alcohol dependence and consumption of alcohol at the time of the suicidal act appeared to be less common in females than in males (Platt & Robinson, 1991). Female alcoholics were more likely to report that their husband, cohabiting partner (Platt & Robinson, 1991) or father (Gomberg, 1989) had a problem with alcohol abuse.

Personality

It has been assumed that suicidal women have personality problems (e.g., Schrut & Michels, 1974). Specifically, it has been noted that suicidal women are excessively dependent (see Canetto & Feldman, 1993, for a review). The evidence cited in support of this idea comes from two main sources: studies of suicidal women's personalities and studies of the antecedents of women's suicidal behavior. Personality studies (e.g., Cantor, 1976; Neuringer & Lettieri, 1982) have found that suicidal women tend to report affiliative needs, feelings of helplessness, and/or feelings of inadequacy. According to studies of the antecedents of suicidal behavior, women experience serious interpersonal conflict (Birtchnell, 1981; Bosch & Schlebusch, 1987; Fieldsend & Lowenstein, 1981; Maris, 1971, 1981; Paykel, Prusoff, & Myers, 1975; Sefa-Dedeh & Canetto, 1992; Suleiman et al., 1989; Weissman, Fox, & Klerman, 1973), marital infidelity (Stephens, 1985), threat of separation and/or actual separation, and/or divorce (Breed, 1967; Robins, Schmidt, & O'Neal, 1957) during the months preceding a suicidal act. Furthermore, suicidal women tend to attribute their suicidal acts to interpersonal problems (Beck, Lester, & Kovacs, 1973; Vinoda, 1966).

A limitation of these two kinds of studies is that conclusions about suicidal women's dependence are made on the basis of self-report measures and without consideration of the relational context. It has been argued (Birtchnell, 1991; Bornstein, 1992) that self-report measures of dependence may be contaminated by social desirability biases, since acknowledgment of dependence is encouraged in women but not in men. According to Bornstein, the solution to such biases is to include projective measures of dependence. Furthermore, according to Birtchnell (1991), dependence should be measured "in relation to the response of the person towards whom it is directed" (p. 282). He pointed out that dependence may be "induced or intensified by another who has an excessive need to be depended upon . . . [or] it can be made to appear exaggerated by the rejection of another who cannot tolerate being depended upon" (p. 282).

When family members of suicidal persons are studied, it is often found that they have significant psychological difficulties of their own. For example, in a personality study by Bhagat (1976), both suicidal females and their male partners were found to be anxious and mistrusting. According to a study by Wolk-Wasserman (1985), approximately one-third of partners of suicidal persons admitted to an intensive care unit had a history of suicidal behavior; many of them "felt desperate about not being able to handle . . . their own problems" (p. 591). Finally, Canetto and Feldman (1993), using projective measures of dependence, noted that suicidal women and their male partners had similar deficits in their covert capacity for autonomy in relationships.

THE EPIDEMIOLOGY OF FATAL SUICIDAL BEHAVIOR

Nationality, Ethnicity, and Culture

Women are less likely to kill themselves than men in *almost* all countries reporting their mortality statistics to the World Health Organization. The latest (1984–1990) WHO suicide mortality rates (per 100,000) and female/male ratios are shown in Table 3.1.

The female/male suicide mortality ratio varies considerably from country to country. In general, the ratio is higher in Asian countries. For example, the female/male ratio ranges from 0.00 in Malta and Egypt, to 0.77 in Hong Kong, and 0.86 for Singapore.

Lester (1982) examined international data on suicide mortality rates for females and males for 1975. He concluded that Asian countries had proportionately more female deaths from suicide than non-Asian countries. In 1975, the female/male ratio was significantly higher in Asia (M = 0.74) than in Europe (0.45), and in South America and Central America/Caribbean countries (0.34). Lester also looked at the distribution of suicide mortality rates by age for women and men in each country as a function of the level of national economic development (defined as the gross national product per capita). For females, the peak age for death by suicide rose from 55 to 64 to 75 + as the level of economic development of the nations increased, with the exception of the least-developed nations, where the peak was for those aged 15 to 24. For males, suicide mortality rates rose with age in nations at all levels of economic development.

Even though women's rates of suicide mortality are lower than men's for most countries for which data are available, in some countries women's absolute rates of suicide mortality are quite high. The countries with the highest rates of suicide mortality for women include Hungary (21.4 per 100,000 in 1990), Sri Lanka (18.9 in 1986), Denmark (16.3 in 1990), and East Germany (16.3 in 1989).

One exception to the male predominance in suicide mortality is Papua New Guinea. Anthropological studies of suicidal behavior in several Papua

TABLE 3.1 Female and Male Suicide Mortality Rates (per 100,000) for Countries of the World

Country	Suicide Mortality Rates Female	Male	Female/Male ratio	Year[a]
Argentina	4.4	10.5	0.42	1987
Australia	5.6	21.0	0.27	1988
Austria	13.4	34.8	0.39	1990
Belgium	14.1	30.9	0.46	1986
Bulgaria	8.8	20.7	0.43	1990
Canada	6.0	20.9	0.29	1989
Chile	2.0	9.2	0.22	1987
China	20.4	14.9	1.37	1987
Colombia	1.6	6.0	0.27	1984
Costa Rica	1.3	8.6	0.15	1988
Czechoslovakia	8.9	27.3	0.33	1990
Denmark	16.3	32.2	0.51	1990
Ecuador	2.8	6.3	0.44	1988
Egypt	0.0	0.1	0.00	1987
El Salvador	6.1	14.8	0.41	1984
Finland	11.5	46.4	0.25	1989
France	11.7	30.5	0.38	1989
Gernamy, East	16.3	36.1	0.45	1989
Germany, West	10.0	23.5	0.43	1989
Greece	2.1	5.6	0.37	1989
Hong Kong	9.1	11.8	0.77	1989
Hungary	21.4	59.9	0.36	1990
Iceland	3.9	27.4	0.14	1990
Israel	4.0	9.7	0.41	1988
Italy	4.4	11.1	0.40	1988
Jamaica	0.1	0.3	0.33	1984
Japan	12.4	20.4	0.61	1990
Korea	4.4	11.5	0.38	1987
Kuwait	0.6	1.0	0.60	1987
Luxembourg	9.8	30.0	0.33	1989
Malta	0.0	4.6	0.00	1990
Martinique	3.0	4.4	0.68	1985
Mauritius	10.5	17.4	0.60	1987
Mexico	0.7	3.6	0.19	1986
Netherlands	7.5	13.0	0.58	1989
New Zealand	6.0	22.2	0.27	1987
Norway	8.4	23.0	0.37	1989
Panama	1.9	5.6	0.34	1987
Papua New Guinea	0.2	0.1	2.00	1987
Poland	4.5	22.0	0.20	1990
Portugal	4.5	13.5	0.33	1990
Puerto Rico	1.9	16.4	0.12	1989
Singapore	13.2	15.4	0.86	1989
Spain	4.0	10.6	0.38	1987
Sri Lanka	18.9	46.9	0.40	1986

TABLE 3.1 Continued

Country	Suicide Mortality Rates Female	Male	Female/Male ratio	Year[a]
Surinam	11.6	31.8	0.36	1985
Sweden	11.5	26.4	0.44	1988
Switzerland	12.7	31.5	0.40	1990
Trinidad & Tobago	7.4	19.0	0.39	1988
United Kingdom	3.8	12.6	0.30	1990
USA	5.0	20.1	0.25	1988
USSR	9.1	34.4	0.26	1990
Uruguay	4.4	18.1	0.24	1989
Venezuela	1.5	6.6	0.23	1987
Yugoslavia	9.9	23.2	0.43	1989

[a]Latest available year from the World Health Organization.

New Guinea ethnic groups (Counts, 1987; Healey, 1979; Johnson, 1981) confirm that people who kill themselves are usually women. In fact, according to Healey (1979), only women of the Maring ethnic group kill themselves.

Another exception is the People's Republic of China, which now reports on about 10 percent of its population, and has a higher suicide mortality rate for women than for men, 20.4 per 100,000 per year for women versus 14.9 for men in 1987 (Lester, 1990). In rural areas these rates were 32.3 and 23.2, respectively, and in urban areas 11.4 and 8.7.

Other exceptions can be found among several ethnic and/or regional groups. In some cases, women's suicide mortality exceeds men's in subgroups of the populations of a given country. For example, In England and Wales, mortality by suicide among immigrants of Indian origin is higher among women than men (Raleigh, Bulusu, & Balarajan, 1990). Furthermore, Brown (1986) has reported that death from suicide among the Aguaruna and Peruvian Amazon region is especially common in women and young men. Finally, in the Deganga region of India, women constituted 79 percent of the deaths by suicide in 1979 (Banerjee, Nandi, Nandi, Sarkar, Boral, & Ghosh, 1990).

In the United States death by suicide is less common in women than men, independent of age, ethnic origin, and relationship status (Lester, 1988). Rates of fatal suicidal behavior, however, vary considerably across time, ethnic group, and locality. Nationwide data show that the female-to-male suicide mortality ratio peaked in the early 1970s; the ratio was 0.27 in 1933, 0.31 in 1940, 0.28 in 1950, 0.29 in 1960, 0.39 in 1970, 0.30 in 1980, and 0.24 in 1990 (National Center for Health Statistics, 1933–1990).

There are large regional variations in suicide mortality across regional and ethnic groups in the United States. In 1980 the female/male ratio ranged from 0.17 in South Dakota to 0.51 in Nevada (Lester, 1988, 1991a).

In 1980, the female/male ratio was similar for Whites (0.21) and non-Whites (0.19) (Lester, 1989).

Age

No consistent relationship was found between age and suicide mortality in women across the world. An international study of suicide mortality rates during the period 1950–1971 by Ruzicka (1976) discerned three age-related patterns of suicide in women. A first pattern, found in Austria, Czechoslovakia, France, Hungary, Italy, Netherlands, Portugal, and West Germany, involved continuously increasing mortality by suicide with age. In a number of countries, including Australia, Belgium, Canada, Denmark, England and Wales, Finland, Israel, New Zealand, Norway, Poland, Sweden, Switzerland, and the United States, rates of death by suicide peaked around middle age and declined thereafter. In the third pattern, suicide rates were high at younger ages, descended to a trough for various periods of time, and then resumed an upward trend. This pattern was found in Bulgaria, Greece, Japan, Singapore, and Yugoslavia.

A review of the mortality data for 1970 and 1980 (Lester, 1991b) revealed some shifts in these age patterns of death by suicide. In a majority of countries women's rates of suicidal deaths rose with age (Austria, Bulgaria, France, Greece, Hong Kong, Hungary, Italy, Japan, Portugal, Singapore, and Spain). Several nations, including the United States, followed Ruzicka's (1976) second pattern of suicide mortality, with a peak in the mid-adulthood years, broadly defined. In some cases, this mid-adulthood peak shifted from decade to decade. For example, the peak suicide rate for Australian women was among those aged 55-64 years of age in 1970, and in those 35 to 44 years of age in 1980. No nation conformed to the third, bimodal pattern described by Ruzicka, although in a few countries (Chile, Thailand, and Venezuela) the peak suicide mortality rate for women fell in the age range 15 to 24.

In the United States, suicide mortality rates for women peak at mid-life. Because female rates decrease after mid-life, and male rates reach their highest levels in late life, the gender differential in rates is least at mid-life (ages 40 to 59, most often ages 45 to 54), and greatest during late life (ages 65 and older) (McIntosh, 1992). It should be noted, however, that rates for middle-aged women are less than half those for middle-aged men (McIntosh, 1991).

The data reviewed earlier indicate, with some exceptions, that women are less likely to kill themselves than men. However, when mortality data are examined by age and gender, one finds more exceptions to the usual preponderance of men among the casualties of suicide. For example, Barraclough (1988) examined women's and men's suicide mortality rates for those aged 15 to 24 for the years 1972–1984. He found that in several Asian and South American countries, including Brazil, Cuba, and the Dominican Republic, Ecuador, Hong Kong, Paraguay, the Philippines, Singapore, and Thailand, females' suicide mortality rates exceeded those of males. Similarly, studies of police and medical records in a province of Fiji (Haynes, 1988) and in the Highlands of Malaysia (Maniam, 1988) showed that young women (under the age of 30) had higher suicide mortality rates than young men. In 1980, countries with high rates of suicide mortality for women aged 15 to 24 included Thailand (19.6 per 100,000 per year) and Switzerland (12.3); for women aged 44 to 54, Denmark (42.8) and Hungary (36.2); and for women aged 75 and older, Hungary (90.6) and Hong Kong (64.6) (Lester, 1991b).

Social Class, Education, Employment and Economic Resources

The relationship between social class and suicide mortality in women is difficult to assess because of the tendency to assign social class to married women on the basis of the social class of their husbands. Furthermore, there are few sound studies on the relationship between social class and suicide mortality in general, let alone studies focusing on women. Available studies have yielded variable findings. On the one hand, in England suicide mortality was found to be more common in the higher social classes (Stengel, 1964). Similarly, Nayha (1977) reported that in Finland women who killed themselves were from a higher social class than men who killed themselves. On the other hand, a study of suicide mortality in Sacramento, California, found that the women were from lower social classes than the men (Bourque, Cosand, & Kraus, 1983).

Several studies have noted that women's suicide mortality rates are high in societies such as China (Wolf, 1975), India (Adityanjee, 1986), Japan (Iga, Yamamoto, & Noguchi, 1975), the Kaliai, Gainj, and Maring people of Papua New Guinea (Counts, 1980, 1987; Healey, 1979; Johnson, 1981) and the Aguaruna of Peru (Brown, 1986), where women's social status is extremely low. In these societies, women's social, educational, vocational and economic opportunities are severely restricted. Yet in many societies suicide mortality is highest among the most privileged. For example, in the United States, suicide mortality is highest among older White males, not among older Blacks or females (Canetto, 1992). Thus, cultural meanings of gender and suicide influence the risk for suicide mortality

Available studies suggest that unemployment is associated with higher rates of suicide mortality for both women and men in most industrialized nations (Pritchard, 1990). Employed women have lower suicide mortality rates than women who are not employed, regardless of age and marital status (Cumming, Lazer, & Chisholm, 1975). Although in the United States suicide mortality rates are lower in women than in men, professional women have suicide mortality rates as high as, and sometimes higher than those of professional men; this is especially well-documented for physicians (Lester, 1992; Yang & Lester, 1995).

Personal Relationships

Suicide mortality rates are higher in the widowed and divorced, and lower in the married and single for both women and men. Smith, Mercy, and Conn (1988) reported these patterns for both Whites and Blacks in the United States. Furthermore, a longitudinal study of Norwegian women aged 25 or older found that the never-married had a higher risk of suicidal death than the married, and that women who had not borne children had a higher risk than women who had borne children; this was found both for premenopausal and postmenopausal women (Hoyer & Lund, 1993).

Several studies, however, indicate that being married provides significantly better protection from suicide mortality for men than for women. For example, Gove (1972, 1979) explored the relationship between gender, marital status, and death by suicide in the United States. He observed that, since World War II, married women have had higher rates of mental disorder than married men, while never-married women have had lower rates of mental disorder than never-married men. Consequently, he hypothesized that marriage may be a better protector from mental disorder and suicide for men than for women. To verify this hypothesis, he compared the suicide mortality rate for the never-married with that of the married, an index called by Durkheim (1897) the "coefficient of preservation." Gove found that, for 1959–1961, the ratio for females aged 26 to 64 years was 1.5, and for males, 2.0. Single females were 47 percent more likely to kill themselves than married females, while single males were 97% more likely to kill themselves than married males. Divorce and widowhood also seemed to be more disadvantageous for males than for females. Gove presented data that showed this same pattern with rates of nonfatal suicidal behavior. He concluded that "as marital roles are presently constituted in our society, marriage is more advantageous to men than to women while being single (widowed, divorced) is more disadvantageous" to men (Gove, 1972, pp. 213–214). These findings have been replicated by Cumming and Lazer (1981) in Canada. Related to this, Bock and Webber (1972) have noted extremely high suicide mortality rates in elderly widowers, as compared to elderly widows. Based on a survey of the elderly in a Florida county, they attributed this pattern to greater social isolation (including more frequent absence of kin and lack of membership in groups and associations) among the widowers, as compared to the widows.

Finally, several studies have noted that societies with high rates of female suicide mortality, such as China (Wolf, 1975), India (Adityanjee, 1986; Gehlot & Nathawat, 1983), Japan (Iga et al., 1975), the Kaliai, Gainj, and Maring people of Papua New Guinea (Counts, 1980, 1987; Healey, 1979; Johnson, 1981), and the Aguaruna of Peru (Brown, 1986) are also societies in which women's family and social status is extremely low. For example, according to Gehlot and Nathawat, Hindu women are "often treated as chattel, living an existence of near slavery" (p. 274); furthermore, "the unfortunate young wife is not only a victim of the in-laws' desire for dominance, and sometimes avarice concerning dowry, but also of her own parents' indifference. . . . Cut off from any support group, the young wife takes her life" (pp. 276–277). Many married women who kill themselves in these societies have a history of being physically abused by their husbands and/or extended family (Counts, 1980, 1987). For example, according to a Chinese study, some of the women who killed themselves had been taunted by their in-laws over childlessness or failure to produce a son (Wolf, 1975). Most importantly, societies with high rates of female suicide mortality have ideologies supporting self-destructive behavior in women. In these societies, female death by suicide is a culturally recognized behavior that permits them, as Counts (1987) says, "to affect the behavior of the more powerful members of their society, or at least allows them to revenge themselves on those who have made their lives intolerable" (p. 195). These women are not allowed "effective, more direct, [non-self-destructive] means of affecting the behavior of others" (Counts, 1980, p. 336). For example, among the Kaliai and Gainj people of Papua New Guinea, killing oneself is a way for a woman "to require her survivors to demand compensation or take revenge on her abusive husband" (Counts, 1987, p. 203). Ironically, a woman's suicide is perceived as shameful by the husband because it is viewed as an act of willfulness and autonomy. "A suicide husband is an object of ridicule among the Gainj," writes Johnson, because "he has failed completely to control his wife" (p. 332).

Method

Many studies report that women tend to use poisoning more than men, while men use firearms more than women (see Lester, 1984, for a review). For example, in the United States in 1988, 27 percent of the women used solid and liquid substances, as compared to only 6 percent of the men. In contrast, 65 percent of the men used firearms/explosives, as compared to 40 percent of the women (National Center for Health Statistics, 1990).

It has been argued that this differences in choice of method accounts for the difference in fatal/nonfatal outcomes for women and men. However, even within each method (e.g., firearms), relatively more of the acts by women are nonfatal, and more of the acts by men are fatal. Thus, choice of method for suicide cannot be the complete explanation of the gender difference in outcome. One reason for this difference may be that, in the United States, killing oneself is considered masculine, and therefore more "unacceptable" for females than for males, independent of the reasons for it (see Canetto, 1992–1993, 1995; Stillion, 1995 for reviews).

Lester (1993) examined international suicide mortality rates for 24 countries (mainly industrialized nations) and found that the female and male mortality rates from poisoning did not differ significantly. Women, however, had much lower rates of suicide mortality by methods other than poisoning than did men. Lester concluded that the gender differences in the use of these other methods accounted for the gender differences in suicide mortality. It is also possible that these data simply reflect the fact that current medical technology is more efficient at rescuing victims of suicide by poison than victims of suicide by other methods.

Availability, familiarity, and cultural acceptability play a crucial role in the choice of suicide method (Marks & Stokes, 1976). The importance of cultural acceptability was highlighted in a recent study by Fisher, Comstock, Monk, and Sencer (1993), where method was found to be significantly associated with sociodemographic characteristics (such as sex, age, ethnicity, place of birth) and occupational characteristics, even after adjustment for individual access to the method. The authors suggested that since "acceptability exerts an independent influence on method," one could focus prevention programs on restricting access to frequently used means "because there is imperfect substitutability among methods" (p. 99).

Availability,, familiarity and cultural acceptability of different methods vary with gender. For example, among Indian immigrants residing in England and Wales, burning is a method that is culturally acceptable and common among women, but not among men (Raleigh, Bulusu, & Balarajan, 1990). On the other hand, in the United States older White females tend to use poison; older Black females, firearms; and older other non-White females, hanging (McIntosh & Santos, 1985–1986).

In some cultures, however, a method may be similarly available, familiar, and culturally acceptable to women and men. According to a study by Marks and Abernathy (1974), firearms are the most common method of suicide for both women and men living in the American South. Similarly, a Malay study found that poisoning by weed killer or insecticide was the most popular method of suicide for women and men (Maniam, 1988). In their study of method by age, sex, and ethnicity, McIntosh and Santos (1985–1986) noted an increase in the use of firearms in most of the groups studied, an indication perhaps of diminishing cultural distinctiveness in method acceptability and easier access to firearms in the United States.

Mental Disorder

Most studies find the highest mortality rates in those diagnosed as having an affective disorder (Lester, 1992). Asgard (1990) studied women who died from suicide in urban Sweden and reported that 35 percent had a depressive disorder at the time of death; a further 24 percent were depressed. Fifty-seven percent had received inpatient or outpatient psychiatric treatment in the final year of their lives. Recent research on the association between eating disorders and subsequent suicidal behavior indicates that suicide mortality is higher in women with eating disorders than in women who do not have an eating disorder (Gardner & Rich, 1988).

An urban study of suicide mortality in the United States reported that women were less likely to be alcohol abusers than the men, but that they had more often sought psychiatric treatment in the past; women and men, however, did not differ in depression or assaultiveness (Breed, 1972). The relative absence of alcohol abuse in women who kill themselves, as compared to men, has been replicated by Nuttall, Evenson, and Cho (1980) in Missouri, and by Barner-Rasmussen, Dupont, and Bille (1986) in former psychiatric patients in Denmark.

SUMMARY AND CONCLUSIONS

In this chapter, we have noted the inadequacies in the data available to make comparisons between the suicidal behaviors of women and men. Thus, any conclusions drawn from these data must be viewed with caution. Based on the available data, some trends emerged. Nonfatal suicidal behavior appears to be more common in women than in men, while fatal suicidal behavior appears to be more common in men than in women.

Of special interest are the variations and exceptions to these patterns. For example, we noted that in Helsinki, Finland, women engage in fewer nonfatal suicidal acts than men, while in China women engage in more fatal suicidal acts than men. Similarly, we noted that, among individuals age 15 to 24, women's mortality by suicide exceeded men's in several Asian and South American countries. These deviations from the general pattern suggest that cultural factors play an important role in influencing whether a person will engage in suicidal behaviors, which suicidal behaviors will be chosen, and under what circumstances such acts will be performed.

This review has highlighted some heretofore overlooked themes in the lives of suicidal women. Several studies have suggested that women who engage in nonfatal suicidal behavior typically come from educationally, socially, and economically disadvantaged backgrounds. There is evidence of a significant association between unemployment and both fatal and nonfatal suicidal behaviors in women. The association between being unmarried (i.e., single, divorced, or widowed) and suicidal behaviors appears to be stronger for men than for women. Finally, several studies have noted that women's fatal and nonfatal suicidal behaviors often occur in the context of serious neglect, hostility and/or abuse by male significant others. Our review of the epidemiology literature thus challenges the traditional view that women's suicidal behavior is simply the outcome of individual pathology.

ACKNOWLEDGMENTS

This chapter benefited from feedback by Eric R. Dahlen, Janet D. Hollenshead, Patricia L. Kaminski, and David B. Wohl.

NOTES

1. Portions of this chapter were published in an article entitled "Gender and the primary prevention of suicide mortality" in the Spring 1995 issue of *Suicide and Life Threatening Behavior.*

REFERENCES

Adityanjee, -. (1986). Suicide attempts and suicides in India: Cross cultural aspects. *International Journal of Social Psychiatry, 32,* 64–73.

Arcel, L. T., Mantonakis, J., Petersson, B., Jemos, J., & Kaliteraki, E. (1992). Suicide attempts among Greek and Danish women and the quality of their relationships with husbands and boyfriends. *Acta Psychiatrica Scandinavica, 85,* 189–195.

Asgard, U. (1990) A psychiatric study of suicide among urban Swedish women. *Acta Psychiatrica Scandinavica, 82,* 115–124.

Banerjee, G., Nandi, D. N., Nandi, S., Sarkar, S., Boral, G. C., & Ghosh, A. (1990). The vulnerability of Indian women to suicide: A field study. *Indian Journal of Psychiatry, 32,* 305–308.

Barnes, R. (1985). Women and self-injury. *International Journal of Women's Studies, 8,* 465–474.

Barner-Rasmussen, P., Dupont, A., & Bille, H. (1986). Suicide in psychiatric patients in Denmark, 1971–81. *Acta Psychiatrica Scandinavica, 73,* 441–448.

Barraclough, B. M. (1988). International variation in the suicide rate of 15–24 year olds. *Social Psychiatry and Psychiatric Epidemiology, 23,* 75–84.

Beck, A. T., Lester, D., & Kovacs, M. (1973). Attempted suicides by males and females. *Psychological Reports, 33,* 865–866.

Bergman, B., & Brismar, B. (1991). Suicide attempts by battered wives. *Acta Psychiatrica Scandinavica, 83,* 380–384.

Bhagat, M. (1976). The spouse of attempted suicides: A personality study. *British Journal of Psychiatry, 128,* 44–46.

Birtchnell, J. (1981). Some familial and clinical characteristics of female suicidal psychiatric patients. *British Journal of Psychiatry, 138,* 381–390.

Birtchnell, J. (1991). The measurement of dependence by questionnaire. *Journal of Personality Disorders, 5,* 281–295.

Bock, E. W., & Webber, I. L. (1972). Suicide among the elderly. *Journal of Marriage and the Family, 34,* 24–31.

Bornstein, R. F. (1992). The dependent personality: Developmental, social, and clinical perspectives. *Psychological Bulletin, 112,* 3–23.

Bosch, B. A., & Schlebusch, L. (1987). Trends in adult parasuicide in an urban environment. *South African Journal of Psychology, 17,* 100–106.

Breed, W. (1967). Suicide and loss in social interaction. In E. S. Shneidman (Ed.), *Essays in self-destruction* (pp. 188–201). New York: Science House.

Breed, W. (1972). Five components of a basic suicide syndrome. *Life-Threatening Behavior, 2,* 3–18.

Bourque, L. B., Cosand, D., & Kraus, J. (1983). Comparison of male and female suicide in a defined community. *Journal of Community Health, 9,* 7–17.

Brown, M. F. (1986). Power, gender, and the social meaning of Aguaruna suicide. *Man, 21,* 311–328.

Canetto, S. S. (1991). Gender roles, suicide attempts, and substance abuse. *Journal of Psychology, 125,* 605–620.

Canetto, S. S. (1992). Gender and suicide in the elderly. *Suicide and Life Threatening Behavior, 22,* 80–97.

Canetto, S. S. (1992–1993). She died for love and he for glory: Gender myths of suicidal behavior. *Omega, 26,* 1–17.

Canetto, S. S. (1995). Elderly women and suicidal behavior. In S. S. Canetto & D. Lester (Eds.), *Women and suicidal behaviors* (pp. 215–233). New York: Springer.

Canetto, S. S., & Feldman, L. B. (1993). Overt and covert dependence in suicidal women and their male partners. *Omega, 27,* 177–194.

Cantor, P. (1976). Personality characteristics found among youthful female suicide attempters. *Journal of Abnormal Psychology, 85,* 324–329.

Cooperstock, R. (1982). Research on psychotropic drug use: A review of findings and methods. *Social Science and Medicine, 16,* 1179–1196.

Counts, D. A. (1980). Fighting back is not the way: Suicide and the women of Kaliai. *American Ethnologist, 7,* 332–351.

Counts, D. A. (1987). Female suicide and wife abuse: A cross-cultural perspective. *Suicide and Life-Threatening Behavior, 17,* 194–204.

Cumming, E., & Lazer, C. (1981). Kinship structure and suicide: A theoretical link. *Canadian Review of Sociology and Anthropology, 18,* 271–281.

Cumming, E., Lazer, C., & Chisholm, L. (1975). Suicide as an index of role strain among employed and not employed married women in British Columbia. *Canadian Review of Sociology and Anthropology, 12,* 462–470.

De Leo, D., & Diekstra, R. F. W. (1990). *Depression and suicide in late life.* Toronto: Hogrefe & Huber.

Diekstra, R. F. W. (1990). An international perspective on the epidemiology and prevention of suicide. In S. J. Blumenthal & D. J. Kupfer (Eds.), *Suicide over the life cycle: Risk factors, assessment, and treatment of suicidal patients* (pp. 533–569). Washington, D.C.: American Psychiatric Press.

Diekstra, R. F. W., & van Egmond, M. (1989). Suicide and attempted suicide in general practice, 1979–1986. *Acta Psychiatrica Scandinavica, 79,* 268–275.

Douglas, J. D. (1967). *The social meanings of suicide.* Princeton: Princeton University Press.

Durkheim, E. (1897). *Le suicide.* Paris: Felix Alcan.

Fidell, L. S. (1982). Gender and drug use and abuse. In Al-Issa, I. (Ed.), *Gender and psychopathology* (pp. 221–236). New York: Academic Press.

Fieldsend, R., & Lowenstein, E. (1981). Quarrels, separations and infidelity in the two days preceding self-poisoning episodes. *British Journal of Medical Psychology, 54,* 349–352.

Fisher, E. P., Comstock, G. W., Monk, M. A., & Sencer, D. J. (1993). Characteristics of completed suicides: Implications of differences among methods. *Suicide and Life-Threatening Behavior, 23,* 91–100.

Gardner, A., & Rich, C. L. (1988). Eating disorders and suicide. In D. Lester (Ed.), *Suicide '88* (pp. 171–172). Denver, CO: American Association of Suicidology.

Gehlot, P. S., & Nathawat, S. S. (1983). Suicide and family constellation in India. *American Journal of Psychotherapy, 37,* 273–278.

Gomberg, E. S. (1989). Suicide risk among women with alcohol problems. *American Journal of Public Health, 79,* 1363–1365.

Gove, W. R. (1972). Sex, marital status and suicide. *Journal of Health and Social Behavior, 13,* 204–213.

Gove, W. R. (1979). Sex differences in the epidemiology of mental disorder. In E. S. Gomberg and V. Franks (Eds.), *Gender and disordered behavior* (pp. 23–68). New York: Brunner/Mazel.

Hawton, K., Fagg, J., & Simkin, S. (1988). Female unemployment and attempted suicide. *British Journal of Psychiatry, 152,* 632–637.

Haynes, R. H. (1984). Suicide in Fiji. *British Journal of Psychiatry, 145,* 433–438.

Healey, C. (1979). Women and suicide in New Guinea. *Social Analysis, 2,* 89–107.

Hettiarachchi, J., & Kodituwakku, G. C. S. (1989). Self-poisoning in Sri Lanka: Motivational aspects. *International Journal of Social Psychiatry, 35,* 204–208.

Hoyer, G., & Lund, E. (1993). Suicide among women related to number of children in marriage. *Archives of General Psychiatry, 50,* 134–137.

Iga, M., Yamamoto, J., & Noguchi, T. (1975). The vulnerability of young Japanese women and suicide. *Suicide, 5,* 207–22.

Jack, R. (1992). *Women and attempted suicide.* Hillsdale, NJ: Erlbaum.

Johnson, P. L. (1981). When dying is better than living: Female suicide among the Gainj of Papua New Guinea. *Ethnology, 20,* 325–335.

Kessler, R. C., & McRae, J. A. (1983). Trends in the relationship between sex and attempted suicide. *Journal of Health and Social Behavior, 24,* 98–110.

Kok, L-P. (1988). Race, religion and female suicide attempters in Singapore. *Social Psychiatry and Psychiatric Epidemiology, 23,* 236–239.

Kreitman, N., & Schreiber, M. (1979). Parasuicide in young Edinburgh women, 1968–75. *Psychological Medicine, 9,* 469–479.

Kushner, H. I. (1985). Women and suicide in historical perspective. *Signs: Journal of Women in Culture and Society, 10,* 537–552.

Kushner, H. I. (1993). Suicide, gender, and the fear of modernity in nineteenth-century medical and social thought. *Journal of Social History, 26*, 461–490.

Lester, D. (1982). The distribution of sex and age among completed suicides. *International Journal of Social Psychiatry, 28*, 256–260.

Lester, D. (1984). Suicide. In C. S. Widom (Ed.), *Sex roles and psychopathology* (pp. 145–156). New York: Plenum.

Lester, D. (Ed.) (1988). *Why women kill themselves*. Springfield, IL: Charles C. Thomas.

Lester, D. (1989). *Questions and answers about suicide*. Philadelphia: Charles Press.

Lester, D. (1990). Suicide in mainland China by sex, urban/rural location, and age. *Perceptual and Motor Skills, 71*, 1090.

Lester, D. (1991a). Patterns of suicide in America. *Proceedings of the Pavese Society, 4*, 118–211.

Lester, D. (1991b). Suicide across the life span: A look at international trends. In A. A. Leenaars (Ed.), *Life span perspectives of suicide* (pp. 71–80). New York: Plenum.

Lester, D. (1992). *Why people kill themselves* (3rd edition). Springfield, IL: Charles C. Thomas.

Lester, D. (1993). Testosterone and suicide. *Personality and Individual Differences, 15*, 347–348.

Maniam, T. (1988). Suicide and parasuicide in a hill resort in Malaysia. *British Journal of Psychiatry, 153*, 222–225.

Maris, R. W. (1971). Deviance as therapy: The paradox of the self-destructive female. *Journal of Health and Social Behavior, 12*, 113–124.

Maris, R. W. (1981). *Pathways to suicide*. Baltimore, MD: Johns Hopkins University.

Marks, A., & Abernathy, T. (1974). Toward a sociocultural perspective on means of self-destruction. *Suicide and Life-Threatening Behavior, 4*, 3–17.

Marks, A., & Stokes, C. S. (1976). Socialization, firearms and suicide. *Social Problems, 5*, 622–639.

McIntosh, J. L. (1989). Official United States elderly suicide data bases: Levels, availability, omissions. *Omega, 19*, 337–350.

McIntosh, J. L. (1991). Middle-age suicide: A literature review and epidemiological study. *Death Studies, 15*, 21–37.

McIntosh, J. L. (1992). Epidemiology of suicide in the elderly. *Suicide and Life-Threatening Behavior, 22*, 15–33.

McIntosh, J. L. (1993). *U.S. suicide: 1990 official final data*. Denver, CO: American Association of Suicidology.

McIntosh, J. L., & Santos, J. F. (1985–1986). Methods of suicide by age: Sex and race differences among the young and old. *International Journal of Aging and Human Development, 22*, 123–139.

Merrill, J., & Owens, J. (1987). Ethnic differences in self-poisoning: A comparison of West Indian and White groups. *British Journal of Psychiatry, 150*, 765–768.

Miller, H. L., Coombs, D. W., Leeper, J. D., & Barton, S. N. (1984). An analysis on the effects of suicide prevention facilities on suicide rates in the United States. *American Journal of Public Health, 74*, 340–343.

Moscicki, E. K., O'Carrol, P., Rae, D. S., Locke, B. Z., Roy, A., & Regier, D. S. (1988). Suicide attempts in the epidemiologic catchment area study. *Yale Journal of Biology and Medicine, 61*, 259–268.

National Center for Health Statistics. (1933–1990). *Vital Statistics of the United States.* Rockville, MD: Author.

Nayha, S. (1977). Social group and mortality in Finland. *British Journal of Preventive and Social Medicine, 31*, 231–237.

Neuringer, C., & Lettieri, D. J. (1982). *Suicidal women.* New York: Gardner Press.

Newson-Smith, J. G. B., & Hirsch, S. R. (1979). Psychiatric symptoms in self-poisoning patients. *Psychological Medicine, 9*, 493–500.

Nuttall, E. A., Evenson, R., & Cho, D. W. (1980). Patients of a public state mental health system who commit suicide. *Journal of Nervous and Mental Disease, 168*, 424–427.

O'Carroll, P. W. (1989). A consideration of the validity and reliability of suicide mortality data. *Suicide and Life-Threatening Behavior, 19*, 1–16.

Paykel, E. S., Prusoff, B. A., & Myers, J. K. (1975). Suicide attempts and recent life events. *Archives of General Psychiatry, 32*, 327–333.

Petronis, K. R., Samuels, J. F., Moscicki, E. K., & Anthony, J. C. (1990). An epidemiologic investigation of potential risk factors for suicide attempts. *Social Psychiatry and Psychiatric Epidemiology, 25*, 193–199.

Phillips, D., & Ruth, T. E. (1993). Adequacy of official suicide statistics for scientific research and public policy. *Suicide and Life-Threatening Behavior, 23*, 307–319.

Platt, S., Bille-Brahe, U., Kerkhof, A., Schmidtke, A., Bjerke, T., Crepet, P., De Leo, D., Haring, C., Lonnqvuist, J., Michel, K., Philippe, A., Pommereau, X., Querejeta, I., Salander-Renberg, E., Temesvary, B., Wasserman, D., & Sampaio Faria, J. (1992). Parasuicide in Europe: The WHO/EURO multicentre study on parasuicide. I. Introduction and preliminary analysis for 1989. *Acta Psychiatrica Scandinavica, 85*, 97–104.

Platt, S., Hawton, K., Kreitman, N., Fagg, J., & Foster, J. (1988). Recent clinical and epidemiological trends in parasuicide in Edinburgh and Oxford: A tale of two cities. *Psychological Medicine, 18*, 405–418.

Platt, S., & Robinson, A. (1991). Parasuicide and alcohol: A 20 year survey of admissions to a regional treatment center. *International Journal of Social Psychiatry, 32*, 159–172.

Ponnudurai, R., Jeyakar, J., & Saraswathy, M. (1986). Attempted suicides in Madras. *Indian Journal of Psychiatry, 28*, 59–62.

Pritchard, C. (1990). Suicide, unemployment and gender variations in the Western world 1964–1986. *Social Psychiatry and Psychiatric Epidemiology, 25*, 73–80.

Raleigh, V. S., Bulusu, L., & Balarajan, R. (1990). Suicides among immigrants from the Indian subcontinent. *British Journal of Psychiatry, 156*, 46–50.

Richman, J. & Rosenbaum, M. (1970). A clinical study of the role of hostility and death wishes by the family and society in suicide attempts. *Israel Annals of Psychiatry and Related Disciplines, 8*, 213–231.

Robins, E., Schmidt, E. H., & O'Neal, P. (1957). Some interrelations of social factors and clinical diagnosis in attempted suicide: A study of 109 patients. *American Journal of Psychiatry, 114*, 221–231.

Rosenbaum, M., & Richman, J. (1970). Suicide: The role of hostility and death wishes from the family and significant others. *American Journal of Psychiatry, 126*, 128–131.

Ruzicka, L. T. (1976). Suicide, 1950 to 1971. *World Health Statistics Report, 29*, 396–413.

Schrut, A., & Michels, T. (1974). Suicidal divorced and discarded women. *Journal of the American Academy of Psychoanalysis, 2*, 329–343.

Sefa-Dedeh, A., & Canetto, S. S. (1992). Women, family and suicidal behavior in Ghana. In U. W. Gielen, L. L. Adler, & N. Milgram (Eds.), *Psychology in international perspective* (pp. 299–309). Amsterdam: Swets & Zeitlinger.

Smith, J. C., Mercy, J. A., & Conn, J. M. (1988). Marital status and the risk of suicide. *American Journal of Public Health, 78,* 78–80.

Sorenson, S. B., & Golding, J. M. (1988). Suicide ideation and attempts in Hispanic and non-Hispanic Whites: Demographic and psychiatric disorder issues. *Suicide and Life-Threatening Behavior, 18* 205–218.

Stengel, E. (1964). *Suicide and attempted suicide.* Harmondsworth, England: Penguin.

Stephens, B. J. (1985). Suicidal women and their relationships with husbands, boyfriends, and lovers. *Suicide and Life-Threatening Behavior, 15,* 77–89.

Stillion, J. M. (1995). Through a glass darkly: Women and attitudes toward suicidal behavior. In S. S. Canetto & D. Lester (Eds.), *Women and suicidal behavior* (pp. 71–84). New York: Springer.

Suleiman, M. A., Moussa, M. A. A., & El-Islam, M. F. (1989). The profile of parasuicide repeaters in Kuwait. *International Journal of Social Psychiatry, 35,* 146–155.

Vinoda, K. S. (1966). Personality characteristics of attempted suicides. *British Journal of Psychiatry, 112,* 1143–1150.

Walsh, B., Walsh, D., & Whelan, B. (1975). Suicide in Dublin: II. The influence of some social and medical factors on coroners' verdict. *British Journal of Psychiatry, 126,* 309–312.

Weissman, M. M. (1974). The epidemiology of suicide attempts, 1960 to 1971. *Archives of General Psychiatry, 30,* 737–746.

Weissman, M. M., Fox, K., & Klerman, G. L. (1973). Hostility and depression associated with suicide attempts. *American Journal of Psychiatry, 130,* 450–454.

Wexler, L., Weissman, M. M., & Kasl, S. V. (1978). Suicide attempts 1970–75: Updating a United States study and comparisons with international trends. *British Journal of Psychiatry, 132,* 180–185.

Whitehead, P. C., Johnson, F. G., & Ferrence, R. (1973). Measuring the incidence of self-injury: Some methodological and design considerations. *American Journal of Orthopsychiatry, 43,* 142–148.

Wolf, M. (1975). Women and suicide in China. In M. Wolf & R. Witke (Eds.), *Women in Chinese society* (pp. 111–141). Stanford, CA: Stanford University Press.

Wolk-Wasserman, D. (1985). The intensive care unit and the suicide attempt patient. *Acta Psychiatrica Scandinavica, 71,* 581–595.

Wolk-Wasserman, D. (1986). Suicidal communications of persons attempting suicide and responses of significant others. *Acta Psychiatrica Scandinavica, 73,* 481–499.

World Health Organization. (1984–1990). *Statistics annual.* Geneva, Switzerland: Author.

Yang, B., & Lester, D. (1995). Suicidal behavior and employment. In S. S. Canetto & D. Lester (Eds.), *Women and suicidal behavior* (pp. 97–108). New York: Springer.

Part III Theories

4
Gender Socialization and Women's Suicidal Behaviors

A. Kay Clifton and Dorothy E. Lee

In the United States, more women than men engage in suicidal acts (Canetto & Lester, 1994). Many women also engage in self-destructive behaviors that are not immediately life-threatening, but that tend to shorten and/or restrict their lives. This chapter will review and integrate the literature on women's gender socialization and self-destructive behaviors.

GENDER SOCIALIZATION

For women, gender socialization results in both positive and negative behaviors. The most positive behaviors women learn are the abilities to nurture and to express a range of emotions, except for anger. Gender socialization may also lead women to distrust their own abilities and to defer to men, behaviors that may reinforce self-destructive tendencies.

Gender socialization begins at birth (Paludi & Gullo, 1986), is carried out largely through parent-child interactions, and is augmented with clothing, toys, books, and television programs. Passivity and dependence in girls may begin with parents discouraging them from engaging in gross motor activity (Maccoby & Jacklin, 1974) or rough physical play (MacDonald & Parke, 1986). Although fathers encourage physical proximity and vocal interaction in daughters, they encourage visual and motor exploration in sons

(Bronstein, 1988). Traditional girl's clothing, such as dresses and ruffles, also inhibits them from engaging in vigorous physical activity and exploration (Shaken, Shaken, & Sternglanz, 1985).

Parent-child interactions may also direct girls and boys toward either an affective or an analytical orientation. Parents speak more to their daughters than to their sons about feelings and emotions (Shapiro, 1990). The stories parents tell daughters tend to include more words pertaining to emotions, except for anger, than the stories they tell boys. Words pertaining to anger are more likely to be used in stories told to boys (MacDonald & Parke, 1986). Parents also question their sons more than their daughters and use more numbers and action verbs in talking with them (Bronstein, 1988; Weitzman, Birns, & Friend, 1985).

Playrooms, bedrooms, books, toys, television programs, and school experiences tend to reinforce different behaviors in girls and boys. Girls are encouraged to limit their physical activity and to practice routine domestic chores. Childrens' books often portray females as crying a lot, getting rescued by a male, and receiving rewards for their attractiveness. Boys, on the other hand, are encouraged to explore and manipulate their environment. Male characters in children's books enjoy and lead adventures and are more often rewarded for accomplishments and displays of intelligence (Bradford, 1985; Miller, 1987; Peretti & Sydney, 1985; Rheingold & Cook, 1975; Stoneman, Brody, & Mackinnon, 1986; Weitzman, Eifler, Hokada, & Ross, 1972; Williams, Vernon, Williams, & Malecha, 1987).

Elementary teachers also respond differently to girls and boys (Sadker & Sadker, 1985a, 1985b). Teachers interact less with girls and are more likely to complete their tasks for them rather than giving them instructions. They are more likely to reprimand girls when they call out answers without raising their hands and to praise them for neatness in their school work. On the other hand, boys are given both more remediation and more challenge, provided with detailed instructions for task completion, praised more for their intellectual achievement, and allowed to call out answers without raising their hands. Parents and teachers alike attribute girls' academic achievements to the ease of the tasks or to luck and explain their failures as being due to lack of intelligence, whereas they attribute boys' successes to their abilities, and their failures to bad luck.

In the identity-formation years, girls are encouraged to achieve esteem and social status through boyfriend relationships, which fosters emphasis on physical attractiveness and denial of one's own interests and abilities (Zuckerman, 1989); this, in turn, may lead to vulnerabilities in self-concept. On the other hand, boys are expected to achieve both self-esteem and social status through athletic challenges, which foster the personal skills of self-confidence, emotional, and physical endurance, and achievement in a teamwork context (Zuckerman, 1989). It is no wonder then that, although girls academically outperform boys in the early grades, their self-confidence and achievement test scores decline as they progress through school (Gilligan, 1990; Sadker & Sadker, 1985a, 1985b). Young women are led to de-emphasize their academic qualities, which in turn produces career aspirations below their abilities (Danziger, 1983; Stanworth, 1983).

The search for explanations of young women's declining self-confidence and limited aspirations has spanned two decades, with neither fear of success (Horner, 1972) nor fear of failure (Dweck, Davidson, Neson, & Enna, 1978) finding widespread support. Early research by Clifton and Lee (1976) suggests that an explanation most consistent with the literature on traditional gender socialization is that many females are prevented from early practice with challenging situations. In this research, college students were asked to anticipate a challenging public situation (defending a student issue in front of an all-campus governance body) and select from a list of adjectives those that would best describe their feelings prior to the event. Women were more likely than men to report negative feelings (discouraged, frustrated, fearful, troubled, anxious, and embarrassed), whereas men were more likely to report positive feelings (pleased, proud, enthusiastic, and eager). The results were interpreted to suggest that, because traditional gender socialization prevents girls from engaging in early practice with small challenges, girls may be disadvantaged when faced with bigger challenges. For example, girls may focus on feelings that inhibit their own assertiveness, or they may look for help rather than viewing challenges as opportunities for learning.

Fortunately, some women may be able to avoid the negative consequences of traditional gender socialization. For both men and women in the study described above (Clifton & Lee, 1976), the anticipatory negative feelings were more likely to be reported by individuals with low self-esteem, low self-confidence, and high self-destructiveness; positive anticipatory feelings were reported by individuals with high self-esteem, high self-confidence, and low self destructiveness. When these relationships were examined by gender, they were found to be stronger among women, and fell to nonsignificance among men. It seems that most males, regardless of self-assessments, have learned to "psych themselves up" for challenges. For females, on the other hand, feeling prepared for challenges seems to be related to high self-esteem, self-confidence, and low self-destructiveness.

SUICIDAL AND SELF-DESTRUCTIVE BEHAVIORS

Many researchers have trivialized suicidal behaviors and self-destructiveness among women because women are less likely to die as a result of a suicidal act. Kushner (1985) has pointed out that, when fatal and nonfatal suicidal acts are considered together, there is little difference between women's and men's suicidality. Fatal and nonfatal suicidal acts, however, represent only the tip of the iceberg of self-destructive behavior. Recently researchers have become interested in behaviors that have the potential for producing a premature, but not immediate, death. These behaviors have been referred to as indirect, hidden, latent, or covert suicide (Lee, 1987).

In a series of studies by Lee (Clifton & Lee, 1976; Lee, 1976, 1985), adults were found to report a large number of personal behaviors that were self-destructive but not directly suicidal: undereating, overeating, eating unhealthful foods, drinking too much, driving too fast, drinking and driving, failing to take needed medication, and physical inactivity. Reasons most often given for engaging in such behaviors were negative feelings about themselves, escape, and lack of discipline. Respondents said they would be most likely to change these behaviors if they had more self-confidence, or believed that the activities would harm them. The latter responses suggested that individuals were not aware, at least at a conscious level, that their acts were actually self-destructive. These same studies also found that scores on scales of Suicide Proneness and Self-Destructiveness were only weakly correlated. This led the authors to the conclusion that suicidal behaviors and self-destructiveness may be only partially overlapping. Some individuals may be suicidal and self-destructive; some suicidal individuals may not be self-destructive; and yet others may be self-destructive but not suicidal. In another study, Lee (1988) found that self-destructiveness was significantly correlated with low self-esteem, and that the correlation was even stronger when the self-esteem measure was not identified as a measure of self-esteem. Furthermore, more self-destructive behaviors were reported when the measure used was not labeled "self-destructiveness."

FEMININE SOCIALIZATION

Several investigators have reported correlations between specific attitudes, cognitive and emotional styles, and suicidal ideation or behaviors. The attitudes and behaviors most commonly associated with suicidality include passivity, pessimism, lack of self-confidence, and inadequate coping skills. Orbach, Bar-Joseph, and Dror (1990) studied the problem-solving process of suicide ideators/"attempters" as compared with other mental health patients. Suicidal persons tended to be avoidant, pessimistic, passive, and rely on others for solutions. Rich and Bonner (1987) and Bonner and Rich (1988) reported similar correlates of suicide ideation among college students—emotional alienation, cognitive distortions, and deficient adaptive resources. According to the authors, these factors combined to form a "coping vulnerability" and a predisposition for suicidal ideation and behaviors. Simonds, MacMahon and Armstrong (1991) found that persons who engaged in nonfatal suicidal behavior were characterized by moderately high levels of distress and depression, high hostility and hopelessness, a diminished sense of self-confidence in their ability to improve their situation, and poor coping skills. Finally, Lester (1989) reported suicidal ideation to be correlated with external locus of control among nonpatients.

Zuckerman (1989) observed that college women and men with low self-confidence, low self-worth, and less coping ability and self-sufficiency, were more likely to experience depression, anxiety, withdrawal and anger when under stress. Women, who generally reported less confidence in their coping ability, self-sufficiency, leadership and public-speaking ability than men, diminished their activity level and reported more symptoms of depression and less self-confidence under conditions of stress. Men, who generally rated themselves higher on leadership and public-speaking ability, increased their activity levels when under stress.

Many investigators have reported that women's suicidal behavior appears to occur in the context of relationship problems, either conflict with, or threat of loss of, a significant other (Beck, Lester, & Kovacs, 1973; Birtchnell, 1981; Breed, 1967; Fieldsend & Lowenstein, 1981; Grumet, 1988; Maris, 1971, 1981; Paykel, Prusoff, & Myers, 1975; Robins, Schmidt, & O'Neal, 1957; Stephens, 1985; Weissman, 1974; Weissman, Fox, & Klerman, 1973). This suicide context is a predictable adult outcome of a feminine socialization that places undue emphasis on intimate relationships with men as a measure of personal success (Canetto, 1992; Canetto & Feldman, 1993). Wandrei's (1985) retrospective comparison of females engaging in nonfatal versus fatal suicidal behavior indicates that the high-risk women experienced more traditional gender socialization—they scored higher in helplessness/hopelessness, feelings of self blame, and a sense of confusion and disorganization. Based on a review of the literature, Canetto (1992) concluded, however, that in Western cultures nonfatal suicidal acts are considered more "feminine" than fatal suicidal acts.

DYSFUNCTIONAL FAMILIES

Family pathology may influence the probability of suicidal behavior, and may be a reason why some depressives are suicidal, and others are not (Hendin, 1986; Keitner & Miller, 1990). According to a review by Hendin (1986), some suicidal youngsters described their parents as hostile and resentful, whereas others indicated a lack of emotional involvement that left them depressed and preoccupied with death and suicide. Adam, Bouckoms, and Steiner's (1982) study found suicidal ideation and nonfatal suicidal behavior to be most prevalent among chaotic families. Linkowski, de Maertelaer and Delanbre (1985) analyzed the family histories of suicidal behavior in 453 female and 260 male depressives. Family history was related to frequency of suicidal behavior for women only. Finally, Stephens (1986) found that suicidal females described their parents as nonnurturing (64%), absent (32%), abusive (30%), mentally ill (26%), or alcoholic (22%).

Some studies have observed that suicidal women's relationships are uncaring. For example, Grumet (1988) noted that the male partners of suicidal women were domineering and chauvinistic, while Goldney (1985) reported that suicidal women received low care, but high overprotectiveness from their parents.

Other investigators (Back, Post, & D'Arcy, 1982; Counts, 1987; Jacobsen & Portuges, 1978; Pagelow, 1984; Stark & Flitcraft, 1985; Stephens, 1985) find women's suicidal behavior to be associated with violent relationships. For example, Stark and Flitcraft noted that up to 40 percent of battered women engaged in acts of nonfatal suicidal behavior, and concluded that abuse may be the single most important precipitant for female nonfatal suicidal behavior yet identified. Others report that victims of sexual abuse, physical abuse, rape, and other crimes appear to be more likely than nonabused and nonvictims to engage in suicidal behavior (Briere & Runtz, 1986; Hart, Mader, Griffith, & deMendance, 1989; Kilpatrick, Best, Vernon, Amick, Villeponteau, & Ruff 1985).

LARGER SOCIAL CONTEXTS

There are many other social contexts that potentially impinge on suicidal tendencies. For example, unemployment has been associated with heightened risk of suicide mortality (Pritchard, 1990). Discrimination in the work place and disapproval of women in nontraditional fields is another factor associated with vulnerability to suicidal behavior (Moore, 1982). A study of female chemists who killed themselves showed that the majority of them had suffered from sex discrimination in the workplace. Isolation appeared to be a factor in their suicidal death (Seiden & Gleiser, 1990).

IMPLICATIONS FOR INTERVENTION

Practitioners should be aware of the varieties of suicidal and self-destructive behaviors. Furthermore, they should be able to recognize that suicidal and self-destructive behaviors represent distinct although somewhat overlapping phenomena. Some suicidal individuals engage in chronic self-destructive behaviors. Many self-destructive individuals, however, are not suicide-prone. Covert self-destructive behaviors may be harder to assess, as they may involve a degree of conscious or unconscious denial.

Some clinicians working with suicidal women have argued that feminist therapy may be the best approach to address vulnerabilities related to gender socialization (Grumet, 1988). Encouraging awareness of the destructive aspects of feminine socialization may help women from overinvesting in relationships with men, or at least to withdraw from rejecting or abusing relationsips. Other goals should be the strengthening of suicidal women's self-esteem, increasing their ability to identify anger and healthfully express it, and a broadening of their problem-solving skills.

CONCLUSIONS

This chapter has reviewed the theoretical and research literature on the connection between women's gender socialization and their suicidal and self-destructive behaviors. There is evidence to suggest that some aspects of gender socialization, while aimed at "protecting" women, may actually limit their development of important social-psychological skills, and thus increase their vulnerability to self-destructive and suicidal behaviors. Three factors may be most important to ensure women's resilience: an individuated self-concept, moderate to high self-esteem, and the ability to cope constructively with challenges and stresses. Women's roles as nurturers can only be enhanced when combined with these often under-developed characteristics.

REFERENCES

Adam, K. S., Bouckoms, A., & Steiner, D. (1982). Parental loss and family stability in attempted suicide. *Archives of General Psychiatry, 39*, 1081–1085.

Back, S. M., Post, R. D., & D'Arcy, G. (1982). A study of battered women in a psychiatric setting. *Women and Therapy, 1*(2), 13–26.

Beck, A. T., Lester, D., & Kovacs, M. (1973). Attempted suicide by males and females. *Psychological Reports, 33*, 865–866.

Birtchnell, J. (1981). Some familial and clinical characteristics of female suicidal patients. *British Journal of Psychiatry, 138*, 381–390.

Bonner, R. L., & Rich, A. R. (1988). A prospective investigation of suicidal ideation in college students: a test model. *Suicide and Life-Threatening Behavior, 18*, 245–257.

Bradford, M. R. (1985). Sex differences in adults' gifts and childrens' toy requests at Christmas. *Psychological Reports, 56*, 969–970.

Breed, W. (1967). Suicide and loss in social interaction. In E. S. Shneidman (Ed.), *Essays in self-destruction* (pp. 188–202). New York: Science House.

Briere, J., & Runtz, M. (1986). Suicidal thoughts and behaviors in former sexual abuse victims. *Canadian Journal of Behavioural Science, 18*, 413–423.

Bronstein, P. (1988). Father-child interaction. In P. Bronstein & C. P. Cowan (Eds.), *Fatherhood today: Men's changing role in the family* (pp. 107–124). New York: Wiley.

Canetto, S. S. (1992). Gender and suicide in the elderly. *Suicide and Life-Threatening Behavior, 22*, 1–16.

Canetto, S. S., & Feldman, L. B. (1993). Overt and covert dependence in suicidal women and their male partners. *Omega, 27*, 177–194.

Canetto, S. S., & Lester, D. (1995). The epidemiology of women's suicidal behavior. In S. S. Canetto & D. Lester (Eds.), *Women and suicidal behavior* (pp. 35–57). New York: Springer.

Clifton, A. K., & Lee, D. E. (1976). Self-destructive consequences of sex-role socialization. *Suicide and Life-Threatening Behavior, 6*, 11–22.

Counts, D. A. (1987). Female suicide and wife abuse: A cross-cultural perspective. *Suicide and Life-Threatening Behavior, 17*, 194–204.

Danziger, N. (1983). Sex-related differences in the aspirations of high school students. *Sex Roles, 9*, 683–695.

Dweck, C. S., Davidson, W., Nelson, S., & Enna, B. (1978). Sex differences in learned helplessness. *Developmental Psychology, 14*, 268–276.

Fieldsend, R., & Lowestein, E. (1981). Quarrels, separations and infidelity in the two days preceding self-poisoning episodes. *British Journal of Medical Psychology, 54*, 349–352.

Gilligan, C. (1990). *Making connections: The relational worlds of adolescent girls at Emma Willard School*. Cambridge, MA: Harvard University Press.

Goldney, R. D. (1985). Parental representation in young women who attempt suicide. *Acta Psychiatrica Scandinavica, 72*, 230–232.

Grumet, G. W. (1988). Suicide attempts in rejected women. *Women and Therapy*, 7(1), 49–71.

Hart, L. E., Mader, L., Griffith, K., & deMendance, M. (1989). Effects of sexual and physical abuse: a comparison of adolescent in-patients. *Child Psychiatry and Human Development, 20*(1), 49–57.

Hendin, H. (1986). Suicide: A review of new directions in research. *Hospital and Community Psychiatry, 37*, 148–154.

Horner, M. S. (1972). Toward an understanding of achievement-related conflicts in women. *Journal of Social Issues, 28*, 157–175.

Jacobson, G., & Portuges, S. H. (1978) Relation of marital separation and divorce to suicide: A report. *Suicide and Life-Threatening Behavior, 8*, 217–224.

Keitner, G. I., & Miller, I. W. (1990). Family functioning and major depression: An overview. *American Journal of Psychiatry, 174*, 1128–1137.

Kilpatrick, D. G., Best, C. L., Vernon, L. J., Amick, A. E., Villeponteau, L. A., & Ruff, G. A. (1985). Mental health correlates of criminal victimization: A random community survey. *Journal of Consulting and Clinical Psychology, 33*, 866–873.

Kushner, H. I. (1985). Women and suicide in historical perspective. *Signs: Journal of Women in Culture and Society, 10*, 537–552.

Lee, D. E. (1976). Exploratory studies of self-destructiveness. *Perceptual and Motor Skills, 43*, 689–690.

Lee, D. E. (1985). Alternative self-destruction. *Perceptual and Motor Skills, 61*, 1065–1066.

Lee, D. E. (1987). The self-deception of the self-destructive. *Perceptual and Motor Skills, 65*, 975–989.

Lee, D. E. (1988). Research note: Reference others and self-destruction. *Perceptual and Motor Skills, 67*, 623–626.

Lester, D. (1989). Locus of control, depression and suicidal ideation. *Perceptual and Motor Skills, 69*, 1158.

Linkowski, P., de Maertelaer, V., & Mendle, J. (1985). Suicidal behavior in major depressive illness. *Acta Psychiatrica Scandinavica, 72*, 233–238.

Maccoby, E., & Jacklin, C. (1974). *The psychology of sex differences*. Stanford, CA: Stanford University Press.

MacDonald, C., & Parke, R. D. (1986). Parent-child physical play: The effects of sex and age on children and parents. *Sex Roles, 15*, 367–378.

Maris, R. (1971). Deviance as therapy: the paradox of the self-destructive female. *Journal of Health and Social Behavior, 12*, 113–124.

Maris, R. (1981). *Pathways to suicide: A journey of self destructive behavior*. Baltimore, MD: Johns Hopkins University Press.

Miller, C. L. (1987). Qualitative differences among gender stereotyped toys: Implications for cognitive and social development in girls and boys. *Sex Roles, 16*, 473–488.

Moore, A. C. (1982). Well being and women psychiatrists. *Journal of Psychiatric Treatment and Evaluation, 4*, 437–439.

Orbach, I., H. Bar-Joseph, H., & Dror, N. (1990). Styles of problem-solving in suicidal individuals. *Suicide and Life-Threatening Behavior, 20*, 56–64.

Pagelow, M. D. (1984). *Family violence*. New York: Praeger.

Paludi, M. A., & Gullo, D. F. (1986). The effect of sex labels on adult's knowledge of infant development. *Sex Roles, 16*, 19–30.

Paykel, E. S., Prusoff, B. A., &. Myers, J. K. (1975). Suicide attempts and recent life events. *Archives of General Psychiatry, 32*, 327–333.

Peretti, P. O., & Sydney, T. M. (1985). Parental toy choice stereotyping and its effects on child toy preference and sex-role typing. *Social Behavior and Personality, 12*, 213–216.

Pritchard, C. (1990). Suicide, unemployment and gender variations in the Western world 1964–86: Are women in Anglophone countries protected from suicide? *Social Psychiatry and Psychiatric Epidemiology, 25*, 73–80.

Rheingold, H. L., & Cook, K. V. (1975). The content of boys' and girls' rooms as an index of parents' behavior. *Child Development, 46*, 459–463.

Rich, A. R., & Bonner, R. L. (1987). Concurrent validity of a stress-vulnerability model of suicidal ideation and behavior: A follow-up study. *Suicide and Life-Threatening Behavior, 17*, 265–270.

Robins, E., Schmidt, E. H., & O'Neal, P. (1957). Some interrelations of social factors and clinical diagnosis in attempted suicide: A study of 109 patients. *American Journal of Psychiatry, 114*, 221–231.

Sadker, M., & Sadker, D. (1985a). Striving for equity in classroom teaching. In A. G. Sargent (Ed.), *Beyond sex roles* (pp. 442–455). New York: West.

Sadker, M., & Sadker, D. (1985b, March). Sexism in the schoolroom of the 80's. *Psychology Today, 19*, 54–57.

Seiden, R. H., & Gleiser, M. (1990). Sex differences in suicide among chemists. *Omega, 21*, 177–189.

Shaken, M., Shaken, D., & Sternglanz, S. H. (1985). Infant clothing: Sex labeling for strangers. *Sex Roles, 12*, 955–964.

Shapiro, L. (1990, May 28). Guns and dolls. *Newsweek, 115*(22), 56–65.

Simonds, J. F., MacMahon, T., & Armstrong, D. (1991). Young suicide attempters compared with a control group: psychological, affective, and attitudinal variables. *Suicide and Life-Threatening Behavior, 21*, 134–151.

Stanworth, M. (1983). *Gender and schooling.* London: Hutchinson.

Stark, F., & Flitcraft, A. H. (1985). *Spouse abuse.* Working papers solicited and edited by the Violence Epidemiology Branch. Atlanta, GA: Centers for Disease Control.

Stephens, B. J. (1985). Suicidal women and their relationships with husbands, boyfriends, and lovers. *Suicide and Life-Threatening Behavior, 15*, 767–789.

Stephens, B. J. (1986). Suicidal women and their relationships with their parents. *Omega, 16*, 289–300.

Stoneman, Z., Brody, G. H., & MacKinnon, C. E. (1986). Same-sex and cross-sex siblings: Activity choices, roles, behavior and gender stereotype. *Sex Roles, 15*, 495–511.

Wandrei, K. E. (1985). Identifying potential suicides among high-risk women. *Social Work, 30*, 511–517.

Weissman, M. M. (1974). The epidemiology of suicide attempts: 1960–1971. *Archives of General Psychiatry, 30*, 737–746.

Weissman, M. M., Fox, K., & Klerman, G. L. (1973). Hostility and depression associated with suicide attempts. *American Journal of Psychiatry, 130*, 450–455.

Weitzman, L. J., Eifler, D., Hokada, E., & Ross, C. (1972). Sex-role socialization in picture books for pre-school children. *American Journal of Sociology, 77*, 1125–1150.

Weitzman, N., Birns, B., & Friend, R. (1985). Traditional and nontraditional mothers' communication with their daughters and sons. *Child Development, 56*, 894–896.

Williams, J. A., Vernon, J. A., Williams, M. C., & Malecha, K. (1987). Sex role socialization in picture books: An update. *Social Science Quarterly, 68*, 148–156.

Zuckerman, D. M. (1989). Stress, self-esteem, and mental health: How does gender make a difference? *Sex Roles, 20*, 429–444.

5
Through a Glass Darkly: Women and Attitudes Toward Suicidal Behavior

Judith M. Stillion

"For now we see through a glass darkly; but then face to face: now I know in part; but then shall I know even as also I am known."

—(I. Corinthians, 13:12)

This chapter must begin with a disclaimer. Our understanding of attitudes toward suicidal behavior is in its infancy. We do, indeed, see this subject matter "as through a glass darkly." Because suicide is an act that has been taboo in Western societies since the rise of Christianity, research programs designed to assess attitudes toward suicide began only in the mid-eighties. Until that time, the accepted wisdom was that people viewed the act of suicide as a sin, a crime, or as evidence of insanity.

As rates of suicidal behavior mounted, however, researchers began to wonder if society's attitudes toward suicidal behavior were possible contributing causes. Because no studies existed on the way in which the general populace had previously viewed suicide, it was impossible to carry out research designed to measure changes in attitudes. It was at this point that a number of researchers began to develop techniques for measuring attitudes toward suicide, with the expectation that future epidemiological changes in suicide might be examined against evidence of changing attitudes. The purposes of this chapter are to examine what is currently known about women and attitudes toward suicidal behaviors, and to point out problem areas in the literature.

GENDER DIFFERENCES SUICIDE ATTITUDES TOWARD SUICIDAL BEHAVIORS

One of the earliest findings was the gender differential in rates of fatal and nonfatal suicidal behavior. Females engage in acts of suicidal behavior three times more often than do males, whereas three times as many males as females actually kill themselves (Stillion, McDowell, & May, 1984). Two early studies probing this difference were conducted by Linehan (1971, 1973). She used the semantic differential (Osgood, Suci, & Tannenbaum, 1969) to determine how female and male college students viewed "attempted" versus "completed" suicide. She concluded that "both males and females who commit suicide were rated as more masculine and more potent than males and females who attempt suicide" (Linehan, 1973, p. 33). This suggests that, if indeed nonfatal suicidal behavior is viewed as weaker and less masculine, females might feel less stigma from surviving an attempt and might, therefore, be more likely to engage in less lethal suicidal actions, while males might be more likely to structure any suicidal act in such a way as to reduce the likelihood of surviving it.

In the 1980s, an instrument for assessing attitudes toward suicidal behavior (the Suicide Opinion Questionnaire [SOQ]) (Domino, 1990; Domino, Domino, & Berry, 1987; Domino, MacGregor, & Hannah, 1989; Domino, Moore, Westlake, & Gibson, 1982; Domino & Swain, 1986; Limbacher & Domino, 1986; Swain & Domino, 1985). The SOQ comprises 100 empirically-derived items. One-third of the items reflect factual knowledge about suicide, whereas two-thirds measure attitudes toward suicidal behavior (Limbacher & Domino, 1986). The scale includes as many as 15 factors, which in the original study accounted for 76.7% of the total variance (Domino et al., 1982). Later studies, however, have shown different factors emerging with different populations (Limbacher & Domino, 1986; Swain & Domino, 1985). Domino has not looked systematically at gender differences, nor has he consistently analyzed attitudes toward nonfatal versus fatal suicidal behavior.

One study, however, did report gender differences among respondents. The study was designed to measure the responses of a large (N = 738) sample of college students who were divided into three groups: "attempters," "contemplators," and "non-attempters" (Limbacher & Domino, 1986). Using discriminant analysis, this study found that female "non-attempters" accepted suicide less frequently than male "non-attempters," and that females were also less likely than males to believe that suicide is an impulsive act. Females were also less likely than males "to believe that attempters are not mentally ill nor show loss of control" (p. 320). The authors concluded that "the most noticeable difference was that males were more accepting of suicide than were females. This was true for attempters, contemplators, and non-attempters" (p. 328). However, if one examines the factor labeled "acceptability" in this study, it appears to be comprised, at least partially, of items that tap the acceptability of suicide in specific situations, such as, "Suicide is an acceptable means to end an incurable illness" and "Suicide is acceptable for aged and infirm persons." Given the pressure on contemporary males to be rational problem-solvers, this gender difference may well reflect a greater acceptance of death by suicide based on the inevitability of death in the situations described, rather than a greater generalized acceptance of suicide. The most accurate conclusion that can be drawn about gender differences in this study is that males, when confronted with insolvable situations, approve of death by suicide as an option more often than do females.

DeRose and Page (1985) used the SOQ to measure attitudes of professional and community groups toward female and male suicidal behavior. They were interested in examining whether knowledge and attitudes toward suicidal behavior differed by occupational groups, as well as in discovering whether these groups had different standards or conceptions about mental health, as revealed in suicidal behavior for females and males. The researchers revised the questionnaire to make 76 of the 100 items applicable to either females or males. Their sample consisted of 168 volunteers representing psychology, social work, nursing, and a comparison group of mixed occupations. The psychologist and social work groups were contacted by mail, and returned the questionnaires by mail. The nurses and the comparison community group were approached individually by the first author. Half of each responding group received the questionnaire with female target figures, and half received the questionnaire with male target figures. When data were collapsed across occupational groups, the authors reported that significant gender differences emerged on twenty-two items. Among them were the following: female targets were viewed as more likely to kill themselves as a form of self-punishment, more likely to consider suicide as a response to failed relationships, less likely to be held responsible for suicide as a response to personal or professional embarrassment, less likely to engage in fatal suicidal behaviors, less likely to use a gun or rifle, and less likely to engage in "heroic" suicidal behavior.

The authors also found that some professional groups believed that females are more likely to give warning signs, to be referred to therapy, and to be recognized as potentially suicidal. They observed that "suicide was seen as a more frequently expected, perhaps less catastrophic option for females as an 'escape from life's problems' whereas such was less true when the item referred to a male target person" (DeRose & Page, 1985, p. 60). Suicide among males was more often tied with a nation's problems and viewed as being more puzzling since "they have everything to live for" (p. 60). The authors concluded that "the results . . . , appeared consistent with the prevalent gender role stereotype of the male as normative, i.e., as having, in essence, 'more to live for' than the female, but also as subject to relatively greater responsibilities or problems in life" (p. 60).

With regard to respondent gender differences, female respondents were significantly less likely to see large families as causal factors in suicidal deaths, less likely to recommend a separate cemetery for those dying by suicide, and less likely to feel that executives engaging in illegal business practices should face punishment rather than seek death by suicide as an escape. Female respondents also viewed suicidal persons as more able to profit from lay counseling than did male respondents. One limitation of DeRose and Page's study is that it did not provide information about the reliability and validity of the revised SOQ.

Another group of investigators has formulated a 51 item questionnaire to "measure participants' knowledge of facts about suicide; their attitudes toward and feelings about suicide; and their own suicide ideation, behavior, and contact with others who had attempted or completed suicide" (Wellman & Wellman, 1986, p. 363). Two studies were carried out. In the first one, participants were 473 students enrolled in an urban New England college. The second study involved 684 students at the same college. The authors found that females and males differed on a number of dimensions. Female respondents reported that they would have a suicidal person talk to them about their feelings, and that they would try to talk a friend out of suicide more often than did male respondents. Males reported more often than did females that they would avoid discussing suicide with anyone who was suicidal, and that they thought that discussing the person's feelings would precipitate a suicidal act. Males also denied that people show warning symptoms, and thought that suicide was more situational and impulsive than females. Males believed more often than did females that suicidal adolescents were from low socioeconomic status. Finally, males also tended to underestimate the incidence of suicide more than did females. In the second study, more males than females reported "that any friend of theirs who threatened suicide would have to be joking; believed that suicidal persons commit suicide after serious adverse events; and believed that anyone has the right to commit suicide" (p. 375). Although this research brought some gender differences to light, it, like the DeRose and Page study discussed above, used a custom made, nonnormed instrument for gathering the data.

In a slightly different approach, Marks (1989) carried out a telephone survey of 491 adults in Arkansas during the summer of 1984. He asked the following six questions, most worded as statements: "A person has the right to take their [*sic*] own life? A normal person would not commit suicide? People who commit suicide are acting immorally? Normal people do not think about committing suicide? People who commit suicide are mentally ill? Do you know anyone who either killed themselves [*sic*] or tried to kill themself? He found that, although only 21% of his sample agreed with the statement "A person has the right to take their own life," females were significantly less likely to agree with it than males. Females were significantly less likely than males to believe that "a normal person would not commit suicide."

Sawyer and Sobal (1987) analyzed public attitudes toward fatal suicidal behavior by examining data from the National Opinion Research Center's (NORC) probability sample of 1982. They found that almost half (45.9%) of the respondents approved of suicide "in the case of an incurable disease," whereas less than 15% approved when the person is "tired of living and ready to die," when the person has "dishonored his/her family" or when the person has "gone bankrupt." In this sample, women were more opposed to suicide than were men. The study also showed geographic, socioeconomic, political, and religious differences in attitudes toward suicide. For example, nonwhites and rural residents as well as those living in Central and Southern States, showed greater opposition to suicide than did whites, urban residents, and residents of the Northeast and far West. In addition, frequent church attenders, strong Democrats, low socioeconomic respondents and the elderly showed higher opposition to suicide.

A different method for assessing attitudes toward suicidal behavior has been used in several studies carried out by Stillion and her colleagues (Stillion, McDowell, & May, 1984; Stillion, McDowell, & Shamblin, 1984; Stillion, McDowell, Smith, & McCoy, 1986; Stillion, White, Edwards, & McDowell, 1989; White & Stillion, 1988). This method focused on nonfatal suicidal behavior, and examined gender differences in target figures and among respondents.

In the original study (Stillion, McDowell, & Shamblin, 1984) designed to develop and validate an instrument for assessing attitudes toward suicide, high school students were asked to indicate their level of sympathy, empathy, and agreement with the suicidal behavior described in ten vignettes. Each vignette focused on a troubled teen-ager who "attempted" suicide because of different situational factors, ranging from failure on a college entrance examination, to lack of acceptance by peers, to coping with terminal illness. The situations in the vignettes were based on conditions surrounding nonfatal suicidal behavior as described in the literature. Two forms of the scale, called the Suicide Attitude Vignette Experience - Adolescent Version (SAVE-A), were utilized, in which the situations remained the same but the sex of the target figure varied.

The sample for the first study consisted of 104 males and 94 females enrolled in the twelth grade of a Southern public high school. Factor analysis of the scale showed three separate factors that accounted for 91% of the variance in the responses: sympathy, empathy, and agreement. Other measures of convergent–discriminant validity included measures of self-esteem, religiosity, depression, and suicide proneness. Students who sympathized more with suicidal actions showed more death concern, were more depressed, and had higher self-esteem than students who were less sympathetic. Students who agreed with suicidal actions were more depressed and tended to have lower self-esteem than those who agreed less often with suicidal behaviors; students who described themselves as high in religiosity agreed significantly less with all motivations for suicide than those who had lower religiosity self-ratings. Test–retest reliability checks given approximately four weeks after the first administration yielded coefficients for each factor that were statistically significant.

Female respondents showed significantly higher levels of sympathy than did males. In addition, they sympathized, empathized, and agreed more with female target figures than they did with male target figures. The authors suggested that "it may be that females expect more sympathy and empathy than do males and, therefore, feel less restraint in attempting to end their lives. Males, on the other hand, may expect less environmental support after an attempt, thereby increasing their determination to succeed if suicide is attempted" (Stillion, McDowell, & Shamblin, 1984, p. 75).

A second study (Stillion, 1984), carried out with 386 participants, was designed to examine developmental differences in attitudes toward nonfatal suicidal behavior among ninth graders, twelfth graders, and first year college students. It used the SAVE-A scale with each group. The results indicated that older adolescents tended to agree less with motivations for the suicidal act. Once again, females in all three age groups sympathized more than males with suicidal target figures. The authors concluded that older students, who were more practiced in formal operations level thinking, better understood the finality of death and were less likely to romanticize suicide.

In an attempt to examine that conclusion more closely, a third study was done with academically gifted and nongifted adolescents. Participants were 190 ninth grade students (75 males and 115 females). Forty-eight of the students were academically gifted students participating in a four-week summer enrichment experience on a college campus, 36 were gifted students enrolled in the public schools of a small southern town, whereas 106 students were nongifted students enrolled in that same school. The results indicated once again that females sympathized more with all reasons for suicidal behavior than did adolescent males (Stillion, McDowell, & May, 1984). They also showed that adolescent females who scored higher on intelligence tests agreed less with all reasons for suicidal behavior than did those who scored lower on intelligence tests, thus partially reinforcing the cognitive development interpretation above.

Stillion and associates also examined the relationship between mental health indicators and attitudes toward nonfatal suicidal behavior, using the SAVE scale. The first study compared attitudes toward suicidal behavior in a group of 15- to 24-year-olds, admitted to a private psychiatric hospital during an eight-month period, with attitudes in a group of college students (Stillion et al., 1986). Results showed that institutionalized females agreed more with all motivations for suicide portrayed in the vignettes than did noninstitutionalized females or institutionalized and noninstitutionalized males. The second study utilized two measures of positive mental health: the Personal Orientation Inventory (POI), which is based on a theory of self-actualization, and the Personal Attributes Questionnaire (PAQ), which is based on the assumption that androgynous people (that is, those who combine the best of feminine and masculine traits, such as cooperative and autonomous respectively) are better adjusted than those who manifest only strong stereotypic feminine or masculine traits. This study showed that students who scored higher on one measure of self-actualization (inner-directedness) sympathized, empathized, and agreed less with all reasons for suicidal behavior than did students who scored lower on the same measure. Furthermore, students who evidenced a more stereotypic "feminine" gender identification showed greater sympathy with all reasons for suicide; individuals with more stereotypic "masculine" gender identification showed less sympathy. The conclusions of these two studies were that better-adjusted people agree less often with suicide than do those who are more disturbed, and that stereotypic "femininity" is associated with sympathizing more with suicidal target figures.

Another study in this series was an attempt to scrutinize more closely the statistically significant difference between females and males on sympathy (White & Stillion, 1988). All earlier research using the SAVE scale had indicated that females sympathized more with suicidal figures than do males. The researchers were interested in examining whether this gender difference would hold up when females and males reacted to nonsuicidal as well as suicidal target figures. Female and male college students responded to cases of troubled adolescents taken from the SAVE scale. The sex of the target figures was varied as usual. The other variation introduced was to delete the reference to "attempted" suicide on half of the vignettes. Females once again gave more sympathy than did males, and nonsuicidal targets received more sympathy than did suicidal ones. There was also a significant interaction between sex of target figure, sex of respondent, and the vignette condition (suicide "attempt" or no suicide "attempt"). Further analysis indicated that female mean ratings were nearly identical in each of the four suicide-by-sex of adolescent conditions. In addition, a separate analysis of variance for female participants indicated that there were no significant main effects or interactions. For male respondents, however, both the main effect of suicidal condition and the suicide-by-sex of adolescent interaction were significant. Males gave least sympathy to suicidal males and most sympathy to nonsuicidal males. On the empathy scale, again, there were no significant findings for females but males empathized most with nonsuicidal males. The authors concluded that the study had "found support for a generalized tendency on the part of women to be more sympathetic, regardless of the situation" (p. 364). However, of much more importance was the finding that males reported more sympathy and empathy with troubled males who did not "attempt" suicide than with females in either condition or males who "attempted" suicide. The low levels of sympathy and empathy given by males to males who "attempted" suicide seemed to support the hypothesis that males stigmatize other males who "attempt" suicide.

A final study in this series introduced a second form of the SAVE Scale to be used to assess attitudes toward elderly nonfatal suicidal behavior (Stillion et al., 1989). Called the SAVE-L (Suicide Attitude Vignette Experience - Elderly form), this instrument contained sixteen vignettes about suicidal elderly people in specific situations. The instrument was normed utilizing samples of college students and retired elderly in a rural area of North Carolina. A factor analysis of the SAVE-L scale yielded the same three factors as in the SAVE-A scale: sympathy, empathy, and agreement. These were unitary factors, weighting only on one factor. Taken together, however, they accounted for only 55% of the variance. The internal consistency of the SAVE-L scale was .96 for the sympathy, .95 for the empathy, and .89 for the agreement scale. "The most striking result was that older female target figures received less sympathy than young female target figures, who in turn received more sympathy than either young males or old ones" (p. 252). Similarly, on the empathy scales, young respondents empathized least with older female targets and most with young female targets. Only elderly females empathized more with elderly female targets than they did with any other group. On the agreement scale, both young and old respondents were more likely to agree with decisions to attempt suicide when they were made by older females than when they were made by any other target figure. Young male respondents were more likely to agree with the suicide decisions of all targets than were the other three respondent groups, although the difference was not statistically significant. The authors concluded that "attempts to measure respondents' attitudes toward suicide are incomplete unless they take into consideration the age and sex of the attempter. Attitudes toward suicide are not unitary measures. Future researchers would be well advised to take into consideration the age and gender of persons responding to their surveys" (p. 255).

Taken together, the findings of the studies by Stillion and her colleagues tend to show that females are more sympathetic than males when confronted by troubled suicidal and nonsuicidal target figures. Males, on the other hand, tend to sympathize with nonsuicidal troubled males more than with suicidal males. In addition, older, academically gifted, and more mentally healthy respondents tend to disagree more with suicide "attempts" than do younger, nonacademically gifted and less mentally healthy respondents. Finally, elderly female target figures receive less sympathy than any other suicidal group.

Deluty (1989) attempted to assess attitudes toward death by suicide using a nonnormed scenario approach. He was interested in assessing attitudes as a function of the age and sex of the suicide victim, the sex of the evaluator, and the type of illness that precipitated the suicide. He utilized twelve vignettes in which the age, sex, and illness of the victim were varied. Participants were 780 undergraduate psychology students enrolled in the University of Maryland. Deluty divided his respondents into twelve groups of 65 participants (40 females and 25 males), each of which received one version of a scenario which varied by gender, age (45 or 70), and type of illness (severe depression, severe physical pain, or malignant bone cancer) of the target figure. Each scenario ended with the sentence, "Jane (John) has decided to kill her/himself." The participants responded to the vignette by utilizing a semantic differential technique (Osgood, Suci, & Tannenbaum, 1967) which included six bipolar adjective pairs: wise–foolish, selfish–unselfish, weak–strong, active–passive; right–wrong, and brave–cowardly. In addition, participants were asked to indicate whether the target figure should be permitted to kill her/himself and how acceptable to them was the decision to kill her/himself. Finally, participants were asked if they would try to convince the target figures not to kill themselves, and if they thought the targets had the right to take their own lives.

Deluty found several significant female-male differences. Suicides by females were rated "significantly more foolish, weaker, more wrong, and less permissible than suicides by males" (Deluty, 1989, p. 320). Female respondents rated suicides as significantly more foolish and wrong and less permissible and acceptable than did male participants. Female respondents also replied affirmatively to the statement that they would try to convince their friend not to kill themselves significantly more often than did male participants. Finally, more female evaluators (30.4%) than male evaluators (14.1%) responding to the 70-year-old suicidal target figure agreed with the statement, "the subject has no right to take her/his life." Over 33% of the females and almost 32% of the males responding to 45–year old target figures denied them that right. Thus female respondents were less affected by the age of the suicidal target figures than male respondents, who tended to agree more often that elderly target figures had the right to take their own lives. Deluty concluded his results section by stating that "participants who were male, who judged the elderly, or who judged males tended to give more favorable evaluations of suicide" (p. 322). He also noted that "suicide by females tended to be evaluated significantly more negatively than suicide by males" and that female evaluators "tended to be significantly more unaccepting of suicide than male evaluators" (p. 324). Finally, the study found support for the hypothesis that the stated cause of suicide affects the respondents' ratings, as those who had malignant bone cancer were rated more favorably than those who suffered from depression or chronic pain. Deluty's research supports the growing number of studies that have found that sex/gender of respondent and sex of target figure, as well as age and disease of target figure, are important variables to be considered when conducting research on suicide attitudes.

METHODOLOGICAL ISSUES IN RESEARCH ON ATTITUDES TOWARD SUICIDAL BEHAVIORS

The preceding review of the literature concerning attitudes toward suicide among females and males presents a picture that is far from clear. At best, we are able to see images dimly reflected from the different worlds of respondents. The main point of agreement among researchers is that attitudinal research, especially when done on a complex topic such as suicide, is very difficult to carry out.

There are several methodological issues to consider when evaluating research on attitudes toward suicidal behaviors. First, the term suicide is used to describe behaviors occurring across a continuum of actions and outcomes. Linehan (1971, 1973) has shown that the outcome of a suicidal act influences the way people respond to the behavior. Researchers wishing to look at attitudes toward suicidal behavior must specify which types of behavior they are addressing in their research. Until researchers on attitudes develop a shared vocabulary concerning the gradient of suicidal behaviors, and fashion their instruments to reflect differential outcomes, our understanding will remain obscured.

Second, because of gender differences in suicidal behavior, studies attempting to assess attitudes toward suicidal behavior must also carefully control for the sex of the suicidal target, as well as for the sex/gender of the respondent. In the past, studies have not routinely examined attitudes toward suicidal behavior by sex/gender of respondent (e.g., Domino et al., 1989; Reynolds & Cimbolic, 1988). In addition, some surveys purporting to measure general attitudes toward suicidal behavior seemed to assume that the sex of the target was not a salient factor (e.g., Domino, 1990), whereas other studies have shown differences based on the target's sex (e.g., Stillion, McDowell, & Shamblin, 1984). The result of these omissions is that we currently have an incomplete and contradictory body of literature. Future research should include information about the sex/gender of respondent, as well as the sex of the suicidal target.

A third methodological issue is that an interaction effect may exist between the type of behavior being studied and the sex/gender of the respondents and/or target figures. Research conducted by White and Stillion (1988) found that, when males responded to males who "attempted" suicide, as compared with troubled males in the same situation who did not "attempt" suicide, their level of sympathy fell. Female levels of sympathy remained the same in both the suicidal and nonsuicidal conditions. In order to gain understanding, future research should be designed to examine interaction as well as main effects of gender differences.

A fourth methodological consideration concerns the role of contextual factors on attitudes toward suicidal behavior. Although the literature is not consistent on this point, attitudes toward suicidal behavior in general appear to differ from attitudes toward specific instances of suicidal behavior. For example, there is evidence to suggest that a decision to kill oneself that is made in the presence of terminal illness is viewed differently from a decision made in the presence of psychological depression (e.g., Deluty, 1989). This may be the most volatile area of change in U.S. society's attitudes toward suicide. For example, between 1977 and 1983, there was an 11% increase in the number of people who believe that terminally ill people have the right to kill themselves—an increase from 39% to 50% (Siegel, 1988). Therefore, when instruments are designed to measure attitudes toward suicidal behavior, they must make sure not only to define the term suicide precisely, but also to place it in a context. Most of the instruments developed to date do not address this issue clearly. Future research should routinely define the circumstances surrounding each decision to engage in suicidal behavior.

A fifth methodological issue is related to the one above. Marks (1989) reported that differences exist in attitudes toward suicidal behavior based on the specificity of the instrument. "Concrete situations in the form of vignettes and general abstract questions differentiated among respondents although the two techniques were moderately correlated in their assessment of tolerance of suicidal behavior" (Marks, p. 328). It is clear that the two techniques mentioned by Marks measure related, but substantially different, aspects of attitudes toward suicidal behavior. Therefore, future instruments should combine approaches in order to assess attitudes as broadly as possible.

A sixth methodological issue in assessing attitudes toward suicidal behavior is the fact that the way people view suicidal behavior is almost certainly dependent upon other values and attitudes they hold, such as their religious beliefs, their view of the rights of the individual, legal considerations, or their view of the sanctity of life (DeRose & Page, 1985; Sawyer & Sobel, 1987; Stillion, McDowell, & Shamblin, 1984). Therefore, future research should systematically measure and examine as many relevant mediating variables as possible.

A final methodological issue in research on attitudes toward suicidal behavior comes from the finding that the general response set of females is different from that of males; that is, females are more likely to admit to feeling emotions than are males (Stillion, 1985). For example, on general death attitude scales, females from childhood through middle age tend to admit higher death anxiety than males (Stillion, 1985). There are at least two possible interpretations of this finding. It could be taken at face value, that is, females are more afraid of death than are males. Alternatively, given male socialization toward stoicism and emotional inexpressiveness (Doyle, 1983), lower scores by males may simply indicate unwillingness to reveal true anxiety levels. As one author has noted, "The rule among many males is simple: Don't show any emotion that may make you appear weak, vulnerable, or feminine" (Doyle, 1983, p. 156). In suicide attitude research, then, females may show higher sympathy scores for suicidal target figures simply because they can admit their feelings more easily than can males. The implication of the response set question for research on attitudes toward suicidal behavior is that researchers should try to invent ways to tease out the effect of socialization for expressiveness or inexpressiveness in the responses of females and males—a difficult, if not impossible task.

CONCLUSION

In spite of the complexities surrounding assessment of suicide attitudes, several consistent findings seem to be emerging. First, females seem to know more factual information about suicidal behaviors than do males (Wellman & Wellman, 1986). Females may thus be in a better position than males to recognize when friends or acquaintainces are considering engaging in suicidal behavior. Second, Wellman and Wellman (1986) found that females seem more willing to discuss the subject of suicide with suicidal people. This suggests that females are more likely to be effective than males both in crisis intervention and peer counseling programs. It may also suggest that females may require less training than males to serve in those programs, since both their baseline knowledge and their inclination to discuss the topic are at higher levels than are those of males.

Third, Stillion and her associates have repeatedly found that females report more sympathy for suicidal target figures (Stillion, McDowell, & May, 1984; Stillion, McDowell, & Shamblin, 1984; Stillion et al., 1986; Stillion et al., 1989; White & Stillion, 1988) Because they report higher levels of sympathy toward individuals who are considering suicide, females may also be more supportive of real suicidal persons than males. If so, this would again argue for the use of females in peer counseling and crisis intervention situations. It may also mean that females are more likely than males to create suicidal conditions which they survive, since their expectations might be that they will receive support, rather than censure.

Fourth, in spite of their greater sympathy toward those suicidal persons, females seem to disapprove of suicidal behaviors more often than do males (Deluty, 1989). Perhaps females have a keener appreciation for life and for the waste that death by suicide engenders. The National Center for Health Statistics has estimated that death by suicide accounted for 631,990 years of potential life lost in the year 1983 alone (Centers for Disease Control, 1986). Although it is doubtful that most women respondents could cite this figure, they may have some understanding of the enormity of the potential lost because of suicidal deaths. Males, on the other hand, may view death by suicide, especially the death of those who are old or terminally ill, as representing decisive action in the face of unchangeable fate (Limbacher & Domino, 1986). Therefore, rather than focusing on the waste involved in suicide, males may see it as a final problem-solving solution. Perhaps it is fortunate that females disapprove more of suicide than males, because females continue to provide a disproportionate amount of the care of elderly and infirm relatives (Canetto, 1992). If women were to take the problem-solving approach that men seem to take in viewing suicide among the elderly or terminally ill, the incidence of suicide among those populations would be likely to increase.

Fifth, the age of target figures has been shown to be a factor that interacts with gender in assessing suicide attitudes. Young female suicidal target figures receive more sympathy, and older female target figures receive less sympathy than male target figures of any age. Both females and males seem to agree more with elderly female suicide than with male suicide or young female suicides (Stillion, et al., 1989). Suicide by elderly persons is generally more accepted than is suicide by younger people (Limbacher & Domino, 1986; Stillion et al., 1989). Such devaluing of elderly persons, especially elderly females, may have grave repercussions in the near future. As the baby boom generation reaches old age, with females outliving males by approximately eight years, elderly females may come to understand that their death by suicide would be viewed less negatively than would deaths of their male counterparts. Such understanding, coupled with increasing acceptance of the right to die (Siegel, 1988), may result in increasing suicide rates among elderly females, especially those who are in ill health.

REFERENCES

Canetto, S. S. (1992). Gender and suicide in the elderly. *Suicide and Life-Threatening Behavior*, *22*, 80–97.

Centers for Disease Control. (1986). *Mortality and morbidity weekly report*, 35, (22).

Deluty, R. H. (1989). Factors affecting the acceptability of suicide. *Omega*, *19*, 315–326.

DeRose, N., & Page, S. (1985). Attitudes of professional and community groups toward male and female suicide. *Canadian Journal of Community Mental Health*, *4*, 51–64.

Domino, G. (1990). Popular misconceptions about suicide: How popular are they? *Omega*, *21*, 167–175.

Domino, G., Domino, V., & Berry, T. (1987). Children's attitudes toward suicide. *Omega*, *17*, 279–286.

Domino, G., MacGregor, J. C., & Hannah, M. T. (1989). Collegiate attitudes toward suicide: New Zealand and United States. *Omega, 19,* 351–364.

Domino, G., Moore, D., Westlake, L., & Gibson, L. (1982). Attitudes towards suicide: A factor analytic approach. *Journal of Clinical Psychology, 38,* 257–262.

Domino, G., & Swain, B. (1986). Recognition of suicide lethality and attitudes toward suicide in mental health professionals. *Omega, 16,* 301–308.

Doyle, J. A. (1983). *The male experience.* Dubuque, IA: William C. Brown.

Limbacher, M., & Domino, G. (1986). Attitudes toward suicide among attempters, contemplators, and non-attempters. *Omega, 16,* 325–334.

Linehan, M. M. (1971). Towards a theory of sex differences in suicidal behavior. *Crisis Intervention, 3,* 93–101.

Linehan, M. M. (1973). Suicide and attempted suicide: Study of perceived sex differences. *Perceptual and Motor Skills, 37,* 31–34.

Marks, A. (1989). Structural parameters of sex, race, age, and education and their influence on attitudes toward suicide. *Omega, 19,* 327–336.

Osgood, C., Suci, G., & Tannenbaum, P. (1969). *The measurement of meaning.* Urbana, Ill: University of Illinois Press.

Reynolds, F. M. T., & Cimbolic, P. (1988). Attitudes toward suicide survivors as a function of survivors' relationship to the victim. *Omega, 19,* 125–133.

Sawyer, D., & Sobal, J. (1987). Public attitudes toward suicide: Demographic and ideological correlates. *Public Opinion Quarterly, 51,* 92–101.

Siegel, K. (1988). Rational suicide. In S. Lesse (Ed.), *What do we know about suicidal behavior and how to treat it* (pp. 85–102). Northvale, NJ: Aronson.

Stillion, J. M. (1985). *Death and the sexes: An examination of differential longevity, attitudes, behaviors, and coping skills.* Washington, D.C.: Hemisphere/McGraw-Hill International.

Stillion, J. M., McDowell, E. E., & May, J. H. (1984). Developmental trends and sex differences in adolescent attitudes toward suicide. *Death Education, 8,* Supplement, 81–90.

Stillion, J. M., McDowell, E. E., & Shamblin, J. B. (1984). The suicide attitude vignette experience: A method for measuring adolescent attitudes toward suicide. *Death Education, 8,* Supplement, 65–80.

Stillion, J. M., McDowell, E. E., Smith, R. T., & McCoy, P. A. (1986). Relationships between suicide attitudes and indicators of mental health among adolescents. *Death Studies, 10,* 289–296.

Stillion, J. M., White, H., Edwards, P. J., & McDowell, E. E. (1989). Ageism and sexism in suicide attitudes. *Death Studies, 13,* 247–262.

Swain, B. J., & Domino, G. (1985). Attitudes toward suicide among mental health professionals. *Death Studies, 9,* 455–468.

Wellman, M. M., & Wellman, R. J. (1986). Sex differences in peer responsiveness to suicide ideation. *Suicide and Life Threatening Behavior, 16,* 360–377.

White, J., & Stillion, J. M. (1988). Sex differences in attitudes toward suicide: Do males stigmatize males? *Psychology of Women Quarterly, 12,* 357–366.

6
The Pseudocidal Female: A Cautionary Tale[1]

B. Joyce Stephens

The literature on suicide is increasingly skeptical about the self-destructive behaviors of females to the point of challenging the notion that these acts are suicidal phenomena (Dorpat & Boswell, 1963; Kessel, 1966; Kreitman, 1977; Kreitman & Philip, 1969; Lester & Lester, 1971; Maris, 1981). A corollary theme in the literature is that females use suicidal behavior to manipulate and change their life situations, often with respect to their relationships with significant others (Katschnig & Steinert, 1975; Maris, 1971, 1981). With these ideas in mind, we began to examine the data we had collected on a group of adult females who survived a suicidal act. We wanted to re-examine the profile of suicidal females described in the literature.

REVIEW OF THE LITERATURE

Stengel (1956, 1960, 1962, 1964) was the first to distinguish between nonfatal and fatal suicidal behavior. Although not rejecting all nonfatal suicidal acts as inauthentic, he argued that there are diverse motivations underlying these acts.

It was Stengel who first identified the appeal function of nonfatal suicidal behavior. Stengel further noted the differing rates of nonfatal suicidal behavior by gender, and linked them with a greater propensity of females to use suicidal behavior as both an aggressive and affiliative strategy to influence their relationships.

Three other studies from the 1950s (Jensen & Petty, 1958; Rubenstein, Moses, & Lidz, 1958; Weiss, 1957) further elaborated on the affiliative and communicative function of nonfatal suicide behavior. Rubenstein, Moses and Lidz, stressing that suicidal acts are not necessarily efforts to die, described such acts as "tests of love" whereby the individual hopes and intends to be saved by a concerned other. Jensen and Petty suggested that the attitude and behavior of the suicidal person express a strong wish to survive, and are the enactment of a fantasy of rescue through the caring intervention of a significant other. The work of Weiss mirrors that of other suicidologists in that he notes the preponderance of females who survive a suicidal act, and emphasizes that such behaviors are intended to effect changes in the individual's relationships.

Research during the 1960s served to sharpen distinctions between fatal and nonfatal suicidal behavior and portrayed the latter as being less aimed at ending life than at changing life. In a study that focused on degrees of lethal intent, Dorpat and Boswell (1963) pictured many nonfatal suicidact acts as a kind of "Sleeping Beauty fairy tale" (p. 124) (the feminization of the metaphor is obvious), in which the individual acts out fantasies of a dangerous ordeal followed by rescue. In a similar vein, Sifneos (1966) claimed that approximately 65% of nonfatal suicidal acts in his experience were manipulative gestures used by individuals who took "artful, covert, fraudulent steps" (p. 528) to gain control over others.

The strongest statements come from certain researchers whose work has greatly influenced current views of the psychodynamics of female nonfatal suicidal behavior (Kessel, 1966; Kreitman, 1977; Kreitman et al., 1969). Kessel opposed the inclusion of many behaviors under the category of "attempted suicide," arguing that they were not efforts to end life, but rather efforts to interrupt distress. He described such acts as a "fashion of self-poisoning" (p. 34) which the person expects to survive. He argued that we should discard the term "attempted suicide" in these cases because "it is now customary and respectable to survive self-poisoning acts. Patients, the public, everybody, knows this" (p. 36).

The skeptical view on female suicidal behaviors received major support in the proposal by Kreitman, Philip, Greer, and Bagley (1969) to use the term "parasuicide"; this term would apply to the "great majority of patients designated as suicide attempters who are not in fact attempting suicide" (p. 747). Parasuicide, they explained, defined those acts in which the individual only simulates suicide. Finally, Kreitman and colleagues linked "parasuicide" with females, pointing out the overrepresentation of young women committing nonlethal acts of self-injury without the intent to die.

In the 1970s, studies of nonfatal suicidal behaviors in women were based on the nonlethal intent assumption (e.g., Bancroft, Skrimshire, & Simkin, 1976; Birtchnell & Alarcon, 1971; Fox & Weissman, 1975; Katschnig & Steinert, 1975; Lester & Lester, 1971; Maris, 1971). The common theme of these studies was a skepticism about the lethal intent of female suicidal behavior. Typical was the claim (e.g., Fox & Weissman, 1975) that a majority of suicidal females had little or no intent to die. For example, Katschnig and Steinert, who adopted the term parasuicide, described nonfatal suicidal acts as "covertly extorting strategies for getting out of emotionally troublesome situations" (p. 292). Bancroft, Skrimshire and Simkin characterized their *male* "attempters" as intending to die, and their *female* "attempters" as not intending to die. Maris summarized the picture of suicidal females in the following manner: the nonlethal suicidal acts of women are efforts to solve interpersonal problems, not actions intended to end life; they are manipulative strategies designed to influence significant others.

Current studies have continued to reflect the view that nonfatal suicidal acts by women are characterized by nonlethal intent (Fieldsend & Lowenstein, 1981; Lester, 1988; Maris, 1981; Pommereau, Delile, & Caule, 1987; Shneidman, 1985). Fieldsend and Lowenstein, in a study of a group of self-poisoners, concluded that, for women, overdosing had a controlling and manipulative quality and served the function of expressing hostility. Maris described suicide attempters as primarily young women, motivated by interpersonal problems, especially sexual and marital conflicts. The suicidal act is a strategy to manipulate significant others with whom the suicidal person is experiencing difficulties. To further emphasize his position, Maris makes the following statement: "we hope this point will not be misunderstood, there is too much faddish preoccupation with the suicides of the young, of women, and of minorities" (p. 334).

Shneidman (1985) recommended the adoption of a separate term for self-inflicted nonlethal acts—"quasi-suicide" (p. 19). He argued that not only are the two acts (fatal and nonfatal suicidal acts) radically different, but also that the individuals who engage in fatal suicidal behavior have different psychological characteristics than individuals who engage in nonfatal suicidal behavior. In addition, he differentiated fatal suicidal acts and "quasi-suicides" in terms of their purposes and goals. The purpose of fatal suicidal acts, he argues, is to seek a solution to an overwhelming problem, whereas the purpose of quasi-suicide is to evoke a response from others. The goal of fatal suicidal acts is to stop life, whereas the goal of quasi-suicide is to change life.

Similarly, Pommereau, Delile, and Caule (1987) argued that many suicidal women have a weak intention to die. Their suicidal behavior is less a deliberate search for death than a desire to escape a difficult situation. The authors likened the suicidal female to Snow White, a woman who falls (overdoses) into a deep, deathlike sleep. Later, thanks to Prince Charming, the woman awakes to a happier life. Summarizing their theory, the authors stated: "In our opinions, most contemporary suicidal women are in search of this kind of temporary death, a step toward possible rebirth" (p. 331).

Finally, Lester (1988) suggested both a sociological theory and a psychological theory to explain the higher prevalence of nonfatal suicidal behavior among women. He hypothesized that nonfatal suicidal behavior is more common among those who are highly socially integrated (females, the young, and the lower classes). According to him, females and young people are likely to possess certain personality traits (low self-esteem, dependency, lack of self-confidence) that make them vulnerable to nonfatal suicidal acts.

Compared to studies of intent in suicidal persons, studies on the consequences of nonfatal suicidal behavior are fewer in number. Several studies have reached the conclusion that nonfatal suicidal behavior by females results in positive changes. Two early studies (Rubenstein et al., 1958; Weiss, 1957) concluded that nonfatal suicidal behavior produces secondary gains for the individual. Weiss argued that in almost all cases the suicidal behavior resulted in immediate changes in the individuals' relationships. Rubenstein, Moses, and Lidz (1958) referred to the "spiteful" (p. 111) character of many suicidal acts. More recently, Lukianowicz (1972), in a study of 100 suicidal females, reported that, following a nonfatal suicidal act, all the women experienced favorable changes, such as removal from a stressful environment, reconciliation with significant others, or attention and expressions of concern.

Some studies, however, have found that the interpersonal consequences of nonfatal suicidal behavior are mixed (Katschnig & Steinert, 1975; Maris, 1981; Sifneos, 1966; Stengel, 1956). Both Maris and Sifneos noted that favorable *and* unfavorable changes followed suicidal acts and, perhaps more importantly, that the changes were transient. Katschnig and Steinert, and Stengel, described a similar pattern of short-term changes. These findings suggest that the positive effects, if achieved, may be of short duration.

THE PRESENT STUDY

The participants for this study were 50 adult females who had engaged in nonfatal suicidal behavior. The participants included referrals from mental health agencies and individuals who contacted the researcher after an article about the study appeared in a local newspaper. Life histories of the participants were obtained from taped interviews and combined with an analysis of personal documents (diaries, letters, and written accounts by the participants). Additional materials were gathered from interviews with the participants' therapists (in those cases where the individual was in therapy) and the researcher's weekly attendance at support group sessions with the participants.

The median age of the participants was 34, ranging from 18 to 63. All income and educational levels were represented. All of the participants were of

European-American descent (one woman was from Puerto Rico). The sample included both one-time and chronically suicidal women: 27 participants had engaged in a single act, and 23 had engaged in more than one act. The chronically suicidal women had engaged in an average of 2.8 suicidal acts. The total number of suicidal acts by all participants was 84. Thirty-one individuals used poisoning, ten combined methods, seven used cutting instruments, and two used firearms.

In order to examine the two issues of this study—degree of lethal intentionality and secondary gains achieved by the suicidal behavior—it was necessary to establish categories which differentiated the participants. To determine the degree of lethal intentionality, we used both objective and subjective criteria. All participants were ranked on the following: (1) potential lethality of the method used, (2) likelihood of rescue, and (3) the individual's motivational account of her intentions. From this we obtained three intent categories: high lethal intent (HLI), medium lethal intent (MLI), and low lethal intent (LLI). Thus, a woman who had used a method of extreme life-threatening potential, took precautions to prevent rescue, and expressed an unambiguous intent to die, was put in the HLI category. Participants who ranked high on two of these criteria were assigned to the MLI category while participants who ranked high on only one or none of the criteria were assigned to the LLI category.

For the variable of secondary gains, we relied essentially upon the women's assessment of the aftermath of their suicidal behavior. We believed that their *experience* of a better or worsening situation was most germane. Our initial attempt to classify the participants into three response categories (positive changes, negative changes, and no changes) required refinement. The resulting classification yielded four response categories: positive changes, mixed changes (both positive and negative), negative changes, and no changes. All of the participants were assigned to one of these four categories.

RESULTS

We first assessed the degree of lethal intent of the suicidal women in this study. The following breakdown was obtained: 38% (n = 19) of the participants had engaged in a suicidal act with HLI, 32% (n = 16) with MLI, and 30% (n = 15) with LLI.

The participants were then compared with respect to the variables of age at the time of the suicidal act, marital status, whether or not they were one-time or chronically suicidal, and method used. The average age of the HLI group was 39 years, the MLI group 33 years, and the LLI group 34 years. Except for a slight tendency for HLI participants to be older, no significant age differences were found among the three groups.

With regard to marital status, the HLI participants were as likely to be married at the time of the suicidal behavior (39%, $n = 7$) as to be separated or divorced from their spouses (39%, $n = 7$). Twenty-two percent ($n = 5$) were single. Over half (56%, $n = 9$) of the MLI participants were divorced or separated at the time of the attempt. The LLI group comprised the most participants (40%, $n = 6$) who had never married.

A definite pattern was found with regard to the variable of one-time versus multiple suicidal acts: women who had engaged in more intentionally lethal suicidal acts were more likely to be multiple attempters. The LLI participants had a very high percentage of one-time suicidal women (73%, $n = 11$), whereas the HLI participants comprised a very high percentage of multiple suicidal actions (68%, $n = 13$). The MLI participants were in between, with 43% ($n = 7$) of them being multiple attempters.

The method used in the suicide act did not differentiate the three groups in any significant way, as self-poisoning had been the method for most (82%) of the participants. However, there was a greater tendency for the HLI participants than the other participants to have combined poisoning with another method.

We next looked at the participants' evaluation of the aftermaths of their suicidal act, to determine whether they found them desirable or undesirable. Most women (46%, $n = 23$) reported no identifiable changes following the suicidal act, 38% ($n = 19$) reported desirable changes, 10% ($n = 5$) reported both desirable and undesirable changes, and 6% ($n = 3$) reported negative changes only.

No correlation was found between the ages of the participants and their assessment of changes after the suicidal act. With respect to marital status, all of the participants ($n = 3$) reporting negative changes were divorced. Those reporting positive changes (44%, $n = 8$) were typically women who had never been married. Multiple attempters were twice as likely as the one-time attempters to report negative changes. In contrast, one-time attempters were more likely to report positive changes than the multiple attempters. No relation was found between the method used and the participants' reports of changes.

DISCUSSION

Discussion of our findings begins with the caveat that we are working with a relatively small sample. Although a sample of fifty is not unusual in this type of study, the resultant percentages may tend to overstate differences and exaggerate their significance. For this reason, statistical analyses were not performed. The nature of the study is explorative. Its purpose is to encourage a re-examination of what has come to be taken for granted in the suicide literature.

An additional caveat should be noted in assessing our findings. Our sample included a majority of individuals who had high or medium lethal intent. We noted an association between multiple suicidal acts and high lethal intent. Samples with fewer multiple attempters may include fewer individuals in the high lethal intent category.

The question remains, nevertheless, whether the typical suicidal woman exhibits little or no lethal intent. Thirty-eight percent of the participants, as assessed by the three stated criteria, intended to die and another 32% showed a seriousness of purpose in that death was at least a partial intent. The remaining 30% fit the "parasuicide" profile described in the literature.

One reason for the disparity between our findings and other studies may lie in the criteria used to evaluate the degree of lethal intentionality. If the criteria used to determine and categorize individuals' intentions are not specified, we cannot know the procedures used to arrive at the classification of intents. If the assessment of suicidal intent was accomplished through the "clinical judgment" of the researcher, we urge caution. Clinical judgments are prone to reliability problems. To properly evaluate such judgments, one would need to know the logic and procedures used in the classification and measurement of intent. Unfortunately, what we are often presented with in published reports is a *stereotypical description* of these suicidal females. Typical adjectives used to describe suicidal women are "hysterical," "emotionally shallow," "immature," and "manipulative." These are rather facile and *demeaning descriptions*. The bottom line is that, given the vague and possibly biased manner in which determinations of intent were arrived at, the validity of the conclusions of many studies may be questionable.

Of course, the determination of individuals' intentions—suicidal or otherwise—is always going to thrust us onto slippery ground. Intent cannot be directly observed or measured. In a sense, intent will be forever inaccessible to direct study. More sobering is the fact that most behavior rarely arises from a single intention, but rather it is accompanied by a complexity of purposes. Even "simple" behaviors may conceal a thicket of intentions, not necessarily similar or even compatible. Surely, suicidal intentionality can not be expected to be less complicated. Indeed, this most powerful and simultaneously powerless of acts reflects in its ambiguities emotional and mental paradoxes. Probably few suicidal people purely and wholly intend to die. Most are tormented by a changing mix of lethal purpose and the wish to survive, albeit under changed circumstances.

Also at issue is the question of the method used by suicidal females. The fallacy of using method as a gauge of intentionality should be rather obvious, and most researchers explicitly take this into account in the evaluations of their findings. It is possible, however, that implicit assumptions may operate to associate inefficient methods with lower suicide intentionality. We cannot overestimate the inexperience of individuals when it comes to the technology of ending life. Few people in suicidal crisis seem to be able or willing to research the most effective ways of doing it. Typically, the women in our study grabbed whatever was available. Individuals who "study up" on better ways to kill themselves are a rarity. A frequent statement made by the participants in our study was that they were surprised to be still alive. We are convinced that many of them thought that a few more Valiums would have done the trick. To use this commonly prescribed drug as an example, how many people are aware of the near impossibility of killing oneself by its ingestion?

If nonfatal suicidal behavior is a manipulative strategy used to obtain secondary gains, we can conclude only that it is a poor tool. Forty-six percent of the participants reported no changes. For many of those who reported positive changes, such changes were short-lived. It is conceivable that participants underreported negative changes. Many of them felt quite embarrassed and foolish after their suicidal act. Perhaps it was too humiliating for them to admit that not only had they "failed" to end their lives, but that their already mortifying condition had become worse.

Ominously, the multiple attempters were twice as likely as the one-time attempters to report undesirable changes following their suicidal acts. This, combined with their higher lethal intent, indicates that they are at increased risk for future life-threatening acts. We wish to stress the dangerous nature of this association and to resist discrediting the multiple attempter, that is, viewing her as not serious. It would be ironic to take less seriously the very group with the most determination to die because their suicide efforts had not *yet* culminated in a self-inflicted death.

Our research has led us to conclude that the issue of female lethal intent in suicidal behaviors remains unresolved, and that characterizations of these women and their presumed lack of suicidal intent are premature. Pending clarification, researchers and suicide prevention workers might adopt a conservative, even skeptical, position, especially refraining from trivializing and ridiculing female nonfatal suicidal behavior. Our data support what Stengel (1956) first described so accurately, namely, the complexity of purposes and motives underlying suicidal behaviors. The model that dismisses female nonfatal suicidal acts as spurious is premature and awaits empirical verification. Therefore, a refinement of prevailing explanations of female suicidal behavior is called for. Otherwise, we risk trivializing women's suicidal behaviors. Theoretical overgeneralizations can become sexist stereotypes.

NOTE

1. This is a revised version of a paper presented at the Meeting of the American Association of Suicidology, May 1987, San Francisco, CA.

REFERENCES

Bancroft, J. H., Skrimshire, A. M., & Simkin, S. (1976). The reasons people give for taking overdoses. *British Journal of Psychiatry, 128*, 538–548.

Birtchnell, J., & Alarcon, J. (1971). The motivation and emotional state of 91 cases of attempted suicide. *British Journal of Medical Psychology, 44*, 45–52.

Dorpat, T., & Boswell, J. W. (1963). An evaluation of suicidal intent in suicide attempts. *Comprehensive Psychiatry, 4*, 117–125.

Fieldsend, R., & Lowenstein, E. (1981). Quarrels, separations and infidelity in the two days preceding self-poisoning episodes. *British Journal of Medical Psychology, 54*, 349–352.

Fox, K., & Weissman, M. M. (1975). Suicide attempts and drugs: Contradiction between method and intent. *Social Psychiatry, 10*, 31–38.

Jensen, V., & Petty, T. A. (1958). The fantasy of being rescued in suicide. *Psychoanalytic Quarterly, 27*, 327–339.

Katschnig, H., & Steinert, H. (1975). The strategic function of attempted suicide. *Mental Health and Society, 2*, 288–293.

Kessel, N. (1966). The respectability of self-poisoning and the fashion of survival. *Journal of Psychosomatic Research, 10*, 29–36.

Kreitman, N. (1977). *Parasuicide*. London: Wiley.

Kreitman, N., Philip, A. E., Greer, S., & Bagley, C. R. (1969). Parasuicide. *British Journal of Psychiatry, 115*, 746–747.

Lester, D. (1988). Toward a theory of parasuicide. *Corrective and Social Psychiatry, 34*(1), 24–26.

Lester, G., & Lester, D. (1971). *Suicide: The gamble with death*. Englewood Cliffs, NJ: Prentice-Hall.

Lukianowicz, N. (1972). Suicidal behavior: An attempt to modify the environment. *British Journal of Psychiatry 121*, 387–390.

Maris, R. W. (1971). Deviance as therapy: The paradox of the self-destructive female. *Journal of Health and Social Behavior, 12*, 113–124.

Maris, R. W. (1981). *Pathways to suicide: A survey of self-destructive behaviors*. Baltimore, MD: Johns Hopkins University Press.

Pommereau, X., Delile, J. M., & Caule, E. (1987). Hypnotic overdoses and fairy tales: Snow White and the uses of disenchantment. *Suicide and Life-Threatening Behavior, 17*, 326–334.

Rubenstein, R., Moses, R., & Lidz, T. (1958). On attempted suicide. *Archives of Neurology and Psychiatry, 79*, 103–112.

Shneidman, E. S. (1985). *Definition of suicide*. New York: Wiley.

Sifneos, P. S. (1966). Manipulative suicide. *Psychiatric Quarterly, 40*, 525–537.

Stengel, E. (1956). The social effects of attempted suicide. *Canadian Medical Association, 74*, 116–120.

Stengel, E. (1960). The complexity of motivations to suicidal attempts. *Journal of Mental Science, 106*, 1388–1393.

Stengel, E. (1962). Recent research into suicide and attempted suicide. *American Journal of Psychiatry, 118*, 725–727.

Stengel, E. (1964). *Suicide and attempted suicide*. Baltimore, MD: Penguin.

Weiss, J. M. A. (1957). The gamble with death in attempted suicide. *Psychiatry, 20*, 17–25.

Part IV Diverse Experiences of Suicidal Women

■ 7
Suicidal Behavior and Employment

Bijou Yang and David Lester

Several features of scholarly research make it difficult to address the association between employment and suicidal behavior in women. First, as Lester (1990a) has noted, suicidologists have preferred to study suicide mortality rather than suicidal ideation or nonfatal suicidal behaviors, despite the fact that nonfatal suicidal acts and suicidal ideation are much more common than fatal suicidal acts (Lester, 1984).

A second bias in the literature on women's employment and suicidal behavior comes from a legacy of long-standing prejudices about the nature of women. It has long been assumed that education and paid employment are not suitable for women (Showalter, 1985). The proposed explanation may have been physiological or psychological, but the assumption was that women's mental and physical health would be better if they were homemakers (Lane, 1990). This bias has been documented by many commentators (Canetto, 1992–1993; Kaplan & Klein, 1989).

These two biases present different problems for the scholar. The first bias, the lack of research on women's nonfatal suicidal behavior and employment, impedes the drawing of sound conclusions. It is our hope that this volume and, in particular, this chapter will stimulate research on this important topic. The second bias, the myth that employment is detrimental to the mental health of women, is more easily dealt with, for we will see in this chapter that there is no research to support this myth, and a good deal of research against it.

SOCIOLOGICAL STUDIES OF SUICIDE AND EMPLOYMENT

Durkheim (1897) proposed that two societal characteristics influenced the suicide rate, social integration (the number and strength of the person's social relationships) and social regulation (the strength of the norms and values which control the person's desires). Durkheim speculated that economic conditions may affect rates of suicidal behavior by modifying these two social characteristics. He hypothesized that suicidal deaths would increase during times of economic change, regardless of the direction of the economic change for, during periods of economic boom and bust, the degree of social integration and social regulation are diminished.[1]

Research, however, has not typically confirmed Durkheim's proposal. For example, Henry and Short (1954) found that, as the economy contracted in the United States, the suicide mortality rate increased and, when the economy expanded, the suicide mortality rate decreased. Araki and Murati (1987) found that the suicide mortality rates of *both* men and women decreased during periods of economic prosperity and increased during periods of economic crisis in Japan.

Unemployment and Suicidal Behavior

Platt (1984) reviewed the published research on the association between rates of suicidal deaths and unemployment, and concluded that the association was well-documented in most research paradigms. A similar association has been confirmed for unemployment and nonfatal suicidal behavior (Platt, 1986). For example, in London (England), Fuller, Rea, Payne, and Lant (1989) found a high rate of unemployment in both women and men aged 16 to 65 who had nonfatally injured themselves (60% and 40%, respectively). In a study of women in England, Hawton, Fagg, and Simkin (1988) also found that the rate of nonfatal suicidal behavior was higher in the unemployed than in the employed, the longer the period of unemployment, and in those unemployed who were aged 30 to 49.

There are several possible explanations for this association between suicidal behavior and unemployment. One possibility is that unemployment is a stressor that increases the likelihood of suicidal behavior, especially if it occurs in combination with other stressors. Another possibility is that certain psychological conditions, such as mental disorders or alcohol abuse, increase both the likelihood of people being fired, laid off or not hired, and of engaging in suicidal behavior. No research study has yet attempted to test these hypotheses in a methodologically sound manner, and in both women and men, and both possibilities have merit.

Women in the Labor Force

Aggregate studies on the relationship of employment and suicidal behavior in women are not as useful for our purpose as studies of individuals, since their implications for the impact of employment on suicidal behavior in women are difficult to identify. However, because aggregate studies are easy to do, several have appeared.

It has been argued that the participation of women in the labor force is a source of conflict between women and men (Miley & Micklin, 1972; Newman, Whittemore, & Newman, 1973). Stack (1978) suggested that employment may result in higher rates of suicide among married women due to the role conflict created between household and employment, which presumably would reduce the level of social integration. These are sexist arguments because the scholars do not typically look at male employment as a source of conflict between women and men (Canetto, 1992–1993, 1993).

The results of studies on women's employment and overall suicide mortality rates have yielded mixed results. Three studies have focused on census tracts within major American cities. In both Atlanta and Chicago, Newman, Whittemore and Newman (1973) found that census tracts with a higher rate of female participation in the labor force had higher overall suicide mortality rates, but Lester (1973) and Diggory and Lester (1976) failed to find any association in the census tracts in Buffalo for the overall suicide mortality rate or for the suicide mortality rates of women and men. Thus, the validity of the study by Newman and his associates is doubtful.

Stack (1978) found a positive association between female participation in the labor force and the overall suicide mortality rate over several countries, even after controlling for the level of industrialization and the rate of economic growth. However, a major limitation of most early studies of female labor force participation and rates of death by suicide is their limited scope and inappropriate statistical techniques. There are many social variables that have an impact on suicide mortality rates, and a simple multiple regression using few social indicators may not be sufficient to enable us to choose one variable as the critical variable.

In a study of American states, Yang and Lester (1988) found that in 1980 participation of married women in the labor market (part-time or full-time) was not associated with male or female suicide mortality rates of the states. (The participation in the labor force of women of all marital statuses combined was positively associated with female suicide mortality rates.) In a later study, Yang and Lester (1989) found that the participation of married women in the labor force was associated with the suicide mortality rates of married men and women, positive for full-time work and negative for part-time work (but not with the suicide mortality rates of men and women of other marital status). This study, however, did not explore the nature of the work engaged in by women and by men.

In a critique of this research, Lester (1990b) found that the participation of women in the labor force in the American states was positively associated with the participation of men in the labor force, and so was probably little more than a measure of employment opportunities. He argued that *aggregate* studies on female participation in the labor force, therefore, shed little light on the impact of women's employment on other behaviors in their lives. Furthermore, in a multivariable study of the American states, Lester (1992) found no association between the participation of women and men in the labor force and the suicide mortality rates of women and men, nor between the unemployment rates of women and men and the suicide mortality rates of women and men. He concluded that, despite occasional significant findings reported by the research reviewed above, there were no reliable aggregate associations between women's employment and suicidal behavior.

In a time-series study of the United States from 1950 to 1969, Davis (1981) found that the overall female participation in the labor force and the participation of married women in the labor force were both positively associated with the female suicide mortality rate, but not with the male suicide mortality rate. However, the participation of women in the labor force has been increasing steadily since the Second World War in the United States, and so the association reported by Davis may be the result of serendipitous concomitant changes in two variables (the suicide mortality rate of women and their participation in the labor force).

Yang (1991, 1992), using more sophisticated time-series analytical methods, found evidence that female participation in the labor force in America from 1940 to 1984 had been accompanied by *lower* suicide mortality rates in women. She also found that economic growth was associated with higher suicide mortality rates in women and lower suicide mortality rates in men, indicating that women may benefit less from economic booms. In contrast, female labor force participation was associated with lower suicide mortality rates for both White and non-White women of all ages. (Female labor force participation was not associated with the suicide mortality rate of White men, but was associated with higher suicide mortality rates for non-White men.)

Thus, new evidence, analyzed using better statistical techniques, suggests that employment may be associated with better mental health for women, a conclusion that is congruent with studies of individuals reviewed in the next section.

INDIVIDUAL STUDIES

Cumming, Lazer, and Chisholm (1975) studied the suicide mortality rates of employed and nonemployed women in British Columbia (Canada) in 1961 and 1971. They found that the rates of suicidal deaths of married women who were employed were lower than the suicide mortality rates of married women who were not employed. They concluded that the benefits of employment must outweigh the costs; their results lent no support to the hypothesis that employment creates role overload and role conflict for women. They suggested that employment may provide augmented social relationships for women, which might lessen their risk of suicidal death. Other possibilities can be suggested, of course. For example, employment provides increased economic resources, and this may lead to greater freedom of action for women and increased power. The results of the research of Cumming and her colleagues supports the thesis put forward by Gove (1979), that the role of housewife is low status, frustrating, powerless, and thus potentially suicidogenic.

Occasional research has focused on negative consequences of employment for women. It has been found, for example, that employment for women can lead to reduced contact with their spouse and children (Staines & Pleck, 1983), reduced affection from the spouse and less harmony (Geeken & Gove, 1983), and more guilt (Mortimer & London, 1984). Compared with other groups, married women with full-time jobs experience the highest general tension, housewives the least, with married women working part-time in between (Michelson, 1985). Baruch, Biener, and Barnett (1987), after reviewing the benefits and costs of employment for women, concluded that employment alone is not a sufficient predictor of women's health. Jobs that demand a great deal from the worker but permit very little autonomy may undermine a woman's health. Such jobs are typically low-paying ones. Taken together, these research findings indicate that employment is more stressful than beneficial to women, mostly because of unsupportive home relationships or unfavorable employment conditions. As noted by Canetto (1992), it is interesting how the existence of unfavorable home and work conditions has been used to argue that employment in general is detrimental for women while, if this were true for men, the argument would be made that the home and employment environment need to be improved.

Several studies find that employment has benefits for women. A variety of well-controlled studies show significant mental and physical health differences that favor employed women over nonemployed women (Merikangas, 1985; Verbrugge, 1982; Waldron & Herold, 1984). Verbrugge (1986) found that having numerous roles was associated with better physical health in both women and men, whereas dissatisfaction with the main role was associated with poorer physical health. Recently, Kritz-Silverstein, Wingard and Barrett-Connor (1992) found a decreased incidence of risk factors associated with heart disease in middle-aged women in managerial positions, as compared to nonemployed women. Overall, the results of the research on suicide mortality, mental disorder and employment appear to indicate that employment is associated with better health and a lowered suicidal death risk for women.

SUICIDE AND OCCUPATION

In North America, there is no relationship between the prestige or socioeconomic status of occupations and the suicide mortality rates of individuals in those occupations (Lester, 1987; Marks, 1980). Most of the research on women, employment and suicide mortality, however, has focused on those occupations with the highest prestige, whereas research on men has considered the full range of occupational types.

Professionals

Although in the United States, women have lower rates of suicidal deaths than men, some categories of professional women appear to have as high a suicide mortality rate as professional men, or even higher. High suicide mortality rates have been found among female chemists (Li, 1969), psychologists (Mausner & Steppacher, 1973), university professors (Arnetz, Horte, Hedberg, Theorell, Allander, & Malker, 1987), and physicians (Arnetz et al., 1987; Craig & Pitts, 1968; Steppacher & Mausner, 1974; Pitts, Scholler, Rich, & Pitts, 1979; Rich & Pitts, 1980; Richings, Khara, & McDowell, 1986; Sakinofsky, 1980). However, Arnetz, Horte, Hedberg, and Malker (1987) did not find an elevated suicide rate in Swedish female dentists, whereas they did in male dentists.

It is possible that some female professionals have higher suicide rates because, as a minority in their profession, they experience discrimination and harassment (Canetto, 1993), an hypothesis that has been confirmed for chemists (Seiden & Gleiser, 1990). Furthermore, as members of a powerful guild, female professionals have more opportunities for self-determination than other women, which may lead to a preference for being in charge of their deaths (Canetto, 1993). Kessler and McRae (1983), and Steffensmeier (1984) suggested that the increase in female suicide mortality rates during the 1960s, and the subsequent stability in the rates during the 1970s, might be related to changes, over time, in the degree of social integration and the role conflict of employed women; these may be responses to the broad societal changes during the 1960s, specifically the development of ideological support for gender role changes in the sexual, marital, and economic realms.

Bowman and Allen (1985) described the special stressors to which female physicians may be subject, including discrimination and minority status, stereotyping, lack of role models, mentors and sponsors, and mixed societal expectations. These variables may be related to the appearance of suicidal behavior in women physicians. The evidence on the role of alcohol and substance abuse is mixed. For example, Bissell and Skorina (1987) reported high rates of nonfatal suicidal behavior in female physicians who abused alcohol and narcotics. However, Bowman and Allen (1985) found little evidence that female physicians have higher rates of substance abuse or of other psychiatric disorder (though they may have a higher incidence of affective disorders).

It may be that female physicians, like other female professionals, face more demands on their time than male physicians who, while often similarly engaged in marital and parenting relationships, may expect, and count on, the women in their lives to take care of their household and family tasks (Canetto, 1993). As discussed by Geeken and Cove (1983), many male partners appear to be unsupportive of, and unaffectionate with, their employed mates.

It is important that future research on suicidal behavior in women professionals include studies of nonfatal suicidal behavior. To date, there has been only one study, an unpublished doctoral dissertation, comparing suicidal and nonsuicidal women professionals (Diamond, 1978). This study found no differences in scores on the California Psychological Inventory (on scales measuring self-acceptance, flexibility, achievement via conformity, achievement via independence or intellectual efficiency), on an androgyny scale, or on an objective measure of role conflict between suicidal and nonsuicidal women. Diamond also interviewed the women and obtained the impression that those who had nonfatally injured themselves had experienced more demands on their time from home and employment than those who had not engaged in such behavior.

Nonprofessionals

Alston (1986) found that suicide rates in women in highly traditional occupations were lower than those of women in nontraditional occupations, which in turn were lower than those of women in moderately traditional occupations. The relationship was not, therefore, linear. As the occupation became less traditional, suicidal behavior first became more common and then less common.

Alston (1988) found that ethnicity played a role in this relationship. African American employed women had higher suicide rates if they had clerical jobs and lower suicide rates if they had service jobs. European-American women had higher suicide rates if they were in service jobs.

WHAT ABOUT THE RELATIONSHIP OF EMPLOYMENT AND NONFATAL SUICIDAL BEHAVIOR?

As must be obvious from the research discussed so far, we have been primarily concerned with suicidal deaths. What would our conclusions be if we considered the relationship between employment and nonfatal suicidal behavior and suicidal ideation, behaviors that are more common in women than in men?

The difficulty here is that there are few good epidemiological studies of nonfatal suicidal behavior. A second difficulty for understanding the relationship between employment and nonfatal suicidal behavior is that the published epidemiological studies have not compared the effect of employment with the roles of being a homemaker, student, or retired. Thus, for example, we cannot compare rates of nonfatal suicidal behavior for married women who are employed and those who are not employed; or, to take another example, female physicians versus male physicians versus female nonprofessionals. This dearth of research suggests an important area for study in the 1990s.

DISCUSSION

The relationship between the risk for suicidal behaviors and employment in women is important because it has been commonly assumed that employment is detrimental to the mental health of women. It is clear from this review that the evidence on suicide mortality does not support this assumption. There is evidence at the aggregate level that female participation in the labor force in the United States is associated with a lowered risk of death from suicide for women. Individual studies also show that employment is associated with a reduced risk of death from suicide in women, though some professional women do appear to have an increased risk of death from suicide.

There are many possible responses to stress. Some individuals may turn to suicidal behavior, whereas others turn to assault and murder; some may injure themselves while others may use drugs and behave in delinquent ways. The choice of symptom can be affected by age, religion, ethnic group, social class, as well as gender socialization (Canetto, 1991; Lester,

1988). Particular symptoms may be more available or acceptable to one group than to another depending upon gender-specific social norms. Therefore, a complete examination of the association between employment and mental health should look at the complete range of symptoms of distress.

The results of this review on employment and suicidal behavior in women suggests that suicidal behavior in women may show the same pattern in response to employment as that found in men. Unemployment in women and in men seems to be suicidogenic (Canetto, 1992–1993). Employment in women seems to be associated with lower rates of suicidal behaviors. Thus, we can agree with Kaplan and Klein (1989) and Canetto (1992–1993) that employment may contribute to the prevention of suicidal behavior in women. Some professional careers, however, are associated with an increased risk of death from suicide in both women and men.

It is notable that most of the research reviewed here has been distal. The investigators have rarely got close to the individuals and interviewed them in detail. The sociological studies have relied on easily collected data from computer tapes, and most of the studies of individuals have looked at easily measured characteristics, such as a history of alcohol abuse or employment status. Moving outside of suicidology, we encounter much better studies of the psychological and social world of employed women. Future research on employment and suicidal behaviors in women should use detailed structured interviews with participants, so that *their* reasons for suicidal behavior can be ascertained.

ACKNOWLEDGMENT

We would like to thank Silvia Sara Canetto for her helpful comments and suggestions for this chapter.

NOTE

1. Johnson (1979) noted that the categories of altruistic suicide and fatalistic suicide in Durkheim's theory of suicide, types of suicide which Durkheim and later sociologists have dismissed as relatively unimportant in modern societies, might describe the suicidal behavior of women quite well, indicating that women and men "inhabit different social worlds."

REFERENCES

Alston, M. H. (1986). Occupation and suicide among women. *Issues in Mental Health Nursing*, *8*, 109–119.

Alston, M. H. (1988). Occupational correlates of suicide in black and other nonwhite women. In D. Lester (Ed.) *Suicide '88* (p. 206). Denver: American Association of Suicidology.

Araki, S., & Murata, K. (1987). Suicide in Japan. *Suicide and Life-Threatening Behavior, 17*, 64–71.

Arnetz, B. B., Horte, L. G., Hedberg, A., & Malker, H. (1987). Suicide among Swedish dentists. *Scandinavian Journal of Social Medicine, 15*, 243–246.

Arnetz, B. B., Horte, L. G., Hedberg, A., Theorell, T., Allander, E., & Malker, H. (1987). Suicide patterns among physicians related to other academics as well as to the general population. *Acta Psychiatrica Scandinavica, 75*, 139–143.

Baruch, G. K., Biener, L., & Barnett, R. C. (1987). Women and gender in research on work and family stress. *American Psychologist, 42*, 130–136.

Bissell, L., & Skorina, J. K. (1987). One hundred alcoholic women in medicine. *Journal of the American Medical Association, 257*, 2939–2944.

Bowman, M. A., & Allen, D. I. (1985). *Stress and women physicians*. New York: Springer-Verlag.

Canetto, S. S. (1991). Gender roles, suicide attempts, and substance abuse. *Journal of Psychology, 125*, 605–620.

Canetto, S. S. (1992, April). *Gender and suicide in the elderly*. Paper presented at the 25th Annual Conference of the American Association of Suicidology, Chicago, IL.

Canetto, S. S. (1992–1993). She died for love and he for glory: Gender myths of suicidal behavior. *Omega, 26*, 1–17.

Canetto, S. S. (1993). *Women and suicidal behavior*. Unpublished manuscript. Colorado State University, Fort Collins, CO.

Craig, A. G., & Pitts, F. N. (1968). Suicide by physicians. *Diseases of the Nervous System, 29*, 763–772.

Cumming, E., Lazer, C., & Chisholm, L. (1975). Suicide as an index of role strain among employed and not employed married women in British Columbia. *Canadian Review of Sociology and Anthropology, 12*, 462–470.

Davis, R. A. (1981). Female labor force participation, status integration and suicide, 1950–1969. *Suicide and Life- Threatening Behavior, 11*, 111–123.

Diamond, H. A. (1978). Suicide by women professionals. *Dissertation Abstracts International, 38B*, 5009.

Diggory, J. D., & Lester, D. (1976). Suicide rates in men and women. *Omega, 7*, 95–101.

Durkheim, E. (1897). *Le suicide*. Paris: Felix Alcan.

Fuller, G. N., Rea, A. J., Payne, J. F., & Lant, A. F. (1989). Parasuicide in central London. *Journal of the Royal Society of Medicine, 82*, 653–656.

Geeken, M., & Gove, W. R. (1983). *At home and at work*. Beverly Hills: Sage.

Gove, W. R. 1979). Sex differences in the epidemiology of mental illness. In E. S. Gomberg & V. Franks (Eds.), *Gender and disordered behavior* (pp. 23–68). New York: Brunner/Mazel.

Hawton, K., Fagg, J., & Simkin, S. (1988). Female unemployment and attempted suicide. *British Journal of Psychiatry, 152*, 632–637.

Henry, A. F., & Short, J. F. (1954). *Suicide and homicide*. New York: Free Press.

Johnson, K. K. (1979). Durkheim revisited. *Suicide and Life-Threatening Behavior, 9*, 145–153.

Kaplan, A. G., & Klein, R. B. (1989). Women and suicide. In D. Jacobs & H. N. Brown (Eds.), *Suicide: Understanding and responding* (pp. 257–282). Madison, CT: International Universities Press.

Kessler, R. C., & McRae, J. A. (1983). Trends in the relationship between sex and attempted suicide. *Journal of Health and Social Behavior, 24*, 98–110.

Kritz-Silverstein, D., Wingard, D. L., & Barrett-Connor, E. (1992). Employment status and heart disease risk factors in middle-aged women. *American Journal of Public Health, 82*, 215–219.

Lane, A. J. (1990). *To* Herland *and beyond*. New York: Pantheon.

Lester, D. (1973). Completed suicide and females in the labor force. *Psychological Reports, 32*, 730.

Lester, D. (1984). Suicide. In C. S. Widom (Ed.), *Sex roles and psychopathology* (pp. 145–156). New York: Plenum.

Lester, D. (1987). Occupational prestige and rates of suicide and homicide. *Perceptual and Motor Skills, 64*, 398.

Lester, D. (1988). Rational choice theory and suicide. *Activitas Nervosa Superior, 30*, 309–312.

Lester, D. (1990a). The study of suicide from a feminist perspective. *Crisis, 11*, 38–43.

Lester, D. (1990b). Women in the labor force and suicide. *Psychological Reports, 66*, 194.

Lester, D. (1992). Patterns of suicide and homicide in America. *Proceedings of the Pavese Society, 4*, 118–211.

Li, F. B. (1969). Suicide among chemists. *Archives of Environmental Health, 19*, 518–520.

Marks, A. (1980). Socioeconomic status and suicide in the state of Washington. *Psychological Reports, 46*, 924–026.

Mausner, J., & Steppacher, R. (1973). Suicide in professionals. *American Journal of Epidemiology, 98*, 463–445.

Merikangas, K. (1985). *Sex differences in depression*. Paper presented at the Murray Center (Radcliffe College) Conference on Mental Health in Social Context, Cambridge, MA, May.

Michelson, W. (1985). *From sun to sun*. Totowa, NJ: Rowman and Allanheld.

Miley, J., & Micklin, M. (1972). Structural change and the Durkheimian legacy. *American Journal of Sociology, 78*, 657–673.

Mortimer, J. T., & London, J. (1984). The varying linkages of work and family. In P. Voydanoff (Ed.), *Work and family* (pp. 20–35). Palo Alto: Mayfield.

Newman, J., Whittemore, K., & Newman, H. (1973). Women in the labor force and suicide. *Social Problems, 21*, 220–230.

Pitts, F. N., Scholler, A., Rich, C., & Pitts, A. (1979). Suicide among US women physicians, 1967–1972. *American Journal of Psychiatry, 136*, 694–696.

Platt, S. D. (1984). Unemployment and suicidal behavior. *Social Science and Medicine, 19*, 93–115.

Platt, S. D. (1986). Parasuicide and unemployment. *British Journal of Psychiatry, 149*, 401–405.

Rich, C. L., & Pitts, F. N. (1980). Suicide by psychiatrists. *Journal of Clinical Psychiatry, 41*, 261–263.

Richings, J. C., Khara, G. S., & McDowell, M. (1986). Suicide in young doctors. *British Journal of Psychiatry, 149*, 475–478.

Sakinofsky, I. (1980). Suicide in doctors and their wives. *British Medical Journal, 2*, 386–387.

Seiden, R. H., & Gleiser, M. (1990). Sex differences in suicide among chemists. *Omega, 21*, 177–189.

Showalter, E. (1985). *The female malady*. New York: Penguin.

Stack, S. (1978). Suicide. *Social Forces, 57*, 644–653.

Staines, G. L., & Pleck, J. H. (1983). *The impact of work on the family*. Ann Arbor: University of Michigan Survey Research Center.

Steffensmeier, R. H. (1984). Suicide and the contemporary woman. *Sex Roles, 10*, 613–631.

Steppacher, R., & Mausner, J. (1974). Suicide in male and female physicians. *Journal of the American Medical Association, 228*, 323–328.

Verbrugge, L. M. (1982). Women: Social roles and health. In P. Berman & E. Ramey (Eds.), *Women: A developmental perspective*, Publication No. 82–2298 (pp. 49–78). Bethesda, MD: National Institutes of Health.

Verbrugge, L. M. (1986). Role burdens and physical health of men and women. *Women and Health, 11*(1), 47–77.

Waldron, I., & Herold, J. (1984, March). *Employment, attitudes toward employment and women's health*. Paper presented at the meeting of the Society of Behavioral Medicine, Philadelphia, PA.

Yang, B. (1991, September). *The impact of the economy on the elderly suicide rate in the USA*. Paper presented at the meeting of the International Association for Suicide Prevention, Brussels, Belgium.

Yang, B. (1992). The economy and suicide: A time-series study of the USA. *American Journal of Economics and Sociology, 51*, 87–99.

Yang, B., & Lester, D. (1988). The participation of females in the labor force and rates of personal violence (suicide and homicide). *Suicide and Life-Threatening Behavior, 18*, 270–278.

Yang, B., & Lester, D. (1989). The association between working and personal violence (suicide and homicide) in married men and women. *Proceedings of the Annual Meeting of the Pennsylvania Economic Association* (pp. 343–350). University Park, PA: Pennsylvania State University.

8 Suicidal Behavior Among Adolescent Females: The Cry for Connection

Brenda J. Bettridge and
Olga Eizner Favreau

It has been theorized that adolescent females who engage in nonfatal suicidal behavior experience difficulty in achieving adequate separation-individuation (Lukianowicz, 1972; Wade, 1987). However, recent contributions to the psychology of adolescence suggest that the achievement of greater interdependency, rather than increased separation, is an important goal for many nonsuicidal adolescent girls. In this chapter we will examine the interpersonal characteristics of suicidal adolescent girls and report on the results of our study into their relational experiences.

A central hypothesis guiding our investigation was that interdependency is a healthy developmental goal during adolescence, and that the pathway toward increased interdependency has been disrupted in the lives of adolescent girls who engage in nonfatal suicidal behavior. In the first part of this investigation (Bettridge & Favreau, in press), we examined the dependency needs and the availability and adequacy of relationships in female suicidal and nonsuicidal adolescents. In a subsequent study (Bettridge & Favreau, 1994), we examined their perceptions of intimacy in relationships.

FEMALE ADOLESCENT DEVELOPMENT

The need to create a model of healthy female psychological development (Miller, 1986) has led clinical and developmental theorists (Gilligan, Lyons, & Hanmer, 1990; Jordan, Kaplan, Miller, Stiver, & Surrey, 1991) to begin outlining a relational theory of women's mental health. This perspective conceptualizes development as taking place only within, and through, relationships (Surrey, 1991). Relational theory thus moves beyond a traditional psychodynamic focus on individual psychological development to encompass relational development (Miller, 1991). Interdependency, reciprocity, and mutual empathy are seen as characteristics of healthy relationships. Relational theorists propose that women and men experience increased psychological difficulties when opportunities to enter into and sustain healthy relationships are unavailable (Bergman, 1991; Jack, 1987; Miller, 1988; Stiver, 1990a, 1990b).

Research in the psychology of female adolescence tends to support the view that increased interdependency is an important task for adolescent girls, and that their psychological development takes place through a process of affiliation and mutuality within relationships (Hodgson & Fisher, 1979; Josselson, Greenberger, & McConochie, 1977; Thornbecke & Grotevant, 1982). According to Hodgson and Fisher (1979), an adolescent girl's identity task "revolves around who she can be in relation to others . . . as if her sense of self rests on the success with which she can resolve issues of getting along with others that satisfy both herself and those important to her" (p. 47). As Cosse (1992) has noted, normal female adolescent development is directly related to the capacity for increased interpersonal relatedness.

SUICIDAL ADOLESCENT FEMALES

It has been theorized that suicidal behavior by adolescent girls signals conflict or failure in their ability to successfully separate and individuate during adolescence (Lukianowicz, 1972; Wold, 1971). Although it is generally accepted that adolescent female suicidal acts are a desperate form of communication regarding unmet interpersonal needs (Rosenthal, 1981), it has also been assumed that these interpersonal needs result from an inability to establish more mature relationships. "It appears that a typical attempter is affiliative; she wants to bring herself into association with others. She is also dependent and relies upon others for help, approval, and support" (Cantor, 1972, p. 254). Female nonfatal suicidal acts have thus been seen as a way of re-establishing dependency within relationships (Wade, 1987) or as a means of gaining power and control 'over' others (Sifneos, 1966). Implicit in this view is the notion that suicidal girls are not simply seeking to create and maintain relationships, but that they are also inappropriately dependent on them.

The assumption that suicidal adolescent females are dependent on their relationships arises, in part, from empirical studies that document the importance of relationships to these girls. Studies indicate that, in the majority of female adolescent nonfatal suicidal acts, the immediate precipitating factors are relational conflict and loss (Bancroft, Skrimshire, Casson, Harvard-Watts, & Reynolds, 1977; Lukianowicz, 1972). These relational precipitants usually occur against a background of ongoing interpersonal dissatisfaction (Cantor, 1976; Lester, 1984). Adolescent girls who engage in nonfatal suicidal behavior report a lack of parental support and a feeling of estrangement from these significant relationships (Simons & Murphy, 1985). They also report feeling distant from those important to them (Marks & Haller, 1977), unfulfilled in their interpersonal needs (Ganzler, 1967), and lacking the security of a close confidant (Topol & Reznikoff, 1982).

On the other hand, the view that suicidal adolescent females are excessively dependent on relationships arises largely from assumptions that have been made based on observations of male adolescent development (Kaplan & Klein, 1989). Traditionally, theories of development have proposed that adolescence entails a process of separation–individuation. This view, as outlined by such writers as Blos (1962), Erikson (1968), and Glenn and Urbach (1981), theorizes that healthy adolescent development involves becoming less dependent on others. "The formation of an independent, autonomously functioning, emotionally self-reliant character is the successful adaptive achievement of a sense of identity" (Glenn & Urbach, 1981, p. 277). From this perspective, adolescent development involves a linear progression away from dependence toward independence.

We decided to test whether adolescent girls who engaged in nonfatal suicidal behavior have excessive dependency needs by comparing them to a matched group of adolescent girls without a history of suicidal behavior, hereafter referred to as "nonsuicidal adolescents" (Bettridge & Favreau, in press). Participants included 21 female adolescents, 12-to-20-years-old, who had presented at an emergency ward at one of four urban Canadian hospitals as a result of a suicidal act. These adolescents were interviewed 2 to 17 weeks after their suicidal act. All adolescents identified their behavior as a suicide attempt, and all suicidal acts were by self-poisonings. Suicidal adolescents were referred to the researchers by hospital staff or by community mental health agencies. Two of the suicidal females referred other suicidal females. The comparison group consisted of 22 female adolescents, 12- to 20 years old, who had no history of suicidal behavior. These adolescents found out about the study via flyers distributed in the community and through their peers.

Dependency was measured using Barnett and Gotlib's (1988) Trait Dependency Scale. In this scale dependency is defined as the "tendency to derive self-esteem primarily from interpersonal relationships' (p. 3). The results of our study indicate that suicidal and nonsuicidal adolescent girls reported similar dependency needs. These findings bring into question assumptions about suicidal adolescent females having excessive dependency needs, unless one is prepared to characterize as excessive the dependency needs of female adolescents in general.

Dependency needs are essential to the development of connectedness within relationships. Stiver (1991), for example, has argued that dependency is a label frequently applied to women as they attempt to create and maintain relationships. "The prevailing belief seems to be that dependency needs belong in childhood and if these needs are not satisfied in childhood, they continue to exert influences . . . in the form of clinging, demanding, helpless personalities" (p. 147).

Using the Interview Schedule for Social Interaction (Henderson, Byrne, & Duncan-Jones, 1981), we also measured the availability and adequacy of both intimate and social network relationships and found highly significant differences between suicidal and nonsuicidal adolescents (Bettridge & Favreau, in press). In addition to a less extensive and less adequate set of intimate relationships in their lives, suicidal girls reported a smaller and less satisfying social network.

We also found that the suicidal adolescents in our sample reported a history of physical and/or sexual abuse more often than nonsuicidal adolescents. In our study, only 3 of the 21 suicidal adolescents did not report having been abused, whereas only 4 of the 23 nonsuicidal adolescents reported a history of abuse. These findings are consistent with recent studies (Briere & Zaidi, 1989; Cutler & Nolen-Hoeksema, 1991; Straus, 1988) documenting high rates of depression, suicide ideation, and suicidal behavior in adolescent girls and women who were physically and sexually abused during childhood.

FROM DEPENDENCY TO DISCONNECTION

In the second part of our investigation (Bettridge & Favreau, 1994), we examined the intimacy imagery of these suicidal and nonsuicidal girls by administering a written Story Completion Test. Each participant received a booklet entitled "Creativity and Imagination." Instructions directed the participant to write a one-page story in response to two written cues. The family cue was: 'A young woman is sitting with her family.' The friendship cue was: 'Two girls are sitting on a park bench.' Participants were told that there were no right or wrong answers and that what was important was to write a complete story with a plot, with characters, and with an ending. All stories were to be written around the following four questions spaced on the page:

1. What is happening?
2. What had led up to the situation?
3. What is being thought? What is wanted? What is being felt? By whom?
4. What will happen? How will it end?

Coding

We obtained an overall intimacy rating for each story by scoring for the presence or absence of negative, unfulfilled, positive, and neutral intimacy imagery as outlined below. The criteria for scoring intimacy were developed from works by Pollack and Gilligan (1982).

Negative Intimacy

Violent intimacy was defined as imagery (that is, statements in the story) that suggested or anticipated negative consequences as a result of, or within intimacy. Violent intimacy imagery included expressions of serious concern about a close, familiar, or warm personal relationship; the occurrence or anticipation of negative affect and/or consequences because of the intimacy (e.g., dispute, physical violence, or suspiciousness); any direct expression of conflict regarding intimacy; explicit denial of intimacy; and/or bizarre, inappropriate, unrealistic, or nonadaptive responses to the situation described by the cue. Defused intimacy was defined as imagery that attempted to prevent the development of intimacy between characters. Defused intimacy imagery included imposing a rule-bound (e.g., sports game or classroom) or impersonal, structured goal-oriented context on the situation described by the cue; placing the characters in a competitive-status relationship to each other; instrumental activity away from intimacy (e.g., constant joking and teasing between characters); and/or introducing other people into the situation.

Unfulfilled Imagery

Unfulfilled intimacy was defined as imagery that suggested or anticipated the nonreciprocity of intimacy between characters. Unfulfilled intimacy imagery included the anticipation or initiation of a close, familiar, or warm personal relationship that was responded to with indifference or negation (e.g., change of subject or leaving the scene); unheeded or ignored requests for present or future plans; commitments, or assistance between characters; feelings of dissatisfaction or disappointment in efforts to obtain intimacy.

Positive/Neutral Intimacy

Positive intimacy was defined as imagery that suggested or anticipated positive consequences as a result of intimacy. Positive intimacy imagery included the occurrence or anticipation of practical positive consequences because of intimacy (e.g., helping someone with homework); positive affect because of the intimacy (e.g., the characters enjoy being with each other); and intentional efforts to attain intimacy. Neutral intimacy was defined as imagery that just describes the intimate situation and does not fall into any of the above categories.

Results

The results of the overall intimacy ratings indicated highly significant differences between suicidal and nonsuicidal girls in their intimacy imagery. Suicidal girls tended to write stories in which there was negative, defused, and unfulfilled intimacy imagery between characters.

These differences between groups were most apparent when we compared the family stories of suicidal and nonsuicidal girls. For example, in her family story, Martha, a 16–year old suicidal girl, wrote of a character's unfulfilled desire for greater authenticity in the mother–daughter relationship. Although the daughter possessed a strong desire to understand her mother and, in turn, to have her feelings understood, she was unable to communicate this desire. As confusion and doubt intensified, the adolescent girl gave up on her attempt to engage her mother:

> The young woman is trying to explain why she is so unhappy. Her mother is crying, thinking it's all her fault. Her brother is nervous and acting like he doesn't care. It's hard for the girl to know that others understand her. Her mother cares more for her new boyfriend whom the girl doesn't like. So the girl is angry and wants to leave home and live somewhere else. But she is also scared for her mother but doesn't tell her this. Maybe her mother cares but can't find the words either. The girl doesn't know what to think. She leaves the room crying.

In comparison, Connie, a 17–year old nonsuicidal girl, wrote a story in which family members verbalize conflict and attempt to work toward a mutual resolution of their differences. Connie's story ends with an understanding that the dialogue is ongoing:

> I am at the dinner table with my parents and Crystal. They are trying to make me feel guilty because I won't move back home. I am getting defensive because they don't understand my reasons, which I'm trying to explain. I still have not found out about my student loan. My parents asked. I told them I didn't know yet. They asked what I will do if I don't get it.

> My parents are upset. They feel that they are no longer needed. I try to make them realize they are needed in other ways. They don't understand my need for independence. I tell them that I'll think it over after I find out if I get my student loan or not. They agree. I ask them about their golf game and the conversation is forgotten (for now).

An analysis of intimacy imagery in their friendship stories indicated that suicidal girls were also more likely to perceive these relationships as negative, defused, and unfulfilled than nonsuicidal girls (although the difference between the groups was not statistically significant). For example, Kathleen, a 14–year old suicidal girl, had the lowest individual score on the Trait Dependency Scale. Coupled with a view of herself as independent and self-reliant, she wrote stories that were disconnected and negative in their intimacy imagery. In addition to writing a family story that was characterized by violence, Kathleen wrote the following friendship story of hopelessness and self-blame:

> The girls are checking out the guys when it starts to rain. It's raining so hard out that they had to find shelter. They were standing under a tree when it got hit by lightening. One girl, Stephanie, was burned badly. But Sherri is dead. When it was raining they should have gone somewhere else. Stephanie was in extreme pain and wished she was dead. Just like Sherri. The pain twisted through her body like electricity. In the end, Stephanie dies from third degree burns and the two girls were buried under a tree.

By contrast, Sheila, an 18-year-old nonsuicidal girl, wrote a friendship story in which empathy, closeness, and dependability characterize the relationship between two girls:

> Tracey and I are talking. She's sitting on the other side of the bench and is crawled up into a ball. Tracey has had another fight with her boyfriend. She called me. I came to her apartment and we went for a walk. We ended up at the park on a bench. I am thinking: Is there any way I can help Tracey? I try to just be there for her and understand. She feels helpless and confused. She doesn't have much confidence. I try to boost it. She needs to be loved, and she needs a hug. As we talk we move closer together. She cries on my shoulder then we hug. When she seems to be done I make a joke and we start laughing. We go watch a movie or something.

In addition to an overall intimacy rating, we analyzed the content of each story by following its course from inception to outcome. The major categories of the content analysis were: (a) the establishment of contact between characters, whether by prearrangement, by chance, or part of an ongoing situation, (b) the presence or absence of expressed feelings and personal experience, (c) the quality of relationships between characters, whether violent, disconnected, unfulfilled, or mutual, and (d) the outcome of the story, whether negative, unfulfilled, positive, or neutral.

The results of the analysis of story content indicated that more suicidal than nonsuicidal girls wrote about relationships that occurred by chance and that ended in disconnection or violence. In comparison to nonsuicidal girls, suicidal girls also depicted the quality of intimacy in relationships, particularly within their family stories, as more unfulfilled and negative. Lastly, feelings and personal experience went unexpressed more often in suicidal girls' stories, suggesting that relationships may be perceived by them as more emotionally constricting. These results lead us to speculate that suicidal adolescent girls may be more likely to censor themselves in relationships (Gilligan, 1990; Miller, 1988) in order to retain a sense of relational connection at all.

THE CRY FOR CONNECTION

Nonfatal suicidal behavior in adolescent females has commonly been defined as an affiliative "cry for help" (Shneidman & Farberow, 1961) arising from unmet interpersonal needs. Rather than being a dependent cry for help, however, a young woman's nonfatal suicidal act can be understood as a cry for connection. From this perspective, an adolescent girl's suicidal act signals "a desperate plea for mutual engagement in which she can make herself known to others, and others will respond so as to make their feelings known to her" (Kaplan & Klein, 1989, p. 260). The suicidal adolescent's unmet need is for greater interdependency in relationships. In the words of one of our participants, relationships need to become "a two-way street."

An understanding of adolescent girls' suicidal behavior in terms of their relational development requires a conceptual shift in how we define and understand the 'self.' It requires the recognition that "for women, the primary experience of self is relational, that is, the self is organized and developed in the context of important relationships" (Surrey, 1991, p. 52).

It has been theorized that the rate of suicide mortality for adolescent girls is lower than that of boys because of girls' greater orientation toward interdependency (Kaplan & Klein, 1989); and that, conversely, adolescent boys' higher suicide mortality rate reflects a male socialization process that discourages boys' dependency needs (Mack, 1988; Sanborn, 1990). It may well be that adolescent girls' interpersonal needs, including their need to depend on others, acts as a protective factor in keeping them alive (Rosenthal, 1981). What is clear at the present time is that a closer examination of the influence of gender provides us with a richer, more accurate understanding of nonfatal suicidal behavior in adolescents.

ACKNOWLEDGMENTS

The authors wish to thank Helene Burt, Michele Phillips, and Lois Sapsford for their thoughtful contributions to this work. The support of Alberta Mental Health and the Calgary District Hospital Group is gratefully acknowledged.

REFERENCES

Bancroft, J., Skrimshire, A. M., Casson, J., Harvard-Watts, O., & Reynolds, F. (1972). People who deliberately poison or injure themselves. *Psychological Medicine, 7*, 289–303.

Barnett, P., & Gotlib, I. (1988, June). *Personality and depression: New scales and a model of relationships.* Paper presented at the meeting of the Canadian Psychological Association, Montreal, PQ.

Bergman, S. J. (1991). Men's psychological development: A relational perspective. *Work in progress no. 48.* Wellesely, MA: The Stone Center.

Bettridge, B. J., & Favreau, O. E. (in press). The dependency needs and perceived availability and adequacy of relationships in female adolescent suicide attempters. *Psychology of Women Quarterly.*

Bettridge, B. J., & Favreau, O. E. (1994). *Intimacy and relationships: The imagery of female adolescent suicide attempters.* Manuscript submitted for publication.

Blos, P. (1962). *On adolescence.* New York: Free Press.

Briere, J. & Zaidi, L. (1989). Sexual abuse histories and sequelae in female psychiatric emergency room patients. *American Journal of Psychiatry, 146*, 1602–1606.

Cantor, P. (1972). The adolescent attempter: Sex, sibling position and family constellation. *Life-Threatening Behavior*, 2, 252–261.

Cantor, P. (1976). Personality characteristics found among youthful female suicide attempters. *Journal of Abnormal Psychology, 85*, 324–329.

Cosse, W. J. (1992). Who's who and what's what? The effects of gender on development in adolescence. In B. Wainrib (Ed.), *Gender issues across the life cycle* (pp. 5–16). New York: Springer.

Cutler, S., & Nolen-Hoeksema, S. (1991). Accounting for sex differences in depression through female victimization: Childhood sexual abuse. *Sex Roles, 24*, 425–438.

Erikson, E. (1968). *Identity: Youth and crisis.* New York: Norton.

Ganzler, S. (1967). Some interpersonal and social dimensions of suicide behavior. *Dissertation Abstracts, 28*, 1192B-1193B.

Gilligan, C., Lyons, N. P., & Hanmer, T. J. (Eds.), (1990). *Making connections: The re-*

lational world of adolescent girls at Emma Willard School. Cambridge, MA: Harvard University Press.

Glenn, J., & Urbach, H. (1981). Adaptive and nonadaptive action in adolescence. In S. Orgel & B. D. Fine (Eds.), *Clinical psychoanalysis* (pp. 259–292). New York: Jason Aronson.

Henderson, S., Byrne, D., & Duncan-Jones, P. (1981). *Neurosis and the social environment*. Sydney: Academic Press.

Hodgson, J. W., & Fisher, J. L. (1979). Sex differences in identity and intimacy development in college youth. *Journal of Youth and Adolescence, 8*, 37–50.

Jack, D. (1987). Self-in-relation theory. In R. Formanek & A. Gurian (Eds.), *Women and depression: A life-span perspective* (pp. 41–45). New York: Springer.

Jordan, J. V., Kaplan, A. G., Miller, J. B., Stiver, I. P., & Surrey, J. L (1991), *Women's growth in connection: Writings from the Stone Center*. New York: Guilford.

Josselson, R., Greenberger, E., & McConochie, D. (1977). Phenomenological aspects of psychosocial maturity in adolescence. Part II. Girls. *Journal of Youth and Adolescence, 6*, 145–167.

Kaplan, A. G., & Klein, R. B. (1989). Women and suicide. In D. Jacobs & H. N. Brown (Eds.), *Suicide: Understanding and responding* (pp. 257–282). Madison, CT: International Universities Press.

Lester, D. (1984). Suicide. In C. P. Widom (Ed.), *Sex roles and psychopathology* (pp. 145–156). New York: Plenum.

Lukianowicz, N. (1972). Suicidal behavior: An attempt to modify the environment. *British Journal of Psychiatry, 121*, 387–390.

Mack, J. E. (1988, April). *Male suicide*. Paper presented at the American Association of Suicidology Conference, Washington, DC.

Marks, P., & Haller, D. (1977). Now I lay me down to sleep: A study of adolescent suicide attempts. *Journal of Clinical Psychology, 33*, 391–400.

Miller, J. B. (1986). *Towards a new psychology of women* (2nd ed.). Boston: Beacon Press.

Miller, J. B. (1988). Connections, disonnections and violations. *Work in progress no. 33*. Wellesley, MA: The Stone Center.

Miller, J. B. (1991). Some misconceptions and reconceptions of a relational approach. *Work in progress no. 49*. Wellesely, MA: The Stone Center.

Pollack, S., & Gilligan, C. (1982). Images of violence in thematic apperception test stories. *Journal of Personality and Social Psychology, 42*, 159–167.

Rosenthal, M. J. (1981). Sexual differences in the suicidal behavior of young people. *Adolescent Psychiatry, 27*, 357–442.

Sanborn, C. J. (1990). Gender socialization and suicide. *Suicide and Life-Threatening Behavior, 20*, 148–155.

Shneidman, E. S., & Farberow, N. L. (1961). *The cry for help*. New York: McGraw-Hill.

Sifneos, P. S. (1966). Manipulative suicide. *Psychiatric Quarterly, 40*, 525–537.

Simons, R., & Murphy, P. (1985). Sex differences in the causes of adolescent suicide ideation. *Journal of Youth and Adolescence, 14*, 423–433.

Stiver, I. P. (1990a). Dysfunctional families and wounded relationships—Part I. *Work in progress no. 41*. Wellesley, MA: The Stone Center.

Stiver, I. P. (1990b). Dysfunctional families and wounded relationships—Part II. *Work in progress no. 44*. Wellesley, MA: The Stone Center.

Stiver, I. P. (1991). The meaning of "dependency" in female-male relationships. In J. V. Jordan, A. G. Kaplan, J. B. Miller, I. P. Stiver, & J. L. Surrey, *Women's growth in connection: Writings from the Stone Center* (pp. 143–161). New York: Guilford.

Straus, M. (1988). Abused adolescents. In M. Straus (Ed.), *Abuse and victimization across the lifespan* (pp. 107–123). Baltimore: John Hopkins University Press.

Surrey, J. L. (1991). The "Self-in-Relation": A theory of women's development. In J. V. Jordan, A. G. Kaplan, J. B. Miller, I. P. Stiver, & J. L. Surrey, *Women's growth in connection: Writings from the Stone Center* (pp. 51–66). New York: Guilford.

Thornbecke, T., & Grotevant, H. (1982). Gender differences in adolescent interpersonal identity formation. *Journal of Youth and Adolescence, 11*, 479–492.

Topol, P., & Reznikoff, M. (1982). Perceived peer and family relationships, hopelessness, and locus of control as factors in adolescent suicide attempts. *Suicide and Life-Threatening Behavior, 12*, 141–150.

Wade, N. (1987). Suicide as a resolution of separation-individuation among adolescent girls. *Adolescence, 22*, 169–177.

Wold, C. (1971). Subgroupings of suicidal people. *Omega, 2*, 19–29.

9
Suicidal Adolescent Latinas: Culture, Female Development, and Restoring the Mother–Daughter Relationship

James K. Zimmerman and
Luis H. Zayas

Adolescent suicidal behavior is a serious social problem in the United States. In fact, suicide is the third leading cause of death among those aged 15 to 24 (National Center for Health Statistics [NCHS], 1992). The risk factors commonly associated with suicidal behaviors include depressive disorders, family turmoil, parental discord and separation, physical and sexual abuse, parental substance abuse, disturbed parent–child relations, major mental disorder in parents, and lack of social supports (Chabrol & Moron, 1988; Husain, 1990; Slaby & MacGuire, 1989; Spirito, Brown, Overholser, & Fritz, 1989). There are, however, significant gender and racial/ethnic differences in the risk for suicidal behaviors (May & Dizmang, 1974; McIntosh & Santos, 1982, 1985–6; NCHS, 1992; Wyche & Rotheram-Borus, 1990).

In this chapter, we focus attention on the suicidal behavior of urban-dwelling adolescent females of Puerto Rican and Dominican descent. Although underrepresented in the empirical literature, this group of suicidal adolescents is frequently seen in the emergency rooms of North American, East Coast, urban hospitals (Razin et al., 1991; Zayas, 1987, 1989).

Before proceeding further, we must note a dilemma in the choice of terms used in this chapter. The term "Hispanic" is problematic because it is overly inclusive; it may apply to Spanish-speaking individuals from Spain, the Caribbean, Central and South America, independent of cultural and "racial" background. The term "Latino" is also problematic because it is masculine. We have chosen to resolve this dilemma by using the word "Hispanic" when referring to the population as a whole, and "Latina" or "Latino" when referring to females or males. Although this is an imperfect choice, we do not see any better alternative.

Our perspective on the problem of suicidal behavior among teen Latinas is drawn from clinical and research experience with inner-city Latinas from socioeconomically disadvantaged backgrounds. Based on this experience, we believe that several themes converge to set the stage for the suicidal behavior. One theme originates in sociocultural and familial processes. Our perspective holds that a complex constellation of issues, such as acculturation, "traditional" child socialization, hierarchical family structures, and immigration influence the suicidal behavior. Another theme emerges from the mother–daughter relationship. We maintain that the connection between the Latina mother and daughter is strained by the daughter's developmental and acculturative strivings, as well as the mother's ambivalence about them. A third theme springs from central issues in adolescent female development, including "self-in-relation" issues (Miller, 1991; Surrey, 1991) and the dilemma of justice versus care (Gilligan, 1982, 1989; Gilligan, Lyons, & Hanmer, 1989).

In this chapter, we integrate these three themes in a model of suicidal behavior based on the observation of inner-city adolescent Latinas. We also present an approach to clinical interventions with the adolescents and their mothers that can be used in concert with individual and family therapy.

Before continuing further in our discussion, there are several points that we need to clarify. First, we recognize that risk factors and precipitants of suicidality among teenage Latinas do not necessarily differ from those observed among youth of other racial/ethnic groups. The families of suicidal adolescent Latinas frequently have problems common to families of other suicidal youths, such as fragmentation, parental discord, and marital turmoil (Pfeffer, 1989).

A second point is that Hispanics in the United States are not a homogeneous ethnocultural or racial group, but rather an amalgam of diverse cultures and nationalities. No one Hispanic subgroup can be considered representative of the population as a whole.

Finally, although our discussion will focus on the mother–daughter relationship, this should not be construed to mean that we intend to blame Latina mothers for the suicidality manifested by their daughters. Rather we suggest that a cultural struggle is played out in the mother–daughter relationship.

SOCIOCULTURAL FACTORS

Based on our clinical experience, two sociocultural factors, acculturation and child socialization patterns, appear to be most significant in the etiology of suicidality of adolescent Latinas. Although these two factors by no means comprise the only ones which impinge on young Latinas—others, such as patriarchal family structure and immigration are important as well—acculturation and child socialization patterns appear to be very salient and deserve in-depth consideration.

Acculturation

One explanation for suicidal behavior in adolescent Hispanics is acculturation differences between adolescents and their parents (Zayas, 1987). Acculturation refers to the process by which immigrants arriving in a new culture gradually adopt the values, behaviors, attitudes, and beliefs of the host culture, while gradually modifying or discarding those of their culture of origin (Olmedo, 1979; Padilla, 1980). Children exposed to the new culture through school, peers, and the media, tend to readily adapt to and adopt the host culture's values, orientations, behaviors, and language.

First-generation parents, on the other hand, often maintain the values and behavioral repertoire of their original culture. Intergenerational tensions and conflicts arise from these differences, leading in some cases to adolescent behavioral dysfunction (Szapocznik, Daruna, Scopetta, & Aranalde, 1977).

Child Socialization

The degree to which immigrant parents hold on to traditional beliefs and methods of child socialization affects Latina youth. Specifically, parents' adherence to traditional female gender-role socialization and their pejorative attitudes toward their daughters' assimilation of mainstream values and behaviors—especially regarding sexuality—may set the stage for suicidal behavior in adolescent Latinas.

Traditional female socialization in Puerto Rican and Dominican cultures, particularly among rural and working-class groups, emphasizes deferential, demure behavior. Sexuality, assertiveness, and autonomy are discouraged. Such proscriptions may be tolerable when experienced within a homogeneous cultural system in which alternatives are few and where accepted social activities may reinforce them. However, in contemporary urban North American communities, restrictive proscriptions about female behavior fuel conflicts between adolescents and their parents. This conflict may manifest itself in suicidal behavior. To explore the etiology of suicidality in adolescent Latinas experiencing this sociocultural struggle, we now turn to a consideration of the mother–daughter relationship.

DYNAMICS OF THE MOTHER–DAUGHTER RELATIONSHIP

The Mother

We focus on the mother–daughter relationship for two reasons. First of all, father–daughter pairs are rarely observed in clinical situations because fathers do not usually participate in their daughers' mental health care. This is not to suggest that fathers are not influential in the development of suicidality in adolescent Latinas, but that their influence has been less directly apparent to us. Second, the mother–daughter relationship is a strong influence in female socialization (Brown & Gilligan, 1992); ways of behaving and thinking of oneself are frequently transmitted along the lines of this relationship. Again, we wish to make it clear that we do not mean to blame the mother in this process, but more to acknowledge that it is often the mother who is the most accessible and influential parent.

It should also be noted that some adolescent Latinas appear to be able to bridge the parent–child conflict in ways that do not lead to serious personal turmoil or family disruption. These tend to be adolescents whose problem solving skills are well-developed and whose families are relatively more able to adapt to cultural change in flexible ways. In particular, the negotiation of conflict seems more successful when parent and child are able to maintain open lines of communication. However, in families where the mother herself has not resolved her own conflicts about female socialization, she may not be able to help her daughter find adaptive solutions to developmental and cultural dilemmas.

Our clinical experience supports the notion of fragmentation and conflict in families of Latinas who engage in nonfatal suicidal behavior (Zimmerman, 1991). Frequently faced with a strong hierarchical, patriarchal family structure, mothers and daughters must elaborate their relationship within a system that is punitive and restrictive for *both* of them. For the adolescent female, there is often disappointment that her mother is not more powerful in freeing her daughter or herself from this oppressive structure.

Most Latina mothers have been socialized within patriarchal cultural systems. Although they may have accepted traditional gender roles, these mothers may not have found adequate resolutions for themselves of conflicts between self-affirmation and acquiescence. They may have "learned to live with it," but may feel ambivalent as they witness their daughters' engagement with a new cultural model that allows, indeed encourages, a freedom of expression that they did not enjoy in their own adolescence. It is this ambivalence—wanting their daughters to advance, yet fearing that the daugthers will become culturally distant from their families—that evokes resentment. As their daughters grow, these mothers come face-to-face with their own missed opportunities. What they see their daughters experiencing is what they often wished for themselves—an opportunity for self-expression. This circumstance often creates a flurry of reactions: a sense of commitment to the culture they know so intimately; envy at their daughters' opportunities; resentment at both their culture and their daughters; and hope that their daughters will genuinely succeed where they were unable to.

Further, some Latina mothers face the fact that they may be poorly equipped to help their daughters move into adulthood and acorss cultural systems. How can they—who did not or could not traverse a similar cultural and developmental transition—offer themselves as an example or as an experienced mentor? Acknowledging that their daughters' situations mark the obsolescence of their own feminine identity and define the limits of their capacity to be of support, Latina mothers are placed in a highly conflicting position, one that may find ultimate expression through a daughter's suicidal act.

Female Adolescent Development

In order to delineate more fully the experience of adolescent Latinas, we draw on female adolescent developmental theory. To set our framework, we offer a brief review of the tenets on which we rely for our theory.

Recent writings (Gilligan, 1982, 1989; Gilligan et al., 1989; Gilligan, Brown & Rogers, 1990; Jordan, Kaplan, Miller, Stiver, & Surrey, 1991; Miller, 1976) have focused on relational development. For example, Miller (1976, 1991) and Surrey (1991) have argued that connectedness, or the "self-in-relation," is a crucial experience in girls' development. "Self-in-relation" refers to the idea that "the primary experience of self is relational, that is, the self is organized and developed in the context of important relationships" (Surrey, 1991, p. 52). Surrey maintains that basic elements of the "core self" in women include interest in, and attention to, others, a sharing of experience, and growth of empowerment and self-knowledge through mutual sensitivity and responsibility.

One task of adolescent girls, then, may be renegotiating the relationship with their mothers through mutual sensitivity and empathy, rather than breaking free. Within this theory, the struggles of adolescence are motivated by a desire to maintain and reshape channels of communication and empathy with the mother, such that reciprocity and mutual connection are supported and deepened (Kaplan, Klein, & Gleason, 1991; Miller, 1976; Surrey, 1991). Included in this struggle is the daughter's need to make her mother see her for who she is, not for who the mother has thought she was or has wanted her to be. There exists, then, a powerful propulsion toward greater authenticity in the relationship, toward increased intimacy and sharing, along with the need to clarify differences. Further, mother–daughter conflict in adolescence is seen as "one mode of intense and abiding engagement" and "essential for the changes that must be made so that the relationship and each person in it can change and grow" (Kaplan et al., 1991, p. 125). Clearly, this stands in stark contrast to the thinking of Erikson (1950, 1968), who maintained that the issue of intimacy becomes ascendant in females only after they have left their parents' home, and of Blos (1962, 1979) who believed that the storms of adolescence were motivated by a need to break away from the family.

One assumption of the above models is that girls are empathically connected to the feelings, attitudes, and beliefs of their mothers; another assumption is that they will search within their mothers' experience for guidelines for the development of their own "self-in-relation." Consequently, when a mother's point of view clashes directly with that of her daughter, creating both a rupture of connection and perhaps a dislocation of empathy, dire circumstances may ensue. We suggest that just such disruptions, combined with discrepancies in acculturational experience, are central conditions for suicidality in adolescent Latinas.

The Experience of the Latina

According to Gilligan and her colleagues (Brown & Gilligan, 1992; Gilligan, 1982, 1989; Gilligan et al., 1989), preadolescent girls in the United States are usually in "contact" with their "voice"—with their unique expression of their self and perspective. However, at some time between the ages of 11 and 15 (if not earlier), this sense of connection dissipates, such that girls in mid-adolescence appear less sure of themselves. It is suggested that girls' "voices" submerge, go "underground," in the face of contact and conflict with the male-dominated society in which they develop. In essence, girls struggle with a sense of who they are in relation to who they are "supposed to be" as nascent women.

We suggest that this struggle has particular overtones in the experience of many adolescent Latinas, and that these unique features are played out in the relationship with their mothers. Adolescent Latinas are confronted with issues at adolescence that are more complex than those of girls in families that have existed within one cultural context for a longer period of time.

Typically, the adolescent Latinas we have seen in treatment complain of restrictions by their mothers, of feeling that their mothers are of the "old culture," maintaining attitudes about adolescent girls that are inappropriate to the North American culture in which the girls feel more at home. These mothers are also seen by their daughters as insisting on interpersonal connectedness, responsibility, and nurturance. This constellation of culturally traditional behaviors, while comparable to the "care" voice described by Gilligan (1982), emphasizes a dysfunctional aspect of care; that is, a focus on the needs of others regardless of the cost to the self.

Latina mothers' desires for their daughters may, however, be more complex than they first appear to be. Although mothers seem to support a view of women that includes selfless (even self-destructive) care for others, passivity, obedience, and sexual chastity, they also support (albeit perhaps covertly) another pathway for their daughters. The adolescent Latinas are thus encouraged, although often in subtly ambivalent ways, to fulfill their potential; in short, they are encouraged to live the dream their mothers did not dare believe could come true for themselves.

The mothers' contradictory messages form the nexus of an "insolvable problem" (Orbach, 1986, 1988) for their daughters. Perhaps because of the adolescent Latina's attunement to her mother through empathy and identification, she internalizes the ambivalence her mother experiences about the direction taken in her own life. Mother and daughter each grapple with the dilemma of being compliant versus fulfilling one's own unique potential. The ambivalence is fed by the pressures and constraints both mother and daughter experience as members of a patriarchal community and culture.

A struggle, based on this ambivalence, ensues. The clash between separation and connectedness (Stern, 1989) is now externalized. For the girls, to feel connected to their mothers means a loss of connectedness to their unique "voice," their sense of self; to separate is to maintain contact with their uniqueness but risk losing connectedness with their family and cultural contexts.

These circumstances can lead to "desperate actions, desperate efforts at connection" (Gilligan, 1989, p. 9). In fact, we maintain that suicidal acts in adolescent Latinas may be understood as desperate efforts at connection to their mothers and at integrating disparate models of self-development.

The Latina mothers we have seen at our clinic are often unable to maintain an empathic connection with their daughters in this struggle. They often come to regard their daughters as "bad" because they have taken on North American values. The adolescent Latinas then experience what Kaplan (1991) refers to as a "sustained state of profound disconnection from a parent who is affectively not available . . . , or who responds to . . . impulses and attempts at contact with disdain, ridicule, or outright hostility" (p. 212). Further, "such experiences . . . can generate . . . a pervasive sense of . . . utter inability to sustain relationship or please the other, which is tantamount to a major disconfirmation of her core sense of self-worth" (p. 212).

Immediately preceding a suicidal act there is a shift in the girls' ability to withstand the pain of the struggle between maintaining contact with their voices and maintaining connection with their mothers. The suicidal act can be understood as a "desperate effort" to resolve this dilemma, to reduce the tension between the potential for loss of nurturance from the mother and the potential loss of nurturance of the self. In the suicidal state, Latinas punish their own voices. They perceive that their mothers only support traditional perspectives and are unable to see or feel their mothers' own ambivalence. Confused and alone, they try to reconnect with their mothers by joining them in an act of self-punishment. The attempt on their own lives is an attempt at reconnection, at re-establishing a sense of "self-in-relation," at resolution of the "insolvable problem" at all costs.

Seen from this perspective, the central need expressed in a suicidal act by an adolescent Latina is to integrate self-expression with connectedness, and to re-establish a mutuality of empathy. The girl desires to elicit her mother's help and support in facing the demands of both the host and the traditional cultures, and of development into adulthood. In a way, the suicidal behavior is a plea for companionship.

Unfortunately, what often follows a suicidal act is an intensified but hostile mother–daughter relationship. In clinical sessions, the adolescent appears to feel a connectedness with her mother through her mother's anger. She may say that her mother is overly intrusive, "breathing down her neck." The mother may feel increasingly controlled by her daughter, and may resent what she perceives as manipulation. She feels she must "walk on eggshells" and give her daughter more autonomy. This "autonomy," however, is given at great cost to any sense of reciprocity and empathy. Both mother and daughter continue to feel misunderstood, disconnected, controlled, and angry. Ironically, both feel connected in a disconnected way—through anger, intrusion, and perceived exploitation—experiencing this circumstance as unfair. This, then, is often the state of the relationship when psychotherapy is sought.

TREATMENT APPROACHES

Engaging suicidal adolescent Latinas and their mothers in psychotherapy requires careful attention to the sociocultural, developmental, and relational variables. One essential feature of such treatment is to arrive at an understanding of historical events in the family's life cycle, its culture of origin and the degree of adherence to that culture, motives for immigration, and mother's and daughter's perceptions about both traditional and North

American values. Another aim of such treatment is to assist both mother and daughter in regaining a sense of empathic connection and mutual concern. This can be attained through delineating the dilemma faced by the adolescent and framing it in terms of her development into female adulthood.

When we treat suicidal Latinas and their families, we do not accept certain cultural characteristics as "static, inherent attributes of a people" (de la Cancela & Martinez, 1983, p. 256); we also do not accept as "cultural" behaviors that are clearly self-damaging (Espin, 1985; Padilla & Salgado de Snyder, 1985). We agree with these writers, and with Sue and Zane (1987), that it is not enough to know the culture to create effective treatments; the unique characteristics of each case must be regarded as salient in psychotherapy.

Based on the sociocultural experience of adolescent Latinas, and informed by our perspective on female adolescent development, we employ three techniques in the treatment of suicidal adolescent Latinas. The techniques are: (1) delineating the dilemma; (2) promoting authorship of, and listening to, narrative (Tappan & Brown, 1989); and (3) reorienting to "good care" and "good justice" (Gilligan et al., 1990).

Delineating the Dilemma

Early in treatment, it is often useful to assist both mother and daughter in defining the dilemma in their own terms. The intent of this intervention is to reframe the suicidal act in terms of its ontological and acculturational components, removing blame and guilt. Elsewhere, Zimmerman (1991) has described how a Latina can articulate under these circumstances "the pain of trying to establish and maintain her sense of self in the face of an intense need to feel her mother's presence and potential for nurturance," and to help her mother understand that "her more 'American' ways of behaving were not intended to be hurtful or rejecting, but were necessary for her ability to evolve in her own uniqueness" (p. 237). Delineating the dilemma can help both the adolescent Latina and her mother understand the girl's need for a connected separateness so that the adolescent's "voice" may survive without damaging her mother or incurring retributive anger and rejection.

Delineating the dilemma can also attenuate the intensity of the " 'dance' of exploitation, intrusion, and mistrust" (Zimmerman, 1991, p. 237) that is so common following a suicidal act by an adolescent Latina. Assisting the adolescent in articulating her experience gives her mother the opportunity to understand that she (the daughter) is not behaving out of disrespect or intending to cause upset. It also allows the adolescent to make clear to her mother that she needs to be trusted to manage her own life, while conveying simultaneously how important it is that mother and daughter share open communication with one another.

Authoring the Narrative

A second restorative, integrating therapeutic technique is to have both the adolescent Latina and her mother describe, in narrative form (Tappan & Brown, 1989), their experience of the suicidal behavior and events surrounding it. Some clinicians may feel that this may activate disturbing memories better left alone; however, our experience has been otherwise. We have observed that having mother and daughter "translate knowing into telling" (Tappan & Brown, 1989, p. 185) can provide an opportunity for empathic entry into each other's experience of the events, often leading to a profound sense of reconnection between them. Narrating can strengthen the mother's understanding that her daughter was not acting from manipulative motives, and can rebuild her sense of trust that the daughter will not repeat such an action. Through her own narrative, the mother is inevitably brought back in touch with the pain of seeing her daughter in dire circumstances. For the daughter, this experience can help reconnect with her mother's care and concern.

Throughout this process the therapist must be focused on assisting both parties in articulating not only the sequence of events as they experienced them, but also the moments when feelings of empathy and reconnection occurred. In helping both mother and daughter to author the narrative, the therapist often serves as an off-stage reader or prompter. The narrative can be heard by both parties as it is articulated by a third person. Mother and daughter can then reabsorb the narrative in a new way.

Reorienting to "Good" Care and "Good" Justice

In the process of delineating the dilemma and authoring the narrative of the suicidal act, adolescent Latinas and their mothers can discover a more positive mutuality of concern. Intrusion and exploitation—manifestations of "bad care" (Brown, 1988; Gilligan, 1989; Gilligan et al., 1990)—can be replaced by understanding and empathy; inequality and unfairness—manifestations of "bad justice"—can be reoriented toward respect.

CONCLUSION

In this chapter, we have described processes of development and acculturation in the lives of many inner-city adolescent suicidal Latinas. Particular attention has been given to the mother–daughter relationship. Finally, we have presented three techniques which we have found to be effective in psychotherapy with suicidal adolescent Latinas and their mothers. These interventions have been specifically designed to foster the ability of adolescent Latinas and their mothers to renegotiate their relationship.

REFERENCES

Blos, P. (1962). *On adolescence: A psychoanalytic interpretation.* New York: The Free Press.

Blos, P. (1979). *The adolescent passage.* New York: International Universities Press.

Brown, L. M. (Ed.). (1988). *A guide to reading narratives of conflict and choice for self and moral voice* (Monograph No. 1). Cambridge, MA: The Center for the Study of Gender, Education, and Human Development, Harvard University.

Brown, L. M., & Gilligan, C. (1992). *Women's psychology and girls' development.* Troy, NY: Emma Willard School.

Chabrol, H., & Moron, P. (1988). Depressive disorders in 100 adolescents who attempted suicide. *American Journal of Psychiatry, 145,* 379.

de la Cancela, V., & Martinez, I. Z. (1983). An analysis of culturalism in Latino mental health: Folk medicine as a case in point. *Hispanic Journal of the Behavioral Sciences, 5,* 251–274.

Erikson, E. H. (1950). *Childhood and society.* New York: Norton.

Erikson, E. H. (1968). *Identity, youth, and crisis.* New York: Norton.

Espin, O. M. (1985). Psychotherapy with Hispanic women. In P. Pedersen (Ed.), *Handbook of cross-cultural counseling and therapy* (pp. 165–171). Westport, CT: Greenwood Press.

Gilligan, C. (1982). *In a difference voice: Psychological theory and women's development.* Cambridge, MA: Harvard University Press.

Gilligan, C. (1989). Teaching Shakespeare's sister. In C. Gilligan, C., N. Lyons, & T. Hanmer (Eds.), *Making connections: The relational worlds of adolescent girls at Emma Willard School* (pp. 6–29). Troy, NY: Emma Willard School.

Gilligan, C., Lyons, N., & Hanmer, T. (Eds.). (1989). *Making connections: The relational worlds of adolescent girls at Emma Willard School.* Troy, NY: Emma Willard School.

Gilligan, C., Brown, L. M., & Rogers, A. G. (1990). Psyche embedded: A place for body, relationships, and culture in personality theory. In A. Rabin, R. Zucker, R. Emmons, & S. Franks (Eds.) *Studying persons and lives* (pp. 86–147). New York: Springer.

Husain, S. A. (1990). Current perspectives on the role of psycho-social factors in adolescent suicide. *Psychiatric Annals, 20*(3), 122–127.

Jordan, J. V., Kaplan, A. G., Miller, J. B., Stiver, I. P., & Surrey, J. L. (1991). *Women's growth in connection: Writings from the Stone Center.* New York: Guilford.

Kaplan, A. G. (1991). The "self-in-relation": Implications for depression in women. In J. V. Jordan, A. G. Kaplan, J. B. Miller, I. P. Stiver, & J. L. Surrey, *Women's growth in connection: Writings from the Stone Center* (pp. 206–222). New York: Guilford.

Kaplan, A. G., Klein, R., & Gleason, N. (1991). Women's self-development in late adolescence. In J. V. Jordan, A. G. Kaplan, J. B. Miller, I. P. Stiver, & J. L. Surrey, *Women's growth in connection: Writings from the Stone Center* (pp. 122–142). New York: Guilford.

May, P. A., & Dizmang, L. H. (1974). Suicide and the American Indian. *Psychiatric Annals, 4*, 22–28.

McIntosh, J. L., & Santos, J. F. (1982). Changing patterns in methods of suicide by race and sex. *Suicide and Life-Threatening Behavior, 12*, 221–233.

Miller, J. B. (1976). *Toward a new psychology of women.* Boston: Beacon Press.

Miller, J. B. (1991). The development of women's sense of self. In J. V. Jordan, A. G. Kaplan, J. B. Miller, I. P. Stiver, & J. L. Surrey, *Women's growth in connection: Writings from the Stone Center* (pp. 11–26). New York: Guilford.

National Center for Health Statistics (1992). Advance report of final mortality statistics, 1989. *National Center for Health Statistics Monthly Vital Statistics Report, 40* (8, suppl. 2).

Olmedo, E. L. (1979). Acculturation: A psychometric perspective. *American Psychologist, 34*, 1061–1070.

Orbach, I. (1986). The "insolvable problem" as a determinant in the dynamics of suicidal behavior in children. *American Journal of Psychotherapy, 40*, 511–520.

Orbach, I. (1988). *Children who don't want to live.* San Francisco, CA: Jossey-Bass.

Padilla, A. M. (Ed.). (1980). *Acculturation: Theory, models, and some new findings.* Boulder, CO: Westview Press.

Padilla, A. M., & Salgado de Snyder, N. (1985). Counseling Hispanics: Strategies for effective intervention. In P. Pedersen (Ed.), *Handbook of cross-cultural counseling and therapy* (pp. 157–164). Westport, CT: Greenwood Press.

Pfeffer, C. R. (Ed.). (1989). *Suicide among youth: Perspectives on risk and prevention.* Washington, DC: American Psychiatric Press.

Razin, A. M., O'Dowd, M. A., Nathan, A., Rodriguez, I., Goldfield, A., Martin, C., Goulet, L., Scheftel, S., Mezan, P., & Mosca, J. (1991). Suicidal behavior among inner-city Hispanic adolescent females. *General Hospital Psychiatry, 13*, 45–58.

Slaby, A. E., & MacGuire, P. L. (1989). Residential management of suicidal adolescents. *Residential Treatment for Children and Youth, 7*(1), 23–43.

Spirito, A., Brown, L., Overholser, J., & Fritz, G. (1989). Attempted suicide in adolescence: A review and critique of the literature. *Clinical Psychology Review, 9*, 335–363.

Stern, L. (1989). Conceptions of separation and connection in female adolescents. In C. Gilligan, N. Lyons, & T. Hanmer (Eds.), *Making connections: The relational worlds of adolescent girls at Emma Willard School* (pp. 73–87). Troy, NY: Emma Willard School.

Sue, S., & Zane, N. (1987). The role of culture and cultural technique in psychotherapy: A critique and reformulation. *American Psychologist, 42*, 37–45.

Surrey, J. L. (1991). The "self-in-relation": A theory of women's development. In J. V.

Jordan, A. G. Kaplan, J. B. Miller, I. P. Stiver, & J. L. Surrey, *Women's growth in connection: Writings from the Stone Center* (pp. 51–66). New York: Guilford.

Szapocznik, J., Daruna, P., Scopetta, M. A., & Aranalde, M. A. (1977). The characteristics of Cuban immigrant inhalant abusers. *American Journal of Drug and Alcohol Abuse, 4*, 377–389.

Tappan, M., & Brown, L. M. (1989). Stories told and lessons learned: Toward a narrative approach to moral development and moral education. *Harvard Educational Review*, 59, 182–205.

Wyche, K. F., & Rotheram-Borus, M. J. (1990). Suicidal behavior among minority youth in the United States. In A. R. Stiffman & L. E. Davis (Eds.), *Ethnic issues in adolescent mental health* (pp. 323–338). Newbury Park, CA: Sage.

Zayas, L. H. (1987). Toward an understanding of suicide risks in young Hispanic females. *Journal of Adolescent Research*, *2*(1), 1–11.

Zayas, L. H. (1989). A retrospective on the "suicidal fit" in mainland Puerto Ricans: Research issues. *Hispanic Journal of the Behavioral Sciences*, *11*(1), 46–57.

Zimmerman, J. K. (1991). Crossing the desert alone: An etiological model of female adolescent suicidality. In C. Gilligan, A. G. Rogers, & D. L. Tolman (Eds.), *Women, girls, and psychotherapy: Reframing resistance* (pp. 223–240). New York: Haworth Press.

■ 10
Suicidal Behavior in African-American Women

Maude H. Alston and
Sharon Eylar Anderson

According to official records, rates of suicide mortality for African-American women are the lowest of all race-by-gender groups in the United States. In 1988, the rate for African-American women was 2.4 per 100,000. In contrast, the rate for European-American women was 6.8. For European-American and African-American men, the suicide rates were 21.7 and 11.5, respectively (U.S. Department of Health and Human Services, 1988).

Because mortality from suicide is rare in African-American women, suicidologists have tended to ignore this group, resulting in limited conceptual and empirical work on self-destructive behavior in African-American women. Another reason for the failure to focus on suicidal behavior in African-American women may be the fairly common assumption that nonfatal and fatal suicidal behaviors are similar in terms of motives, precipitants, and sociodemographic characteristics. Since the rate of fatal suicidal behavior is so low for African-American women, it may also be assumed that nonfatal suicidal behavior is also infrequent among African-American women. Canetto (1992), Cantor (1976) and Wilson (1981), however, remind us that there are a number of characteristics differentiating fatal and nonfatal suicidal behaviors. These differentiating characteristics include age, gender, marital status, race, and precipitants. Fatal suicidal behavior occurs most frequently in older White males who are socially isolated (Canetto, 1992).

In contrast, nonfatal suicidal behavior is most common among young females from lower socioeconomic backgrounds and with a history of "interpersonal problems such as marital conflict, divorce, or separation" (Wilson, 1981, p. 134). With regard to etiology, it has been suggested that nonfatal suicidal behavior is a response to powerlessness (Wilson, 1981), loss of significant social supports (Hickman, 1984), and hopelessness (Beck, Steer, Kovacs, & Garrison, 1985; Topol & Reznikoff, 1982). In fact, hopelessness seems to be a better predictor of suicidal behavior than depression (Beck et al., 1985).

In the next sections, the evidence and methodological limitations of data on fatal and nonfatal suicidal behaviors among African American women will be reviewed. Based on indirect evidence, we suspect that African-American women may be at higher risk for nonfatal suicidal behavior than traditionally assumed.

SUICIDAL BEHAVIORS IN AFRICAN-AMERICAN WOMEN

Nonfatal Suicidal Behavior

The terms "attempted" and "completed" suicide have recently come under question. Some suicidologists (e.g., Canetto, 1992) have argued that the term "attempted" suicide inaccurately implies that all suicidal persons have a definite commitment to kill themselves. Canetto (1992) suggests instead that the term "nonfatal" be used to describe suicidal acts that did not result in death. Yet, according to Garrison, Lewinsohn, Marsteller, Langhinrichsen, and Lann (1991), a classification of "suicidal" is often assumed to imply a definite intent to die. Intent may, however, be difficult to establish since motives may be unconscious, although actions may be clearly self-injurious. For purposes of this chapter, the term "nonfatal" suicidal behavior is used broadly to reflect "any willful, self-inflicted, life-threatening action that does not lead to death" (Simonds, McMahon, & Armstrong, 1991, p. 135). This definition includes overt nonfatal suicidal behavior, that is, actions that can be documented as deliberate attempts at self-injury or death, as well as covert, indirect nonfatal actions that could have led to injury or death.

Fatal Suicidal Behavior

Although the focus of this chapter is on nonfatal suicidal behavior among African-American women, a word needs to be first said about fatal suicidal behavior. The question concerned the possibility of systematic underreporting of fatal suicidal behavior in African-American women.

It is widely acknowledged that published fatal suicide rates account for approximately half of the actual suicides (e.g., Jobes, Berman, & Josselsen, 1986; Monk, 1987; U.S. Department of Health and Human Services, 1985). It is also widely known that there are geographical variations in certification of suicide (Monk, 1987). What may be less known is that there may be systematic underreporting of mortality by suicide for some American ethnic minorities. For example, Warshauer and Monk (1978) found that fatal suicide rates for African-Americans were underestimated by 80%; for European-Americans the underestimation of suicide mortality rates was 42%. According to Peck (1983) "a systematic racial and social class bias continues to exist as part of the recording process" (p. 23).

Gibbs (1988) has also questioned validity of national suicide statistics for African-Americans. She found that ambiguous death classifications were particularly common for African-American men.

It is possible that many deaths by homicide in African-American women may, in fact, represent an indirect type of suicide. According to the Subcommittee on Human Services of the Select Committee on Aging (1984), such action occurs "when an individual plays an indirect, covert, partial, or unconscious role in his [*sic*] own demise (p. 48)." Wolfgang (1968) was the first to call this behavior "victim-precipitated homicide," that is, nondefensively provoking a confrontation with someone as a means of hastening one's death. As evidence for the notion of victim-precipitated suicide, the homicide rate for African-American women is more than four times that for European-American women, exceeded only by the homicide rate for African-American men (McClain, 1982; Subcommittee on Human Services of the Select Committee on Aging, 1984; U.S. Department of Health and Human Services, 1988). Research on African-American women homicide victims has been neglected, with research instead focusing on African-American men (McClain, 1982).

Overt, Nonfatal Suicidal Behavior

It is difficult to document the epidemiology of overt nonfatal suicidal behavior because of incomplete data sources. According to Whitehead, Johnson, and Ferrence (1973), the incidence of overt nonfatal suicidal behavior is seriously under-reported. Sources of data for nonfatal suicidal behavior are often hospital emergency rooms (Hickman, 1984) or police records (Kessler & McRae, 1983). These data sources may miss persons engaging in overt nonfatal suicidal acts that do not require medical or legal intervention.

The limitations of the information on overt nonfatal suicidal behavior also apply to the information on suicidal behaviors in African-American women. One has to rely on local studies that included African-American women and extrapolate from these about possible national trends. On the basis of available information, we know that the gender ratio of nonfatal suicidal behavior among African-Americans is similar to the gender ratio in other ethnic groups. In this country, nonfatal suicidal behavior is at least three times more frequent among women than among men (Maris, 1981). A study of nonfatal suicidal acts seen at a large hospital's emergency department found that the ratio of women to men among African-Americans was 4:1 compared to 3:1 for European Americans (Hickman, 1984).

Just as it is difficult to establish the true incidence of nonfatal suicidal behavior among African-American women, it is also difficult to identify the motives for these acts. In studies by Hendin (1969) and Hickman (1984), the prime precipitant of nonfatal suicidal behavior in African-American women was described as desperation over being abandoned by a lover. A study of suicidal African-American women conducted by Howze (1977), however, noted that many of these women had severe and repeated experiences of neglect and abuse, beginning in childhood.

According to Hendin (1978) and Howze (1977), African-American suicidal women are in a perpetual state of simmering, intense, explosive anger. Hendin (1978) suggested that one of the means by which these women deal with rage and anger is to turn these impulses inward in the form of suicidal behavior.

Clearly the dynamics of overt nonfatal suicidal behavior posited by Howze (1977) and Hendin (1978) are simplistic and victim-blaming. It is also obvious that theories of nonfatal suicidal behavior in African-American women need to move beyond the stereotype of the dependent, rejected woman (Canetto, 1992, 1992–1993).

Covert, Nonfatal Suicidal Behavior

According to the Subcommittee on Human Services of the Select Committee on Aging (1984), covert nonfatal suicidal behavior involves actions that have a high probability of resulting in one's injury or even death, such as alcohol and drug abuse, avoidable accidents, falls from heights, and risky sexual behavior. Gibbs (1988) speculated that the disproportionate increase of HIV infection in African-American women may be a covert, perhaps even unconscious form of suicidal activity. It has been speculated that many suicidal behaviors may take a covert form because of the religious disapproval of suicidal activity (Gibbs, 1988). For instance, it is well-documented that the African-American community imposes severe sanctions on overt suicidal behavior based on religious interpretations (Gibbs, 1988). An example of such sanctions would be to exclude a suicidal individual from church membership.

In summary, the true prevalence of overt nonfatal suicidal behavior in African-American women is unknown. There is a distinct possibility that the rate of covert suicidal behavior may be higher within this population than estimated.

OCCUPATIONAL CORRELATES

Questions have always abounded as to why one person engages in self-destructive behavior while another does not, although both experience comparable life stressors. Although we recognize that the complexity of forces contributing to nonfatal suicidal behavior defies simple answers, we would like to draw attention to two factors that we believe may be important predictors of nonfatal suicidal behavior in African-American women: occupational and social-system factors.

Troll (1975) argued that occupation impacts on every aspect of one's life. An occupation can provide both material (e.g., money) and emotional (e.g., support from others) rewards. There is little doubt that African-American women share the burden common to all women—sexism in the labor market (e.g., Amott & Matthaei, 1991; Gwartney-Gibbs & Taylor, 1986; Hesse-Biber, 1986; Wallace, 1980). Hesse-Biber (1986) stated, "both black and white women, for instance, share a disadvantaged position in the labor market in terms of earning, occupational status, and job mobility" (p. 26). African-American women, however, have to deal with racism as well (Amott & Matthaei, 1991).

Although African-American women have made progress in the occupational arena (Amott & Matthei, 1991), the picture is not a rosy one. For instance, while African-American women were better represented in professional and managerial occupations in 1980 than in previous years, many African-American women (32%) remain concentrated in low status, low-paying jobs (Amott & Matthaei, 1991; Gwartney-Gibbs & Taylor, 1986; Hesse-Biber, 1986; Wallace, 1980). Furthermore, African-American women are eight times more likely than women in other racial/ethnic groups to live in poverty resulting from underemployment or unemployment (Amott & Matthei, 1991; Horton & Smith, 1990; Wallace, 1980).

In addition to underemployment, African-American women are more likely than those in other race-by-gender groups to be unemployed or to be "discouraged" workers, that is, workers who sought employment for a long time without success (Rexroat, 1978; Wallace, 1980). It has been shown consistently that unemployment erodes self-concept and motivation (e.g., Dunston, 1990; Rexroat, 1978).

It is conceivable that African-American women's occupational and economic disadvantage (Gwartney-Gibbs & Taylor, 1986; Hesse-Biber, 1986; Rexroat, 1978) may contribute to their suicidal behavior. It has been extensively documented that a lack of control over one's destiny, combined with poverty, leads to extreme hopelessness (Dill & Feld, 1982; Dunston, 1990).

PRIMARY SUPPORT SYSTEMS

Another factor that may contribute to African-American womens' suicidal behavior is an inadequate social support system. Primary support systems include family, friends, and religious institutions.

It is commonly accepted that primary support systems provide some protection against suicidal behavior (Wilson, 1981). Social support from family and friends (Dunston, 1990) has historically been a mechanism for coping among African-American women (Gary, Brown, Milburn, Thomas, & Lockley, 1984). According to Barnes (1986) and Gibbs (1985), five primary social institutions have traditionally contributed protective functions against suicidal behavior among African-Americans. These social institutions include families, friendships, churches, and schools. Gibbs (1985) stated that protection against suicidal behavior is mediated through these institutions by "social cohesion, shared values, and mutual support" (p. 82). In contemporary African-American life these primary support systems may provide only limited instrumental and emotional support because of migration, urbanization, and social and economic changes. Hence, for many African-American women, these support networks may not exist or may be inadequate.

According to Dunston (1990), African-American women require a great deal of support from their primary support networks because of racial *and* gender discrimination. Some of these primary social systems may, however, serve as stressors rather than reducing stress for African-American women. There is also some question as to whether the African-American church continues to function in its historical roles of social support, affirmation, and nurturance (Alston, 1991; Gibbs, 1988). Alston (1991), citing others, suggested that the African-American church has not fully addressed suicidal behavior, choosing instead to deny the importance of this problem or to project a sense of guilt onto the suicidal person. Thus, it should not be assumed that social support systems for African-American women are always in place and that the quality of these support systems is optimal.

SECONDARY SUPPORT SYSTEM

A secondary support system is a bureaucratic structure, such as the welfare system, providing services to the individual. Some features of the secondary support system, however, may contribute to a sense of hopelessness and despair, and perhaps even to suicidal behavior.

For many African-American women, the welfare system may be the only secondary support system available (Marshall, 1982). As such, the welfare system may turn into a dehumanizing institution. Although African-American women are not inordinately represented on welfare rolls (Marshall, 1982), they may be treated as if they were "lazy, cheating, promiscuous, dependent free-loaders, and daughters of mothers of equally poor character" (Marshall, 1982, p. 96). Marshall argued that persons who are stigmatized tend to accept the stigma. Self-derogation results, adding to the sense of powerlessness and hopelessness.

Health care services provided by the social welfare system may also create a sense of powerlessness and hopelessness for African-American women. In our experience, we have seen African-American women with bored and hungry children in tow wait for hours in depressing waiting rooms to receive services from insensitive, condescending providers. Treatment as a second-class citizen, especially when the individual is powerless to affect change in this treatment, may contribute to depersonalization, depression, and anger.

Bureaucratic structures may unwittingly perpetuate powerlessness. For example, a recent issue of *Time* magazine (Sancton, 1992) chronicled the trials of a young African-American woman who was trying to escape the vicious cycle of intergenerational welfare. This young woman worked diligently to save money for college. When state officials learned that she had a modest sum in her savings account, they invoked the federal law that prohibits families on welfare from having more than $1,000 in assets. The state then demanded that the woman spend the money that had been saved. In addition, her mother was ordered to refund over $9,000 that had been received from Aid to Families of Dependent Children (AFDC) during the period in which the aspiring college student maintained her savings. This case is an example of how an ineffective secondary social support system may generate a sense of futility.

A CASE STUDY OF A SUICIDAL AFRICAN-AMERICAN WOMAN

Ms. J., a 42-year-old African-American woman, was raised by her mother in a major metropolitan city. She never knew her father but was emotionally attached to her mother's boyfriend. Although Ms. J.'s mother was employed, the sporadic nature of her job, along with its inadequate salary, necessitated supplemental assistance from AFDC.

Ms. J. recalls being taught from an early age to fear the "welfare lady," since the latter had the power to stop the family's assistance if a number of rules were violated. She was also taught to avoid the police, any white male, and anyone asking questions about the family. She characterized her childhood as "normal" and relatively happy despite her fear of those whom she felt exerted control over her family. She attended local public schools and, in high school, dated a man who drank heavily and who introduced her to alcohol.

Ms. J. made the first of several overt nonfatal suicidal acts by overdosing on alcohol when her mother was preparing to move the family to another state. In response to Ms. J.'s overt suicidal behavior, her mother allowed her to remain with friends in the neighborhood. Ms. J. became pregnant in her junior year of high school and dropped out of school. When the pregnancy resulted in a stillbirth, the father of her child ended the relationship and she cut her wrists.

When she was 18, Ms. J. moved in with an older man and began using street drugs. Her third overt nonfatal suicide act occurred 3 years into the relationship when she was told by medical personnel that she would be unable to have children because of various gynecological problems. She used a combination of street drugs and alcohol, was found in a comatose state by her partner, and was hospitalized. After recovering physically from this third overt suicidal act, Ms. J. was admitted to a psychiatric facility for treatment of drug abuse and "depression." Upon being released from the psychiatric hospital, she returned to the same relationship, friends, and environment.

Ms. J. continued to use street drugs and alcohol for several years after the third overt suicidal act, but reduced her substance abuse to what she considered a "reasonable" level. She believed that since she continued to hold a job she was in control of her addiction.

By age 40, Ms. J. had become involved with a man who was a substance-abuser. He was also physically abusive. After 2 years of physical and psychological abuse by her mate, Ms. J. made her fourth overt nonfatal suicidal act, using street drugs and alcohol. She voluntarily admitted herself to a psychiatric hospital for treatment of her chronic substance dependence and suicidal behaviors.

Because there is probably no "typical" suicidal behavior in African-American women, this case study simply describes how one African-American woman may have perceived that death was her only option, or the only method at her disposal to convey her needs to others. First, Ms. J. was limited educationally and occupationally, thereby limiting her options for escaping from socioeconomic disadvantage. She may also have learned self-destructive coping mechanisms in her early relationships. Substance abuse may have been a self-destructive attempt at coping.

It also seemed that Ms. J. was unable to develop other support systems outside of her family and male partner relationships. She had been socialized into believing that the more others knew about her situation, the more this information could be used to her detriment, as with the "welfare lady." In sum, losses, limited coping skills, and inadequate support systems may have been contributing factors in her chronic suicidal behaviors.

ASSESSMENT AND INTERVENTION

Assessment

Assessment of the suicidal African-American woman should take into account her self-awareness as a woman and as an African-American, and her perception of the relationship between the current suicidal crisis and her ethnicity and gender. For example, it is well-documented that African-American women tend to view the feminist movement with some wariness (e.g., Higginbotham, 1992; Smith & Stewart, 1983). Higginbotham (1992) felt that this is because African-American women see race as more important than gender in determining their disadvantaged status in society. Although both gender and racial discrimination erode self-concept (e.g., Gwartney-Gibbs & Taylor, 1986), the effects of gender discrimination may be experienced and perceived differently by African-American women than European-American women.

Intervention

Just as assessment of suicidal precipitants among African-American women should be individualized, so should intervention. A primary focus of intervention may be to debunk the myth that the African-American woman is forever adaptive and strong. The African-American woman who is suicidal should be helped to accept her responses to the stressors that provoked a suicidal crisis. It is only then that she may feel safe enough to accept assistance in exploring adaptive coping strategies.

At the same time, it is important to remind African-American women of their historical resilience and adaptation to a system that has devalued, victimized, and disenfranchised them. African-American women have survived and continue to survive against incredible odds.

We need to acknowledge that there may be a subgroup of African-American women who lack, or who perceive themselves as lacking, the human and material resources for coping with stressors. These women may feel they ought to fit the standard profile of the "strong African-American woman," but also feel that they cannot for various reasons.

Dick Gregory, the comedian, once quipped in a tongue-in-cheek manner that African-Americans do not kill themselves because it is not possible to kill oneself by jumping out of a basement window. Part of Mr. Gregory's nonchalance may be reflected in the minimal attention given to suicidal behavior in African-American women. Hopefully, this attitude will change.

REFERENCES

Alston, M. (1991). *The African-American church in suicide prevention.* Paper presented at the meeting of the American Association of Suicidology, Boston, MA.

Amott, T. L., & Matthaei, J. A. (1991). *Race, gender, and work.* Boston: South End Press.

Barnes, A. S. (1986). *Black women: Interpersonal relations in profile.* Bristol, IN: Wyndham Hall Press.

Beck, A. T., Steer, R. A., Kovacs, M., & Garrison, B. (1985). Hopelessness and eventual suicide: A 10-year prospective study of patients hospitalized with suicidal ideation. *American Journal of Psychiatry, 142*, 559–563.

Canetto, S. S. (1992). Gender and suicide in the elderly. *Suicide and Life-Threatening Behavior, 22*, 80–97.

Canetto, S. S. (1992–1993). She died for love and he for glory: Gender myths of suicidal behavior. *Omega, 26*, 1–17.

Cantor, P. (1976). Frequency of suicidal thought and self-destructive behavior among females. *Suicide and Life-Threatening Behavior, 6*, 92–100.

Dill, D., & Feld, E. (1982). The challenge of coping. In D. Belle (Ed.), *Lives in stress* (pp. 179–210). Beverly Hills, CA: Sage.

Dunston, P. J. (1990). Stress, coping, and social support: Their effects on Black women. In D. S. Ruiz (Ed.), *Handbook of mental health and mental disorders among Black Americans* (pp. 133–147). New York: Greenwood Press.

Garrison, C. Z., Lewisohn, P. M., Marsteller, F., Langhinrichsen, J., & Lann, I. (1991). The assessment of suicidal behavior in adolescents. *Suicide and Life-Threatening Behavior, 21*, 217–230.

Gary, L. E., Brown, D. R., Milburn, N. G., Thomas, V. G., & Lockley, D. S. (1984). *Pathways: A study of Black informal support networks*. Washington, DC: Howard University.

Gibbs, J. T. (1985). City girls: Psychological adjustment of urban black adolescent females. *Sage, 2*, 28–36.

Gibbs, J. T. (1988). Conceptual, methodological, and sociocultural issues in Black youth suicide: Implications for assessment and intervention. *Suicide and Life-Threatening Behavior, 18*, 73–89.

Gwartney-Gibbs, P. A., & Taylor, P. A. (1986). Black women workers' earnings progress in three industrial sectors. *Sage, 3*, 20–25.

Hendin, H. (1969). *Black suicide*. New York: Basic Books.

Hendin, H. (1978). Suicide: The psychosocial dimension. *Suicide and Life-Threatening Behavior, 8*, 99–117.

Hesse-Biber, S. (1986). The black woman worker: A minority group perspective on women at work. *Sage, 3*, 26–33.

Hickman, L. C. (1984). Descriptive differences between Black and White suicide attempters. *Issues in Mental Health Nursing, 6*, 293–310.

Higginbotham, E. B., (1992). African-American women's history and the metalanguage of race. *Signs, 17*, 251–274.

Howze, B. (1977). Suicide: Special references to black women. *Journal of Non-White Concerns, 5*, 65–72.

Jobes, D. A., Berman, A. L., & Josselsen, A. R. (1986). The impact of psychological autopsies on medical examiners' determination of manner of death. *Journal of Forensic Sciences, 31*, 177–189.

Kessler, R. C. & McRae, J. A. (1983). Trends in the relationship between sex and attempted suicide. *Journal of Health and Social Behavior, 24*, 98–100.

Maris, R. W. (1981). *Pathways to suicide: A survey of self-destructive behavior*. Baltimore, MD: Johns Hopkins University Press.

Marshall, N. (1982). The public welfare system: Regulation and dehumanization. In D. Belle (Ed.), *Lives in stress* (pp. 96–108). Beverly Hill, CA: Sage.

McClain, P. D. (1982). Cause of death: Homicide: *Victimology*, *7*, 204–212.

Monk, M. (1987). Epidemiology of suicide. *Epidemiological Reviews*, *9*, 51–73.

Peck, D. L. (1983). "Official documentation" of the Black suicide experience. *Omega*, *14*, 21–31.

Rexroat, C. (1978). The changing cost of being a Black woman. *Sociology of Work and Occupation*, *5*, 341–359.

Sancton, T. (1992, May 25). How to get America off the dole. *Time*, pp. 44–47.

Simonds, J. F., McMahon, T., & Armstrong, D. (1991). Young suicide attempters compared with a control group: Psychological, affective, and attitudinal variables. *Suicide and Life-Threatening Behavior*, *21*, 134–151.

Smith, A., & Stewart, A. J. (1983). Approaches to studying racism and sexism in Black womens' lives. *Journal of Social Issues*, *39*, 1–15.

Subcommittee on Human Services of the Select Committee on Aging, House of Representatives (1984). *Suicide and suicide prevention* (Comm. Pub. No. 98–497. Washington, DC: U.S. Government Printing Office.

Topol, P., & Reznikoff, M. (1982). Perceived peer and family relationships, hopelessness, and locus of control as factors in adolescent suicide. *Suicide and Life-Threatening Behavior*, *12*, 143–150.

Troll, L. C. (1975). *Early and middle adulthood*. Monterey, CA: Brooks/Cole.

U.S. Department of Health and Human Services (1985). *Mental Health, United States 1985*. Rockville, MD: National Institute of Mental Health.

U.S. Department of Health and Human Services (1988). *Monthly Vital Statistics Report*. Atlanta, GA: Centers for Disease Control.

Wallace, P. A. (1980). *Black women in the labor force*. Cambridge, MA: M.I.T. Press.

Warshauer, M. E, & Monk, M. (1978). Problems in suicide statistics for whites and blacks. *American Journal of Public Health*, *126*, 309–312.

Whitehead, P. C., Johnson, F. G., & Ferrence, R. (1973). Measuring the incidence of self-injury: Some methodological and design considerations. *American Journal of Orthopsychiatry*, *43*, 142–148.

Wilson, M. (1981). Suicidal behavior: Toward an explanation of differences in female and male rates. *Suicide and Life-Threatening Behavior*, *11*, 131–140.

Wolfgang, M. F. (1968). Suicide by means of victim precipitated homicide. In H. L. P. Resnik (Ed.), *Suicidal behaviors: Diagnosis and management* (pp. 87–103). Boston, MA: Little, Brown.

11
Suicidal Behavior in Asian-American Women

Farah A. Ibrahim

This chapter focuses on suicidal behavior among Asian-American women and explores the following: (a) the epidemiology of suicidal behavior among Asian-American women, (b) women's status in Asian-American cultures, (c) cultural factors in Asian-American women's suicidal behavior, (d) the impact of migration on Asian-American women's suicidal behavior, and (e) recommendations for therapy.

EPIDEMIOLOGY OF SUICIDAL BEHAVIOR AMONG ASIAN-AMERICAN WOMEN

Asian-American women are at high risk for suicidal behavior (Takaki, 1989). Asian-American immigrant women experience higher levels of depression, alienation, and anomie and are at higher risk for suicidal behavior than Asian-American immigrant men (Merrill & Owens, 1986, 1988).

The most vulnerable ages for Asian-American women are 15 to 30 (Handy, Chitiramohan, Ballard, & Silviera, 1991; Raleigh, Bulusu, & Balarajan, 1990). Being married also increases the risk for suicidal behavior (Raleigh et al., 1990). Vulnerability to suicidal and life-threatening behavior increases with social isolation, alienation, cultural incompatibility, religious differences, lack of a supportive community, and pressure of the family to conform to old cultural traditions (Ibrahim, 1992; Mohan, 1989; Takaki, 1989).

Because Asian-American women often adhere strongly to Asian traditions, it is important to explore the status of women in Asian cultures. McGoldrick (1982) points out that ethnic and cultural roots can define immigrants lives even four or five generations after migration.

Epidemiological reports from Japan, India, and Singapore indicate that female suicide mortality is nearly as high as that of men for these countries (Chadda, Shome, & Bhatia, 1991; Iga, Yamamoto, & Noguchi, 1975; Kok, 1988). Suicide mortality is higher in the groups that subscribe to Confucian, Buddhist, or Hindu faiths than in Christian or Moslem groups. Confucianism, Buddhism, and Hinduism have no strong prohibitions against suicide, whereas Christianity and Islam prohibit suicide. The rate of death by suicide is higher among Asian women than among women of African, European or Middle Eastern origin (Handy et al., 1991; Haynes, 1984; Raleigh et al., 1990).

Asian refugee women who emigrate to the United States are at high risk for stress-related disorders due to war trauma and abuse (Rozee, 1989). Research reveals a higher incidence of depressions and suicidal behavior among Asian and Central American immigrants to the United States, when compared to immigrants from other continents (Portes & Rumbaut, 1990). High rates of psychopathology among Asian immigrant women may be influenced by a number of factors, including acculturation stress, emigration circumstances (voluntary or involuntary), and resettling experiences. Research also reveals a higher incidence of suicidal behavior among Asian populations who have immigrated to Fiji, South Africa, and England (Glover, Marks, & Nowers, 1989; Handy et al., 1991; Haynes, 1984; Merrill & Owens, 1986, 1988; Raleigh et al., 1990; Wood & Wassenaar, 1989).

McIntosh and Santos (1982) noted changes in suicide methods in the United States. They reported that the use of firearms was increasing, and the use of poisons decreasing in all ethnic groups, including Asian-American women. According to McIntosh and Santos, Chinese and Japanese women prefer hanging. Asian-Indian women, on the other hand, are more likely to burn themselves to death (Raleigh et al., 1990). Chadda, Shome, and Bhatia (1991) suggest that fatal suicide by burning parallels the custom of "suttee" (burning oneself on one's husband's funeral pyre).

The use of violent methods of ending one's life (such as self-burning, hanging, and shooting) may be a manifestation of frustration and anger. Asian-American women live in a patriarchal system that frustrates their attempts to have any power over their lives. Suicide may be viewed as a way to gain some power (Bumiller, 1990). More specifically, self-burning may be a culturally meaningful way to regain "lost" honor. For example, among the Hindu, burning oneself can announce the end of a failed, "dead" marriage and the hope for a new life through reincarnation. Bumiller (1990), however, argues that, considering the powerless status of women in Asian-Indian societies, self-burnings should be considered murders. Her conclusion is that repressive and abusive conditions may leave many women no "option" but to take their lives.

WOMEN'S STATUS IN ASIAN-AMERICAN CULTURES

It is important to recognize the diversity that exists in Asian-American cultures. Asians come to the United States from countries as different as Pakistan in the West and Japan in the East, Mongolia in the North and the Pacific Rim in the South. Still, there are some characteristics common to all Asian-Americans that differentiate them from European-Americans. Most Asian-Americans are influenced by Confucianism (Ho, 1987; Ryan, 1985). Confucianism emphasizes specific roles based on gender, age, and social status (Keyes, 1977). According to this philosophy, "the quest for spiritual fulfillment is to achieve harmony in this world and in this life through observing five basic relationships of society: those between a ruler and his [*sic*] subjects, father and son, husband and wife, elder and younger siblings, and friends" (Keyes, 1977, p. 175).

Ho (1987) notes that these five relationships demand loyalty and respect. Obligation to the family is reinforced by shaming. If family members behave improperly, they not only "lose face" but also cause the family and community to "lose face." Families may abandon rule-breaking family members to "save face." For example, if an unmarried woman becomes pregnant, she may be abandoned by her family. Her public shame may absolve her family. Because interdependence is very important to Asians, the threat of losing familial or community support can be a strong deterrent to breaking community rules.

A woman in Confucianism is "instructed to obey her father as a daughter, her husband as a wife, and her eldest son as a widow" (Takaki, 1989, p. 36). Female children are seen as a burden for their families; male children are valued because they are expected to provide economically for the family (Takaki, 1989).

A good wife is expected to be tolerant and patient and to accept her fate, good or bad, in her husband's home. In the Confucian tradition, a wife is given three pathways to follow (daughter, wife, and mother), all of which involve subjugation to a man (Ho, 1987). It is believed that a woman should work to fit into her husband's family, whatever the circumstances.

A woman is blamed for the failure of a marriage, for it is assumed that the failure is due to her inability to adapt to her spouse's family. A man can divorce his wife for infertility, filial impiety (e.g., "inappropriate" behavior toward the family or lack of "respect"), jealousy of his relationship with other women and/or his family, and even "talkativeness" ("too much" talking by a woman is seen as inappropriate) (Ho, 1987). Ho maintains that a divorce for a woman, or a threat of divorce, leads to loss of support from both her family of origin and her spouse's family.

Asian-American women learn to turn family discord inward leading to depression and, possibly, vulnerability to life-threatening behavior. In this sense Asian-American women are not different from North American women. Canetto (1991, 1992) and Gilligan (1982) have noted that women internalize social roles and gender-specific values. Among Japanese-American women, life-threatening behavior may be manifest as death pacts between a mother and her children when the mother cannot overcome the familial and societal oppression (Leong & Silva, 1989; Takaki, 1989).

The other major influence on Asian-American values is Buddhism (Ryan, 1985). Buddhism focuses on qualities considered essential for harmonious living, such as compassion, respect for life, moderation in behavior, self-discipline, patience, modesty, and selflessness (Ho, 1987). The Buddhist system of thinking reflects influences from Judeo-Christian-Islamic traditions, due to invasions and colonialization, but these influences are only a few centuries old. Women, in Buddhist cultures, are expected to be patient, selfless, empathic, and concerned about others.

Asian-American women have a distinctively different history and culture from mainstream and other ethnic minority women (Takaki, 1989). Their migration and acculturation to the United States reveals a unique pattern of discrimination (Amott & Matthaei, 1991). It is important to remember that, from the 1850s to the early 1900s, a much larger proportion of Asian men than Asian women was allowed to come to the United States under the exclusionary immigration laws. Many Asian women were brought over as prostitutes (Takaki, 1989). Thus, the way in which Asian-American women came to the United States reduced them to the status of sexual objects and even sexual deviants, whereas, in fact, they were victims of a racist exclusionary society, and victims of exploitation by their own ethnic group.

Asians are noted in the United States for their work ethic and stoicism (Takaki, 1989). At the same time, Asians may be rejected and discriminated against because of their tenacious bonds with their cultures of origin, faiths, and racial and religious distinctiveness (Mohan, 1989; Takaki, 1989). As noted earlier, Asian cultures emphasize the unquestioned authority of men over women. Men are supposed to be the leaders of the family and society. Women are to be virtuous, patient, and tolerant (Noda, 1989; Tajima, 1989). They must maintain the family honor by remaining virgins until they marry, remain faithful to their spouse in spite of his infidelities (that are to be expected); they are to be patient and responsive to the family's and spouse's needs, even when they are abandoned or abused (Rimonte, 1989).

Ironically, women are expected to transmit to the next generation a culture that is often uniquely oppressive to them. Although Asian-American women are expected to be virtuous, patient, and tolerant, men have license to be "Western" (Brainard, 1989). As a result of migration to the United States, Asian women drop to fourth-class status. Migration takes them from second-class status in their country (where men are first-class citizens) to the lowest rung of this society, where Caucasian men come first, then Caucasian women, then ethnic minority males and, last, ethnic minority females.

CULTURAL FACTORS IN ASIAN-AMERICAN WOMEN'S SUICIDAL BEHAVIOR

Durkheim (1951) originally described three basic types of suicide: altruistic, egoistic, and anomic. Tseng and Hsu (1980) differentiated between suicide, which fulfills sociocultural functions, such as suttee, and "personal-psychiatric" suicide, which occurs for individual-emotional reasons. An example of a sociocultural suicide would be suttee. Death by suttee is viewed as a culturally appropriate behavior from a loyal and honorable wife, following the death of her husband. Using Durkheim's system, this kind of suicidal behavior would be classified as altruistic. Suicide for personal-psychiatric problems would be classified under egoistic or anomic categories. It is unclear whether Asian women kill themselves for personal-psychiatric reasons, or because of family and community pressures, in which case their death may be more accurately described as murder (Bumiller, 1990).

One cultural factor for Asian-American women's suicidal behavior is the conflict between the cultural belief that the family should provide support and intimacy, and the reality of their status within the family (Ryan, 1985). It is assumed that Asian women derive stability and interpersonal intimacy from their family (Hsu, 1972). In reality, Asian-American women are often oppressed within the family, beside being racially segregated and discriminated against by the larger society (Mazumdar, 1989). A main precipitant of suicide for women, especially young mothers, may be isolation (Glover et al., 1989).

A second major factor in Asian-American women's suicidal behavior may be shame or "loss of face." Asian-American women have an external locus of control and an internal locus of responsibility (Sue & Sue, 1990). When an Asian-American woman fails, she will tend to take full responsibility for the failure. For example, although Asian-American women are aware that racism exists in the United States, it is still difficult for them not to take responsibility for it. Additionally, the mythology of the "model minority" may reinforce the sense of personal responsibility.

A third factor in Asian-American women's suicidal behavior may be that suicidal behaviors receive a certain degree of social approval. The fact that suicidal behavior is culturally approved is evident in the Japanese custom of "Hara Kiri." Death by suicide is also an accepted option in the Indian subcontinent. It is stated that, before you bring shame on your family, you "should drown yourself in a handful of water" (chulu bhar pani may doop jao). Additionally, the patriarchal Indian subcontinent culture reveres "suttee," a custom in which the wife burns herself on her husband's funeral pyre. Suttee was practiced until about a century and a half ago, and is still being practiced in some parts of India (Chadda, Shome, & Bhatia, 1991). This ritual signifies that a woman lacks the right to an existence once the man in her life dies.

To summarize, Asian-American women may be at greater risk for suicidal behavior due to racism, sexism, lower social status, and cultural barriers (Ibrahim, 1992; Lalinec-Michaud, 1988; Merrill & Owens, 1988; Portes & Rumbaut, 1990; Ryan, 1985). Asian-American women may find themselves in a double-bind (Ibrahim, 1992). On the one hand, they are forced to preserve their Asian ethnic identity in a culturally different world; on the other hand, these same values they are expected to defend are a source of oppression and discrimination. When we consider ethnicity, race and gender identity from a psychological point of view, we find Asian-American women caught between two worlds, neither of which supports them or encourages them to be their own person (Ibrahim, 1992; Noda, 1989).

IMPACT OF MIGRATION ON ASIAN-AMERICAN WOMEN'S SUICIDAL BEHAVIOR

Migration is a major source of stress for Asian-American women. Refugees appear to have the greatest amount of stress due to "the context of their exit" and the "context of their reception" (Portes & Rumbaut, 1990, p. 156). Luu (1989) maintains that the highest stress is experienced by Asian refugee women. For example, she states that Vietnamese refugee women face unique challenges, including economic adjustment, changes in power in the marital situation due to husband's joblessness, violence toward women, and language and cultural differences (Luu, 1989).

Portes and Rumbaut (1990) consider refugees to be at greater risk because of their involuntary decision to emigrate, often due to coercive political conditions. They consider the context of exit as critical to understanding depression among Southeast Asians (Vietnamese, Cambodians, and Hmong). They report, however, that the effect of the traumatic experience declines over time, and that the focus shifts to survival in the new country.

A study of Canadian immigrants (Portes & Rumbaut, 1990) found that

Vietnamese refugees exhibited the highest level of stress. Higher stress was also found for females, the elderly, those unable to speak English, the uneducated and the unemployed. Portes and Rumbaut reported greater stress among immigrant professionals who were unable to pursue their careers, who had to work in their occupations in an "underground" capacity, or who were significantly underemployed. According to other authors (Steinberg, 1989; Takaki, 1989), Asian-American professionals, especially women, also exhibit particularly high levels of stress after immigration.

Migration to the United States was severely restricted prior to 1965. When Asian migration resumed, the new wave of immigrants came better educated and sought better jobs and opportunities for themselves (Steinberg, 1989). They were unable to procure jobs at the highly skilled level they deserved due to racism and sexism; so they took lower status jobs to survive (Takaki, 1989). Rumbaut (1985, 1989) noted that there was a considerable difference in depression rates among the various groups he studied, with the highest rate for Cambodians and Hmong, and the lowest for Chinese and first-wave Vietnamese arrivals.

IMPLICATIONS AND RECOMMENDATIONS FOR THERAPY

Asian-Americans do not readily utilize mental health services (Ho, 1987; Kim, 1985; McGoldrick, 1982; Sue & Sue, 1990), mostly due to cultural factors. Takaki (1989) notes that the notion of "self-help" is a Christian concept, and stems from the belief that God helps those who help themselves. Asian-Americans are influenced by a belief in fatalism, an acceptance of difficulties in life as part of a person's fate (Kim, 1985). In Asia, psychological pain is often experienced as a somatic problem. It may be very difficult for an Asian-American woman to (a) identify the problem as psychological, when the symptoms are somatic, and (b) reach out and ask for help, especially in a crisis, given prevalent Asian fatalistic attitudes. It is also possible that, when faced with a crisis, people may cling to the values of their country of origin. It may even be more difficult to break from cultural tradition and seek help from outside agencies in times of crisis.

Asian-American women may also be deterred from seeking help for suicidal behavior because they want to avoid hospitalization and even involving their family in therapy. First, hospitalization may be viewed as shameful. Second, the family may actually support suicidal behavior as a culturally appropriate method of dealing with the crisis (Bumiller, 1990).

McGoldrick (1982) noted that culture of origin is often alive and well in immigrant families for four or five generations, or even longer. In circumstances in which it is difficult to accurately assess women's acculturation level, it is imperative that the client's suicidal ideation be considered within the Asian cultural context. The assumption cannot be made that, because she is removed from the migrating generation, she is acculturated. Further, McGoldrick (1982) and Portes and Rumbaut (1990) both emphasize the context of exit and the context of reception for each ethnic group in the United States. If the reception was traumatic, as is the case with many Asian groups (Takaki, 1989), the trauma experienced is covertly or overtly passed from generation to generation, and affects the client's trust level (McGoldrick, 1982).

In working with refugee and immigrant women, it is important to recognize their stage of social adaptation, and to design the intervention accordingly. Further, reports exist documenting paranoid thinking among refugees and immigrants. It is important to recognize that refugees, immigrants and illegal aliens experience real threats to security and that therefore their "paranoia" is at least somewhat justified (Jack, Nicasso, & West, 1984). The therapist can help a client establish a sense of comfort by discussing issues related to their immigration status, and accept their anxieties as a normal reaction to the process of immigration.

It is also critical to understand culturally approved communication patterns among Asian-American women. Traditional Asian logic and communication are circular and indirect (e.g., respecting everyone's status and sensibilities, recognizing that there is no one truth but many realities). American logic and communication are linear, even blunt (Hall & Hall, 1987; Lebra, 1976; Nakamura, 1960; Takaki, 1989). The lower the status of the woman in her system (for example, youngest daughter or youngest daughter-in-law), the more circular and indirect her communication will be. She will appear to be "beating around the bush," focusing on minor details. There is an expectation that the listener can make decisions regarding the importance of the communication (Takaki, 1989). Such a communication style requires that a therapist be highly skilled in cross-cultural communication, and tuned in to verbal and nonverbal communication.

In order to accurately determine the needs of severely depressed and suicidal Asian-American women, the therapist must be aware of not just cultural characteristics and expectations, but also verbal and nonverbal behaviors. Further, it is important to understand that the reticence exhibited by Asian-American women is culturally approved as the culture demands that they examine all issues before discussing them. Further, from early childhood people learn to guess what others think, rather than ask direct questions. Silence, therefore, must be interpreted in the context of the client's culture (Takaki, 1989).

Depressive symptomatology varies across cultures (Kleinman & Kleinman, 1985; Lalinec-Michaud, 1988; Tseng & Hsu, 1985). For example, among the Chinese, depression may lead to hypochondriacal complaints and somatization. Because the Chinese language has a paucity of terms to describe emotional pain, and because socioculturally it is more acceptable to discuss physical than psychological pain, depression is often somatized (Lalinec-Michaud, 1988). In this context, it is up to the therapist to decide the level of anguish the woman is experiencing, without making her uncomfortable, and to realistically address treatment issues without causing her shame over the psychological pain. If the woman feels that sharing her crisis is a sign of weakness, she may feel shame and may be reluctant to pursue treatment.

If a woman appears to be suicidal, or has considered suicide, I explore the risk of shame and loss of face to the client and her family. Takaki (1989) states that two variables pose a threat to the family: (a) introverted aggression directed at family members (due to the prohibition against revealing hostile feelings) and (b) family suicide pacts (Fusé, 1985). Leong and Silva (1989) describe the case of a Japanese woman living in the United States who tried to drown herself and her two children in the Pacific Ocean, after discovering her husband's infidelity and intention to divorce her. She survived the attempt, though her two children did not. She was charged with double murder. To save the woman from penalty of murder, four thousand members of the Japanese-American community signed a petition stating that this act of *Oyako Shinju* would not be considered murder in Japan.

Asian-American women come from a "shame" (external sanctions for good behavior) culture. Thus, Asian-American women may be more concerned about others' reactions to their behavior than about what they are experiencing (Takaki, 1989). Further, the open, direct, and honest approach of mainstream American therapists may be perceived as threatening. Takaki (1989) notes that sensitive questions about suicidal ideation should not be approached directly or "in haste," say, within the first 10 minutes of the interview. Such a direct approach may shock the clients, and may inhibit sharing their real concerns. I recommend that a much longer period be spent establishing a relationship before focusing on the lethality of the client's behavior.

TREATMENT INTERVENTIONS

Treatment strategies for Asian-American women clients need to be focused more on understanding the role of acculturation stress and adaptation processes, rather than on psychopathology. I recommend that, in the treatment of a suicidal woman, an elder, possibly a female, who has status in the family, be invited to become involved as co-therapist. This elder needs to advocate to the family that the suicidal woman is not the problem and that she should be encouraged to live (Kim, 1985). Treatment must involve the entire family, including extended kin, so as to educate them about the meaning of the familial conflict, the woman's depression, acculturation stress, the status of the woman in the family, and value differences between the United States and Asia regarding suicide. Bicultural psychoeducational treatment strategies are often useful. For example, Szapocznik, Rio, Perez-Vidal, Kurtines, and Santisteban's (1986) propose interventions for enhancing family effectiveness among ethnic minority and immigrant families. The roles of cultural conflict and the stress of acculturation need to be examined with the family. Further, methods to alleviate the stress for the whole family need to be sought. Here it is critical, especially if the therapist is from a different cultural group than the family, that the woman and the family's world-views are mapped out before an intervention is considered (Ibrahim & Schroeder, 1990). Both the client and her family need to be educated about the practical consequences (e.g., hospitalization) of suicidal behavior in the United States.

If the client remains committed to her goal of killing herself, a systematic desensitization approach (Wolpe, 1958) may be useful. Guided imagery may be used to ritualistically walk through the suicidal sequence. The ritual may help alleviate the anxiety and stress experienced by the woman, and assist her in exploring whether the suicide would truly solve the problem. Following the desensitization, the intervention should shift to increasing the client's self-control and coping behaviors (Coelho & Ahmad, 1980; Goldfried, 1971; Meichenbaum, 1972). Self-control is enhanced by increasing the woman's self-observation skills and the development of new self-statements (Meichanbaum, 1977).

Goldfried and Goldfried (1975) maintain that cognitive behavior modification techniques are useful for Asian-American clients as a form of self-control. The objectives of cognitive behavior modification are consistent with Eastern religious experiences such as yoga, transcendental meditation, and trance induction (Shapiro & Zifferbaltt, 1976).

It is also important to help increase the suicidal woman's social support (Ibrahim & Herr, 1987; Lefley, 1989) and enhance her bicultural effectiveness (Szapocznik et al. 1986). She should be helped to integrate her Asian beliefs into her North American cultural context. If a sizable Asian-American community exists, it would be important for the woman to find a support group to help her cope with the ongoing stress of negotiating two cultures and the role conflicts it generates for her. I recommend that members of the support group represent multiple acculturation levels. The new social network may provide the support she seeks, but cannot get from her family.

ACKNOWLEDGMENT

The author gratefully acknowledges the assistance and support provided by Catina Caban-Owen and Maria A. Tocyska in the preparation of the chapter, and the technical support provided by Naeem A. Khan.

REFERENCES

Amott, T. L., & Matthaei, J. A. (1991). *Race, gender, and work*. Boston: South End Press.

Brainard, C. M. (1989). Waiting for Papa's return. In Asian Women United of California (Eds.), *Making waves* (pp. 223–227). Boston: Beacon Press.

Bumiller, E. (1990). *May you be the mother of a hundred sons*. New York: Random House.

Canetto, S. S. (1991). Gender roles, suicide attempts, and substance abuse. *Journal of Psychology, 125*, 605–620.

Canetto, S. S. (1992). Gender and suicide in the elderly. *Suicide and Life Threatening Behavior*, 22, 80–97.

Chadda, R. K., Shome, S., & Bhatia, M. S. (1991). Suicide in Indian women. *British Journal of Psychiatry, 158*, 434.

Coelho, G. V., & Ahmed, P. I. (Eds.) (1980). *Uprooting and development: Dilemmas of coping with modernization*. New York: Plenum Press.

Durkheim, E. (1951). *Suicide* (J. A. Spaulding & G. Simpson, Trans.). New York: The Free Press.

Fusé, T. (1985). *Suicide and culture*. Tokyo: Shinchosa.

Gilligan, C. (1982). *In a different voice: Psychological theory and women's development*. Cambridge, MA: Harvard University Press.

Goldfried, M. R. (1971). Systematic desensitization as training in self-control. *Journal of Consulting and Clinical Psychology*, 37, 228–234.

Goldfried, M. R., & Goldfried, A. P. (1975). Cognitive change methods. In F. H. Kanfer & A. P. Goldstein (Eds.), *Helping people change* (89–116). New York: Pergamon.

Glover, G., Marks, F., & Nowers, M. (1989). Parasuicide in young Asian women. *British Journal of Psychiatry, 154*, 271–272.

Handy, S., Chithiramohan, R. N., Ballard, C. G., & Silveira, W. R. (1991). Ethnic differences in adolescent self-poisoning: A comparison of Asian and Caucasian groups. *Journal of Adolescence, 14*, 157–162.

Haynes, R. H. (1984). Suicide in Fiji: A preliminary study. *British Journal of Psychiatry, 145*, 433–438.

Ho, M. K. (1987). *Family therapy with ethnic minorities*. Newbury Park, CA: Sage.

Hsu, F. (1972). *American museum science book*. Garden City, NY: Doubleday.

Ibrahim, F. A. (1992). Asian-American women: Identity issues. *Women's Studies Quarterly, 20*, 41–58.

Ibrahim, F. A., & Herr, E. L. (1987). Battered women: A developmental life career counseling perspective. *Journal of Counseling and Development*, 65, 244–248.

Ibrahim, F. A., & Schroeder, D. G. (1990). Cross-cultural couple counseling: A developmental, psychoeducational approach. *Journal of Comparative Family Studies, 21*, 193–205.

Iga, M., Yamamoto, J., & Noguchi, T. (1975). The vulnerability of young Japanese women to suicide. *Suicide and Life Threatening Behavior*, 5, 207–227.

Jack, R. A., Nicassio, P. M., & West, W. S. (1984). Acute paranoid disorder in Southeast Asian refugees. *Journal of Nervous and Mental Disorders*, 172, 495–497.

Keyes, C. (1977). *The golden peninsula*. New York: Macmillan.

Kleinman, A., & Kleinman, J. (1985). Somatization: Interconnections in Chinese society among culture, depressive experience, and the meaning of pain. In A. Kleinman & B. Good (Eds.), *Culture and depression* (pp. 429–490). Berkeley: University of California Press.

Kim, S. C. (1985). Family therapy for Asian-Americans: A strategic-structural framework. *Psychotherapy*, 22, 342–348.

Kok, L. P. (1988). Race, religion, and female suicide attempted in Singapore. *Social Psychiatry and Psychiatric Epidemiology*, 23, 236–239.

Lalinec-Michaud, M. (1988). Three cases of suicide in Chinese-Canadian women. *Canadian Journal of Psychiatry*, 33, 153–156.

Lebra, T. S. (1976). *Japaneses patterns of behavior*. Honolulu: University of Hawaii Press.

Leong, G. B., & Silva, J. A. (1989). Asian American forensic psychiatrists. *Psychiatric Annals*, 19, 629–368.

Luu, V. (1989). The hardships of escape for Vietnamese women. In Asian Women United of California (Eds.), *Making waves* (pp. 60–74). Boston: Beacon Press.

Mazumdar, S. (1989). General introduction: A woman-centered perspective on Asian-American history. Asian Women United of California (Eds.), *Making waves* (pp. 1–24). Boston: Beacon Press.

McGoldrick, M. (1982). Ethnicity and family therapy: An overview. In M. McGoldrick, J. Pearce, & J. Giordano (Eds.), *Ethnicity and family therapy* (pp. 3–30). New York: Guilford.

McIntosh, J. L., & Santos, J. F. (1982). Changing patterns in suicide. *Suicide and Life-Threatening Behavior*, 12, 221–233.

Meichenbaum, D. (1972). Ways of modifying what clients say to themselves: A marriage of behavior therapies and rational-emotive therapy. *Rational Living*, 7, 23–27.

Meichenbaum, D. H. (1977). *Cognitive behavior modification: An integral approach*. New York: Plenum Press.

Merrill, J., & Owens, J. (1986). Ethnic differences in self-poisoning: A comparison of Asian and White groups. *British Journal of Psychiatry, 148*, 708–712.

Merrill. J., & Owens, J. (1988). Self-poisonings among four immigrant groups. *Acta Psychiatrica Scandinavica*, 77, 77–80.

Nakamura, H. (1960). *The ways of thinking of Eastern peoples*. New York: UNESCO.

Noda, K. E. (1989). Growing up Asian in America. In Asian Women United of California (Eds.), *Making waves* (pp. 243–250). Boston: Beacon Press.

Portes, A., & Rumbaut, R. G. (1990). *Immigrant America: A portrait*. Berkeley: University of California Press.

Raleigh, V. S., Bulusu, L., & Balarajan, R. (1990). Suicides among immigrants from the Indian subcontinent. *British Journal of Psychiatry, 156*, 46–50.

Rimonte, N. (1989). Domestic violence among Pacific Asians. In Asian Women United of California (Eds.), *Making waves* (pp. 327–336). Boston: Beacon Press.

Rozee, P. D. (1989). The psychological effects of war trauma on older Cambodian refugee women. *Women and Therapy, 8*, 23–50.

Rumbaut, R. G. (1985). Mental health and refugee experience. In T. C. Owan (Ed.), *Southeast Asian mental health* (pp. 433–486). Rockville, MD: National Institute of Mental Health.

Rumbaut, R. G. (1989). Portraits, patterns, and predictors of refugee adaptation process. In D. Haines (Ed.), *Refugees as immigrants: Cambodians, Laotians, and Vietnamese in the United States* (pp. 138–192). Totowa, NJ: Rowman & Littlefield.

Ryan, A. S. (1985). Cultural factors in casework with Chinese-Americans. *Social Casework, 66*, 333–340.

Shapiro, D. H., & Zifferblatt, S. M. (1976). Zen meditation and behavioral self-control: Similarities, differences, and clinical applications. *American Psychologist, 31*, 519–523.

Steinberg, S. (1989). *The ethnic myth.* Boston: Beacon Press.

Sue, D. W., & Sue, D. (1990). *Counseling the culturally different: Theory and practice* (2nd ed.). New York: Wiley.

Szapocznik, J., Rio, A., Perez-Vidal, A., Kurtines, W., and Santisteban, D. (1986). Family effectiveness training (FET) for Hispanic families. In H. P. Lefley and P. B. Pedersen (Eds.), *Cross-cultural training for mental health professionals* (pp. 245–261). Springfield, IL: Charles C. Thomas.

Tajima, R. E. (1989). Lotus blossoms don't bleed: Images of Asian women. In Asian Women United of California (Eds.), *Making waves* (pp. 308–317). Boston: Beacon Press.

Takaki, R. (1989). *Strangers from different shores.* Boston, MA: Little Brown.

Tseng, W-S., & Hsu, J. (1980). Minor psychological disturbances of everyday life. In H. Triandis & J. G. Draguns (Eds.), *Handbook of cross-cultural psychology: Psychopathology* (Vol. 6, pp. 61–98). Boston: Allyn-Bacon.

Wolpe, J. (1958). *Psychotherapy by reciprocal inhibition.* Stanford, CA: Stanford University Press.

Wood, N., & Wassenaar, D. R. (1989). Family characteristics of Indian parasuicide patients: A controlled study. *South African Journal of Psychology, 19*, 172–174.

12 Suicidal Behavior in American Indian Female Adolescents

Teresa D. LaFromboise and Beth Howard-Pitney

Adolescence may be characterized as a period of great risk to healthy development. During adolescence, the stress surrounding social, physical, cognitive, and academic growth increases. It is a time when negative emotional outcomes may arise over conflict between desires for autonomy and control, and perceptions of restricted opportunities in the environment (Eccles et al., 1993). Feelings of helplessness may intensify due to new challenges and limited experiences (Pfeffer, 1989). These feelings often result in depression, which occurs along with other symptoms and disorders, the most serious of which is suicidal behaviors. Suicide rates of adolescents in the United States almost tripled among 10- to 14-year-olds, and doubled among 15- to 19-year-olds between 1968 and 1985, to become the second leading cause of death within this age group (Children's Safety Network, 1991).

While certain characteristics of adolescence have been ascribed to adolescents in general, their effect may vary depending on cultural and ethnic background. For American Indian adolescents, this difficult developmental period is further challenged by (1) acculturation pressures, which threaten personal identity and interfere with involvement in traditional ceremonies, such as initiation and puberty rituals; (2) poverty, which limits perceptions of present and future opportunities; (3) the multigenerational effects of alcoholism, which interfere with family functioning; and the (4) frequent occurrence of accidental deaths among parents, other relatives, or friends. These additional stressors may account for the findings that American Indian adolescents are three times as likely to rate their health status as poor than European American adolescents, and to have a death rate twice that of adolescents from other ethnic backgrounds (Blum, Harmon, Harris, Bergeisen, & Resnick, 1992). One cannot rule out the possibility of a relationship between mourning over these losses and increased vulnerability toward suicidal behavior.

Suicide is the second leading cause of death for American Indian and Alaska Native adolescents. However, suicide deaths for American Indian adolescents 10 to 14 years of age are approximately four times higher than for adolescents of other ethnic groups (U.S. Congress, 1990; Wyche & Rotheram-Borus, 1990). Suicide death rates for American Indian females aged 10 to 19 peaked in 1985 with 9.0 deaths per 100,000 population. In contrast, the figure for females of other United States ethnic groups aged 10 to 19 was 2.3 deaths per 100,000 population (U.S. Congress, 1990).

This chapter empirically explores the psychological and sociocultural predictors of suicidal behavior (suicidal ideation and nonfatal suicidal behavior) among American Indian adolescent females. The Indian Adolescent Health Survey indicates that 13% of the respondents (30% who came from families with a suicide history) reported having tried to kill themselves in the past year (Blum et al., 1992), a finding which concurs with our earlier results (Howard-Pitney, LaFromboise, Basil, September, & Johnson, 1992). Rates of nonfatal suicidal behavior are very high among female American Indian adolescents (May, 1987). Nearly 20% of American Indian females and 12% of American Indian males report that they have engaged in suicidal behavior (U.S. Congress, 1990). American Indian adolescent females made up 70% of all suicide-related Indian Health Service hospitalizations in 1989 (U.S. Congress, 1990).

RISK FACTORS

What follows is a synopsis of selected literature on the complex web of psychological states (such as depression, anxiety, and anger) that, in combination with social and environmental factors, may lead to suicidal behavior.

Depression

Depression is common in adolescence, and a better understanding of adolescent depression is particularly important since it has a long-term effect on adult psychological functioning. Even though depression is the most common factor in youth suicidal behaviors (Hafen & Frandsen, 1986), it must be kept in mind that most depressed youth are not suicidal. The relationship between depression and suicidal behaviors is complex. It appears to be most directly related to suicidal ideation (Lester & Gatto, 1989; Pfeffer, Zuckerman, Plutchik, & Mizruchi, 1984). Yet "the relation between depression and suicidal ideation may be mediated both by deficits in cognitive coping strategies and hopelessness" (Berman & Jobes, 1991, p. 90).

Depression is a frequent problem among American Indian youth (Beiser & Attneave, 1982; Dauphinais, LaFromboise, & Rowe, 1980; May, 1983). Recent studies of American Indian adolescent suicidal behavior report depression to be a primary risk factor (Dinges & Duong-Tran, 1993; Manson, Beals, Wiegmen, & Duclos, 1989). Young American Indian women are much more prone to depression than young American Indian men (Ackerson, Dick, Manson, & Baron, 1990; Blum, et al., 1992; Manson, Ackerson, Dick, Baron, & Fleming, 1990; Manson, Shore, & Bloom, 1985). Women's depression is consistently higher than men's at every grade level in high school. Females endorse items pertaining to negative affect ("depressed," "sad," "crying"), somatic complaints ("bothered," "could not get going"), and interpersonal difficulties ("disliked") far more frequently than males (Manson et al., 1990).

Hopelessness

Hopelessness is one of the core characteristics of depressed and suicidal persons. Beck defines hopelessness as a desire to escape from what one considers to be an insoluble problem and having no hope that relief is possible in the future. Hopelessness involves a system of cognitive schemata that share the common element of negative expectations, thus leading to an overall sense of despair and feeling of a lack of purpose in life (Beck, Weissman, Lester, & Trexler, 1974). According to Freese (1979) some adolescents do not have adequate coping skills, which makes them feel helpless. After a series of events involving feelings of helplessness, they begin to experience hopelessness.

Beck hypothesized that specific cognitive aspects of depression were more closely associated with suicide than were affective aspects of depression. A number of studies focusing on hopelessness and its relationship with depression and suicidal behavior in adults lent credence to his theory (Petrie & Chamberlain, 1983). Over the years, additional evidence has accumulated to support hopelessness as a key cognitive variable in the assessment of suicidal adolescents (Brent et al., 1986). However, Cole (1989) recently questioned whether these assertions hold true for adolescents, given their ability to attenuate extreme despair by focusing on upcoming life events (e.g., leaving school, finding a mate) that may bring about perceived positive changes for the future. His research found that depression was more strongly related to suicidal behavior than hopelessness among adolescents. Gender differences regarding hopelessness and depression were also found. Hopelessness was only modestly related to suicidal behaviors for young women and unrelated to suicidal behaviors for young men.

Hopelessness is often experienced by young American Indian women who witness continuous cultural, spiritual, social, and economic loss. Blum et al. (1992) found differential rates of hopelessness related to gender among American Indian adolescents. Fourteen percent of the young American Indian females and 8% of the young American Indian males in this nationwide survey indicated that they felt so sad and hopeless in the last month that they wondered if anything was worthwhile. Even young American Indian women who are successful in school often suffer feelings of apathy and low self-esteem (Manson, Dinges, Grounds, & Kallgren, 1984; Young, 1991). Many young American Indian women also experience helplessness due to victimization associated with racism and sexual abuse (U.S. Congress, 1990). Further research on the cognitive factors related to suicide in young American Indian women might help determine whether there are cultural as well as developmental and gender differences in the impact of depression and hopelessness on suicidal behavior.

Alcohol and Drug Use

Most suicidal acts are carried out when young people are enraged, intoxicated, or in a state of terror (Shaffer, 1988). Adolescents who engage in alcohol and drug abuse to combat depression are more likely to lose control or act on impulse (Wodarski & Harris, 1987). At least half of adolescent suicidal acts are committed while the person is under the influence of alcohol or drugs (Porter, 1985). Substance abuse alone or in combination with an affective disorder emerges as an important factor in one-third of psychological autopsies of youthful suicide victims (Brent et al., 1988). The feelings of helplessness and powerlessness that lead youth to use drugs or alcohol may be the same feelings that lead youth to suicide. The substance itself may serve as a ready method for experimenting with self-destructive behavior (Neiger & Hopkins, 1988).

Several studies have found an association between alcohol and suicidal behavior among American Indian adults (Levy, 1965; Miller & Shoenfeld, 1971; Travis, 1983). This association appears to hold true for young American Indian women and men. For example, Conrad and Kahn (1974) found alcohol was involved in 8 of the 10 suicide deaths among young members of the Tohono O'odham (Papago) tribe. Alcohol abuse was also common among female members of suicide victims but not as common as among suicide victims. Alcohol abuse or solvent sniffing was also involved in 75% of the deaths by suicide of the Intermountain tribal cultural group (Shore, 1974). Finally, Manson et al. (1989) found a relationship between suicidal behavior and alcohol consumption quantity and frequency.

Recent reports of American Indian adolescent female substance abuse are staggering. The alcohol/substance abuse death rate of American Indian females aged 15 to 24 years exceeds that of Indian boys by 40% (Indian Health Service, 1991). "Girls are more likely than boys to use alcohol on schooldays, both during school hours and in the evenings. They also experienced blackouts more frequently while drinking" (Dick, Manson, & Beals, 1993, p. 174). Frequent use of alcohol by American Indian girls may be a factor in their prominent involvement in nonfatal suicidal behaviors.

Family Dysfunction

Physical or sexual abuse, lack of good parent child communication, instability, discord, and/or violence are typical signs of a dysfunctional family. Dysfunctional families may decrease a child's self-esteem, threaten a child physically and psychologically, and the combination may contribute to a young woman's sense of vulnerability and motivation for suicide (Dukes & Lorch, 1989).

Family is a major source of identity, self-worth, and social support among American Indians. Most young American Indian women live near a large number of relatives with whom they maintain frequent interaction in a system of reciprocal exchanges of moral, emotional, and tangible support. However, a substantial number of young American Indian women live in families where those exchanges are dysfunctional because of sexual abuse, substance abuse, or frequent loss or grief (Dizmang, Watson, May, & Bopp, 1974; Willis, Dobrec, & BigFoot, 1992). Young American Indian women are six times more likely than young American Indian men to have been physically and sexually abused (U.S. Congress, 1990). Twenty-four percent of American Indian females report physical abuse and 22% report experiences of sexual abuse by the twelfth grade (Blum et al., 1992). Many Indian communities suffer high rates of alcohol abuse causing a breakdown in family and community relationships and causing extreme hardship for children (Lujan, DeBruyn, May, & Bird, 1989). Finally, given the high rates of suicide in many tribes and the extended family systems typical of American Indian society, it would not be unusual for a young American Indian woman to have experienced directly or indirectly the loss of a family member through suicide. Families that model suicidal behavior and act in other dysfunctional ways may lead a young American Indian woman to consider suicidal behaviors as a viable option.

PROTECTIVE FACTORS

Social Support

Aside from the treatment of the psychological precursors of suicidal behavior, social support is perhaps the single most important protective factor in suicide intervention (Blumenthal & Kupfer, 1990). Even when stressful life events, depression, and loss occur together, rarely does this result in a suicidal act if the social support system (i.e., family, friends, or confidant and community or religious affiliations) is of high quality and vigorously maintained.

Most young American Indian women prefer not to be isolated from culture and community. Their family and culture are inseparable and intricately linked to an understanding of their sense of self. Group activities focusing on community support and participation are often the driving force in many Indian communities. A young American Indian woman who feels estranged from her family or community may be especially vulnerable to suicide.

Self-Efficacy

Challenging situations together with greater arousal in such situations may produce anxiety, especially during adolescence. Individuals who feel little control or confidence in their ability to manage those situations may subsequently become depressed (Petersen, 1988). Suicidal individuals often have a low sense of efficacy concerning their ability to influence stressful events and maintain a rather indifferent attitude toward life (Schotte & Clum, 1987). Petersen (1988) asserts that both situational factors (e.g., uncontrollable situations), personal response styles (e.g., negative expectations), and low perceived self-efficacy (Bandura, 1982) may play a role in the adolescent adjustment process. Petersen further suggests that young women are more likely to experience challenging situations associated with pubertal change than young men, rendering them more susceptible to anxiety and thus to depressive affect. Gender differences in negative self-appraisal are widely found by middle adolescence in the general population (Kandel & Davies, 1982; Petersen, 1988). Unfortunately, empirical information does not exist concerning the role of self-efficacy in American Indian female coping efforts.

Liking for School

During adolescence, school becomes the training ground for earning a living and developing other life skills. Extreme academic difficulties (e.g., learning disability) or social alienation at school is often associated with teen suicide in the general population (Dukes & Lorch, 1989). Eccles et al. (1993) assert that if the social environment of school does not fit the psychological needs of adolescents, then interest, motivation and performance decline. Poorer school performance, underachievement, and school disciplinary problems have been noted among suicidal adolescents (Berman & Carroll, 1984).

A recent report of the Indian Nations At Risk Task Force characterized the climate of many schools serving American Indian youth as unfriendly and unsupportive of the academic, social, cultural, and spiritual development of students. A young American Indian woman's liking for school might be further hampered by low self-esteem or fears of "re-living" the unpleasant educational experiences often recounted by parents and elders. Some American Indian educators like Travis (1983) blame the school environment as "the ultimate culprit" of suicide since most schools are staffed with non-Indian personnel who impart "skills and values of the majority culture" (p. 23) thus applying pressure for acculturation. Travis found that death by suicide was more frequent among native youth in the northwestern part of Alaska with greater educational attainment. Another study of factors associated with suicide completion found that school problems occurred along with a previous psychiatric contact, parental separation, previous suicidal attempt, suicidal ideation, and suicidal threats among Indian youth in Manitoba, Canada (Thompson, 1987).

The variables reviewed above represent some of the better explored predictors of suicidal behavior in adolescents. They represent both factors that protect against suicidal behavior (e.g., social support) and factors that increase risk for suicidal behavior (e.g., alcohol and drug use). The current research has explored the relationship of these protective and pathogenic factors in two samples of American Indian adolescent females. Data on each sample were examined separately for two primary reasons. First, the two groups of females represent distinctly different tribes. Second, the school and social environment of the two samples differ in a number of aspects; for example, one sample was drawn from a small village public school, while the other was drawn from a boarding school attended by youth from around the country.

OUR STUDY

Young American Indian women were recruited to participate in this study from two high schools, one in New Mexico and one in Oklahoma. One-hundred-and-seventy-six females (84 from Zuni Public High School and 92 from Sequoyah High School) ranging in age from 14 to 20 agreed to participate.

The Zuni Public High School is located in Zuni, New Mexico. The Zuni Pueblo has approximately 9,000 tribal members living on the reservation which encompasses 324,000 acres and is located about 150 miles west of Albuquerque, New Mexico. Poverty affects a large number of Zuni people even though 75% of tribal members are employed on a full- or part-time basis. Those who are unemployed are supported by tribal, state or federal programs, as well as support provided by extended family members. The tribe has been characterized as being traditional in terms of its contact with the mainstream North American culture and maintains much of its culture, language, and tribal beliefs and practices.

Sequoyah High School is located in Tahlequah, Oklahoma, about 50 miles east of Tulsa in the Cherokee Nation. Its student population is almost evenly divided between students from tribes all across the nation and students from tribes in the local area. Approximately 120,000 members of the Cherokee tribe live in a 14 county area in Eastern Oklahoma. The Cherokee Nation, in contrast to Zuni, has become more acculturated to mainstream America. The tribe has grown tremendously in recent years. Major economic development activities like the Cherokee Nation Industry and Cherokee Bingo Outpost have provided employment opportunities for its members, allowing many who once lived in distant urban areas to return home.

Measures

Students at both sites completed a battery of questionnaires that were administered by members of the research team over two class periods on separate days. While the surveys were somewhat different for the two schools, measures were identical for all the major predictor and dependent variables included in this report.

Suicidal behavior

To determine risk for suicidal behavior, students were asked (1) whether they had ever engaged in suicidal behavior, (2) the number of times they had engaged in suicidal behavior, (3) the recency of that behavior, (4) whether they told anyone about it, and (5) whether the suicidal act had led to a visit to a medical clinic.

Suicide probability

The Suicide Probability Scale (Cull & Gill, 1982), a 36-item self-report inventory was used to assess suicide risk. Respondents indicated on a four-point scale, from none or little of the time to most or all of the time, how frequently they experienced various subjective states related to hopelessness, suicide ideation, negative self-evaluation, and hostility.

Depression

Depression was measured by a 5-item, 7-point scale taken from the emotional health section of the Indian Adolescent Health Survey (Greer, 1988). Sample items include: "How depressed or cheerful have you been (during the past month)?" and "How much energy, pep, vitality have you felt (during the past month)?"

Hopelessness

Feelings of hopelessness were assessed by the 20-item true-false Hopelessness Scale (Beck, Weissman, Lester, & Trexler, 1974) that assesses the extent of pessimism. For example, "I look forward to the future with hope and enthusiasm."

Alcohol use

The extent and nature of alcohol use was measured by asking students to indicate how often they used beer/wine and hard liquor on a scale ranging from never to daily. This item was taken from the Indian Adolescent Health Survey (Greer, 1988).

Family dysfunction

This index was composed of three, 5-point scale items that asked about how much the student was concerned or worried about arguments and fights in the family, parental use of marijuana or other drugs, and parental use of alcohol.

Social support

Participants responded to eight, 7-point scale items designed to measure the extent to which they believed they had access to social support, for example, "There are people who care for me" and "There is someone with who I would feel perfectly comfortable talking about any problems I might have with drugs or alcohol."

Self-efficacy

Twenty-four items for Zuni and 29 items for Sequoyah assessed perceived self-efficacy on a range of skills indicating ability to cope well in life. For each item, participants rated how well they could successfully enact each skill on a 5-point scale ranging from not well to very well. These items were originally developed to assess self-efficacy for skills that were taught in a life skills and suicide prevention curriculum for American Indian adolescents (LaFromboise, in press). The following skills important for coping with stressful life situations were measured: suicide prevention skills (e.g., "How well can you get a suicidal person to agree not to commit suicide?"); communication (e.g., "How well can you help a friend describe their feelings?"); stress management (e.g., "How well can you cope with stress?"); anger regulation (e.g., "How well can you control your temper when people get angry with you?"); problem solving (e.g., "How well can you break down a big problem into smaller problems to make it easier for you to solve?"); and self-talk or the ability to turn negative thoughts into positive thoughts (e.g., "How well can you use self-talk to control anger?").

Liking for school

This was a single 5-point scale item, "How do you feel about going to school?" with a 1 = I like school very much, to 5 = I hate school.

RESULTS[1]

The median ages of the two samples were equivalent, but the Sequoyah had a much more even distribution of girls across grade level. At Zuni, all students were from the Zuni tribe; at Sequoyah over half of the students were Cherokee, 23% Creek, and the rest evenly divided between Seminole and other tribal representation. The two samples differed somewhat in measures of suicidal behavior. While an equal percentage (20%) of the two samples scored in the severely suicidal range of the suicide probability scale, more Zuni girls (67%) scored in the moderate range than Sequoyah girls (44%), and correspondingly fewer Zunis scored in the mild range. While more Sequoyah students had a history of nonfatal suicidal behaviors, Zuni girls were more than twice as likely to have acted suicidal, three or more times than Sequoyah girls. Zuni students were also more likely to have a history of suicidal behavior within the last year. For both samples, past nonfatal suicidal acts were serious enough to have caused them to visit a clinic in about 15% of the cases. In most cases, students had told someone (e.g., a friend, parent, or teacher) about the nonfatal suicide act, but in almost a fifth of the cases the students had told no one. Overall, these results indicate that a substantial proportion (64%–83%) of these adolescent females reported moderate to severe suicidal thinking, 20 to 30% have engaged in nonfatal suicidal acts, many of them repeatedly, and more than half of these girls had engaged in this behavior within the last year.

Overall, the pattern of correlation between the measures conformed to expectations; liking for school, self-efficacy, and social support were positively correlated with each other, while negatively correlated with depression, hopelessness, family dysfunction, alcohol use and the suicidal behavior measures. Likewise, the variables indicating more psychological and social distress were positively correlated with each other and with the suicidal behavior measures.

Comparisons in the correlations between predictor variables in the Zuni and Sequoyah samples were fairly similar. There were, however, a few notable differences. There were strong negative correlations between liking for school and hopelessness, and social support and hopelessness, in the Sequoyah sample; these same correlations were nonsignificant in the Zuni sample. This suggests that Sequoyah students who lacked social support from friends and family and did not enjoy their school environment were likely to feel hopeless about the future, while the same was not necessarily true for Zuni students. In the Zuni sample, social support was strongly, but negatively correlated with family dysfunction; this correlation was nonsignificant in the Sequoyah sample. This may indicate that the Zunis draw more of their social support from families than do the Sequoyah students.

We conducted separate regression analyses on two measures of suicidal behavior for each sample because we believe it is important to study tribal-specific differences in suicidal behavior to gain a clearer understanding of appropriate factors for intervention. An OLS (Ordinary Least Square) regression analysis was performed with suicide probability as the dependent variable and a maximum likelihood logistic regression analysis was performed with past nonfatal suicidal acts (ever attempted or never attempted) as the dependent variable. The independent variables in each equation were depression, hopelessness, alcohol use, family dysfunction, social support, self-efficacy, and liking for school

For the Zuni sample, alcohol use (beta = .43) and hopelessness (beta = .25) were significant predictors of suicide probability. For the Sequoyah sample, hopelessness (beta = .50) and family dysfunction (beta = .21) produced coefficients which were significantly different than zero, while alcohol use (beta = .13) approached significance. Although not significant, other coefficients were in the expected direction: positive for depression and negative for social support and liking for school.

For nonfatal suicidal acts, depression, alcohol use, and social support were predictors among Zuni women, and were statistically different than zero. For the Sequoyah sample, alcohol use was the sole predictor of nonfatal suicidal acts.

COMMENTS

Findings from this survey indicated that suicidal behaviors are significant problems for young American Indian women students at Sequoyah and Zuni high schools. A very high rate of nonfatal suicidal behavior, 31% for Sequoyah and 22% for Zuni, was found. This rate is disconcertingly higher than the 4 to 13% rate reported in recent studies of female and male high school students in the general population (Friedman, Asnis, Boeck, & Di-Fiore, 1987; Provonost, 1990; Smith & Crawford, 1986). The rate, however, is consistent with the 30% attempt rate of American Indian and Alaska Native boarding school adolescents reported by Dinges and Duong-Tran (1993) and the 23% attempt rate of American Indian students at Sequoyah reported by Manson et al. (1989). Clearly suicidal behavior is a serious issue for American Indian adolescents.

The degree of suicide severity among young Zuni women as indicated by multiple acts and a higher percentage of moderate to severe suicidal thinking (as compared to young Sequoyah women) runs counter to theories of the protective factors inherent in socially integrated communities, such as pueblos (Van Winkle & May, 1986; 1993). Zuni leaders have recently expressed concern over eroding cultural beliefs and decreasing adherence to traditional practices; such erosion may represent severe, but not openly discussed, interpersonal conflict and disturbance (H. Lewis, personal communication, September 17, 1993) which could lead young Zuni women to engage in self-destructive ideation and activities.

It is generally thought that living away from home to attend a group home or boarding school, such as Sequoyah High School, is an additional risk factor for suicidal behavior (Shore, 1972). The pattern of findings in the current research are not fully supportive of such a claim. Perhaps the added support from dormitory aides and suicide crisis management teams, available on an hourly basis in the boarding school setting, helps monitor and intervene with those most vulnerable to repeated suicidal acts.

One striking finding in the regression analyses is that alcohol use was a strong predictor across both samples. In the Zuni sample, alcohol use was the strongest predictor of suicide probability and a highly significant predictor of nonfatal suicidal behavior. In the Sequoyah sample, alcohol use was the sole predictor of nonfatal suicidal behavior and a modest predictor of suicide probability. The consistency of these findings are interesting and give a clear direction for prevention.

The early onset of alcohol use, abuse and dependence has been noted as the major mental health problem of many American Indians. Earlier, we examined the literature suggesting that alcohol use is a special problem for female adolescents; they drink more, and more frequently than boys. Their drinking may lead to poor academic performance, deteriorating social relationships with friends and family, and depression, as well as make them more susceptible to sexual abuse and rape. These experiences may in turn lead them to consider suicide as the only viable outlet.

Many studies in the general population (e.g., Brent et al., 1986) and studies of American Indian suicidal behavior (Berlin, 1985; Conrad & Kahn, 1974; Dinges & Duong-Tan, 1993; Manson et al., 1989; Shore, 1975) have established a clear and powerful relationship between alcohol use and suicide ideation and behaviors. Our data are no exception to these consistent findings and suggest that substance abuse prevention activities are of vital importance in reducing the frequency of suicidal behavior in young American Indian women. Suicide intervention programs must include a focus on alcohol use and provide the necessary personal and community supports, so that young American Indian women can choose means other than alcohol to cope with the problems endemic to their lives.

The regression analyses also reveal that hopelessness and depression are important predictors of suicidal behavior. Hopelessness was predictive of suicide probability in both tribal samples, but was not predictive of nonfatal suicidal behavior in either sample. Therefore the role of hopelessness in nonfatal adolescent suicidal behavior documented by Petrie and Chamberlain (1983) was not clearly supported by these data. One explanation for why hopelessness was more predictive of suicide probability than depression may have been the similarity between these two independent and dependent measures; both dealt with pessimistic thoughts and low expectations about the future. When looking at behavior rather than thought patterns, the data revealed that depression was predictive of nonfatal suicidal behavior, but only in the Zuni sample. This pattern of data is not easily explained and, as others have found, the relationship between hopelessness, depression, and suicidal behavior is a complex one (Cole, 1989; Lester & Gatto, 1989).

Social support and family dysfunction were found to be important predictors of suicidal behavior in two of the regression analyses. For Zuni students, lack of perceived social support predicted nonfatal suicidal behavior. One potential explanation for why the lack of social support was predictive of nonfatal suicidal behavior in the Zuni sample but not in the Sequoyah sample may hinge on specific tribal differences. The small, tradition-bound pueblo of Zuni draws part of its tribal strength from a complex network of extended families, clans, and religious orders. Being a part of this social network is integral to Zuni identity. Feeling apart from this social support system may increase one's sense of loneliness which is often a precursor to suicidal thoughts and actions. Tribal life and the social support that derives from close knit extended family and clan life may not be as central to the lives of Sequoyah students, who are often either boarding away from home or belong to more acculturated tribes.

Social support networks can not only support distressed young women, but can also help cultivate the desire for personal change and aid in the development of patterns of healthy behavior. Prevention efforts directed at American Indian female adolescents could focus on building stronger social support networks.

One might expect that family dysfunction would be a stronger factor predicting suicide probability among young women in the Zuni sample, rather than the Sequoyah sample; young Zuni women are continuously living with their "dysfunctional families," while young Sequoyah women have "escaped" these circumstances. However, the results of the regression equations predicting suicide probability suggest the contrary: Family dysfunction is a significant variable among young women in Sequoyah boarding school but not among those in Zuni day school. Apparently the young women at the Sequoyah school continue to be affected by their families since they undoubtedly learn about incidents that take place at home even though they are not present.

This information about psychological and social indicators of suicidal behavior for young Zuni and Sequoyah high school women, although limited in scope, contributes to knowledge about the risk factors for young American Indian women. Our results point to several important predictors of suicidal thinking and behavior, including alcohol use, feelings of depression and hopelessness, the lack of social support systems, and dysfunctional families. Each of these areas lends itself to the development of a culturally appropriate skill-training approach that could be presented in school- or community-based prevention programs. As we have pointed out (Howard-Pitney et al., 1992), increased skills in each of these areas would not only help decrease suicidal behavior, but also as enhance one's coping with a variety of life situations.

ACKNOWLEDGMENTS

We thank the Henry J. Kaiser Family Foundation, the Zuni Public School District, and the Cherokee Nation Health Department for supporting this research. We especially thank Hayes Lewis, Ruby Wolf, and the Zuni High School administration and teachers; Linda Guy Goodrich, and the Sequoyah High School administration and teachers for facilitating our involvement in both schools. We thank Geetu Melwani for her assistance in the data analysis. Finally, we extend our appreciation to the students at Zuni High School and Sequoyah High School for their cooperation and willingness to participate in this research.

NOTE

1. Fuller results in tabular form are available from the first author.

REFERENCES

Ackerson, L. M., Dick, R. W., Manson, S. M., & Baron, A. E. (1990). Properties of the Inventory to Diagnose Depression in American Indian adolescents. *Journal of the American Academy of Child and Adolescent Psychiatry, 29*, 601–607.

Bandura, A. (1982). Self-efficacy mechanism in human agency. *American Psychologist, 37*, 122–147.

Beck, A. T., Weissman, A., Lester, D., & Trexler, L. (1974). The measurement of pessimism: The Hopelessness Scale. *Journal of Consulting and Clinical Psychology, 42*, 861–865.

Beiser, M., & Attneave, C. (1982). Mental disorders among Native American children: Rates and risk periods for entering treatment. *American Journal of Psychiatry, 139*, 193–198.

Berlin, I. N. (1985). Prevention of adolescent suicide among some Native American tribes. In S. C. Feinstein (Ed.), *Adolescent psychiatry: Developmental and clinical studies* (pp. 77–93). Chicago: University of Chicago Press.

Berman, A. L., & Carroll, T. A. (1984). Adolescent suicide: A critical review. *Death Education, 8* (Suppl.), 53–64.

Berman, A. L., & Jobes, D. A. (1991). *Adolescent suicide assessment and intervention*. Washington, DC: American Psychological Association.

Blum, R. W., Harmon, B., Harris, L., Bergeisen, L., & Resnick, M. D. (1992). American Indian-Alaska Native youth health. *Journal of the American Medical Association, 267*, 1637–1644.

Blumenthal, S. J., & Kupfer, D. J. (Ed.) (1990). *Suicide over the life cycle*. Washington, DC: American Psychiatric Press.

Brent, D. A., Kalas, R., Edelbrock, C., Costello, A. J., Dulcan, M. K., & Conover, N. (1986). Psychopathology and its relationship to suicidal ideation in childhood and adolescence. *Journal of the American Academy of Child Psychiatry, 25*, 666–673.

Brent, D. A., Perper, J. A., Goldstein, C. E., Kolko, D.J., Allan, M. J., Allman, C. J., & Zelenak, J. P. (1988). Risk factors for adolescent suicide: A comparison of adolescent suicide victims with suicidal inpatients. *Archives of General Psychiatry, 45*, 581–588.

Children's Safety Network. (1991). *A data book of child and adolescent injury*. Washington, DC: National Center for Education in Maternal and Child Health.

Cole, D. A. (1989). Psychopathology of adolescent suicide: Hopelessness, coping beliefs, and depression. *Journal of Abnormal Psychology, 98*, 248–255.

Conrad, R. D., & Kahn, M. W. (1974). An epidemiological study of suicide and attempted suicide among the Papago Indians. *American Journal of Psychiatry, 131*, 69–72.

Cull, J., & Gill, W. (1982). *Suicide probability scale manual*. Los Angeles: Western Psychological Services.

Dauphinais, P., LaFromboise, T., & Rowe, W. (1980). Perceived problems and sources of help for American Indian students. *Counselor Education and Supervision, 20*, 37–46.

Dick, R. W., Manson, S. M., & Beals, J. (1993). Alcohol use among male and female native American adolescents: Patterns and correlates of student drinking in a boarding school. *Journal of Studies on Alcohol, 54*, 172–177.

Dinges, N. G., & Duong-Tran, Q. (1994). Suicide ideation and suicide attempt among American Indian and Alaska Native boarding school adolescents. *American Indian and Alaska Native Mental Health Research: The Journal of the National Center Monograph Series, 4*, 167–188.

Dizmang, L., Watson, J., May, P., & Bopp, J. (1974). Adolescent suicide at an Indian reservation. *American Journal of Orthopsychiatry, 44*, 43–49.

Dukes, R. L., & Lorch, B. D. (1989). The effects of school, family, self-concept, and deviant behavior on adolescent suicide ideation. *Journal of Adolescence, 12*, 239–251.

Eccles, J., Midgley, C., Wigfield, A., Buchanan, C., Reuman, D., Flanagan, C., & MacIver, D. (1993). Development during adolescence: The impact of stage-environment fit on young adolescents' experiences in schools and in families. *American Psychologist, 48*, 90–101.

Freese, A. (1979). *Adolescent suicide: Mental health challenge*. USA: Public Affairs Committee.

Friedman, J. M. H., Asnis, G. M., Boeck, M. B., & DiFiore, J. (1987). Prevalence of specific suicidal behavior in a high school sample. *American Journal of Psychiatry, 144*, 1203–1206.

Greer, L. (1988). *Adolescent health survey (American Indian Version)*. Minneapolis, MN: University of Minnesota Adolescent Health Program.

Hafen, B. Q., & Frandsen, K. J. (1986). *Youth suicide: Depression and loneliness*. Evergreen CO: Cordillera Press.

Howard-Pitney, B., LaFromboise, T. D., Basil, M., September, B., & Johnson, M. (1992). Psychological and social indicators of suicide ideation and suicide attempts in Zuni adolescents. *Journal of Consulting and Clinical Psychology, 60*, 473–476.

Indian Health Service (1991). *Indian women's health care: Consensus statement*. Rockville, MD: U.S. Department of Health and Human Services, Public Health Service.

Kandel, D. B., & Davies, M. (1982). Epidemiology of depressive mood in adolescents. *Archives of General Psychiatry, 39*, 1205–1212.

LaFromboise, T. D. (in press). *American Indian life skills curriculum*. Palo Alto, CA: Health Promotion Resource Center, Stanford University School of Medicine.

Lester, D., & Gatto, J. (1989). Self-destructive tendencies and depression as predictors of suicidal ideation in teenagers. *Journal of Adolescence, 12*, 221–223.

Levy, J. E. (1965). Navaho suicide. *Human Organization, 24*, 308–318.

Lujan, C., DeBruyn, L. M., May, P.A., & Bird, M.E. (1989). Profile of abused and neglected Amrican Indian children in the southwest. *Child Abuse and Neglect, 13*, 449–461.

Manson, S. M., Ackerson, L. M., Dick, R. W., Baron, A. E., & Fleming, C. M. (1990). Depressive symptoms among American Indian adolescents. Psychometric characteristics of the Center for Epidemiologic Studies Depression Scale (ES-1). *Psychological Assessment: A Journal of Consulting Clinical Psychology, 67*, 231–237.

Manson, S. M., Beals, J., Wiegmen, D., & Duclos, C. (1989). Risk factors for suicide among Indian adolescents at a boarding school. *Public Health Reports, 104*, 609–614.

Manson, S. M., Dinges, N. G., Grounds, L. M., & Kallgren, C. A. (1984). *Psychosocial research on American Indian and Alaska Native youth*. Westport, CT: Greenwood.

Manson, S. M., Shore, J. H., & Bloom, J. D. (1985). The depressive experience in American Indian communities: A challenge for psychiatric theory and diagnosis. In A. Kleiman, & B. Good (Eds.), *Culture and depression* (pp. 331–368). Berkeley: University of California Press.

May, P. A. (1983). *A survey of the existing data on mental health in the Albuquerque Area*. Unpublished report prepared under Indian Health Service Contract 3–200423.

Miller, S. I., & Shoenfeld, L. S. (1971). Suicide attempt patterns among the Navajo Indians. *International Journal of Social Psychiatry, 17*, 189–193.

Neiger, B. L., & Hopkins, R. W. (1988). Adolescent suicide: Character traits of high-risk teenagers. *Adolescence, 23*, 471–475.

Petersen, A. C. (1988). Adolescent development. *Annual Review of Psychology, 39,* 583–607.

Petrie, K., & Chamberlain, K. (1983). Hopelessness and social desirability as moderator variables in predicting suicidal behavior. *Journal of Consulting and Clinical Psychology, 51,* 485–487.

Pfeffer, C. (1989). Life stress and family risk factors for youth fatal and non-fatal suicidal behavior. In C. Pfeffer (Ed.), *Suicide among youth: Perspectives on risk and prevention* (pp. 143–164). Washington, DC: American Psychiatric Press.

Pfeffer, C. R., Zuckerman, S., Plutchik, R., & Mizruchi, M. (1984). Suicidal behavior in normal school children: A comparison with child psychiatric inpatients. *Journal of American Academy of Child Psychiatry, 23,* 416–423.

Porter, W. (1985). *Inservice and resource guide for children and adolescent suicide prevention.* Unpublished manuscript, Cherry Creek Schools, Denver, CO.

Provonost, J. (1990). Epidemiological study of suicidal behavior among secondary school students. *Canada's Mental Health, 38,* 9–14.

Schotte, D. E. & Clum, G. A. (1987). Problem-solving skills in suicidal psychiatric patients. *Journal of Consulting and Clinical Psychology, 55,* 49–54.

Shaffer, D. (1988, April). School research issues. In K. Smith (Chair), *How do we know what we've done? Controversy in evaluation.* Symposium conducted at the meeting of the American Association of Suicidology, Washington, DC.

Shore, J. H. (1972). Suicide and suicide attempts among American Indians of the Pacific Northwest. *International Journal of Social Psychiatry, 2,* 91–96.

Shore, J. H. (1974). Psychiatric epidemiology among American Indians. *Psychiatric Annals, 4,* 56–66.

Shore, J. H. (1975). American Indian suicide—Fact and fantasy. *Psychiatry, 38,* 86–91.

Smith, K., & Crawford, S. (1986). Suicidal behavior among "normal" high school students. *Suicide and Life Threatening Behavior, 16,* 313–325.

Thompson T. R. (1987). Childhood and adolescent suicide in Monitoba. A demographic study. *Canadian Journal of Psychiatry, 32,* 264–269.

Travis, R. (1983). Suicide in northwest Alaska. *White Cloud Journal, 3*(1), 23–30.

U. S. Congress, Office of Technology Assessment (1990). *Indian adolescent mental health,* OTA-H-446. Washington, DC: U. S. Government Printing Office.

Van Winkle, N. W., & May, P. A. (1986). Native American suicide in New Mexico, 1957–1979: A comparative study. *Human Organization, 45,* 296–309.

Van Winkel, N. W., & May, P. A. (1993). An update on American Indian suicide in New Mexico, 1980–1987. *Human Organization, 52,* 304–315.

Willis, D. J., Dobrec, A., & BigFoot, D. S. (1992). Treating American Indian victims of abuse and neglect. In L. A. Vargas & J. D. Koss-Chioino (Eds.), *Working with culture* (pp. 276–299). San Francisco, CA: Jossey-Bass.

Wodarski. J. S. & Harris, P. (1987). Adolescent suicide: A review of influences and the means for prevention. *Social Work, 32,* 477–484.

Wyche, K. F., & Rotheram-Borus, M. J. (1990). Suicidal behavior among minority youth in the United States. In A. R. Stiffman & L. E. Davis (Eds.), *Ethnic issues in adolescent mental health* (pp. 323–338). Newbury Park, CA: Sage.

Young, T. J. (1991). Suicide and homicide among Native Americans: Anomie or social learning? *Psychological Reports, 68,* 1137–1138.

13 Women, Physical Illness and Suicidal Behavior

Sharon M. Valente and
Judith M. Saunders

The relationship between physical illness and suicidal behavior in women merits attention because physical illness could be an important contributor to their suicide mortality (Bolund, 1985a; Dorpat, Anderson & Ripley, 1968; Louihivuori & Hakama, 1979). Bolund (1985a) reported that many women (and men) who died by suicide had experienced a deterioration in their health. Conwell, Caine, and Olsen (1990) found poor physical health in 37% of those who died by suicide.

In this chapter the empirical and theoretical literature on women, illness and suicidal behavior will be reviewed. To start, we will address the meanings of physical illness and disease and the impact of women's roles on their experiences with illness. After examining these background issues, we will review the existing literature on physical illness and suicidal behavior in general, and as applied to women specifically. We will examine the suicidal pathways of physically ill women and suggest research questions to be addressed.

DEFINITIONS OF PHYSICAL ILLNESS

Conceptualizing what qualifies as a physical illness is controversial. Although ordinary people rarely differentiate the terms illness and disease, experts disagree on the nature and definitions of both illness and disease. Moos (1984) conceptualized physical illness as an acute health crisis, a definition that omits chronic illnesses. Disease is typically defined as a disruption in body function that results in diminished capacity or reduced life span (Twaddle, 1977).

Kidel (1988) suggested avoiding rigid divisions among notions of illness, sickness, health, wellness, and disease. If a person has cancer, but has no symptoms and does not feel ill, then one could argue that disease exists in the absence of illness. One can also experience the reverse, that is, have symptoms and feel ill, but lack a defined disease.

A new conceptualization of illness focuses on the mind–body interaction. Researchers have recently identified relationships among psychological-social-behavioral processes, stressful physical and behavioral states, and immune function (Birney, 1991). The emerging field of psychoneuroimmunology examines illnesses with associations between psychological stress and immune function (Hillhouse & Adler, 1991).

Finally, what the medical profession classifies as a disease changes over time. Disorders that used to be thought as psychological may be viewed as physical, and vice versa.

Women are diagnosed as having psychosomatic disorders or are assigned psychogenic etiology for somatic complaints more often than are men (Williams, 1987). Only recently has a diagnosis emerged, General Fatigue Syndrome, to give medical legitimacy to the symptoms that women had taken to physicians, but that were met with skepticism and often diagnosed as neuroses. In the last decade, medicine has begun to give more serious attention to other common medical complaints of women, such as headaches and backaches.

WOMEN'S GENDER ROLES AND THE DYNAMICS OF PHYSICAL ILLNESS

In her classical work, Chodorow (1971) argues that women have been ascribed roles that society devalues. In all settings, at home, at work and in the community, women learn that they "are," while boys and men "do." Women are taught to be nurturing, while men are taught to be wage earners. In most societies, women who care for children, spouses and other family members occupy less desirable and less powerful social roles than men (Williams, 1987).

According to Kaplan and Klein (1989) a woman's sense of self depends upon being actively engaged in relationships. Socialization into femininity begins early as girls are taught the importance of nurturing (Chodorow, 1971).

Physical illness may disrupt a woman's social role and relationships because pain, fatigue, and medical appointments hinder her caretaking ability. As a woman fails to meet the internalized commitment to nurture, her sense of self may decline.

WOMEN, CANCER AND SUICIDE

A majority of the literature on women, physical illness, and suicidal behaviors has focused on cancer. Cancer has been associated with heightened suicidal risk in women (Black, Warrick, & Winokur, 1985; Bolund, 1985a, 1985b; Fox, Stanek, Boyd, & Flannery, 1982; Louihivuori & Hakama, 1979), men (Farberow et al., 1971; Fox et al., 1982), and older individuals (Maris, 1992; Sainsbury, 1955). Black and colleagues reported that the risk of suicide mortality increased for women during the first two years after diagnosis of cancer. Louihivuori and Hakama (1979) examined records to determine the risk of death by suicide among 28,857 cancer patients registered by the Finnish Cancer Registry in 1955, 1960, and 1965. By the end of 1970, 63 of these people had killed themselves. The rate of suicide mortality among females was 1.9 times higher than the rate in the general population, and higher than among males. The highest risk for suicide mortality occurred among those with gastrointestinal cancer and cancer patients without surgery or radiation treatment.

Multiple Illnesses

Bolund (1985a) analyzed the 1973–1975 medical, forensic, and police records of all persons who killed themselves and had cancer diagnosis. The sample included eighty-eight persons, one-third women and two-thirds men. Bolund found that most persons had been diagnosed with a second serious illness (e.g., tuberculosis, cardiac infarction, aortic aneurysm). Some killed themselves before receiving treatment expected to cure the cancer, or after treatment had cured the cancer (see Table 13.1). In three cases, a diagnosed physical illness other than cancer was responsible for prominent symptoms and apparently affected the patient more than the cancer.

Unrelieved Pain and Symptoms

Physical illnesses are associated with varying degrees of suffering. Pain may influence the risk of suicide mortality (Bolund, 1985a). Unrelieved pain may lead to suicidal behavior if suicide is seen as the only option for relief.

In a study by Bolund (1985b), most of the women with cancer had experienced moderate to severe suffering before their fatal suicidal act. Al-

Table 13.1 Case Examples of Physically Ill Women Who Killed Themselves

1. A woman had been treated for uterine cancer for many years and had suffered from recurrent depressions before as well as after the diagnosis of cancer. She hung herself a few days before a scheduled psychiatric consultation.

2. A middle-aged woman wanted to kill herself because she had Alzheimer's disease and did not want to continue to waste away and become a burden on her family.

3. A middle-aged woman with multiple sclerosis asked for help to kill herself as she did not want to continue living with a chronic illness.

4. A woman of 58 had been examined a number of times for abdominal pain. Surgery revealed disseminated pancreatic cancer which was treated by cytostatic therapy. A fortnight later, she was discharged from the hospital, after being told that she could not count on living for more than a month or so. A few hours later she was found to have hanged herself at home.

5. A young woman's HIV antibody test was positive. The counselor who informed her of her test results arranged for a mental health consultation but the woman killed herself the same day.

though some women had no physical symptoms, some suffered sequelae from cancer treatment. Twenty six of the 29 women who died by suicide suffered slight to severe symptoms from pain, nausea, and loss of appetite.

Social Isolation

Social isolation is considered a factor in suicidal behavior. Bolund (1985a) reported, however, that women with cancer who died by suicide were not socially isolated. Most lived with spouse or family or had neighbors and people around. Having people around did not "mean that these cancer patients did not feel alone with their threatening disease" (Boland, 1985a, p. 29). The impact of disrupted social role or relationships on suicide requires further study, because active relationships are often considered central to women's sense of self (Kaplan & Klein, 1989).

METHODOLOGICAL ISSUES IN STUDYING SUICIDE AND PHYSICAL ILLNESS AMONG WOMEN

Suicidal behavior among physically ill women has been difficult to study partly because (1) women's baseline rates of suicide mortality are relatively low, (2) women may easily conceal their nonviolent suicidal acts, (3) women's nonfatal suicidal behavior is rarely examined (Bolund, 1985a), and (4) conceptualizations of physical illness are inconsistent. Physical illness rather than the suicide is usually listed as the mode of death when a medically ill patient dies by a nonviolent method or overdose (Boland, 1985a; Saunders & Valente, 1988). Finally researchers have reported difficulty controlling relevant variables such as age, gender, or knowledge of a medical diagnosis, and agreeing on appropriate comparison groups (Fox et al., 1982).

FROM PHYSICAL ILLNESS TO SUICIDAL BEHAVIOR

Untreated depression, a frequent concomitant of cancer treatment among physically ill patients, may be a critical link between physical illness and suicidal behavior (Bolund, 1985a, 1985b; Holland & Rowland, 1990; Massie, 1990; Saunders & Valente, 1988). Bolund (1985a) reported that 50 percent of the women who died by suicide exhibited some mental distress during the course of cancer. Massie (1990) reviewed nine studies of cancer and depression; she concluded that 24 percent of cancer patients were depressed, and that major depression was the most common diagnosis. Similar rates of depression are reported in other studies of physically ill patients (Geringer, 1989; Henderson-Brown, Hentcleff, Barakat, & Rowe, 1986; Massie, 1990).

Massie and Holland (1990) reported data on consultations with 546 cancer patients. Forty-nine percent of these patients were diagnosed as depressed, and 70% of these had a reactive depression. Patients experiencing pain and those whose cancer was advanced were the most depressed. Much of the emotional distress experienced by cancer patients resulted from treatments rather from the disease (Massie, 1990). Patients with a history of affective disorder or alcoholism (Massie, 1990), advanced stages of cancer (Bolund, 1985b; Massie, 1990), poorly control pain, treatment symptoms (Bolund, 1985b; Massie, 1990), cancer of the breast, gastrointestinal cancer (Farberow et al., 1971; Louihivuori & Hakama, 1979), pancreatic or lung cancer, and metastatic disease and neoplasms, were at high risk for depression (Saunders & Valente, 1988).

Maguire and colleagues (Maguire, 1985; Hardman, Maguire, & Crowther, 1989; Maguire, 1985) explored depressive symptoms and treatment in 75 mastectomy patients one year after surgery by conducting in-depth interviews with general practitioners and nurses treating these patients. Twenty-five percent of the post-mastectomy patients were found to have developed an anxiety or depressive disorder, but only 42% of these patients were recognized as distressed and were offered help for these symptoms; finally, only 10% considered the help they received appropriate to their needs. These researchers concluded that inadequate detection of depression stems from the physician's failure to evaluate depressive symptoms, the misconception that depressed patients would request treatment, and a reluctance to encounter a patient's strong feelings of anger or despair. In a comparative study of a random sample of 505 depressed and nondepressed women with cancer, Lansky and colleagues (Lansky et al., 1985) reported that depressed women experienced more pain and greater physical disability than the nondepressed women. No differences in disease-related parameters, diagnosis, time since diagnosis, stage of illness and treatment were found between depressed and nondepressed groups. Evaluating depression among medically ill individuals may be difficult because the same symptoms (e.g., anorexia and fatigue) may indicate physical illness and depression. After comparing 325 physically ill and 101 psychiatric patients experiencing depression, Cavanaugh, Clark, and Gibbons (1983) reported that psychological, but not somatic, criteria accurately indicated depression among the medically ill.

Medications such as analgesics, antiinflammatory agents, antihypertensives, antimicrobials, hormones, cytoxic agents, antineoplastics, sedatives, and steroids, may cause depression as a side effect (Geringer, 1989). Steroids have reportedly precipitated suicidal ideation (Holland & Rowland, 1990).

In sum, medications, treatment, diagnosis, poorly controlled pain and advanced disease associated with physical illness, such as cancer, increase the risk of depression. Untreated depression may increase the risk of suicide among physically ill women. Gender socialization is essential in explaining physically ill women's suicidal behavior.

CONCLUSIONS

Many studies have examined the relationship between cancer and fatal suicidal behavior; some studies either focused on women primarily, or included women in their sample and discussions (Black et al., 1985; Bolund, 1985a, 1985b; Cella et al., 1990). These studies have provided some understanding of how cancer increases the risk of women's suicidal behavior. It is not clear how other physical illnesses may affect women's risk for suicidal behavior. Most research on physically ill women who kill themselves has been retrospective (Bolund, 1985a). There is a dearth of information about physical illness and nonfatal suicidal behaviors.

Prospective research is needed that provides insight into the experience of physical illness and the development of suicidal ideation in physically ill women (Bolund, 1985b). Research is also needed that can guide clinical intervention with suicidal physically ill women. One interesting empirical question may be how health care resources help or hinder women's depressive and suicidal responses to illness. It is also important to learn more about clinicians' experiences in assessing and managing suicidal clients (Massie, 1990). Finally, it may be useful to explore what resources would improve clinicians' assessment and treatment of depression among physically ill women (Massie, 1990).

REFERENCES

Birney, M. H. (1991). Psychoneuroimmunology: A holistic framework for the study of stress and illness. *Holistic Nursing Practice, 5*, 32–38.

Black, D. W., Warrick, G., & Winokur, G. (1985). Excess mortality among psychiatric patients: The Iowa linkage study. *Journal of the American Medical Association, 253*, 58–61.

Bolund, C. (1985a). Suicide and cancer: I. Demographic and social characteristics of cancer patients who committed suicide in Sweden, 1973–1976. *Journal of Psychosocial Oncology, 3*, 17–30

Bolund, C. (1985b). Suicide and cancer: II. Medical and care factors in suicides by cancer patients in Sweden, 1973–1976. *Journal of Psychosocial Oncology, 3*, 31–52.

Cavanaugh, S., Clark, D. C., & Gibbons, R. D. (1983). Diagnosing depression in hospitalized medically ill. *Psychosomatics, 24*, 809–815.

Cella, D. F., Mahon, S. M., & Donovan, M.I. (1990). Cancer recurrence as a traumatic event. *Behavioral Medicine, 16*(1), 15–22.

Chodorow, N. (1971). Being and doing: A cross-cultural examination of the socialization of males and females. In V. Gornick & B. K. Moran (Eds.), *Woman in sexist society: Studies in power and powerlessness* (pp. 259–291). New York: Basic Books.

Conwell, Y., Caine, E. D., & Olsen, K. (1990). Suicide and cancer in late life. *Hospital and Community Psychiatry, 43*, 1334–1338.

Dorpat, T. L., Anderson, W. F., & Ripley, H. S. (1968). The relationship of physical illness to suicide. In H. L. P. Resnik (Ed.), *Suicidal behaviors: Diagnosis and management* (pp. 209–219). Boston: Little Brown.

Farberow, N. L., Ganzler, S., Cutter, F., & Reynolds, D. (1971). An eight-year survey of hospital suicides. *Suicide and Life-Threatening Behavior, 1*, 184–202.

Fox, B. H., Stanek, E. J., Boyd, S. C., & Flannery, J. T. (1982). Suicide rates among cancer patients in Connecticut. *Journal of Chronic Diseases, 35*, 89–100.

Geringer, E. S. (1989). Treating major depressive disorder in the patient with a medical illness. *Medical Aspects of Human Sexuality, 23*(4), 22–34.

Hardman, A., Maguire, P., & Crowther, D. (1989). The recognition of psychiatric morbidity on a medical oncology ward. *Journal of Psychosomatic Research, 33*, 235–239.

Henderson-Brown, J., Henteleff, P., Barakat, S., & Rowe, C. J. (1986). Is it normal for terminally ill persons to desire death? *American Journal of Psychiatry, 143*, 208–211.

Hillhouse, J., & Adler, C. (1991). Stress, health, and immunity: A review of the literature and implications for the nursing profession. *Holistic Nurse Practitioner, 5*(4), 22–31.

Holland, J. C., & Rowland, J. H. (1990). *Handbook of psychooncology* (pp. 283–299). Oxford, England: Oxford University Press.

Kaplan, A. G., & Klein, R. B. Women and suicide. (1989). In D. Jacobs & H. N. Brown (Eds.), *Suicide: Understanding and responding* (pp. 257–282). Madison, CT: International Universities Press.

Kidel, M. (1988). Illness and meaning. In M. Kidel & S. Rowe-Leete (Eds.), *The meaning of illness* (pp. 4–21). New York: Routledge.

Lansky, S. B., List, M. A., Herrmann, C. A., Ets-Hakin, E. G., Tapas, K., Das Gupta, Wilbanks, G. D., & Hendrickson, F. (1985). Absence of major depressive disorder in female cancer patients. *Journal of Clinical Oncology, 3*, 1553–1559.

Louhivouri, K. A., & Hakama, M. (1979). Risk of suicide among cancer patients. *American Journal of Epidemiology, 109*, 59–65.

Maguire, P. (1985). Improving the detection of psychiatric problems in cancer patients. *Social Science and Medicine, 20*, 819–823.

Maris, R. W. (1992). An overview of the study of suicide assessment and prediction. In R. W. Maris, A. L. Berman, J. T. Maltsberger, & R. L. Yufit (Eds.), *Assessment and prediction of suicide* (pp. 3–22). New York: Guilford.

Massie, M. J. (1990). Depression. In J. C. Holland & J. H. Rowland (Eds.), *Handbook of psycho-oncology* (pp. 283–290). Oxford, England: Oxford University Press.

Massie, M. J., & Holland, J. C. (1990). Depression and the cancer patient. *Journal of Clinical Psychiatry, 51*, (July Supplement), 12–17.

Sainsbury, P. (1955). *Suicide in London*. London: Chapman and Hall.

Saunders, J. M., & Valente, S. M. (1988). Cancer and suicide. *Oncology Nursing Forum, 15*, 575–581.

Twaddle, A. C. (1977). *A sociology of health*. St. Louis, MO: Mosby.

Whitlock, F. A. (1978). Suicide, cancer and depression. *British Journal of Psychiatry, 132*, 269–274.

Williams, J. H. (1987). *Psychology of women: Behavior in a biosocial context* (3rd ed.). New York: Norton.

14
Leisure Attitudes and Social Adjustment of Women Who Are Depressed and Suicidal

Marjorie J. Malkin

Leisure research, like suicide research, lacked an emphasis on the issue of gender until the early 1980s. Leisure researchers (e.g., Glancy, 1991; Henderson, 1990, 1991) then began to critique androcentric (male-centered) definitions and research orientations, and recommended reference to the social, economic, and political context of women's lives. Thus, while earlier definitions of leisure were based on a compartmentalized male-oriented work/leisure dichotomy, current definitions take into account the varied, interwoven multiple roles experienced by women (paid and unpaid work, caretaker, parent, homemaker).

Gender may be defined as the "interaction between the environment and biological sex" (Henderson, 1990a, p. 229). Gender involves the culturally and socially determined definitions of appropriate female/male behavior. Issues of gender-role socialization and the changing roles of women are clearly relevant to investigations of leisure in women.

One goal of feminism has been the "freeing of all people from the restrictions of their culturally defined sexual roles" (Mander & Rush, 1974, p. 39). Furthermore, feminism is a philosophy and a practice that "embodies equality, empowerment, and social change for women and men and that seeks to eliminate the invisibility of women" (Henderson, Bialeschki, Shaw, & Freysinger, 1989, cited in Henderson, 1990a, p. 230). A feminist approach to leisure research, therefore, promises important insights (Henderson, 1990b).

SUICIDAL BEHAVIOR IN WOMEN

In the United States females are more likely to engage in nonfatal suicidal behaviors (Canetto, 1991, 1992; Canetto & Lester, 1995; Kaplan & Klein, 1989; Lester, 1988). The suicide/depression link is well documented (Kaplan & Klein, 1989), as are higher rates of depressive disorders in women (Nolen-Hoeksema, 1990).

SUICIDAL BEHAVIOR AND LEISURE ATTITUDES

In a 1982 study, Neuringer and Lettieri observed that suicidal women appeared to be unable to take pleasure from life and enjoy themselves. Inspired by Neuringer and Lettieri's findings, Malkin and colleagues (Malkin, 1991; Malkin, Howe, & Del Ray, 1989) examined leisure attitudes of suicidal and depressed women. Within this study, leisure was defined as an experience or subjective state characterized by enjoyment, intrinsic motivation, perceived competence, perceived control, pleasure, satisfaction, and enjoyment. Perceived freedom of choice was assumed to be a primary dimension of the leisure experience. The research participants were 33 women aged 25 to 55 who had been hospitalized at a Southern state psychiatric hospital. Research participants were divided into three groups on the basis of their physician's rating of suicidality: highly suicidal (a recent nonfatal suicidal act, $N = 13$), moderately suicidal (suicidal ideation, $N = 9$), and depressed but nonsuicidal ($N = 11$).

The main finding was that, among women who had recently engaged in suicidal behavior, leisure satisfaction and perceived freedom in leisure significantly decreased as levels of depression, suicidality, and "life dissatisfaction" increased. Furthermore, highly suicidal women rated life, leisure, and women more negatively than moderately suicidal and nonsuicidal women.

SUICIDAL BEHAVIOR AND SOCIAL INTEGRATION

Neuringer and Lettieri (1982) also noted that suicidal women were socially isolated, suggesting the importance of examining the social context of mental disorders (Fine & Gordon, 1989; Weissman & Paykel, 1974). Essential aspects of social context for women are the beliefs and attitudes about femininity and the "proper" social roles women should occupy. Nolen-Hoeksema (1990) has documented how women are devalued and discriminated against both in family and employment settings. According to her, this domestic and social victimization has implications for depression; "girls and women come to expect that they will have little control over the events at work, at home and in relationships. As a result they show lowered motivation and self-esteem—in other words, helplessness and depression" (p. 19). Jack (1992) noted that suicidal women are often not well integrated in their societies, "in terms of involvement with family, with community activities and occupational integration" (p. 171).

Social adjustment had been the focus of an early study of depressed women by Weissman and Paykel (1974), which focused on work, social and leisure, extended family, marital, and parental roles. Weissman and Paykel found that depressed women who were withdrawn and isolated from people, and who did not have interesting leisure pursuits, or supporting friends and relatives had a more guarded prognosis.

Inspired by the study by Weissman and Paykel (1974), we decided to explore the social adjustment of suicidal and/or depressed women. Like Weissman and Paykel, we used a structured interview. This methodology is consistent with the recommendation by Bella (1989) for studies of the meaning of social and leisure activities. The research questions were: (1) to what extent are personal, social, work, and gender-role factors related to the attitudes toward, and functions of leisure; and (2) what is the relationship between attitudes toward leisure (perceived freedom, perceived control, competence, enjoyment) and social adjustment?

A NONSEXIST RESEARCH APPROACH

Previous studies of leisure and suicidal behavior have tended to neglect women as participants; furthermore, findings from studies with male participants have been generalized to females (Canetto, 1992; Unger, 1983). Feminist leisure scholars call for an examination of leisure within "a broader social context, as part of life-styles . . . rather than as a separate dimension" (Wimbush & Talbot, 1988, p. xv). Qualitative methodology is often chosen by feminists in order to examine leisure in the context of life style (Wimbush & Talbot, 1988).

Howe (1993) and Glancy (1993) recommend qualitative research methods such as interviewing, because they elicit responses from people in their own language. The researcher's task is to clarify the participants' experiences based on their cultural and social contexts. Unger (1983) argues that the sex/gender of the researcher may affect the research outcome.

The in-depth interviews reported below constitute the qualitative phase of a larger study of suicidal women (Malkin, 1991; Malkin et al., 1989). Based on the research recommendation discussed above, my study of suicidal women used only a female interviewer.

PARTICIPANTS

Three women were chosen from the original group of 33 hospitalized women (Malkin, 1991; Malkin et al., 1989). One woman had recently engaged in a nonfatal suicidal act; another women had been thinking about suicide; and a third woman was depressed but nonsuicidal. The technique for selecting representative interviewees was the same as that adopted by Neuringer and Lettieri (1982). Relevant variables considered in selection were age, race/ethnicity, education, marital status, previous therapeutic contacts, and previous suicidal communications. A women was considered typical or representative for her group if she occupied a modal position on a majority of the six variables.

PROCEDURES

The interview was semi-structured. All respondents were presented the same questions in the same order; equal attention was given to all areas. The standardized format facilitated data analysis, and served to minimize interviewer bias effects (Patton, 1980). At the same time, the open-ended questions allowed individual responses. It was assumed that such flexible format would facilitate exploration of contextual meanings and facilitate situation-explicit and value-resonant grounding (Guba & Lincoln, 1981).

The interview questions were derived from leisure surveys (Malkin et al., 1989) and from Weissman and Paykel's (1974) interview format. Attitudes toward leisure, identity through work and/or leisure, interpersonal and social relationships, perceived control (internal/external orientation), and gender roles in leisure were explored.[1]

Extensive notes were taken by the interviewer during the interview. In addition, an audio-tape was made as back-up. The interview data were integrated with the medical records data in the form of a written case study.

CLINICAL CASE STUDIES

A Case of Nonfatal Suicidal Behavior

At the time of the interview, Ms. S., a 31-year-old European-American woman was heavily bandaged on both wrists from recently self-inflicted butcher-knife wounds. According to the attending physician, she was depressed and seriously suicidal. Chronic psychological difficulties were noted in her medical records. Ms. S. had been unemployed for over a year, was separated from her husband, and had lost custody of her three-year-old son to her brother. She had a history of outpatient and inpatient psychological treatment.

Ms. S. reported that she was satisfied with her leisure activities, but that she had too much free time. She enjoyed fishing, swimming, song-writing, and reading. Ms. S. enjoyed socializing with friends, but prior to her hospitalization she had been spending more time alone. Lack of money and "feeling bad" caused her to reduce her participation in activities. She reported that she was "not having fun" lately. She stated that leisure activities were more satisfying than work because, as a woman, her career choices were limited. She felt that her work and leisure activities were mainly under the control of other people, a fact she disliked. However, she reported more control in leisure than in other areas.

Ms. S. seemed to apologize for not having what she thought were "feminine" leisure pursuits. She was concerned about her inability to have more children. She reported that she enjoyed leisure activities that others may see as masculine, such as playing the guitar and writing music. In terms of interpersonal relationships, Ms. S. reported that she socialized weekly with two close friends, but avoided drinking situations. Recently, she noted some social discomfort, boredom, and loneliness. She had "felt so far down" like someone was "crushing" her heart. Ms. S. reported recent friction with friends and family, especially with her mother, with whom she lived, and her brother. She said that her boyfriend was not "serious" about her because of her inability to have more children.

A Case of Suicidal Ideation

Ms. M., a 27-year-old European-American woman, was hospitalized for the eighth time. Ms. M. lived with her three children and parents in the suburbs. She had attended a year and a half of technical school after high school, but was unemployed. Ms. M. had a history of losing jobs due to poor performance and friction with coworkers. Prior to her divorce, she lost jobs because she had to move whenever her husband moved. She was judged by the attending psychiatrist to be depressed and "moderately" suicidal at the time of the interview.

Ms. M. reported a recent lack of energy and participation in recreational or social activities. She stated, however, that she was satisfied with her leisure interests. She reported having too much free time since she had lost her job as a day-care center cook. Ms. M. had disliked being alone, but reported that she was becoming more self-focused and therefore more comfortable when alone. She continued to participate in church activities. Ms.

M. reported that she used to measure fun as "boredom versus excitement." She now looked at how rewarding life was, an outlook she considered more positive. She commented "how very different for 'Miss Near-Suicide' herself to say that." Ms. M. believed that many aspects of her life, both in work and in leisure were under the control of other people.

Ms. M. reported "social discomfort"—she had only two friends, both female, from her church. She said she often felt uncomfortable and shy in social situations. She used to avoid most social interactions but through psychotherapy had learned to "confront" them. She had divorced two years after her husband left her. During her marriage, she had been emotionally and economically dependent on her husband. Ms. M. reported current friction with her sister, but close relationships with her parents and brother.

Ms. M. reported that she previously enjoyed "masculine" activities, such as repairing cars and riding motorcycles with her husband. She also spoke enthusiastically about her cake-decorating talents.

A Case of Nonsuicidal Depression

Ms. C., a 39-year-old African-American, never married, unemployed woman, was hospitalized for alcohol-abuse treatment. She lived in an urban apartment with her parents, several younger siblings, and her son. She had had 2 years of outpatient therapy and several inpatient hospitalizations for depression and alcohol abuse. She stated that she drank only during leisure time.

Ms. C. attended family dinners and church activities, played baseball and softball, and enjoyed dancing at parties. Some activities were limited by her jealous boyfriend, lack of energy, money, motivation, and family responsibilities. She felt that her recent depression had "slowed her down." Ms. C. valued work more than leisure. She had been drinking more heavily since being laid-off from work several months ago, and she felt that she now had too much free time. She felt that her personal ambitions could best be realized on the job rather than in leisure. In terms of perceived control over events and happenings in her life, Ms. C. felt that most events in her life were under the control of other people.

Ms. C. had six close friends, but said she rarely discussed feelings with these friends. She did not report social discomfort. She never married, but she had a boyfriend who also drank. She had little friction with her family, but hoped soon to be able to move into her own apartment.

DISCUSSION

All three women, especially the two suicidal women, reported limited participation in leisure activities. Psychological difficulties, lack of money, energy, and motivation, as well as family responsibilities, were listed as constraints to leisure. There was evidence, however, of previous satisfaction with leisure experiences.

Leisure researchers have commented that women's ability to exercise real choice in leisure is limited by their low social and economic status. In this study, typical constraints included jealous, unsatisfied or absent partners, unemployment, and lack of funds.

All three women interviewed were unemployed but valued work over leisure. The work history of the two suicidal women was sporadic and generally less successful than that of the depressed nonsuicidal woman. All three women had returned home to live with parents due to financial difficulties and the break-up of a relationship with a male partner. Kushner (1985) and Canetto (1992–1993) have noted that the impact of unemployment and restricted job mobility is often ignored in discussions of suicidal behavior in women. The three women interviewed for this study clearly emphasized their frustration with their unemployed status, noting that they felt their work opportunities were limited due to gender discrimination, as well as their lack of education and training. Kaplan and Klein (1989) noted the relationship between poverty, conflict, isolation, disempowerment, and suicidality.

Social and interpersonal problems and, hence, a lack of "social adjustment," were noted most clearly in the two suicidal women. There were difficulties with family, co-workers, relatives and former partners, as well as limited social contacts with friends. All three women had problems in their primary relationship. This suggests the importance of exploring suicidal women's relationship with their "significant other" (Canetto & Feldman, 1993; Stephens, 1988).

Lester (1988) discussed the association of suicidal behavior, social relationships, and feelings of "being in control." He characterized suicidal individuals as interpersonally isolated and disengaged. According to him, suicidal individuals have poorer relationships and less active social lives than other individuals. Suicidal individuals "have less confidence in their ability to control their future" (pp. 6–7). This lack of control over their lives is a theme which emerges clearly from the interviews. All three women stated that most events in their lives were under the control of other people. Such a feeling may lead to "learned helplessness" (Dattilo & Kleiber, 1993; Nolen-Hoeksema, 1990). It is noteworthy that all three women interviewed felt they had more control over events in leisure or recreation than in other aspects of their lives.

The final topic explored in this study was that of gender identity in leisure. All three women demonstrated an "apologetic" attitude for not having typically "feminine" leisure pursuits. Henderson (1991) states that certain recreational activities may be perceived as more appropriate for women.

Such assumptions may serve as an interpersonal constraint inhibiting women from making free leisure choices.

SUMMARY AND CONCLUSIONS

The depressed and suicidal women interviewed showed "dysfunction" in all of the social roles examined—as worker, parent, partner, relative, and friend. Social isolation, social discomfort, and lack of participation in recreation and social activities were greater in the suicidal women, as compared with the depressed nonsuicidal woman.

Feminist researchers stress that "successful" leisure experiences may be an opportunity for women to gain personal empowerment and autonomy. "Opportunities for empowerment throughout the leisure aspects of women's lives may have a relationship to other areas of women's lives" (Henderson & Bialeschki, 1991, p. 5). The freedom and opportunity found in leisure may contribute to an improved quality of life for suicidal women, and may ameliorate their feelings of powerlessness and hopelessness.

NOTE

1. The full interview protocol can be obtained from the author.

REFERENCES

Bella, L. (1989). Women and leisure: Beyond androcentrism. In E. L. Jackson & T. L. Burton (Eds.), *Understanding leisure and recreation: Mapping the past, charting the future* (pp. 151–179). State College, PA: Venture Publications.

Canetto, S. S. (1991). Gender roles, suicide attempts, and substance abuse. *Journal of Psychology, 125*, 605–620.

Canetto, S. S. (1992). Gender and suicide in the elderly. *Suicide and Life-Threatening Behavior, 22*, 80–97.

Canetto, S. S. (1992–1993). She died for love and he for glory: Gender myths of suicidal behavior. *Omega, 26*, 1–17.

Canetto, S. S., & Feldman, L. B. (1993). Overt and covert dependencies in suicidal women and their male partners. *Omega, 27*, 179–194.

Canetto, S. S., & Lester, D. (1995). The epidemiology of women's suicidal behavior. In S. S. Canetto & D. Lester (Eds.), *Women and suicidal behavior* (pp. 35–57). New York: Springer.

Dattilo, J., & Kleiber, D. A. (1993). Psychological perspectives for therapeutic recreation research: The psychology of enjoyment. In M. J. Malkin & C. Z. Howe (Eds.), *Research in therapeutic recreation: Concepts and methods* (pp. 57–76). State College, PA: Venture.

Fine, M., & Gordon, S. S. (1989). Feminist transformations of/despite psychology. In M. Crawford & M. Gentry (Eds.), *Gender and thought* (pp. 146–174). New York: Springer-Verlag.

Glancy, M. (1991). The androcentrism complex. In T. L. Goodale & P. A. Witt (Eds.), *Recreation and leisure: Issues in an era of change* (3rd ed., pp. 413–428). State College, PA: Venture.

Glancy, M. (1993). The analysis of subjective information: A process for perspective taking. In M. J. Malkin & C. Z. Howe (Eds.), *Research in therapeutic recreation: Concepts and Methods* (pp. 257–278). State College, PA : Venture.

Guba, E., & Lincoln, Y. (1981). *Effective evaluation*, San Francisco: Jossey-Bass.

Henderson, K. A. (1990a). Anatomy is not destiny: A feminist analysis of the scholarship on women leisure. *Leisure Science, 12*, 229–339.

Henderson, K. A. (1990b). The meaning of leisure for women: An integrative review of the research. *Journal of Leisure Research, 22*, 228–243.

Henderson, K. A. (1991). The contribution of feminism to an understanding of leisure constraints. *Journal of Leisure Research, 23*, 363–377.

Henderson, K. A., & Bialeschki, M. D. (1991). Women and leisure: An introduction. *World Leisure and Recreation, 33*(3), 4–5.

Howe, C. L. (1993). Naturalistic research design. In M. J. Malkin & C. L. Howe (Eds.), *Research in therapeutic recreation: Concepts and methods* (pp. 235–256). State College, PA: Venture.

Jack, R. (1992). *Women and attempted suicide*. Hillside, NJ: Lawrence Erlbaum.

Kaplan, A. G., & Klein, R. B. (1989). Women and suicide. In D. Jacobs & H. N. Brown (Eds.), *Suicide: Understanding and responding* (pp. 257–282). Madison, CT: International Universities Press.

Kushner, H .I. (1985). Women and suicide in historical perspective. *Signs: Journal of Women in Culture and Society, 10*, 537–52.

Lester, D. (1988). Suicide in women: An overview. In D. Lester (Ed.), *Why women kill themselves* (pp. 3–15). Springfield, IL: Charles C. Thomas.

Malkin, M. J. (1991). Cognitive evaluations of suicidal women: Implications for therapeutic recreation intervention. *Therapeutic Recreation Journal, 25*(1), 34–49.

Malkin, M. J., Howe, C. Z., & Del Ray, P. (1989). Psychological disability and leisure dysfunction of female suicidal psychiatric clients. *Therapeutic Recreation Journal, 23*(1), 36–46.

Mander, A. V., & Rush, A. K. (1974). *Feminism as therapy*. New York, NY: Random House.

Neuringer, C. , & Lettieri, D. J. (1982). *Suicidal women: Their thinking and feeling patterns*. New York, NY: Gardner Press.

Patton, M. Q. (1980). *Qualitative evaluation methods*. Beverley Hills, CA: Safe.

Nolen-Hoeksema, S. (1990). *Sex differences in depression*. Stanford, CA: Stanford University Press.

Stephens, B. J. (1988). The social relationships of suicidal women. In D. Lester (Ed.), *Why women kill themselves* (pp. 73–85). Springfield, IL: Charles C. Thomas.

Unger, R. H. (1983). Through the looking glass: No wonderland yet! (The reciprocal relationship between methodology and models of reality). *Psychology of Women Quarterly*, 8, 9–32.

Weissman, M. M., & Paykel, E. S. (1974). *The depressed woman: A study of social relationships*. Chicago: University of Chicago.

Wimbush, E., & Talbot, M. (Eds.) (1988). *Relative freedoms: Women and leisure*. Philadelphia, PA: Open University Press.

■ 15
Suicidality in Female Survivors of Child Sexual Abuse

Karen M. Fondacaro and
William M. Butler

Survivors learn early that they have no voice
They see no evil
They hear no evil
They speak no evil
They just feel evil

Jo Ann Hernandez (1986, p. 11)
Writer, Survivor of Child Sexual Abuse

Current research indicates that at least 25% of females in the United States have experienced child sexual abuse by the time they reach 18 years of age (e.g., Finkelhor, Hotaling, Lewis, & Smith, 1990; Russel, 1984). In our clinical practice we often encounter female survivors of child sexual abuse who, as the poem above aptly puts it, "feel evil" and somehow blame themselves for their own abuse. This feeling, and others stemming from the sexual abuse experience, seem to lead to suicidal ideation and behavior in some survivors. It has been our experience that many child sexual abuse survivors report suicidal ideation during the course of treatment. An important question for both clinicians and researchers is whether or not suicidality is as common in child sexual abuse survivors as it is in other clinical and nonclinical populations. Also, if it is demonstrated that child sexual abuse and suicidal ideation or behavior are related, it is important to understand if this is a causal relationship and, if so, what it is about the sexual abuse experience that leads to suicidality. Finally, it is important to assess whether gender differences play a role in the risk of suicidality for sexual abuse survivors. With this information, professionals working with survivors can be sensitive to those survivors who may be at increased risk for suicidal behavior.

Although clinical lore and past empirical reviews (see for example, Browne & Finkelhor, 1986) have held that self-destructive behavior is one of the most frequently noted long-term effects of child sexual abuse, our review of the literature indicates that this connection is far from empirically established. In this chapter we review and critique the available empirical studies of the alleged relationship between child sexual abuse and suicidal behaviors. Based on our clinical experience and the conceptual work of others (e.g., Browne & Finkelhor, 1986) we also present a theoretical formulation which outlines individual, interpersonal, and societal factors that may be related to suicidality in survivors. Hopefully, this review will provide information that will assist prevention and clinical interventions as well as guide future research.

Due to space limitations we have excluded from our review the literature on women sexually assaulted as adults. Also, we do not consider male survivors of sexual abuse who are now thought to comprise upwards of one-third of all child sexual abuse survivors (Finkelhor, 1990). Some studies that we reviewed (e.g., Adams-Tucker, 1982) included small numbers of male sexual abuse survivors within the overall sample. Unfortunately, due to the small number of male participants, gender comparisons could not be made. We did, however, include these studies in our review since there were, over all, so few studies on sexual abuse and suicidality. Only one study was found that compared male and female survivors in terms of suicidality (Briere, Evans, Runtz, & Wall, 1988). No gender differences were found for either suicidal ideation or behavior.

The link between child sexual abuse and suicidality has been investigated using two different survivor populations: children/adolescents and adults. This division roughly breaks down the effects of child sexual abuse into short and long-term outcomes. In our review, we first consider studies that assess children and adolescents, and then ones that assess adults. Studies with child, adolescent and adult participants were placed in the child/adolescent section if the average age of participants was 18 or under, and in the adult section if the average age was above 18. Due to the paucity of research assessing children/adolescents as survivors, we included studies without control groups. A greater number of studies with adult survivors of child sexual abuse were found, and we reviewed, therefore, only controlled studies in that section. We excluded unpublished studies and dissertations.

Throughout the literature, suicidality and sexual abuse are frequently defined in vague terms. Therefore, in the course of reviewing each study, we point out the definitions, if any, used by the author(s).

REVIEW OF EMPIRICAL STUDIES

Child/Adolescent Survivors of Sexual Abuse

Five studies were found that assess the relationship between sexual abuse and suicidality in children/adolescents as survivors. Only one of these studies included a comparison group.

Adams-Tucker (1982) conducted one of the first studies that assessed suicidal ideation (undefined) in an outpatient clinical sample ($N = 28$) of child sexual abuse survivors soon after the abuse occurred. Sexual abuse was not defined by the author but the abuse ranged from genital fondling to intercourse. In some cases the type of abuse was unknown. Information regarding the abuse was obtained through child and parent interviews. The authors found that 21% of childhood sexual abuse survivors (age 2½ to 15½ years) reported suicidal ideation. Their sample was 79% female and included survivors of intrafamilial and extrafamilial child sexual abuse. There was no control group in this study with which to make comparisons.

Wozencraft, Wagner and Pelligrin (1991) conducted a study specifically designed to assess depression and suicidal ideation in a clinical sample ($N = 65$, mean age = 10.7) of sexually abused children (undefined). Ninety-one percent of the sample was female and 9% was male. They found that 42% of the childhood sexual abuse survivors experienced suicidal ideation seven to 72 days after the abuse investigation. Fifty-eight percent reported that they did not want to kill themselves, 37% indicated that they thought about suicide but indicated they would not do it, and 5% reported that they wanted to kill themselves. It was also found that suicidal ideation was more likely if the child was molested by a family member, if she was not removed from home, if she was older and if she had a parent who was less compliant with treatment recommendations.

Goodwin (1981) reviewed the records of a protective service agency for nonfatal suicidal behavior in cases where child sexual abuse had been substantiated. These cases had occurred during a 2½ year period. Intrafamilial sexual abuse was defined as "exploitative sexual behavior toward a child by a socially defined family member (this includes stepfathers and stepbrothers)" (p. 218). Incest was further defined as "oral, anal or vaginal penetration of the child by a family member" (p. 218). "Suicide attempts" were defined as "self-destructive behaviors taking place in the context of a suicidal plan" (p. 218). Participants reporting only suicidal ideation were excluded. Records were reviewed for suicidal acts that occurred between three and 33 months following substantiation of abuse. It was found that out of 201 families with substantiated sexual abuse, eight female victims (4%) had engaged in nonfatal suicidal acts.

In a study of adolescent rape victims, Felice, Grant, Reynolds, Gold, Wyatt, and Heald (1978) assessed a range of psychological symptoms experienced by females who entered the emergency room of a hospital after having been raped. Rape was defined as "violent sexual assault without consent" (p. 311). Of the initial 102 females screened, 39, between the ages of 11 and 19 years, returned for follow-up and were assessed within one month of the assault. Among other problems, they found that 10% of the survivors had engaged in suicidal behavior and required hospitalization as a precaution against suicide.

In the only controlled study of child survivors of sexual abuse, Edwall, Hoffman, and Harrison (1989) investigated the psychological correlates of sexual abuse in a sample of 210 females receiving chemical dependency treatment. Ninety-one percent of the females were White and their mean age was 16. A semi-structured interview during the second week of treatment was used to obtain the data. Two questions relating to sexual abuse in the interview were: "Has anyone in your family ever been sexual with you?" and "Has anyone else ever sexually abused you?" (p. 282). The criteria for coding the answers to these questions as sexual abuse were not defined. Suicidal ideation and behaviors were not defined other than by the labels "suicidal ideation" or "suicide attempt" in the last year. Participants were divided into four groups: nonvictims, victims of extrafamilial sexual abuse, victims of intrafamilial sexual abuse, and victims of both intrafamilial and extrafamilial sexual abuse. Significant differences between groups were found on measures of suicidal ideation and behaviors. Fifty-seven percent of intrafamilial abuse survivors, 36% of extrafamilial abuse survivors, 44% of survivors of both intrafamilial and extrafamilial abuse and 20% of nonabused controls reported past suicidal behavior. Sixty-five percent of intrafamilial abuse survivors, 64% of extrafamilial abuse survivors, 74% of survivors of both types of abuse and 52% of nonabused controls reported suicidal ideation. It should be noted that the groups also differed on a measure of physical abuse experience. Thus, it cannot be determined if the differences in suicidal behavior between sexual abuse survivors and controls are due to being a sexual abuse survivor, or due to the experience of physical abuse, or both.

Summary

Our review indicates that there is insufficient data at this time to determine whether child survivors of sexual abuse are at greater risk of suicidal ideation and behavior than nonabused children. The one controlled study (Edwall et al., 1989) did find a significantly higher rate of suicidal ideation and behavior in child abuse survivors than in nonabuse controls. In that study, however, the sexual abuse survivors also experienced significantly more physical abuse than nonsexually abused controls. The frequency of suicidal ideation and behavior in child sexual abuse survivors reported in the uncontrolled studies did not differ markedly from reported rates in comparable community and clinical samples. For example, Bongar (1991) reviewed several studies and found rates of suicidal ideation as high as 63% in nonclinical samples of high school students. In his review, Bongar (1991) also noted rates of suicidal behavior as high as 8% in nonclinical adolescent samples and as high as 20% in clinical samples. Other reviewers reported similar findings (e.g., Blumenthal & Kupfer, 1990; Patros & Shamoo, 1989; Pfeffer, 1986). It should be noted, however, that three of the studies we reviewed found higher rates of suicidality soon after the abuse occurred than one would expect over such a short time period, even in clinical samples (Felice et al., 1978; Goodwin, 1981; Wozencraft et al., 1991).

Adult Survivors of Child Sexual Abuse

Five controlled studies were found that investigated the relationship between child sexual abuse and suicidality in adult survivors. A study by Herman (1981) was one of the first to explore the link between child sexual abuse and suicidality in a clinical sample of adult female survivors (*N* = 60). Paternal incest was defined as "any sexual relationship between a child and an adult in a position of paternal authority" (p. 70). Using a combination of interviews and therapist reports, Herman found that 37½% of adult survivors of "paternal incest" reported at least one nonfatal suicidal act. This rate was not statistically significantly different from a suicidal behavior rate of 5% found in a control group consisting of women whose father was described as seductive (undefined).

Sedney and Brooks (1984) conducted one of the first studies investigating the connection between child sexual abuse and suicidality in a nonclinical sample of adult female survivors (*N* = 301). The authors of this study defined sexual abuse as "some kind of sexual experience with another person while they were growing up" (p. 215). In this study, significantly more survivors of child sexual abuse (39%) had "thoughts of hurting oneself" (p. 217) than did nonabused controls (16%). The groups did not differ significantly on the self-report of (undefined) "suicide attempts" (survivors 16% versus controls 6%). Significantly more survivors of intrafamilial (43%) than extrafamilial abuse (31%) reported past suicidal ideation. The two subgroups, however, did not differ significantly in terms of nonfatal suicidal acts.

As research into child sexual abuse has progressed, more rigorous methodology has become the norm. The three more recent studies reviewed below exemplify this maturation.

Briere and Runtz (1986) explored the relationship between child sexual abuse and suicidality in a sample of adult women (*N* = 195) seeking services at a community crisis counseling center. In this study sexual abuse was defined as "any self reported sexual contact (ranging from fondling to sexual intercourse) experienced by a client on or before age 16, initiated by someone five or more years her senior" (p. 415). Women sexually abused by near-age peers and victims of noncontact abuse (e.g., exhibitionism) were excluded. Significantly more of the child sexual abuse survivors (55%) had a history of past "suicide attempts" (undefined) than did controls (23%). Also, clients who were suicidal (undefined) at intake were significantly more likely to be child sexual abuse survivors (36%) than not (23%).

The authors also investigated several potential moderating variables. A history of both child sexual abuse and physical abuse was significantly positively correlated with past and current suicidality. The number of perpetrators was significantly positively correlated with current suicidality but not with past suicidal behavior. Also, women whose first suicidal act occurred in adulthood were not statistically more likely to have been child sexual abuse victims, while women whose first suicidal act occurred in childhood or adolescence were statistically more likely to have been sexually abused as children. Other abuse variables including age at the time of abuse, the presence of intrafamilial sexual abuse and intercourse were not significantly correlated with the number of past suicidal acts or current suicidality.

Briere and Runtz (1988) also investigated suicidality in adult survivors (*N* = 152) of child sexual abuse as part of a broader study of the psychological effects of sexual abuse in a sample of women seeking crisis services at a community mental health clinic. While this study included females as young as 14, the mean age of the sample was 27. In this study child sexual abuse was defined in the same way as noted above in Briere and Runtz (1986). Using a semistructured clinical interview, Briere and Runtz (1988) found that significantly more survivors of child sexual abuse (51%) had a history of "suicide attempts" (undefined) than did nonabused controls (34%). There was, however, no significant difference between child sexual abuse survivors and controls on a measure of current "desire to hurt self" (p. 371). Thirty-one percent of the survivors had a "desire to hurt self" compared to 19% of the controls.

Briere and Zaidi (1989) conducted a study of self-mutilation, suicidal ideation and nonfatal suicidal behavior in a clinical sample (*N* = 100) of adult female survivors of child sexual abuse. Sexual abuse was defined as "sexual contact, ranging from fondling to intercourse, that occurred before age 17 and was initiated by someone 5 or more years older" (p. 1603). Significantly more survivors (66%) reported a history of "suicide attempts" (undefined) than did nonabused controls (33%). Also, significantly more survivors (77%) reported current or past suicidal ideation (undefined) than did controls (33%). Survivors did not differ significantly from controls in terms of self-mutilative (undefined) behavior (survivors 17% versus controls 0%).

Summary

Several controlled studies were reviewed that investigated the frequency of suicidal ideation and behavior in adult survivors of child sexual abuse. The results of these studies are mixed. Three of the four studies assessing suicidal ideation (Briere & Runtz, 1986; Briere & Zaidi, 1989; Sedney & Brooks, 1984) found a significantly higher rate of suicidal ideation in adult survivors than in nonabused controls. Three of the six comparisons assessing suicidal behavior found higher rates for adult survivors versus controls (Briere & Runtz, 1986; Briere & Runtz, 1988; Briere & Zaidi, 1989) while the remaining three found no significant differences between groups (Briere & Zaidi, 1989; Herman, 1981; Sedney & Brooks, 1984).

Summary of Child and Adult Research

Our review of the empirical literature indicates that there is no clear evidence for a link between child sexual abuse and suicidality. Despite the lack of clear statistical support, we would note that in all the studies reviewed the survivors reported more suicidal ideation and behavior than did the nonabused controls. It may be that in the mostly clinical samples used, the base rate of suicidality is so high that very large differences would be needed to reach statistical significance. It is equally possible, however, that there is no relationship between sexual abuse and suicidality.

Also, even if child sexual abuse survivors are found to have a higher rate of suicidal ideation and behavior than nonabused controls, this does not prove a cause and effect relationship. In all but one of the studies reviewed it is not clear that the suicidality followed the abuse experience. In two of the studies comorbid physical abuse was identified as a third variable that could account for the differences between groups. Many other third variables are potential precipitants, including family dysfunction, depression and the effects of sexual abuse disclosure (e.g., family disruption and stigmatization).

It may also be that certain subtypes of child sexual abuse lead to a greater risk of suicidality. Two studies in this review found significantly greater rates of suicidality in survivors of intrafamilial abuse (Edwall et al., 1989; Wozencraft et al., 1991).

CLINICAL AND THEORETICAL CONSIDERATIONS

While our review of the empirical literature did not clearly find that child sexual abuse survivors are at greater risk for suicidal behavior, in our clinical experience, sexual abuse and suicidality seem to be intimately linked for some survivors. In fact, the majority of the child and adult survivors we have worked with have contemplated suicide. We believe that the disparity between the empirical literature and our clinical experience may be due to heterogeneity within the child sexual abuse survivor population. In other words, it is possible that some female survivors are at increased risk for suicidal behavior, whereas other female survivors are not. In the following theoretical discussion we detail several factors that may place some survivors at increased risk of suicidal ideation and behavior. While this list of factors is not exhaustive, it provides the clinician and researcher with ideas of how sexual abuse might result in suicidality for the female survivor.

In general, we view the relationship between sexual abuse and suicidality from a multidimensional perspective, based on the integration of individual, interpersonal (family and community) and societal factors. We believe that the suicidal ideation and behavior experienced by some female survivors is a product of numerous factors that function within each of these three levels.

Individual Level

Factors at the individual level, such as life experiences a woman has had prior to, during and after the abuse, and behavioral patterns that result from these life experiences, may increase the survivors' risk for suicidal behaviors. These life experiences may include sexual victimization and other forms of abuse, parental loss, or medical illness. With respect to multiple victimizations, it is possible that a survivor of sexual abuse who is battered within an adult relationship may "re-experience" the initial trauma and ultimately feel an increased level of helplessness and depression.

Also included at the individual level are psychological variables related to "the self" that the survivor brings with her to the abuse experience. These include variables such as a survivor's low self-esteem, depression, or limited coping repertoire prior to the abuse. These individual factors often represent "third variables" that may be linked to suicidality in their own right. In this respect, they are difficult to separate from the influences of the sexual abuse itself. It is also possible that individual psychological factors may serve as buffers in the relationship between sexual abuse and suicidality. For example, a survivor with extensive coping abilities may be at less risk of suicidal behaviors.

Interpersonal Level

Interpersonal factors may also play a role in the suicidality of sexual abuse survivors. Interpersonal factors include the reactions of significant others to the abuse, the type of abuse experienced and the dynamics that sometimes stem from the abuse (e.g., stigmatization and powerlessness). Our model of the link between interpersonal factors and suicidality builds upon the work of Briere and Runtz (1986, 1988) and Finkelhor and Browne (1985).

According to Finkelhor and Browne (1985), stigmatization refers to the negative messages survivors receive from others about the abuse. These messages have an impact on self-image and can lead to feelings of worthlessness, shame, evilness, and guilt. For example, survivors sometimes feel guilty because they may have enjoyed the sexual contact or special attention that was part of the abuse experience. It is often difficult for survivors to understand that their feelings (e.g., arousal) are natural and not an indication that they are to blame for the abuse. Perpetrators may also convey the message that the abuse is shameful and that the victim is to blame in order to assuage their own guilt and encourage secrecy. Survivors are also often coerced to keep the abuse "secret," with threats of family dissolution or imprisonment of the offender. This secrecy may in turn enhance the sense of stigma experienced by the victim. Stigmatization is represented at the community level when people react to the knowledge of the abuse with disgust and attribute negative characteristics to the survivor. We have frequently heard of neighbors no longer allowing their children to associate with a child who has been abused. This type of reaction may enhance guilt and the sense of shame experienced by the child survivor, and therefore increase the risk of suicidality.

According to Finkelhor and Browne (1985) betrayal occurs in most abuse situations and represents the discovery that someone whom the child trusted and cared for has caused the child harm. Betrayal also refers to the actions of the perpetrator and/or significant others who may not believe the survivor or who blame her for the abuse. For example, the survivor may be told by the perpetrator or by family members that she is to blame for the abuse because she was "seductive" in the way she dressed. We have sometimes encountered nonoffending spouses who do not believe the abuse occurred, or who may blame the survivor for the abuse in an attempt to preserve their relationship with the perpetrator.

Another interpersonal factor that can influence the survivor's risk of suicidal ideation and behavior is the type of abuse experienced. Two studies reviewed (Edwall et al., 1989; Wozencraft et al., 1991) found that survivors of intrafamilial child sexual abuse may be more at risk than survivors of extrafamilial abuse. Other potential mediating factors of this sort include the duration and frequency of abuse, degree of force or threats used, presence of ritualistic components, gender of the perpetrator, location of abuse, survivor age at time of abuse and number of perpetrators.

Briere and Runtz (1988) point out that conditioned anxiety stemming from the abuse experience may be an important factor in the development of suicidal ideation and behavior in survivors. It is thought that various stimuli associated with the abuse experience may come to elicit anxiety through classical conditioning. Suicidal behavior may then develop as a way to cope with, and lessen, this anxiety. For example, we have treated survivors in whom physical touch elicits memories of the abuse that lead the survivor to carve their arms in order to "turn off" the anxiety-provoking memories. Finkelhor and Browne (1985) have also identified feelings of powerlessness as a result of abuse-related anxiety over the survivors inability to "control noxious events" (p. 536). It is hypothesized that powerlessness may subsequently lead to depression and suicidality. In the case of ongoing abuse as opposed to past abuse, suicidal behavior may serve as one way to escape the abuse and anxiety associated with it (Briere & Runtz, 1986).

Societal Level

There are a variety of ways that societal factors may impact the abuse survivor and her risk of suicidal ideation and behavior. As is the case at the interpersonal level, stigmatization and powerlessness play a role at the societal level (Browne & Finkelhor, 1986).

Victims in our society are seen as "getting what they deserve" (Finkelhor & Browne, 1985). Underlying this idea is the belief that the world is fair, and only those who do something wrong will be harmed. This viewpoint serves to lessen one's anxiety about being harmed by random, nonsensical violence. It also leads, however, to stigmatization of the victim as "bad" in some way. In the case of child sexual abuse, this can lead to the victim being labelled as "seductive" or as "damaged goods." These societal beliefs can be incorporated by the victim and may lead to increased risk of suicidality.

Victims, women and children in our society are in many ways powerless. Thus, female child sexual abuse survivors are at particular risk of feeling powerless. As the poem that opens this chapter puts it, "survivors learn early that they have no voice. . . . " Child sexual abuse survivors often have "no voice" when they attempt to speak about the abuse. Society prefers to "see no evil," especially in the case of otherwise "respectable" families. Historically, mental health professionals, police, courts and government agencies have colluded in this collective denial. Fortunately, this is now changing in many locales. However, even when the abuse is taken seriously, the child sexual abuse survivor can still feel powerless in many ways. For example, in cases of intrafamilial abuse, the child may be removed from her home, or the perpetrator may be asked to leave. The child survivor often has little or no say in this matter. In addition, throughout the court process the child survivor can often experience re-victimization and powerlessness. Our judicial system is in many ways disempowering to victims and children. Child survivors often lack the cognitive and emotional maturity required to adequately confront the perpetrator in the courtroom setting. This can serve to re- traumatize the child via the court process and increase feelings of powerlessness. Also, the courtroom environment is often not set up to accommodate child victims. Adult size chairs and the formality of the courtroom are often threatening to children. Many courts are attempting to limit the potential for re-traumatizing child victims by using video taped testimony and providing children with comforting toys when they are in the courtroom. It is very difficult, however, to balance the rights of the defendant with the needs of child survivors.

Child sexual abuse survivors may feel powerless if they complete the entire court process regardless of the outcome of the case. A guilty verdict, in the case of intra- familial abuse, may lead to incarceration of the perpetrator and result in poverty for the child survivor due to a loss of the perpetrator's income. This economic powerlessness is something the survivor must deal with on a daily basis. A guilty verdict may also lead to increased guilt for the survivor for "putting the perpetrator in jail," especially if the perpetrator is a family member. If the perpetrator is not found guilty, the survivor may question herself or fear retribution for speaking out.

Repeated experiences with powerlessness might lead to a sense of "learned helplessness" in the survivor, that is, a sense that her actions do not affect the consequences she experiences (e.g., Gold, 1986). This feeling may lead to depression and suicidality.

A final societal factor that may influence the risk of suicidality in child survivors of sexual abuse is the way in which females are socialized to deal with problems. Although males are often encouraged to "externalize" problems, females are socialized to "internalize" their problems (e.g., Brehm, 1981). With respect to sexual abuse, this emphasis on internalizing problems may serve to increase self-blame and maintain secrecy about the abuse. In our clinical experience, females who have internalized the sexual abuse, by keeping quiet and blaming themselves, seem to be at increased risk for suicidality. Our clinical experience with child victims of sexual abuse seems to indicate that girls are more likely than boys to turn the abuse inward and become re-victimized, whereas boys seem more likely than girls to externalize the abuse and become abuse-reactive. Similarly, in his review of the sexual abuse literature, Finkelhor (1990) notes that gender differences in internalizing and externalizing behavior are commonly reported.

FUTURE DIRECTIONS FOR RESEARCH

In conducting our empirical review we discovered many methodological flaws in studies assessing the connection between child sexual abuse and suicidality. Although the more recent studies (e.g., Briere & Runtz, 1986) avoided many of these pitfalls, we outline below some of the problems encountered.

Many of the studies reviewed (e.g., Adams-Tucker, 1982) did not have control groups. Also suicidality and sexual abuse were often poorly defined and it was often unclear when the suicidal ideation occurred in relation to the sexual abuse.

Future research should control for the apparent mediating effect of concurrent physical abuse. Future research should also rely on direct questioning rather than on record reviews (e.g., Goodwin, 1981) as research has shown that such reviews are often inaccurate (e.g., Briere & Zaidi, 1989). Research will need to include both clinical and community samples since the rates of suicidality in these populations differ so greatly (see Bongar, 1991, for a review).

Although studies have begun to focus on gender differences with respect to the relationship between sexual abuse and suicidality (Briere, Evans, Runtz, & Wall, 1988), no differences have been found. Further research is needed to determine if there are gender-related differences. From a clinical perspective we have presented the factors at an individual, interpersonal and societal level that may place female survivors at increased risk of suicidality. Although empirical investigation is needed to test these hypotheses, it is possible that women who have experienced multiple victimizations, betrayal and stigmatization within the context of the abuse, and who tend to internalize their problems, may be more likely to become suicidal than those who do not share those characteristics and experiences.

REFERENCES

Adams-Tucker, C. (1982). Proximate effects of sexual abuse in childhood: A report on 28 children. *American Journal of Psychiatry, 134*, 1252–1256.

Blumenthal, S. J. & Kupfer, D. J. (1990). *Suicide over the life cycle: Risk factors, assessment, and treatment of suicidal patients*. Washington, DC: American Psychiatric Press.

Bongar, B. (1991). *The suicidal patient: Clinical and legal standards of care*. Washington, DC: American Psychological Association.

Brehm, S. S. (1981). Oppositional behavior in children: A reactance theory approach. In S. S. Brehm, S. M. Kassin, & F. X. Gibbons (Eds.), *Developmental social psychology* (pp. 96–126). New York: Oxford University Press.

Briere, J., & Runtz, M. (1986). Suicidal thoughts and behaviors in former sexual abuse victims. *Canadian Journal of Behavioural Science, 18*, 413–423.

Briere, J., Evans, D., Runtz, M., & Wall, T. (1988). Symptomatology in men who were molested as children: A comparison study. *American Journal of Orthopsychiatry, 58*, 457–461.

Briere, J., & Runtz, M. (1988). Post sexual abuse trauma: Data and implications for clinical practice. *Journal of Interpersonal Violence*, 2, 367–379.

Briere, J., & Zaidi, L. Y. (1989). Sexual abuse histories and sequelae in female psychiatric emergency room patients. *American Journal of Psychiatry, 146*, 1602–1606.

Browne, A., & Finkelhor, D. (1986). Impact of child sexual abuse: A review of the research. *Psychological Bulletin*, 99, 66–77.

Edwall, G. E., Hoffman, N. G., & Harrison, P. A. (1989). Psychological correlates of sexual abuse in adolescent girls in chemical dependency treatment. *Adolescence, 24*, 279–288.

Felice, M., Grant, J., Reynolds, B., Gold, S., Wyatt, M., & Heald, F. P. (1978). Follow-up observations of adolescent rape victims. *Clinical Pediatrics, 17*, 311–315.

Finkelhor, D. (1984). *Child sexual abuse: New theory and research*. New York: The Free Press.

Finkelhor, D. (1990). Early and long-term effects of child sexual abuse: An update. *Professional Psychology: Research and Practice, 21*, 325–330.

Finkelhor, D., & Browne, A. (1985). The traumatic impact of child sexual abuse: A conceptualization. *American Journal of Orthopsychiatry*, 55, 530–541.

Finkelhor, D., Hotaling, G., Lewis, I. A., & Smith, C. (1990). Sexual abuse in a national survey of adult men and women: Prevalence, characteristics, and risk factors. *Child Abuse and Neglect, 14*, 19–28.

Gold, E. R. (1986). Long-term effects of sexual victimization in childhood: An attributional approach. *Journal of Consulting and Clinical Psychology, 54*, 471–475.

Goodwin, J. (1981). Suicide attempts in sexual abuse victims and their mothers. *Child Abuse and Neglect, 5*, 217–221.

Herman, J. L. (1981). *Father-daughter incest*. Cambridge, MA: Harvard University Press.

Hernandez, J. Y. (1986). *Victim's voices: A collection of facts and short stories*. Unpublished manuscript.

Patros, P. G., & Shamoo, T. K. (1989). *Depression and suicide in children and adolescents*. Needham Heights, MA: Simon & Schuster.

Pfeffer, C. R. (1986). *The suicidal child*. New York: Guilford.

Russel, D. E. H. (1984). *Sexual exploitation*. Beverly Hills, CA: Sage.

Sedney, M. A., & Brooks, B. (1984). Factors associated with a history of childhood sexual experience in a nonclinical female population. *Journal of the American Academy of Child Psychiatry, 23*, 215–218.

Wozencraft, T., Wagner, W., & Pelligrin, A. (1991). Depression and suicidal ideation in sexually abused children. *Child Abuse and Neglect, 15*, 505–511.

16 By Her Own Hand: The Acquiescent Suicide of Older Women[1]

Nancy J. Osgood and
Susan A. Eisenhandler

In the United States, people 65 years of age and older have a suicide mortality rate over 50 percent higher than the suicide mortality rate for the general population (Osgood, 1992). Although males are considerably more at risk than females for death by suicide in late life, during the last decade we have witnessed an increase in the rate of suicide mortality for older females. Females 65 and older have a higher rate of suicide mortality than females aged 15 to 24 (Osgood, 1992).

In 1986 there were over 1.5 million elders living in nursing homes (Osgood, Brant, & Lipman, 1991). Compared to older adults living in the community, nursing home residents are older and sicker, and they are less likely to have any family support system. The average age of nursing home residents is 82 years. The majority of nursing home residents are women (71%) and most have no living spouse (85%). Half of the residents living in nursing homes have no living blood relatives. Most nursing home residents have multiple physical health problems and over one-third of them suffer from some form of mental disorder. For a variety of reasons, older women are much more likely than older men to live in nursing homes. Women live longer than men, and the current cohort of older women also tended to marry men 5 to 10 years older than themselves. Older women also suffer more physical health problems that require constant medical monitoring and attention than older men (Osgood et al., 1991).

In a recent study, Osgood et al. (1991) found that residents in 20% of the 1,080 long-term care facilities surveyed engaged in some form of suicidal behavior. Over 80% of the suicidal residents engaged in indirect life-threatening behavior (ILTB), whereas 20% engaged in overt suicidal behavior. The most widely used form of ILTB was refusal to eat or drink, or refusal of medications. The most common form of overt suicidal behavior was wrist slashing. A comparison of suicidal behavior of females and males revealed that females were significantly less likely than males to engage in overt suicidal behaviors.

Current discussions of suicidal behavior (Battin, 1982; Humphry, 1991; Osgood et al., 1991) raise ethical questions regarding the active or tacit roles played by others in the decision to kill oneself. The focus of the recent debate have centered on the legitimacy and adequacy of decisions made by adults whose social roles (physician, nurse, spouse, daughter, son, friend) have provided them with the power and authority to influence the individual's thinking and behavior regarding an exit from life.

The shift in emphasis described above, from discussions of the individual's direct role in suicide to discussions of the roles of others and of contextual factors, demands an examination of acquiescent suicide.[2] This chapter examines two cases of elderly women who lived in long term care facilities, hereafter called nursing homes. Through a qualitative analysis of these case studies, we argue that these women's deaths illustrate acquiescent suicide. Acquiescent suicide represents a form of suicide that occurs in relatively isolated settings with hierarchical patterns of interaction that intensify powerlessness. As is the case with other forms of indirect suicide, acquiescent suicide in nursing homes is easy to overlook.

In order to enrich the theoretical basis of our argument, we will interpret our case studies in light of the insights offered by Charlotte Perkins Gilman (1892/1980) and May Sarton (1973/1982). Their respective literary works, the short story, "*The yellow wallpaper*," and the novella, "*As we are now*," present images and ideas about the struggles of women within institutions. This kind of analysis falls within feminist theory because it delineates central processes and patterns of institutionalization which have a strong influence on women's lives (Harding, 1986; Heilbrun, 1988). We also analyze acquiescent suicide by working across traditional disciplinary boundaries in order to show the ways in which patriarchal norms and values have framed much of our substantive knowledge about gender and suicidal behavior (Kushner, 1985). This analysis of suicide among elderly, institutionalized women emphasizes the situational (Morawski, 1990) and relational (Gilligan, 1982) aspects of the problem. We agree with Canetto

(1992, p. 91) that "for elderly females, the social norms regarding suicidal behavior appear to be complex and contradictory." Our case studies and interpretive analysis reveal that the coercive normative structure of institutions, social isolation from significant others her despair, are powerful explanatory factors in acquiescent suicide.

TOTAL INSTITUTIONS AND ACQUIESCENT SUICIDE

Goffman's 1961 text on total institutions, *Asylums*, provided a framework for understanding institutionalization in a nursing home. As Goffman noted, "processes of mortification," succeed and define total institutions because "total institutions disrupt or defile precisely those actions that in civil society have the role of attesting to the actor and those in his [*sic*] presence . . . that he [*sic*] is a person with 'adult' self-determination, autonomy, and freedom of action" (Goffman, 1961, p. 43). Nursing home living exposes residents to the depersonalization and control which affects even those with the strongest identities. Within the context of the nursing home, older women may engage in only two "lines of adaptation" to preserve self and identity—withdrawal and intransigence (p. 61). The silent struggle against confinement—rejecting medication, refusing food and interaction—mounted by many older women in nursing homes becomes their means of release from the environment. In Wilson's (1981) terms, this kind of suicidal behavior may be treated as a deviant form of coping.

Acquiescent suicide is not simply an outcome of learned helplessness (Seligman, 1975). It is a response to the powerlessness and marginalization which women experience in nursing homes. To underscore the meaning of acquiescent suicide, we turn to a fictional treatment of institutionalization. In "*As we are now*," May Sarton (1973/1982) creates a fictional convalescent home where the protagonist, Caro Spencer, lives out her final days. Early in the novella, Caro comments on a friend's situation: "he cannot be beaten down yet . . . . So he is tortured in mean little ways—made to wait too long for the bedpan. Very often he refuses to eat. . . . I sometimes think he is trying to starve himself to death" (p. 13).

Initially Caro states that she "would not wish to end . . . [her life] by unnatural means" (p. 13). She attempts to adjust to the home through writing a journal and interacting with other residents, but to no avail. "I am amazed at the vitality I had when I came here—about six months ago," she notes. "My mind was alive. Now it is only alive in spots and at moments . . . I no longer function as a human being" p. 111). Before she sets fire to the home, killing herself and others, Caro describes the nursing home to a visiting minister as a "locked world."

A similar process unfolds in an earlier fictional treatment of institutionalization, "*The yellow wallpaper*," by Charlotte Perkins Gilman (1892/1980). The protagonist and narrator of this story is a young, married woman who is being treated for an emotional disorder. Her physician-directed therapy involves total withdrawal from writing, which was her source of expression and her vocation. She spends a summer resting in a room that had once been a nursery. Its prominent feature is yellow wallpaper. As the narrator spends more and more time in the room, she becomes aware that the wallpaper is alive and aware that a woman behind it seeks release. Working together one evening, "I pulled and she shook. I shook and she pulled, and before morning we had peeled off yards of that paper" (p. 17). The narrator has freed herself from behind the wallpaper but has become part of the room with no desire to leave.

Apart from documenting the dangers of rest cures, which historically were often prescribed for women (Lane, 1990; Showalter, 1985), Gilman's (1973/1980) imagery highlights how acquiescence eventually undermines the individual's ability to break free from the surrounding context. The socially isolated, yet "cared for" person slowly gives up autonomy. In the novel, the narrator loses her desire to leave the room. "It is so pleasant to be out in this great room and creep around as I please! I don't want to go outside" (p. 18).

Nursing homes are institutions where women wrestle with confinement. As Suter (1976) has noted, in such circumstances women do not have the resources to assert themselves and consequently may become even more susceptible to suicidal behavior.

CASE STUDIES

Nursing home residents, who were identified by staff as depressed and/or suicidal, or whose medical record revealed symptoms of depression and/or suicidal ideation, were asked to be interviewed. The semi-structured interview for residents focused on past family relations, past employment, reason for living in a nursing home, satisfaction with the facility, concerns about life in the institution, depression and suicidal ideation. Data from the medical record were also used. It was not, however, possible to interview the residents' family members and friends. The following case studies describe the circumstances of two elderly women nursing home residents.[3]

Sadie

A former supervisor with the local phone company in a New England city, Sadie retired after the death of her husband to tend her home and to spend more time with her grown children and grandchildren. For fifteen years after her husband's death Sadie was active in civic affairs, maintained an interest in reading, handwork, and current events, and managed her life independently.

At one point, her children, noticing subtle changes in behavior, admitted Sadie to a nursing home. Sadie, perceiving herself as able to manage herself independently at home, was bewildered and angered by the family's insistence that she go to a nursing home, "your new home" as her son referred to it, against her wishes.

Admission assessment revealed an adequately nourished, alert individual who was functional in all activities of daily living. A medical history revealed that Sadie experienced occasional but well-managed urinary incontinence. Her family physician had been treating her for cardiac irregularities, borderline hyperglycemia, hypertension, arthritis, and possible Alzheimer's disease.

Since she seemed to be adjusting well to the nursing-home routine, Sadie was moved to a room with a roommate for company. Within weeks Sadie was unable to eat her meals. When staff expressed concern about her diminishing appetite, she responded, "I'm too angry with my son to eat. When he comes to take me out of here, I may; otherwise, I don't care whether I ever eat." Increased irritability, severe facial pain and a fall ensued during this period, accompanied by social withdrawal and requests to be left alone. Finally, Sadie was hospitalized after episodes of vomiting and weakness. "Passing out" on the unit occurred with frequency. Following hospitalization, she communicated little and refused to leave her room for meals or activities.

Sadie attempted unsuccessfully to leave the nursing home with few prized possessions. Unable to do so, she asked for the "big pill" and stopped accepting most medications. Finally, she confined herself to bed, spat out food and medicine. Dependence on nursing staff for ordinary daily needs increased. The family told Sadie that the consequences of her actions may be to "become very ill again, or worse, die!" Smiling, Sadie rejected the family's concern.

Confusion, physical deterioration, and ultimate refusal of all treatment culminated in the development of respiratory complications. The family requested a "no code."[4] Sadie died six months after moving in to the nursing home.

Irene

Because of her youthful presence, one could barely believe that Irene was 81 years of age, and that she had raised 11 children. At the time of her first interview she had lived in the nursing home approximately one week. She had moved there at the insistence of the family.

The last time the interviewer saw Irene alive, just 2 months after the initial meeting, she was barely recognizable. Her appearance was disheveled, her face pale and sunken, and her lips a bluish color, she rapidly paced back and forth near the pay phone. A healing laceration was observed over her left eye.

Recovering from the shock of seeing Irene in this state, the interviewer asked what was going on with her and how she could help. With a look of recognition, she replied: "I can't go on like this anymore. I feel like a caged animal. If I don't get out of here soon, I am going to die!" It was obviously difficult for her to call her son, a professor at a nearby university, to ask him to take her out of the nursing home. Eventually she did call but there was no answer.

Irene's overall health state had seriously deteriorated. Before her admission to the nursing home, she had been able to keep her late-onset diabetes and hypertension under control. At the time of the last interview, she was recovering from a mild heart attack. She had also suffered from congestive heart failure.

Notations in the medical record, and interviews with staff members and Irene revealed that she showed signs of depression. At one point she had refused to eat, drink, or take the medication. Frequent expressions of loneliness and periods of crying were also noted.

During her adult years, life had been very difficult for Irene. A creative, resourceful, and independent woman, she had managed to clothe and feed her family and contribute to their education. She scrubbed other people's homes, took in laundry and sewing, and farmed the land with her husband, often working from dawn to dusk.

A few of Irene's children had completed college; all were married and were financially independent. She was especially proud of her oldest son, a professor at a local university. Neither the children nor the grandchildren visited Irene very often in the nursing home. One of her granddaughters was employed by the facility, but seldom visited her grandmother. Irene felt totally rejected and abandoned by the children she devoted her life to. "I just want to be wanted. When you get old, your family just forgets you and you have no purpose in life anymore. Eleven children and no place to go in the end."

Irene's financial situation contributed to her depression and suicidal ruminations. She and her husband had suffered the loss of the family farm. After her husband's death she was destitute and ashamed that she was forced to live on welfare. As a Medicaid resident in the nursing home, she received less than $35 dollars a month for necessities and had little left over for extras. Unless her friends treated her to a night out, she could not afford that luxury she so enjoyed. As she put it: "I hardly ever have a nickel to my name. Who wants to waste their time and money on a poor old woman? Not even the children. I have nothing to leave them in my will. They must be ashamed of me now."

Irene could not adjust to the dependent status of being in a nursing home. She viewed herself as trapped and likened her feelings to those of a caged animal, stating "If they make me stay here, then my life is over. I might just as well be dead."

Recognizing the seriousness of Irene's situation, the family was contacted, but they refused to help in any way. During the last two months of her life, Irene gave up hope of ever leaving the nursing home or of seeing her family. One of the last statements was: "I don't have much to live for now. I sit and cry myself to sleep every night and pray that I will die. When I awaken, I cry again. It's hopeless." She fell, was admitted to a care unit for treatment, and died there of congestive heart failure.

ACQUIESCENT SUICIDE: YIELDING TO RESIDENTIAL CONFINEMENT AND DESPAIR

It is perhaps unremarkable that a confining environment leads to "thanatopsis"[5] and ultimately to acquiescence and indirect forms of suicide. It is, however, remarkable that the developmental stages for this kind of suicide unfold in full view of several kinds of witnesses. Just as the female protagonists of Gilman's (1892/1980) and Sarton's (1973/1982) novels undertake actions that culminate in self-destruction under the eyes of significant others, the elderly women described in the case studies withdrew from life under the observant eyes of family and paid caregivers. Like the narrator of "*The yellow wallpaper*," Sadie and Irene attempted to strip the context (they rejected food and medication, and withdraw from interaction), the wallpaper, away. Although they were "free" to be alone in their rooms, they had become part of the context, part of the wallpaper.

The Relationship between Health and Despair

Health problems played a role in Sadie's and Irene's move to nursing homes. Once in residence, other health problems arose, some very serious. Yet, it is not clear whether deteriorating health diminished these women's will to live (Eisenhandler, 1989). It is clear they sought to control their health by controlling food, sleep and levels of social interaction. Sadie's and Irene's refusal of food may represent efforts to maintain "physiological autonomy" (Frank, 1959). The consequence of refusing food and medication results, paradoxically, in freeing the self while at the same time killing the body.

A Traumatic Displacement

For both women, moving into the nursing home was emotionally traumatic. Younger family members were key players in the process of their institutionalization, and both women came to rue these family members. The move challenged Sadie and Irene's sense of identity. The meaning, purpose, and value of their lives seemed lost.

Staff and Family Influences

Many older people living in nursing homes have very little if any contact with family or friends (Osgood et al., 1991). Nursing home staff members become the residents' major source of support. Many staff members fail to recognize their importance to residents and see their role solely in terms of work responsibilities. This difference in the "definition of the situation" between the two groups is a source of problems. Older residents need and want a friend and confidant, someone to bond with emotionally, someone who cares about them. Staff members, on the other hand, may be primarily concerned with keeping rooms tidy and clean, providing adequate meals and physical care, and meeting the physical health needs of residents.

The majority of institutionalized elders have no family members (Osgood et al., 1991). Unfortunately, many of those who do have family feel they have none. Many older residents feel family members have abandoned them and left them to die alone in a strange place.

CONCLUSIONS

If suicidal behavior in nursing homes is the result of acquiescence to a depersonalizing context, solutions may not be found merely in counseling individuals or in providing more opportunities for staff and family input. The organization of nursing home care may need to be reconsidered.

There are, of course, traditional techniques that might blunt the edge of isolation and impersonality of nursing homes. One such technique, guided sessions in reflection and life-review, has been shown to be effective with female nursing home residents by Brody (1990). Developing and offering programs in what Birren and Deutchman (1991) call "guided autobiography" may also create opportunities for older women to talk, work and interact with others. Such small efforts to reforge social connections with others are likely to enhance the quality of life in nursing home residents.

Serious questions about institutionalization remain. Under what social and personal circumstances do elderly women need to be in nursing homes? What can we do to prevent the harmful and iatrogenic effects that institutionalization has on some individuals? These questions loom large because, as Matthews (1979) stated, "in the resolution of the conflict between the social identity of the old promoted by gerontologized professionals and the self-identity held by the old themselves, the professionals have the upper hand" (p. 163). Nursing homes must become homes. They need to become places where elderly women can define and assert themselves rather than acquiesce to the surroundings and giving up.

NOTES

1. Portions of this chapter were published earlier in an article entitled "Gender and assisted and acquiescent suicide: A suicidologist's perspective in *Issues in Law and Medicine*, 9, 361–374, 1994.

2. An acquiescent suicide is one in which a person, who feels powerless, simply turns away from life and passively accepts death. However, this simple definition misses the deeper meaning of the concept, as we illustrate in this chapter.

3. The case studies are reprinted by permission of Greenwood Publishing Group Inc, Westport, Connecticut, and Osgood, Brant, and Lipman, the co-editors of *Suicide among the elderly in long-term care facilities*, 1991, pp. 95, 88, and 91.

4. "No code" means that, if the person is in a life-threatening situation, you do not call for medical help; you allow the person to die.

5. A state of contemplation or reverie focused on death.

REFERENCES

Battin, M. P. (1982). *Ethical issues in suicide.* Englewood Cliffs, NJ: Prentice-Hall.

Canetto, S. S. (1992). Gender and suicide in the elderly. *Suicide and Life-Threatening Behavior*, 22, 80–97.

Eisenhandler, S. A. (1989). More than counting years: Social aspects of time and the identity of elders. In L. E. Thomas (Ed.), *Research on adulthood and aging: The human science approach* (pp. 163–181). Albany, NY: State University of New York Press.

Frank, L. K. (1959). Cultural control and physiological autonomy. In C. Kluckhohn & H. A. Murray (Eds.), *Personality in nature, society, and culture* (pp. 119–122). New York: Knopf.

Gilligan, C. (1982). *In a different voice.* Cambridge, MA: Harvard University Press.

Gilman, C. P. (1980). The yellow wallpaper. In A. J. Lane (Ed.), *The Charlotte Perkins Gilman reader* (pp. 3–19). New York: Pantheon. (Original work published 1892)

Goffman, E. (1961). *Asylums: Essays on the social situation of mental patients and other inmates.* Garden City, NY: Anchor.

Harding, S. (1986). The instability of the analytical categories of feminist theory. *Signs: Journal of Women in Culture and Society, 11*, 645–664.

Heilbrun, C. G. (1988). *Writing a woman's life.* New York: Norton.

Humphry, D. (1991). *Final exit: The practicalities of self-deliverance and assisted suicide for the dying.* Eugene, OR: Hemlock Society.

Kushner, H. I. (1985). Women and suicide in historical perspective. *Signs: Journal of Women in Culture and Society, 10*, 537–552.

Lane, A. J. (1990). *To herland and beyond: The life and work of Charlotte Perkins Gilman.* New York: Pantheon Books.

Morawski, J. G. (1990). Toward the unimagined: Feminism and epistemology in psychology. In R. T. Hare-Mustin & J. Marecek (Eds.), *Making a difference* (pp. 150–183). New Haven, CT: Yale University Press.

Osgood, N. J. (1992). *Suicide in later life: Recognizing the warning signs.* New York: Lexington Books.

Osgood, N. J., Brant, B. A., & Lipman, A. (1991). *Suicide among the elderly in long-term care facilities.* Westport, CT: Greenwood Press.

Sarton, M. (1982) *As we are now.* New York: Norton. (Original work published 1973)

Seligman, M. E. P. (1975). *Helplessness.* San Francisco, CA: W. H. Freeman.

Showalter, E. (1985). *The female malady.* New York: Pantheon.

Suter, B. (1976). Suicide and women. In B. B. Wolman & H. H. Krauss (Eds.), *Between survival and suicide* (pp. 129–157). New York: Gardner Press.

17 Elderly Women and Suicidal Behavior

Silvia Sara Canetto

In the social sciences, misunderstandings about human experience have often resulted from narrowly construed conceptual models. A common error has been to define human experience based on categories derived exclusively from men's experiences (Riger, 1992). This approach has rendered women's experiences at best invisible, and at worst, deviant, since analytical categories appropriate for men do not always apply to women. Without the benefit of information about women, the meaning of men's experiences has also been distorted. Finally, issues relevant to both women and men that most readily emerge through the study of women have been overlooked (Baruch, Biener, & Barnett, 1987).

One example of this conceptual error can be found in the United States' literature on late life suicidal behavior. In the United States, patterns of suicidal behavior in the elderly vary greatly by gender. A fairly consistent finding is that elderly women are less likely to kill themselves than elderly men. In 1988, the female/male suicide mortality rate for individuals ages 65 and older was 1:6 (McIntosh, 1992). Yet, theories based on elderly males' suicidal patterns and life experiences have often been proposed as *generic* models of elderly suicidal behavior (Canetto, 1992, 1994). As a result, elderly women's patterns of suicidal behavior have remained invisible and largely unexplained. Paradoxically, this invisibility has been enhanced in recent years since male-based theories have begun to be presented in gender-neutral language.

In this chapter, women's behavior and experiences are made central to an analysis of the theoretical and empirical literature on elderly suicidal behavior. The strategies of analysis adopted in this review are not found in a majority of earlier reviews, reflecting different heuristic and epistemological commitments. Although most previous reviews have focused on elderly men and have sought an understanding of their high rates of suicide mortality, this review will focus on elderly women and aim at explaining their apparent resilience. "General" theories of elderly suicidal behavior will be evaluated in terms of their capacity to account for women's experiences. One guiding question of this analysis is: Are elderly women protected from the conditions assumed to increase the risk for suicidal behavior in the elderly? A negative answer to this question will be taken to indicate that current "general" theories have failed to "build women in" and will need to be expanded to account for women's experiences. The assumption is that looking at theories and data on suicidal behavior from a woman's perspective, or as Harding (1991) put it, "thinking from women's lives," will enhance our understanding not only of women but of men as well.

Studies of suicidal behavior have not usually included simultaneous consideration of gender and ethnicity, social class, relationship status, or sexual orientation. Due to limitations in the available data, this review will deal with women and men as if they were homogeneous groups. Hopefully, future reviews will be able to draw on more specific data and make progress in disentangling the effect of gender from those of ethnicity, social class, relationship status, and sexual orientation.

Previous reviews of the literature have combined data from different countries, based on the assumption that there are general laws of suicidal behavior. However, since historical (Kushner, 1995) and current epidemiological (Canetto & Lester, 1995) evidence shows that patterns of suicidal behavior vary according to culture, this review will utilize data from the United States only. As Riger (1992) says, social sciences may benefit from "descriptions of how people act in certain places at certain times in history" (Riger, 1992, p. 730).

Although gender patterns of suicide mortality are fairly well documented, relatively little is known about the gender epidemiology of nonfatal suicidal behavior, except for the fact that rates of nonfatal suicidal behavior decline with age (Canetto, 1992, 1994). This analysis, therefore, will rely primarily on suicide mortality data and will be most relevant to an understanding of fatal suicidal behavior.

THEORIES OF ELDERLY SUICIDAL BEHAVIOR AND THEIR APPLICABILITY TO WOMEN

A review of the United States' literature on elderly suicidal behavior reveals a fairly consistent array of theories. The most commonly cited theories focus on retirement, financial resources, widowhood, living arrangements, physical health, and mental health. Other less frequently mentioned but promising theories examine coping styles and the acceptability of suicidal behavior. In the following sections, each of these theories will be described and then discussed in terms of its fit with the data on elderly women.

Retirement

Retirement is often mentioned as a factor in suicide mortality among older persons (De Leo & Diekstra, 1990; Kirsling, 1986; Lyons, 1984). Retirement theories of suicidal behavior are usually stated in gender-neutral terms, as if they were equally applicable to women and men. A closer analysis of these theories, however, reveals that they have been derived from the experience of retired males. For example, retirement is usually defined as "separation from paid employment" (Hatch, 1987, p. 131), rather than separation from a primary productive activity. Employment-focused definitions render the retirement experience of (mainly female) homemakers invisible.

According to a review by De Leo and Diekstra (1990), the risk for death by suicide is especially high in the first few years after termination of employment. Typically, what is considered suicidogenic about retirement are changes in income, social status, social interaction and family roles.

Given the historically limited participation of women in the extradomestic, paid labor force (Hatch, 1990), occupational retirement is more normative for men than for women among recent cohorts of older adults. Are elderly women less likely to kill themselves because they are less likely to be exposed to the stresses of occupational retirement than elderly men?

In attempting to answer this question, one needs to first verify whether occupational retirement is typically stressful. According to Hatch (1987), there is no evidence that occupational retirement has a universally negative effect on well-being and life-satisfaction. On the contrary, many studies have documented that most retirees look forward to, and are satisfied with, retired life. A common conclusion is that the effect of retirement depends on specific situational variables, such as income, health, and occupational status.

If retirement from employment is not universally stressful, could it be that occupational retirement is more stressful for elderly men than for elderly women? Available evidence does not support this hypothesis. In fact, according to a review of the research by Hatch (1987), retirement from employment appears to be more stressful for women than for men. A recent study (Hatch, 1992) suggests that differences in women's and men's occupational and economic opportunities and family circumstances may be responsible for the gender differences in adjustment to retirement. For many older women, retirement is difficult if they have had interrupted work careers (Atchley & Corbett, 1977), and thus less time to attain personal career goals and/or accumulate sufficient retirement income (Hatch, 1987). According to Atchley and Corbett, the assumption that older women can easily refocus their energy on domestic and familial roles ignores the fact that it is partly because of the loss of such roles at midlife that some women become involved in jobs. It is not surprising, therefore, that "losses in social contacts as well as in income may be especially problematic for women at the time of retirement" (Hatch, 1992, p. 140).

Women whose primary productive activities involved domestic and parental responsibilities may experience retirement when the children leave home. It has been speculated that this transition may be particularly stressful for women whose self-esteem centered around being a mother (Suter, 1976). More often, however, the "emptying of the nest" appears to be associated with improved well-being and life-satisfaction for women (Lowenthal, Thurnher, Chiriboga, & Associates, 1975; Neugarten, 1970). Some women may experience retirement vicariously through their husbands' retirement and associated lifestyle changes.

In sum, available empirical evidence indicates that although not universally stressful, occupational retirement is typically more stressful for women than for men. For many women, retirement-related experiences (retirement from parental roles, the husband's occupational retirement, the anticipation of one own's occupational retirement) cluster around mid-life. Thus, retirement may be worth exploring as a factor in women's high rates of mortality by suicide at mid-life. At the same time, retirement theories do not account for women's low rates of suicidal behavior in late adulthood.

Financial Resources

Suicidal behavior in the elderly has been attributed to insufficient economic resources (Stenback 1980). Are elderly women less likely to kill themselves because they are better off financially than elderly men? Evidence from recent reviews of studies of gender and income in late adulthood does not support such a hypothesis (Arber & Ginn, 1991; Hess, 1990).

Elderly women have more limited financial resources than elderly men (Arber & Ginn, 1991; Hess, 1990). For example, 80% of women age 65 and older have annual incomes of under $13,000 (Hess, 1990). Taking a different perspective, women constitute nearly 75% of the elderly poor, although they are only 59% of all elderly people (Arber & Ginn, 1991). Furthermore, households headed by elderly women are almost twice as likely as those headed by elderly men to have incomes below the 1989 poverty level of $5,500 for a single person over 65, and $6,900 for a two-person household

(Hess, 1990). Elderly women's disadvantaged economic status is typically the result of a lifetime of occupational disadvantages, including brief and discontinuous work histories and segregation in low-paying occupations (Hatch, 1990). These occupational disadvantages are particularly devastating to women who have been homemakers much of their adult lives and end up supporting themselves in late adulthood following divorce or widowhood (Hatch, 1990).

Elderly women are more likely than elderly men to exhaust their financial resources because they live longer, are more likely to have chronic illness, and are less likely to have private insurance coverage (Canetto, 1992, 1994). More women than men depend on government programs such as Medicaid (Thomas & Kelman, 1990).

In sum, elderly women are more likely to be poor but are less likely to kill themselves than elderly men. Thus, insufficient income, often mentioned as a risk factor for suicidal mortality in the elderly in general, does not appear to be a predictor of suicide mortality in elderly women.

Widowhood

Many have linked elderly suicide mortality to widowhood (Kirsling, 1986; Lyons, 1984). Are elderly women less suicidal than elderly men because they are less likely to experience widowhood? In the United States, the opposite is actually true. Females age 65 and over are three-and-a-half times more likely to be widowed than their male peers (Hess, 1990); elderly widows are also less likely to remarry than older widowers (Zarit, 1980). As Zarit puts it, "widowhood is principally a problem of older women and not of men" (p. 103).

Mortality statistics indicate that widowhood is a weaker predictor of suicide mortality in older women than in older men. For example, the 1988 rates of mortality by suicide for elderly (age 65 and above) widows was 8.1 per 100,000, as compared with a rate of 87.2 per 100,000 for elderly widowers (McIntosh, 1992).

An analysis of the ways in which loss of a spouse affects women and men may shed light on some of the possible reasons why widowhood is associated with a lesser risk for death by suicide in elderly females than in males. First of all, women may be more psychologically prepared for widowhood because widowhood is more normative for women than for men; women may also have more access to models and support for positive adjustment.

A second gender difference in the experience of widowhood results from the commonly adopted gender division of household labor. There is evidence that, among married couples, household responsibilities become increasingly segregated over time. Women typically take care of repetitive, menial but essential family tasks, such as cooking, cleaning, and laundry. Men, on the other hand, are usually responsible for infrequent, more prestigious, but relatively less essential family tasks, such as car maintenance, yard work, household repair, and financial management (Blieszner, 1993).

When a spouse dies, the surviving spouse needs to take over the tasks fulfilled by the deceased person. Because domestic tasks usually performed by women are essential to daily living, widows are often better prepared to manage their household independently than are widowers (Blieszner, 1993; Canetto, 1992). Furthermore, widows' self-esteem may benefit from the positive connotation associated with tasks traditionally performed by males: "tasks that require independent decision making provide an opportunity to develop individual autonomy, and success in meeting this challenge can greatly enhance a widow's self-esteem" (Blieszner, 1993, p. 176). Conversely, widowers' self-image may be diminished by the negative connotation associated with tasks previously performed by their wives.

In contrast, since tasks usually performed by men include the management of financial assets, widows are often less well equipped than widowers to manage their economic resources. More importantly, because in many couples men are the sole or main financial providers, losing a spouse exacts a permanent financial toll on widows, but not on widowers (Holden & Smock, 1991). Not only do widows lose access to any income that was previously paid solely to the husband; they may also not receive sufficient life insurance coverage because husbands generally fail to purchase adequate life insurance to protect their wives (Holden & Smock, 1991).

A third important gender difference in the experience of widowhood occurs in the social and emotional domains. According to a review of the literature by Zarit (1980), older women have more emotional connections with friends than do older men. Although men have a greater quantity of social contacts through their employment, these contacts often lack the quality of emotional support that women's contacts have. While women typically name another woman as a confidant, many men view their wives as their sole confidant. Thus, losing a spouse may not disrupt an older woman's support system and emotional functioning to the degree that it might for an older man (Canetto, 1992).

In sum, a number of factors may make widowhood less suicidogenic for elderly women than for elderly men. Because widowhood occurs with greater frequency among elderly women, older women may have more access to positive coping models and support than older men. Elderly women may also be better prepared than elderly men to run their household independently and to maintain supportive emotional relationships. Elderly widows may even benefit from the positive connotation associated with assuming tasks previously performed by their husbands (Canetto, 1992). Other factors, however, appear to make widowhood uniquely stressful for elderly women. The loss of a husband often has a disastrous effect on a woman's income. With this in mind, it is surprising that the suicide mortality rates of elderly widows, although relatively high (8.1 per 100,000 in 1988), when compared with rates of elderly married women (5.3 per 100,000 in 1988), are so much lower than the suicide mortality rates of elderly widowers (87.2 per 100,000 in 1988) (McIntosh, 1992). Taken together, available data indicate that widowhood is associated with a higher suicidal mortality risk for men than for women, a conclusion which is consistent with the data on widowhood and suicidal behaviors throughout adulthood (Gove, 1972; Smith, Mercy, & Conn, 1988).

Living Alone

Living alone is frequently assumed to increase the risk for suicidal behavior among the elderly (Stenback, 1980). Living alone is thought to be suicidogenic because it is assumed to imply isolation. Are elderly women less suicidal than elderly men because they are less likely to live alone? The data on living arrangements by gender do not support this hypothesis. Elderly women are more likely to live alone (Hess, 1990) but are less likely to be suicidal than elderly men. For example, in 1988 there were 6.5 million women age 65 and over living alone, in contrast with fewer than 2 million men in that situation. Women age 65 and over are almost half as likely as their male age peers to be married.

One of the reasons for the lack of correlation between living alone and suicidal mortality in women may be that, for women, living alone does not necessarily mean being isolated. As discussed earlier, older women have more emotionally meaningful connections with friends than older men (Zarit, 1980).

In conclusion, elderly women's low rates of suicidal mortality do not appear to result from more protected living arrangements. Elderly women are more likely to live alone but are less likely to be suicidal than elderly men. Living alone, however, is not the same as being socially isolated. It is possible that elderly women living alone may actually be less isolated than elderly men in the same situation, because elderly women may have more contact with friends and family.

Physical Health

Physical illness and/or disability are often mentioned as risk factors for suicidal behavior in the elderly (De Leo & Diekstra, 1990; Lyons, 1984), especially fatal suicidal behavior (Stenback, 1980). Are elderly women less likely to kill themselves because they enjoy better physical health than elderly men? Evidence from studies of morbidity does not support such a hypothesis. Women have higher rates of physical illness and disability than men (Ory & Warner, 1990; Smith, 1990; Verbrugge, 1990). Women are also more likely than men to suffer from most acute and chronic nonfatal illnesses (Smith, 1990; Verbrugge, 1990), although men are more likely than women to be struck by fatal illnesses (Verbrugge, 1990). According to Verbrugge (1990), women's high rates of illness result from social factors, such as lesser employment, insufficient physical activity, and high levels of stress.

Are elderly women less suicidal because they have better access to medical care than elderly men? According to a review of studies by Hess (1990), older women are less likely than older men to be able to afford costly medical services, to have short hospitalizations, and to have a spouse at home who takes care of them. Although they are less likely to be hospitalized, older women tend to remain longer in acute-care beds and are more likely to be transferred to long-term care facilities for their recovery than older men (Hess, 1990). When discharged, older women are not usually cared for by their husbands; rather, they tend to rely on an adult daughter or another female relative (Hess, 1990; Montgomery & Datwyler, 1990). Older women are also more likely than older men to move to a nursing home. Three out of four nursing home residents are women (Hess, 1990). In conclusion, neither physical health nor medical care appear to account for elderly women's lower rates of suicide mortality.

Mental Health

Mental disorders, especially depression and alcohol abuse/dependence, are often associated with suicidal behavior in the elderly (Stenback, 1980). Are elderly women less suicidal because they enjoy better mental health than elderly men? The relationship between mental health and suicidal behavior in elderly women and men is difficult to ascertain because information on gender patterns of mental disorders in late adulthood is limited (George, 1990). People age 65 and older are less likely to be diagnosed as having nonorganic mental disorders than people under age 65. It has been argued, however, that lower rates of mental disorders in late life reflect the inadequacy of diagnostic criteria based on adult patterns rather than higher levels of psychological well-being (George, 1990).

Although studies of the general population consistently find that women are more likely to suffer from depression than men (Nolen-Hoeksema, 1987), studies of depression in the elderly have produced more variable findings (Brown, Milburn, & Gary, 1992). Although a majority of studies reports higher rates of depression in elderly women than in elderly men, a significant minority does not (Brown et al., 1992). These mixed findings have been interpreted by some (George, 1990) as an indication of increasing gender similarities in rates of depression among older persons.

There is evidence (George, 1990; Nolen-Hoeksema, 1987) that gender similarities in late adulthood depression result from declining rates in women rather than increasing rates in men. Based on these findings, elderly women's exceptionally low rates of death by suicide, as compared with elderly men, cannot be attributed to dramatic gender differences in the rates of depression.

There is, however, evidence indicating that older women tend to become depressed when their health is poor (Thomas & Kelman, 1990), whereas older men are likely to become depressed when they lose a close family member (Siegel & Kuykendall, 1990). With regard to the course of depression, several studies have reported that older men are less likely than older women to recover from depression within a year of diagnosis (Baldwin & Jolley, 1986; Murphy, 1983); however, one study (George, Blazer, & Hughes, 1989) found that adequate social support increased the likelihood of recovery from depression only among older men.

Another condition often associated with suicidal behavior is alcoholism (Canetto, 1992; Stenback, 1980). Chronic alcohol abuse is typically reported in cases of nonfatal suicidal behavior, particularly among males over 65. Chronic alcoholism, however, is more common in suicidal persons under age 65 (Stenback, 1980). Thus, alcohol abuse/dependence may not play a significant role in elderly men's high rates of suicide mortality. In sum, based on the available evidence, it seems unlikely that elderly women's low rates of suicide mortality, as compared with elderly men, are simply the consequence of gender differences in depression and/or alcohol abuse/dependence.

Coping

A promising but insufficiently explored theory is that gender differences in suicidal mortality reflect differences in coping. One version of this theory states that elderly women are less likely to kill themselves because they are more passive, suggestible and malleable than elderly men: "those personality characteristics that are so frequently viewed as psychologically and intellectually crippling to a woman may also be influential in her ability to survive. That is, the passivity, suggestibility, and malleability of women may, ironically, translate into adaptability" (Breed & Huffine, 1979, p. 301). According to Breed and Huffine, older women's adaptability is the result of socialization and developmental experiences involving change. Women's roles often shift during adulthood: "as the child progresses through the developmental stages . . . the demands of the mother's role qualitatively shift and change. In addition, during this period of mothering, the woman may well be in and out of the labor market, further varying her roles" (p. 302). Breed and Huffine also hypothesize that older men's vulnerability to suicidal behavior results from their lack of preparedness in dealing with change. According to them, a man "is not likely to experience major qualitative change after the first few years of adulthood and marriage. In his developmental process, each stage prepares him for the next, and the demands and expectations on him are consistent throughout—he is expected to be assertive, to seek mastery over his environment, and to strive for achievement" (p. 302). A strength of Breed and Huffine's theory is that it recognizes the adaptability and survival potential of women's coping behavior. Its limitations are the use of pejorative labels (e.g., women as passive, suggestible, malleable) and the exclusive focus on women's "passive" strategies.

A more recent version of the coping theory (Canetto, 1992) proposes that elderly women are less likely to kill themselves than elderly men because elderly women are more flexible. Within this theory, flexibility is defined not as "passivity," but as a willingness and capacity to adopt a range of coping strategies, including accommodating to ("being passive"), and transforming ("acting upon"), situations. Older women's capacity to accommodate is thought to involve a sensitivity to others and situational conditions, not just simple "malleability." This theory builds upon evidence suggesting that older women are actually more active, resourceful, and independent in terms of personal self-care and social networking, than older men.

Evidence pertinent to the coping theory is found in a psychological autopsy study of seventy-two elderly (mostly—80% —males) suicides by Clark (1991, 1992). According to Clark (1992), one of the most salient characteristics of these individuals was their inflexible style of coping. This inflexibility was inferred to have been a persistent feature of their personality rather than a recent reaction to difficult life circumstances: a "fundamental adaptational capacity . . . was never present," writes Clark (p. 8). Their sense of self was described as narrow and dependent on "their productivity as a worker" (p. 8). According to Clark, these individuals' coping inflexibility became ominous when life confronted them with acute but ordinary stressors of aging. Interestingly, the life circumstances of these elderly individuals did not involve extraordinary stress, illness, or isolation. Clark's theory, like Breed and Huffine's (1979), emphasizes the suicidal person's failure to accommodate (or to be passive, in Breed and Huffine's language). His case summaries, however, suggest a concomitant failure to take constructive, independent initiative.

In sum, preliminary evidence suggests that styles of coping may play a role in the vulnerability to suicidal behavior. It has been hypothesized that gender differences in socialization and life experiences may affect coping styles and, thus, also the likelihood of self-inflicted death in late adulthood.

Acceptability of Suicide

An increasingly well-documented theory is that variations in rates of suicidal behaviors in different social groups reflect cultural variations in the perceived acceptability of suicidal behaviors (Canetto, 1993; Deluty, 1988–1989a; Deluty, 1988–1989b; Harry, 1983; Johnson, Fitch, Alston, & McIntosh, 1980; Lewis & Shepeard, 1992; Linehan, 1973; Stillion, White, Edwards, & McDowell, 1989; White & Stillion, 1988). It has been suggested that suicidal acts are influenced by perceptions of their social meanings and appropriateness. Are elderly women less likely to kill themselves than elderly men because taking one's life is considered less acceptable for elderly women than for elderly men? The data on attitudes toward suicidal behavior suggest that people hold gender- and age-specific opinions about the meaning and acceptability of different kinds of suicidal behaviors. It is, therefore, likely that these attitudes play a role in elderly women's decisions not to kill themselves.

Fatal Versus Nonfatal Suicidal Behavior

There is evidence indicating that, in the United States, fatal suicidal behavior is considered masculine (Linehan, 1973). Fatal suicidal behavior in females is also evaluated more negatively than fatal suicidal behavior in males (Deluty, 1988–1989b; Shepeard & Lewis, 1992). For example, in Deluty's study, the age and gender of the suicide victim and the context (terminal, chronic, and psychiatric illness) of suicidal death were manipulated to see how these factors affected the acceptability of suicide. One of his main findings was that death by suicide in females was rated as more "wrong," "foolish," "weaker," and less "permissible" than death by suicide in males, independent of context. It is important to note that in Deluty's vignettes, family members and friends were described as opposing suicide. According to him, "a woman who chooses to kill herself may be regarded as particularly 'abnormal' and, therefore, may be evaluated more negatively . . . [because] the decision to suicide . . . [may be] viewed as an abandonment of family" (p. 325). In other words, women who take their own lives, especially women who kill themselves against family wishes, may be perceived negatively because, by taking ownership of their body and control of their destiny, they challenge the assumption of femininity as passive and compliant. In another study (Lewis & Shepeard, 1992), women who killed themselves were viewed as less well-adjusted than men who killed themselves, independent of context.

Conversely, the research on attitudes toward nonfatal suicidal behavior indicates that such acts are viewed as feminine (Linehan, 1973). Furthermore, acts of nonfatal suicidal behavior are perceived as most deserving of sympathy when performed by young women (Stillion et al., 1989). Yet, there is evidence indicating that the decision to kill oneself is viewed as most "understandable" when it is made by older women (Stillion et al., 1989). According to Stillion et al.'s (1989) study, people are most likely to "agree," and least likely to sympathize, with older women's "attempting" to kill themselves. Stillion and associates note that "the elderly do not enjoy a great deal of status and prestige . . . unless they have outstanding attributes, such as wealth and power" (p. 249); therefore, older women, who are most likely to lack status, wealth and power, may not be seen as worthy of survival or sympathy, following a suicidal act. According to Stillion and associates, these findings suggest that the "devaluing of females' lives . . . may become more pronounced in old age" (p. 247).

In addition, it has been found that women and men have different attitudes toward suicidal behavior. Women are less accepting of death by suicide than men (Deluty, 1988–1989b; Johnson et al., 1980) while men are most critical of people—especially other males—who survive a suicidal act (White & Stillion, 1988). According to White and Stillion, "attempted suicide by troubled males may be viewed by other males as violations of the sex-role messages of strength, decisiveness, success, and inexpressiveness" (p. 365).

Finally, the acceptability of death by suicide varies according to the circumstances and (assumed) motivations of the suicidal person. Killing oneself is viewed as most acceptable if the victim is suffering from a terminal physical illness, less acceptable in the case of chronic illness, and least acceptable in the case of "psychiatric illness" (Deluty, 1988–1989a; 1988–1989b). There is also evidence that certain reasons for suicidal behavior are viewed as more understandable and appropriate for women, and other reasons for men. For example, in a study exploring the role of context (athletic vs. relationship failure) in evaluations of suicidal death, Lewis and Shepeard (1992) found that males who killed themselves because of an achievement failure were rated as more well-adjusted than males who killed themselves because of a failed relationship. In addition, a review of the empirical literature on gender and suicidal behavior (Canetto, 1992–1993) indicated that theorists and researchers tend to assume that women are suicidal because of relationship problems, and men because of achievement-related failures. One consequence of these gendered assumptions is that very little research has been conducted concerning the role of extra-personal factors (e.g., poverty, unemployment) in women's suicidal behavior, and interpersonal factors (e.g., failures in personal relationships) in men's suicidal behavior. The lack of information is then mistaken for confirmation of basic differences in the motivations of suicidal women and men.

It is interesting to note that the findings on the acceptability of suicide by gender and age are congruent with epidemiological trends of suicidal behaviors. Nonfatal suicidal behavior is most acceptable and common in young women, and least acceptable and common in men; fatal suicidal behavior is most permissible and frequent in elderly males. Both fatal and nonfatal suicidal behaviors, however, are considered unacceptable for elderly women, a group in which these behaviors are relatively uncommon.

Taken together, the findings on the acceptability of suicidal behaviors suggest that elderly women may be discouraged from killing themselves. First, women in general are expected to "attempt" but "fail" at suicide. Second, "suicide attempts" are seen as most fitting for young adult women. The empirical literature, however, also suggests that people are more likely to agree with the suicidal actions of elderly women than with those of any other group, a finding which has been interpreted as an indication of a devaluing of female life.

Physician-Assisted Suicide

Earlier in this chapter I have suggested that taking one's life may be considered unacceptable in women because it requires self-determined, active choice. If suicidal death could appear passive and compliant, would it be seen as compatible with femininity and, therefore, permissible for women? Would physician-assisted suicide fit such requirements?

Physician-assisted suicide is usually defined as a suicide performed in collaboration with a physician (American Medical Association, 1992). According to the Council on Ethical and Judicial Affairs of the American Medical Association, an assisted suicide involves a physician facilitating a patient's death "by providing its necessary means and/or information to enable the patient to perform the life-ending act" (p. 2229). Individuals are assumed to have made a voluntary and firm request to be assisted in bringing about their own death, basing their decision on a well-informed and dispassionate assessment of their physical health, prospects for recovery, and suffering (Battin, 1991).

The most controversial issue in assisted-suicide is whether one is in fact assisted or pressured into killing oneself. It is precisely to minimize the possibility of misjudgment or coercion that, in countries where physician-assisted suicide is tolerated (e.g., the Netherlands), physicians are expected to consult with a second physician "whose judgment is expected to be independent" (Battin, 1991, p. 299) regarding the physical and mental status of the person requesting an assisted suicide: "every attempt is to be made to rule out depression, psychopathology, pressure from family members, unrealistic fears, and other factors compromising voluntariness" (p. 300). In the Netherlands, pain is not usually considered an acceptable reason for euthanasia because pain can usually be relieved. What is required is "intolerable suffering," meaning suffering that the patient views as intolerable and may include "a fear or unwillingness to endure . . . [the] loss of personal identity that characterizes the end stages of many terminal illnesses" (p. 300).

Systematic data on physician-assisted suicide in the United States are not available because physician-assisted suicide is ethically controversial and generally against the law (Canetto & Hollenshead, 1993). A number of well-publicized cases, however, have been described in newspapers and professional journals, offering a window onto what may be the critical circumstances and issues in United States' physician-assisted suicide. The most well-documented cases to date are those assisted by Dr. Jack Kevorkian. The unique and most problematic feature of Kevorkian's cases, as compared with Dutch patterns, is that Dr. Kevorkian did not consult with another physician to confirm the medical diagnosis and mental status of the persons whose suicide he assisted. An analysis of 20 suicides assisted by Dr. Kevorkian reveals some interesting patterns (Canetto & Hollenshead, 1993). Sixty percent of these assisted suicides involved women. A majority (67%) of these women were in their 40s and 50s. Although poor physical health was mentioned as a factor in all cases, one of these women did not have a terminal illness, and another did not report suffering; all male cases involved an advanced, painful terminal illness. Another well-publicized case, Diane, (Conwell & Caine, 1991; Quill, 1991) also involved a woman being assisted in killing herself by a male physician.

The available evidence on physician-assisted suicide, although unsystematic, suggests that, unlike self-inflicted suicide, physician-assisted suicide may be as frequent, and as socially acceptable, in women as in men. Available data also lead one to wonder whether women may, in fact, be more likely than men to feel obligated to kill themselves, when sick and/or elderly.

Finally, a question raised by available cases is whether physicians in the United States may be more likely to take at face value a woman's decision to suicide than a man's. There are several reasons for considering this possibility. First, people are more likely to agree with an elderly woman's decision to suicide than a man's (Stillion et al., 1989). Second, in the United States more men than women are physicians, and men are more accepting of death by suicide than women (Deluty, 1988–1989; Johnson et al., 1980). Finally, more elderly women than elderly men are poor, widowed, live alone, suffer physical disabilities and chronic diseases, and have limited access to medical insurance and family care. Thus, elderly women may be at greatest risk to be (and/or feel) pressured into assisted suicide in order to relieve others of the financial and emotional burden of care. In a country such as the United States, where medical decisions include financial considerations, and where health care delivery is impersonal, "the line between believing that [a specific sort of care] would not provide benefit to the patient and that it would not provide benefit worth the investment of resources in the patient can be very thin" (Battin, 1991, p. 303).

Summary and Conclusions

There appears to be fairly consistent evidence that people tend to view suicidal behavior in elderly women as particularly aberrant and pathological, and that these views are based on the perceived masculinity of self-inflicted death and the youthfulness of "suicide attempts." It is highly plausible that such prevailing negative views may discourage elderly women from engaging in suicidal behavior. However, there is also evidence suggesting that people are most likely to agree with the suicidal acts of older women. Finally, there is indirect evidence that the disapproval of elderly women's suicidal death may not be as great if death is accomplished with the assistance of a physician. Women are already more likely to experience those conditions—such as advanced age, physical disability, chronic health problems, poverty, widowhood, living alone—which in this country are viewed as diminishing the quality of life (Bell, 1992; Van Der Wal, 1993). If, in fact, it is confirmed that assisted suicide is perceived as compatible with femininity, then women may be at greater risk than men of viewing themselves (and being viewed by others) as acceptable candidates for assisted suicide.

SUMMARY AND IMPLICATIONS

Elderly women are less likely to kill themselves than elderly men. Are elderly women protected from the conditions traditionally assumed to increase the risk for suicidal behavior in the elderly in general?

From available evidence, it does not appear that elderly women enjoy any particular advantages over elderly men, at least with regard to the suicide risk factors most commonly mentioned in the literature. In fact, elderly women are more likely to be exposed to the conditions (e.g., stressful retirement, limited financial resources, widowhood, living alone, poor health) which, in elderly men, have been thought to precipitate suicidal behavior. For women, the transition to retirement can be difficult, perhaps even more difficult than for men. Elderly women tend to live alone following divorce and widowhood. They also tend to have fewer financial resources than elderly men. Elderly women have higher rates of physical illnesses and disabilities than elderly men, but are less likely to be able to afford costly medical services; furthermore, elderly women are less likely to have a spouse who can take care of them at home. Finally, elderly women are more likely than elderly men to live in a nursing home. In sum, traditional theories do not explain women's low rates of suicidal mortality in late adulthood. One reason traditional theories do not account for elderly women's experiences is that they have been developed based on elderly men's suicidal patterns and life experiences.

Two less frequently mentioned theories of elderly suicidal behavior focus on coping and the acceptability of suicide. These two theories articulate specific hypotheses for the gender differences in suicidal behaviors. According to these two theories, elderly women may enjoy an advantage over elderly men with regard to coping flexibility and the social acceptability of suicide. While the coping theory remains largely unexplored, the notion that the acceptability of suicidal behaviors is gender- and age-specific has received support from a variety of independent studies. Put concisely, killing oneself is perceived as masculine and active, and therefore unacceptable in women, while nonfatal suicidal behavior is seen as feminine but youthful, and therefore inappropriate for elderly women. The possibility that suicidal behavior may become acceptable in older women if performed with the assistance of a physician has been suggested, based on the available data on physician-assisted suicide.

This review of the literature has revealed that the most popular theories of elderly suicidal behavior do not account for women's experiences. In fact, the predictions one would make based on such presumably general theories conflict with elderly women's patterns of suicidal behavior. As in many other domains of social research, in studies of suicide "women are alienated from their own experience by having to frame that experience in terms of men's conceptual schemes" (Riger, 1992, p. 733). It is apparent that traditional theories will need to be revised and expanded to capture women's experiences. It is also clear that without the benefit of information about women, traditional theories of suicidal behavior may distort the meaning of men's behavior. For example, the data on elderly women lead one to wonder whether retirement should continue to be considered a suicide risk factor for elderly men. Based on the data on women, strong consideration should be given to men's socialized dependence on women for personal care and socioemotional tasks, and the devaluation of such tasks.

This literature review has also shown that theories which consider gender—such as the coping theory and the acceptability of suicidal behaviors theory—help in articulating more complex questions about the suicidal behavior of both women and men. An even greater sophistication in our theories and research methodologies will be achieved when not only gender experiences but also ethnic, racial, socioeconomic, or sexual orientation experiences will be considered.

ACKNOWLEDGMENTS

A shortened version of this chapter was presented at the pre-conference seminar, *Suicide and the Elderly*, held at the annual convention of the American Association of Suicidology, San Francisco, CA, April, 1993. This chapter benefited from comments and suggestions by Alicia Skinner Cook, Sandra Deraney-Reilly, Jeremy Gersovitz, Sandra Haynes, Patricia L. Kaminski, and David B. Wohl.

REFERENCES

American Medical Association, Council on Ethical and Judicial Affairs. (1992). Decisions near the end of life. *Journal of the American Medical Association, 267,* 2229–2233.

Arber, S., & Ginn, J.(1991). *Gender and later life.* Newbury Park, CA: Sage.

Atchley, R. C., & Corbett, S. L. (1977). Older women and jobs. In L. Troll, J. Israel, & K. Israel (Eds.), *Looking ahead: A woman's guide to the problems and joys of growing older* (pp. 121–125). Englewood Cliffs, NJ: Prentice-Hall.

Baldwin, R. C., & Jolley, D. J. (1986). The prognosis of depression in old age. *British Journal of Psychiatry, 149,* 574–583.

Baruch, G. K., Biener, L., & Barnett, R. C. (1987). Women and gender in research on work and family stress. *American Psychologist, 42,* 130–136.

Battin, M. P. (1991). Euthanasia: The way we do it, the way they do it. *Journal of Pain and Symptom Management, 6,* 298–305.

Bell, N. K. (1992). If age becomes a standard for rationing health care. . . . In H. B. Holmes & L. M. Purdy (Eds.), *Feminist perspectives in medical ethics* (pp. 82–90). Bloomington, IN: Indiana University Press.

Blieszner, R. (1993). A socialist-feminist perspective on widowhood. *Journal of Aging Studies, 7*(2), 171–182.

Breed, W., & Huffine, C. L. (1979). Sex differences in suicide among older white Americans: A role and developmental approach. In C. J. Kaplan (Ed.), *Psychopathology of aging* (pp. 289–309). New York: Academic Press.

Brown, D. R., Milburn, N. G., & Gary, L. E. (1992). Symptoms of depression among older African-Americans: An analysis of gender differences. *The Gerontologist, 32,* 780–795.

Canetto, S. S. (1992). Gender and suicide in the elderly. *Suicide and Life-Threatening Behavior, 22,* 80–97.

Canetto, S. S. (1992–1993). She died for love and he for glory: Gender myths of suicidal behavior. *Omega, 26,* 1–17.

Canetto, S. S., & Hollenshead, J. D. (1993). *Gender and physician-assisted suicide: The Kevorkian cases.* Manuscript submitted for publication.

Canetto, S. S. (1994). Gender issues in counseling the suicidal elderly. In D. Lester & M. Tallmer (Eds.), *Now I lay me down: Suicide in the elderly* (pp. 88–105). Philadelphia, PA: Charles Press.

Canetto, S. S., & Lester, D. (1995). The epidemiology of women's suicidal behavior. In S. S. Canetto & D. Lester (Eds.), *Women and suicidal behavior* (pp. 35–57). New York: Springer.

Clark, D. C. (1991, January). *Suicide among the elderly.* Unpublished final report to the AARP Andrus Foundation, Rush-Presbyterian-St. Luke's Medical Center, Chicago.

Clark, D. C. (1992, April). *Narcissistic crises of aging and suicidal despair.* Paper presented at the 25th Annual Conference of the American Association of Suicidology, Chicago.

Conwell, Y., & Caine, E. D. (1991, October). Rational suicide and the right to die: Reality and myth. *New England Journal of Medicine, 325,* 1100–1103.

De Leo, D., & Diekstra, R. F. W. (1990). *Depression and suicide in late life.* Toronto: Hogrefe & Huber.

Deluty, R. L. (1988–1989a). Physical illness, psychiatric illness, and the acceptability of suicide. *Omega, 19,* 79–91.

Deluty, R. L. (1988–1989b). Factors affecting the acceptability of suicide. *Omega, 19,* 315–326.

George, L. K. (1990). Gender, age and psychiatric disorders. *Generations, 14,* 22–27.

George, L. K., Blazer, D. G., & Hughes, D. C. (1989). Social support and the outcome of major depression. *British Journal of Psychiatry, 154,* 478–485.

Gove, W. R. (1972). Sex, marital status and suicide. *Journal of Health and Social Behavior, 13,* 204–213.

Harry, J. (1983). Parasuicide, gender and gender deviance. *Journal of Health and Social Behavior, 24,* 350–361.

Harding, S. (1991). *Whose science? Whose knowledge? Thinking from women's lives.* Ithaca: Cornell University Press.

Hatch, L. R. (1987). Research on men's and women's retirement attitudes: Implications for retirement policy. In E. F. Borgatta & R. J. V. Montgomery (Eds.), *Critical issues in aging policy: Linking research and values* (pp. 129–160). Newbury Park, CA: Sage

Hatch, L. R. (1990). Gender and work at mid-life and beyond. *Generations, 14,* 48–52.

Hatch, L. R. (1992). Gender differences in orientation toward retirement from paid labor. *Gender and Society, 6,* 66–85.

Hess, B. H. (1990). The demographic parameters of gender and aging. *Generations, 14,* 12–16.

Holden, K. C., & Smock, P. J. (1991). The economic cost of marital dissolution: Why do women bear a disproportionate cost? *Annual Review of Sociology, 17,* 51–78.

Johnson, D., Fitch, S. D., Alston, J. P., & McIntosh, W. A. (1980). Acceptance of conditional suicide and euthanasia among older Americans. *Suicide and Life-Threatening Behavior, 10,* 157–166.

Kirsling, R. A. (1986). Review of suicide among elderly persons. *Psychological Reports, 59,* 359–366.

Kushner, H. I. (1995). Women and suicidal behavior: Epidemiology, gender and lethality in historical perspective. In S. S. Canetto & D. Lester (Eds.), *Women and suicidal behavior* (pp. 11–34). New York: Springer.

Lewis, R. J., & Shepeard, G. (1992). Inferred characteristics of successful suicides as function of gender and context. *Suicide and Life-Threatening Behavior, 22,* 187–198.

Linehan, M. M. (1973). Suicide and attempted suicide: Study of perceived sex differences. *Perceptual and Motor Skills, 37,* 31–34.

Lowenthal, M. F., Thurnher, M., Chiriboga, D. A., & Associates (1975). *Four stages of life: A comparative study of women and men facing transitions.* San Francisco: Jossey-Bass.

Lyons, M. J. (1984). Suicide in later life: Some putative causes with implications for prevention. *Journal of Community Psychology, 12*, 379–388.

McIntosh, J. L. (1992). Epidemiology of suicide in the elderly. *Suicide and Life-Threatening Behavior, 22*, 15–33.

Montgomery, R. J. V., & Datwyler, M. M. (1990). Women and men in the caregiving role. *Generations, 14*, 34–38.

Murphy, E. (1983). The prognosis of depression in old age. *British Journal of Psychiatry, 142*, 111–119.

Neugarten, B. L. (1970). Adaptation and the life cycle. *Journal of Geriatric Psychiatry, 4*, 71–87.

Nolen-Hoeksema, S. (1987). Sex differences in unipolar depression: Evidence and theory. *Psychological Bulletin, 101*, 259–282.

Ory, M. G., & Warner, H. R. (1990). Introduction: Gender, health, and aging: Not just a women's issue. In M. G. Ory & H. R. Warner (Eds.), *Gender, health, and longevity* (pp. xxiii-xxix). New York: Springer.

Quill, T. E. (1991, March). Death and dignity: A case of individualized decision making. *New England Journal of Medicine, 324*, 691–694.

Riger, S. (1992). Epistemological debates, feminist voices: Science, social values, and the study of women. *American Psychologist, 47*, 730–740.

Siegel, J. M., & Kuykendall, D. H. (1990). Loss, widowhood, and psychological distress among the elderly. *Journal of Consulting and Clinical Psychology, 58*, 519–524.

Smith, D. W. E. (1990). The biology of gender and aging. *Generations, 14*, 7–11.

Smith, J. C., Mercy, J. A., & Conn, J. M. (1988). Marital status and the risk for suicide. *American Journal of Public Health, 78*, 78–80.

Stenback, A. (1980). Depression and suicidal behavior in old age. In J. E. Birren & B. Sloane (Eds.), *Handbook of mental health and aging* (pp. 616–652). Englewood Cliffs, NJ: Prentice Hall.

Stillion, J. M., White, H., Edwards, P. J., & McDowell, E. E. (1989). Ageism and sexism in suicide attitudes. *Death Studies, 13*, 247–261.

Suter, B. (1976). Suicide and women. In B. B. Wolman & K. H. Krauss (Eds.), *Between survival and suicide* (pp. 129–161). New York: Gardner Press.

Thomas, C., & Kelman, H. R. (1990). Gender and the use of health services among elderly persons. In M. G. Ory & H. R. Warner (Eds.), *Gender, health, and longevity* (pp. 137–156). New York: Springer.

Van Der Wal, G. (1993). Unrequested termination of life: Is it permissible? *Bioethics, 7*, 330–339.

Verbrugge, L. M. (1990). The twain meet: Empirical explanations for sex differences in health and mortality. In M. G. Ory & H. R. Warner (Eds.), *Gender, health, and longevity* (pp. 159–199). New York: Springer.

White, H., & Stillion, J. M. (1988). Sex differences in attitudes toward suicide: Do males stigmatize males? *Psychology of Women Quarterly, 12*, 357–272.

Zarit, S. H. (1980). *Aging and mental disorders: Psychological approaches to assessment and treatment*. New York: The Free Press.

Part V *Pre*vention, *Inter*vention, and *Post*vention

■ 18
Suicidal Women: Prevention and Intervention Strategies

Silvia Sara Canetto

The literature on interventions for suicidal behaviors is unique in four respects. First, it rarely deals with questions of primary prevention, that is how to reduce the incidence (the number of new cases) of suicidal behavior. A majority of this literature focuses on secondary prevention, namely the reduction of distress and impairment following a suicidal act, or on tertiary prevention, namely the prevention of repeated suicidal behavior.

Second, the intervention literature for suicidal behaviors is quite meager, as compared to the intervention literature for related disorders, such as depression. As Lesse argued in the mid-1970s in a paper entitled "The range of therapies in the treatment of severely depressed suicidal patients," there continues to be a "dangerous void in the development of pragmatic guidelines and techniques in the management of patients who have suicidal ideas" (1975, p. 308). One reason for this void may be that suicidologists have tended to focus on suicide mortality, a rarer and mostly male phenomenon, rather than on nonfatal suicidal behaviors, a more common and typically female phenomenon (Lester, 1989).

Third, a majority of the intervention literature focuses on "management" and "pragmatic guidelines" for suicidal behavior (Harris & Meyers, 1968; Lesse, 1975) rather than on treatment; on "reasonable and prudent" practice and on "standard[s] of due care" (Bongar, 1991, p. 51), especially as concerns the decision to hospitalize, rather than on the content and context of the suicidal individual's distress or the process of psychotherapy. This focus on "management" is at least partially justified by the potential liability, for the therapist, of a client's suicidal death. Yet, it seems there ought to be greater attention devoted to treatment and client issues beyond the important, but narrow, commitment to preventing a suicidal act. As Fremouw, de Perczel, and Ellis (1990) noted, once the suicidal crisis is resolved, it is generally assumed that the treatment of the suicidal person "will be resumed as with any other client" (p. 98).

Finally, the intervention literature does not explicitly deal with the fact that the prototypical suicidal person is a woman. In fact, many authors (e.g., Olin, 1976; Tabachnick, 1961b) use generic male pronouns to refer to the suicidal person even though they feature only females in their case examples. A majority of the treatment literature simply ignores what Jack (1992) considers the most important question of nonfatal suicidal behavior: Why women? Why is nonfatal suicidal behavior more common among women than men in most industrialized countries?

The focus of this chapter is on the primary prevention and treatment (secondary and tertiary prevention) of suicidal behavior in women. Risk factors will be briefly summarized. Primary prevention issues will be discussed next. The treatment literature will then be reviewed and critiqued.

RISK FACTORS

National and international studies indicate that nonfatal suicidal behavior is most prevalent among working class, uneducated, unemployed, impoverished young females with a history of severely neglectful and/or abusive relationships (see Canetto & Lester, 1995, for a review). In the United States, nonfatal suicidal behavior is perceived as feminine. Conversely, fatal suicidal behavior in females is evaluated more negatively than fatal suicidal behavior in males, independent of context. Finally, there is evidence to indicate that in the United States, being suicidal in response to relationship difficulties is perceived as congruent with femininity (see Canetto, 1991, 1992–1993, 1994; Stillion, 1995, for reviews).

PRIMARY PREVENTION

Some of the most interesting findings regarding the primary prevention of suicidal behavior come from studies of help-seeking patterns. A number of researchers (Hawton & Blackstock, 1976; Hawton, O'Grady, Osborn, & Cole, 1982; Turner, 1980) have reported that people who engage in suicidal behavior typically contact a physician within a month of the act. Most of these individuals report social and interpersonal difficulties but are treated with psychotropic drugs, which they overdose on a short time later.

Several primary prevention studies have sought to evaluate the effectiveness of suicide prevention services. Studies conducted in the United States, West Germany and the former Yugoslavia (Miller, Coombs, Leeper, & Barton, 1984; Tekavcic-Grad, Farberow, Zavasnik, Mocnik, & Korenjak, 1988; Wolfersdorf, Blattner, Grober, Nelson, & Dalton-Taylor, 1989) indicate that women make the most use of suicide prevention telephone services. It has, therefore, been of interest whether these services are effective in reducing women's rates of suicidal behaviors. A study of a metropolitan community in the United States found that suicide prevention phone services reduced the rates of mortality by suicide in White women under age 25 (Miller, Coombs, Leeper, & Barton, 1984). A meta-analysis of the results of 18 studies (Dew, Bromet, Brent, & Greenhouse, 1987), however, did not produce evidence that suicide prevention centers affect community suicide mortality rates. It would be interesting to know whether suicide prevention centers affect community rates of nonfatal suicidal behavior.

In sum, available primary prevention studies indicate that contact with physicians and/or suicide prevention services may not affect rates of suicidal behaviors. In fact, it appears that contact with physicians may facilitate access to suicidal method in individuals who plan to poison themselves. It could be argued that it is too late to prevent suicidal behavior when the person is already thinking about suicide, and that it may be more effective to focus on preventing the conditions leading to suicidal ideation.

In the field of public health, it is generally agreed that primary prevention works best when it focuses on the distal causes of a disorder (the "cause of causes"), rather than on proximal "opportunistic" precipitants (see Albee & Canetto, in press, for a review). General ("macro") programs are considered more effective than targeted ("micro") interventions, such as crisis services. In suicidology, macro primary prevention programs have been proposed concerning male suicidal behavior. For example, McIntosh (1992) has argued that a reduction in elderly White male suicide mortality will require a focus on their economic security needs and on society's negative attitudes toward aging. A similar kind of macro analysis could be applied to understanding and preventing female nonfatal suicidal behavior. Yet one rarely sees proposals for macro suicide prevention programs that address risk factors for suicidal behavior in women, specifically unemployment and the cultural reinforcement of nonfatal suicidal behavior as feminine coping (Canetto, 1992–1993; Kaplan & Klein, 1989).

SECONDARY AND TERTIARY PREVENTION

Most of the literature on secondary and tertiary prevention of nonfatal suicidal behavior focuses on individual interventions, such as medication, electroconvulsive therapy, or individual psychotherapy. A few authors have advocated family therapy (Richman, 1986) or group psychotherapy (Farberow, 1968; Linehan, Armstrong, Suarez, Allmon, & Heard, 1991). As was the case with primary prevention, secondary and tertiary prevention programs focusing on social, economic, and cultural factors are conspicuously absent.

INDIVIDUAL INTERVENTIONS

The earliest, and most commonly described, interventions for suicidal behavior draw on the assumption that nonfatal suicidal behavior is a private problem, the expression of an individual disorder or deficiency (Birtchnell, 1983; Maltsberger & Buie, 1974, 1989; Schwartz, Flinn, & Slawson, 1974; Tabachnick, 1961b). Where these interventions differ is in the presumed sources of such individual pathology, whether biochemical imbalance, intrapsychic deficits, personality disorders, irrational cognitions or impaired problem-solving.

Somatic Interventions

One group of treatments commonly described in the literature are somatic interventions. These interventions are based on the assumption that the etiology of suicidal behavior and/or its resolution depend on biological factors. Somatic treatments for suicidal behavior include medication and electroconvulsive therapy (Harris & Myers, 1968; Kaplan & Sadock, 1988; Lesse, 1975; Reid, 1989). Antidepressant or antipsychotic drugs are the medications most often recommended for suicidal patients (see Goldblatt & Schatzberg, 1990; Hirsch, Walsh, & Draper, 1983, for reviews).

Psychological Interventions

The second most discussed intervention for suicidal behavior is individual psychotherapy. Psychodynamically oriented psychotherapy is the approach most commonly proposed; behavioral and cognitive approaches have also been suggested.

Psychodynamically Oriented Psychotherapies

Of all individual therapies, psychodynamically oriented psychotherapy has received the most coverage in the clinical literature (Birtchnell, 1983; Hendin, 1951, 1981; Lesse, 1975; Maltsberger & Buie, 1974, 1989; Olin, 1976; Schwartz et al., 1974; Tabachnick, 1961b; Zinberg, 1989). Psychodynamic interventions are based on the assumption that the basic fault of suicidal persons is intrapsychic (see Kaplan and Klein, 1989, for a dissenting psychodynamic perspective). Specifically, suicidal behavior is assumed to be a manifestation of problems in autonomy and individuation. It is postulated that the suicidal person has suffered from some deficiency or disruption in nurturance, and that such deficiency and/or disruption has led to the development of an oral dependent personality. The family of suicidal individuals is often caricatured to feature a dominant mother and an inadequate and distant father (e.g., Simpson, 1976). Yet, it is the suicidal person's mother who is usually blamed for the suicidal behavior, as is the case with many other psychological disorders (see Caplan & Hall-McCorquodale, 1985, for a review). For example, according to Tabachnick (1961b, p. 64) a person "who makes a suicide attempt has had considerable developmental difficulty in terms of achieving a satisfactory relationship with his [*sic*] mother." This early difficulty with mother is assumed to lead to "the development of a strong passive and oral orientation on the part of the patient" and ultimately to the suicidal act, which presumably occurs when the patient symbolically re-experiences a "rejection by a mother figure" (p. 64).

Diagnostically, the suicidal person is often labeled as dependent (Birtchnell, 1983), immature (Kiev, 1975), borderline (Novotny, 1972), or hysterical (Schrut & Michels, 1974). For example, Birtchnell, in a paper entitled "Psychotherapeutic considerations in the management of the suicidal patient" (1983) writes that "suicidal behavior is a common feature of the dependent personality. Dependent individuals respond to stress by adopting the posture of helplessness, clinging, asking to be told what to do, and wanting to be looked after" (p. 29).

A recurring theme (Furst & Ostow, 1979; Novotny, 1972; Simpson, 1976) is that suicidal behavior is "masochistically" gratifying. Some authors even suggest that self-cutting may represent the symbolic fulfillment of an incestual wish: "the question arises whether the 'self-penetration,' which is one aspect of the self-cutting also represents symbolically the wished for and feared penetration by the father" writes Novotny in a paper on suicidal self-cutters (p. 508). Having noted that a high proportion of self-cutters are women, Novotny concludes that "one might raise the question whether the close relation of the typical female introceptive mode to the incorporative mode might account for the higher freqency [*sic*] of this symptom in women" (p. 511).

Many psychoanalytically oriented clinicians allude to having observed that the relationships of suicidal persons tend to be uncaring and even hostile. For example, according to Schwartz (1979) "the patient is a person with needs for mothering which are *inadequately* [emphasis added] met" (p. 67). In a case example, Maltsberger and Buie (1989) report that "only in retrospect was it noticed that this dependent woman was *without support* [emphasis added] in her social and family context" (p. 288).

Yet, paradoxically, the recognition that the suicidal person has experienced inadequate emotional nurturance is often followed by a warning against providing such nurturance in therapy. Schwartz, Flinn, and Slawson (1974) postulate that "in the person with a suicidal character the need for mothering is expressed as suicidality. The mothering response may avert the suicidal impulse but does so at the expense of reinforcing the suicidal character structure" (p. 206); since, according to them, "as a means of coercing others to catch him [*sic*], he [*sic*] must be helped to recognize that the treatment plan will gradually remove some of those catching arms, leaving him [*sic*] with increasing responsibility for not letting himself [*sic*] go" (pp. 204–206). Along the same lines, it has been argued that "hospitalization of suicidal characters should be as brief as possible" because "prolonged hospitalization fosters precisely the kind of dependency that promotes the suicidal character formation" (Schwartz, 1979, p. 69).

In sum, it seems that psychodynamically oriented psychotherapists are exhorted to replicate the unempathic environment suicidal individuals are said to have experienced in their personal relationships. The insistence that the suicidal person be responsible and independent is striking because psychodynamic approaches are often associated with the theory that the therapist should foster a temporary dependence and provide a nurturing "corrective" emotional experience.

An alternative psychodynamically oriented perspective on treatment of suicidal women is offered by Kaplan and Klein (1989). Like others, they argue that suicidal behavior in women often has an interpersonal matrix and may represent a "plea for mutual engagement" (p. 260). Instead of viewing such a "plea" as a symptom of manipulative dependence, they define it as a manifestation of women's "interacting sense of self": "because they experience action-in-relationship as their primary source of growth, women will take major steps to avoid breaking a connection. This involves taking responsibility for the relationship, including responsibility for relational difficulties" (p. 259). According to Kaplan and Klein, "women will act so as to preserve a relationship, not because of dependency on the other or inadequacy in other realms, but because connection provides them with the fullest context for their own active participation in a growth enhancing situation" (p. 259). Suicidal women, they write, are often "seeking connection with others in a context that is neither mutual nor empathic. Their behavior is often experienced as controlling by those who, for their own reasons, need to resist it" (p. 271). Kaplan and Klein therefore recommend that psychotherapy provide suicidal women with an opportunity for a nurturing emotional experience where they may learn to feel deserving of a mutually caring connection.

Behavioral and Cognitive Therapies

Behavioral theories and therapies of suicidal behavior have been proposed by Frederick and Resnik (1971), Bostock and Williams (1974), and Liberman and Eckman (1981). The common theme across behavioral approaches is that suicidal behaviors are coping responses that are learned and then maintained by reinforcing social consequences. Consequently, behavioral treatments tend to focus on learning non-self-destructive coping responses. Behavioral treatments usually consist of a package of interventions targeting behavioral deficits or excesses. For example, Liberman and Eckman's treatment package for chronic suicidal behavior featured social skills training, anxiety management training, and contracting of responsibilities and privileges between suicidal persons and family members.

Cognitive approaches (Ellis, 1986) deal with suicidal behavior in much the same way as with depression, namely by identifying and correcting dysfunctional cognitive processes, such as "misinterpretation of events, irrational beliefs, and logical errors" (p. 126). According to a review of empirical studies by Ellis, the value of a cognitive approach is underscored by the association between suicidal behavior and cognitive rigidity, as manifested through dichotomous thinking, impaired problem solving, and preoccupation with the present. There is evidence indicating that hospitalized suicidal individuals are less capable of active interpersonal problem solving (Linehan, Camper, Chiles, Strosahl, & Shearin, 1987, $N = 139$, 59% females; Schotte & Clum, 1987, $N = 50$; percentage females unknown; Schotte, Cools, & Payvar, 1990, $N = 36$, 61% females); hospitalized suicidal individuals ($N = 60$, 56% females) were also found to have significantly more stable and global attributions for negative events than hospitalized nonsuicidal controls (Jack & Williams, 1991a). Recommendations for cognitive therapy with suicidal individuals therefore include patient education concerning dichotomous thinking, interpersonal problem solving training, and disputation of irrational beliefs about the self, the world, and the future (Ellis, 1986).

Combined cognitive-behavioral treatments emphasizing the development of problem solving skills (Linehan, 1987; Linehan, Armstrong, Suarez, Allmon, & Heard, 1991; Nidiffer, 1980; Salkovskis, Atha, & Storer, 1990) are the latest development in this literature. These treatments take a psychoeducational, directive, problem-oriented approach. The suicidal person is taught how to identify problems, generate solutions and goals, develop strategies, and assess outcomes. Two models have been proposed. The first model (Salkovskis et al., 1990) is short-term (five sessions) and very focused, involving a combination of individual sessions and homework assignments. The second model (Linehan et al., 1991) is long-term (one year) and addresses a wide range of problems through a variety of techniques, delivered via a combination of individual and group therapy, and between-sessions phone contact.

GROUP, COUPLE, AND FAMILY INTERVENTIONS

Because prevalent conceptual frameworks assume that suicidal behavior is a manifestation of individual psychopathology, there have been very few proposals for interventions focusing on contextual factors. Available contextual interventions focus on the suicidal individual's personal relationships. With the exception of Linehan's group therapy (Linehan, 1987; Linehan et al., 1991), these interpersonal interventions are typically informed by traditional psychodynamic or system perspectives. No proposals have been made for interventions focusing on contextual factors other than interpersonal relationships, such as unemployment or poverty.

Group Psychotherapy

One of the earliest papers on group psychotherapy of suicidal individuals is Farberow's (1968). He described a brief and crisis-oriented group treatment and reported "a clinical impression of usefulness and significance" (p. 340). More recently, Linehan and colleagues (Linehan, 1987; Linehan et al., 1991) incorporated group psychotherapy in their manualized package of intervention, dubbed dialectical behavior therapy. In Linehan's system, group therapy was held once a week for a year and focused on the development of interpersonal skills, stress tolerance, and emotional regulation skills.

Couple and family therapy

Several authors have advocated involving significant others in therapy (e.g., Bedrosian, 1986; Kiev, 1975; Lesse, 1975; Linehan, 1981; Moss & Hamilton, 1956). Only Richman (1986), however, has written in great detail about family therapy for suicidal individuals. His perspective focuses on traditional psychodynamic and system concepts of separation–individuation. According to him, characteristics of families with suicide potential include "an inability to accept necessary change . . . role . . . conflicts . . . a disturbed family structure . . . unbalanced . . . relationships . . . affective difficulties . . . transactional difficulties . . . [and] . . . an intolerance for crises" (p. 58). His suggestions for family therapy are to include as many relatives as possible, to inquire about family members' death wishes, to develop a healing relationship based on commitment and hope, and to monitor transferential and countertransferential processes.

THE THERAPEUTIC RELATIONSHIP

The quality of the therapeutic relationship has long been recognized as an important predictor of psychotherapy outcome: "the positive quality of the relational bond . . . is more clearly related to patient improvement than any of the particular treatment techniques used by the therapist" wrote Kaplan in a review of the literature on gender and psychotherapy (1987, p. 12). What are the characteristics of the relationship between suicidal persons and care providers, and how may this relationship affect outcome?

Studies have shown that care-providers (emergency room personnel, physicians, psychiatric residents, and nurses) tend to be unsympathetic and even hostile toward suicidal persons (Ansel & McGee, 1971; Dressler, Prusoff, Mark, & Shapiro, 1975; Hawton, Marsack, & Fagg, 1981; Patel, 1975; Ramon, Bancroft, & Skrimshire, 1975). Two studies (Ansel & McGee, 1971; Ramon et al., 1975) found that negative attitudes were most likely to be elicited by persons who appeared to be less "serious" in their intent to die. For example, in Ramon et al.'s study of nurses and physicians using a case vignette method, physicians were especially unsympathetic toward, and unwilling to help, patients whose suicidal behavior was depicted as having interpersonal motives, such as the wish to influence others or to make others sorry (motives usually attributed to women), in contrast to patients with depressive motives, such as the wish to die or escape (motives usually attributed to men). Taken together, these studies suggest that care providers may not consider that a woman would have to feel completely powerless and desperate to attempt to influence a significant other via a suicidal act. Given that many suicidal women are involved in hostile and abusive relationships, the possibility that care-providers may be unsympathetic and unwilling to help is particularly ominous.

Care providers' lack of empathy for the interpersonal difficulties of suicidal individuals appears to be compounded by their tendency to assume that most nonfatal suicidal acts have "interpersonal" motives. According to evidence reviewed by Zich (1984), care-providers often assume that nonfatal suicidal behavior is "a sham, a way to manipulate people who could not otherwise be manipulated" (p. 37). In fact, "manipulative" is a ubiquitous term in the nonfatal suicidal behavior literature (Zich, 1984). Empirical studies by Bancroft and colleagues (Bancroft, Skrimshire, & Simkin, 1976; Bancroft, Hawton, Simkin, Kingston, & Whitwell, 1979) reveal that a majority of psychiatrists, but only a minority of suicidal persons, listed interpersonal motivations, such as trying to influence someone. Most suicidal persons explained their actions in terms of despair, not knowing what to do about a terrible situation, or "a terrible state of mind."

Clinical analyses of long-term interpersonal processes between clinicians and suicidal persons (transference and countertransference) (e.g., Tabachnick, 1961b) show that clinicians tend to portray suicidal persons in a critical manner. Suicidal persons are labeled "uncooperative" (Maltsberger & Buie, 1989, p. 287), "gesturing" (Maltsberger & Buie, 1989, p. 290), provocative (Maltsberger & Buie, 1974) and spiteful (Hendin, 1951). Tabachnick (1974, quoted in Zich, 1984, p. 37) summed it up this way: "after all, suicidal people are often hostile, nagging, and irritating individuals who relate to others in an ambivalent fashion." According to Maltsberger and Buie (1974), suicidal patients stimulate "countertransference hate . . . a mixture of aversion and malice" in therapists (p. 625): "suicidal patients tend to evoke the sadism of others; often they can only maintain ties in the sadomasochistic mode. . . . [and attempt] to arouse hate in others through the seductive and inductive conduct known as provocation" (p. 626).

In this clinical literature the suicidal person is often referred to as a "she" and the therapist as a "he." The gender and power dynamics of the therapeutic relationship are, however, not addressed except in a stereotypical fashion; for example, Maltsberger and Buie (1974) write that "the patient is likely to become unconsciously equated in the therapist's mind with the adversary mother of his anal stage; he will be tempted into a fight to 'show her who is boss' " (p. 631).

In sum, empirical and clinical evidence indicates that care-providers tend to have critical and rejecting reactions toward suicidal persons. This negativity appears to be based on a misunderstanding of the motivations of suicidal persons, as well as a lack of empathy for their powerlessness in relationships. Given the importance of a positive therapeutic relationship for the client's recovery, it is not surprising that treatments of suicidal individuals have not typically been successful, as the evidence reviewed in the next section shows.

EFFECTIVENESS OF TREATMENT INTERVENTIONS

According to a 1982 review of studies of treatment effectiveness by Hirsch, Walsh, and Draper, there is little evidence that "any particular intervention strategy is better than any other for preventing repeat parasuicide," although it appears that "prolonged and repeated contact in any form, by telephone or interview, may be of benefit" (p. 310). Evidence from two recent controlled studies using a cognitive-behavioral, problem-solving approach is consistent with previous trends. In one study (Salkovskis et al., 1990) ($N = 20$, 58% females), suicidal patients at high risk for suicide were assigned to either cognitive-behavioral problem-solving treatment or a "treatment as usual" control condition. Suicidal patients in the experimental group showed more improvement on all problems and had a lower rate of repetition at 6 months, but not at the 18-month follow-up. In the second study (Linehan et al., 1991), a group of severely dysfunctional chronically parasuicidal women ($N = 44$) was divided between a manualized cognitive-behavioral treatment and a "treatment as usual" control condition. Progress was assessed every four months, while treatment was in progress. At most assessment points suicidal women in the experimental group had fewer and less medically severe episodes of suicidal behavior, were more likely to stay in individual therapy, and had fewer inpatient days. However, since no post-treatment follow-up data were collected, it is impossible to assess the stability of the experimental group's gains, as compared with the control group.

CONCLUSIONS AND RECOMMENDATIONS

The literature on the treatment of suicidal behaviors offers some diversity of perspectives on management and intervention techniques. One recurrent limitation, however, is the disregard of gender and contextual factors in suicidal behavior. Only two treatment approaches (Jack & Williams, 1991b; Kaplan & Klein, 1989) were designed based on the recognition that suicidal behavior is most common among young adult women from economically and educationally disadvantaged backgrounds with a history of emotional and/or physical abuse.

A second recurrent weakness of the treatment literature is its neglect of the social meanings of suicidal behaviors. Treatments have tended to overlook how suicidal behavior is culturally meaningful and socially structured (Cloward & Piven, 1979; Heshusius, 1980; Johnson, 1979). For example, we know that in the United States nonfatal suicidal behavior is perceived as congruent with youthful femininity (see Canetto, 1991, 1920–1993, 1994; Stillion, 1995, for reviews). Thus, such behavior in young adult women can not be dismissed as the idiosyncratic, aberrant response of an irrational mind. It is behavior that conforms, perhaps even overconforms, to gender stereotypes. Similarly, some of the psychological characteristics of suicidal women—such as their negative beliefs about self, the world and the future, and their indirect ways of relating to others—do not appear so irrational if examined in light of information about women's socialization and cultural values about femininity (Kaplan, 1983).

One place where consideration of gender and other contextual factors would be critical is at the time of assessment. Traditional suicide risk assessment (Bongar, 1991) could be supplemented with a gender role analysis (Brown, 1986; 1990; Canetto, 1994; McGrath, Keita, Strickland, & Russo, 1990). A gender role analysis requires being knowledgeable about the scholarship on gender socialization and its effects on mental health; it also involves being familiar with the interaction of gender, age, social class, ethnicity, culture and other demographic factors, in terms of risk factors and fit of interventions. Gender-aware clinicians inquire into the meanings of gender for clients and the consequence of gender noncompliance, based on the clients' family history, culture and age cohort. Gender-aware clinicians are also aware of their own assumptions about gender and how such assumptions may affect their judgments regarding diagnoses and treatment goals. A gender-role analysis with a suicidal woman should lead a clinician to ask questions such as: Are her symptoms exaggerations of stereotypical femininity? What does her suicidal behavior mean to her? How is suicidal behavior by females interpreted in her culture? How do significant others interpret and react to her suicidal behavior? Does she have a history of interpersonal neglect, exploitation, victimization? What are her financial, educational and employment resources? Is she a member of a marginalized group?

Each of the treatments proposed in the literature has advantages and drawbacks. Given the nature of suicidal women's problems, some treatments, however, may be more helpful than others. Biological interventions have the advantage of not requiring psychological self-awareness; on the other hand, they may promote passivity and reliance on external solutions; as Jack and Williams (1991b) put it, they "may be deskilling and create dependency" (p. 349).

Individual psychotherapies offer the suicidal person an opportunity to develop an exclusive relationship with a psychotherapist and to explore personal concerns in total privacy. One risk of individual interventions, however, especially psychodynamically oriented treatments, is that they may overemphasize an inner focus and overlook external influences, including familial, socioeconomic, cultural, and gender dynamics. Since introspection and privatization of problems are already encouraged by feminine socialization, and since suicidal women appear to be particularly vulnerable to negative and self-blaming cognitions, individual psychotherapies may end up reinforcing an already well-developed focus on internal states. As Nolen-Hoeksema (1987) concluded in her review of the literature on gender and depression, "if a ruminative response style amplifies women's vulnerability to depression, then the recommended interventions . . . should be ones that distract them from their mood" (p. 276).

There are no published empirical studies evaluating the effectiveness of group psychotherapy with suicidal persons (except for Linehan et al.'s 1991 study combining individual, group, and phone contact). Based on Farberow's (1968) and Linehan's work, as well as the literature on group psychotherapy for the treatment of depression (see McGrath et al., 1990, for a review) and the literature on self-help groups for substance abuse (see Canetto, 1991, for a review), there is reason to believe group formats could be uniquely suited to the treatment of suicidal women. For example, group formats could provide suicidal women an expanded source of social support, as well as opportunities for understanding the role of contextual factors. Group formats would also diminish the likelihood of exclusive emotional dependence on the psychotherapist (Canetto, 1991). Group therapy formats may be particularly relevant for suicidal women, as these women often are socially isolated (Arcel et al., 1991) and may have learned to view their problem as unique and self-generated (Cloward & Piven, 1979).

Although there are no systematic studies of the effectiveness of spouse involvement/family psychotherapy with suicidal persons, there are many reasons to believe that family modalities could be beneficial to suicidal women. First, according to a review by Canetto and Lester (1995), there is evidence that suicidal persons tend to be involved with significant others who are ambivalent, controlling, hostile, rejecting, and even physically abusive. In many cases, significant others communicate death wishes to the suicidal individual (Fellner, 1961; Richman, 1986; Richman & Rosenbaum, 1970; Rosenbaum & Richman, 1970; Wolk-Wasserman, 1985b). Finally, family members of suicidal persons often report having serious psychological problems of their own, including problems with autonomy (Canetto & Feldman, 1993) and a history of suicidal behavior (Wolk-Wasserman, 1985a).

A second line of evidence supporting the potential usefulness of family approaches are studies of communication, negotiation, and power in the relationships of suicidal persons (Arcel et al., 1991; Canetto & Feldman, 1993; Kirsch, 1982; Sefa-Dedeh & Canetto, 1992). It has been noted that suicidal women are involved in relationships in which their ability to negotiate is seriously restricted. Typically, these restrictions are not simply the result of insufficient assertiveness on the part of suicidal women, but rather the result of family and social structures supporting women's subordination. Family interventions may help address these negotiation and power inequities. Finally, the potential value of spouse involvement/family therapy for suicidal behavior is supported by the efficacy of these approaches in the treatment of other predominantly female disorders, such as depression and agoraphobia (Jacobson, Holtzworth-Munroe, & Schmaling, 1989).

Family involvement in the treatment of suicidal persons may take different forms. At the very least, the clinician may ask family members to provide information about the suicidal person. For example, Lesse, (1975) expects family members "to observe the patient . . . and to report to the therapist" (p. 321). One limitation of this approach is that it assumes that family members are psychologically healthy, genuinely concerned with, and/or capable of promoting, the well-being of the suicidal person, which may not be the case. The clinician may also choose to assess family members and engage them as full participants in treatment. This approach has several advantages, as it provides the therapist opportunities (a) to directly observe the family's dynamics; (b) to intervene in family dynamics that may trigger or maintain the suicidal behavior; (c) to provide support to concerned family members; (d) to help family members become more aware of their potential contribution to dysfunctional interactions and more supportive of the suicidal person; and (e) to reduce the suicidal person's and the family's reliance on the therapist. The use of family therapy would be limited in cases where family members are seriously abusive, uncooperative, or simply unavailable.

While therapy has its role and beneficial effects, it is important to remember that, to date, no treatment has been shown to be successful in preventing the long-term (18-month) risk of repeated suicidal behavior. One way to improve the success of treatments may be to make them more focused on the social, economic, employment, family, age and gender factors associated with the risk for suicidal behavior.

The problem with all treatments, however, is that they do not affect the incidence of suicidal behavior. As Albee (1990) has written in a paper entitled "The futility of psychotherapy," "no mass disease or disorder afflicting humankind has ever been eliminated by attempts at treating affected individuals" (p. 370). Another problem with treatments is that it may be hard to find enough helpers to provide the intense and long-term support suicidal individuals may need (see Linehan et al.'s 1991 one-year therapy package).

It has been suggested that sociocultural influences may prove more important than any treatment approach, and that a real reduction in rates of suicidal behavior will come only "when the nature of society itself changes" (Hirsch et al., 1983, p. 193S). Based on work by Hirsch and colleagues and Albee (Albee, 1986, 1990) it seems reasonable to conclude that the most promising development in the field of nonfatal suicidal behavior may be primary prevention programs targeting social and cultural risk factors. The incidence of women's nonfatal suicidal behavior is likely to drop if women are going to have improved access to employment. Rates of nonfatal suicidal behavior in women are also likely to be reduced if we stop socializing women into believing that "attempting suicide" is a reasonable "feminine" solution to problems in living.

ACKNOWLEDGMENT

I thank Jeremy Gersovitz and David B. Wohl for their editorial comments.

REFERENCES

Albee, G. W. (1986). Toward a just society: Lessons from observations on the primary prevention of psychopathology. *American Psychologist, 41*, 891–898.

Albee, G. W. (1990). The futility of psychotherapy. *The Journal of Mind and Behavior, 11*, 369–384.

Albee, G. W., & Canetto, S. S. (in press). The role of the family in prevention. In C. A. Heflinger (Ed.), *Families and mental health services for children and adolescents: Policy, services, and research*. Newbury Park, CA: Sage.

Ansel, E. L., & McGee, R. K. (1971). Attitudes toward suicide attempters. *Bulletin of Suicidology, 8*, 22–28.

Arcel, L. T., Mantonakis, J., Petersson, B., Jemos, J., & Kaliteraki, E. (1991). Suicide attempts among Greek and Danish women and the quality of their relationships with husbands or boyfriends. *Acta Psychiatrica Scandinavica, 85*, 189–195.

Bancroft, J. H. J., Skrimshire, A. M., & Simkin, S. (1986). The reasons people give for taking overdoses. *British Journal of psychiatry, 128*, 538–548.

Bancroft, J. H. J., Hawton, K. E., Simkin, S., Kingston, B., & Whitwell, D. (1979). The reasons people give for taking overdoses: A further inquiry. *British Journal of Medical Psychology*, 52, 353–365.

Bedrosian, R. C. (1986). Cognitive and family interventions for suicidal patients. *Journal of Psychotherapy and the Family, 2*, 129–152.

Birtchnell, J. (1983). Psychotherapeutic considerations in the management of the suicidal patient. *American Journal of Psychotherapy, 37*, 24–36.

Bongar, B. (1991). *The suicidal patient: Clinical and legal standard of care*. Washington, DC: American Psychological Association.

Bostock, T., & Williams, C. L. (1974). Attempted suicide as an operant behavior. *Archives of General Psychiatry, 31*, 482–486.

Brown, L. S. (1986). Gender-role analysis: A neglected component of psychological assessment. *Psychotherapy, 23*, 243–248.

Brown, L. S. (1990). Taking into account of gender in the clinical assessment interview. *Professional Psychology: Research and Practice, 21*, 12–17.

Canetto, S. S. (1991). Gender roles, suicide attempts, and substance abuse. *Journal of Psychology, 125*, 605–620.

Canetto, S. S. (1992–1993). She died for love and he for glory: Gender myths of suicidal behavior. *Omega, 26*, 1–17.

Canetto, S. S. (1994). Gender issues in the treatment of suicidal individuals. *Death Studies, 18*, 513–527.

Canetto, S. S., & Feldman, L. B. (1993). Overt and covert dependence in suicidal women and their male partners. *Omega, 27*, 177–194.

Canetto, S. S., & Lester, D. (1995). The epidemiology of women's suicidal behaviors. In S. S. Canetto & D. Lester (Eds.), *Women and suicidal behaviors* (pp. 35–57). New York: Springer.

Caplan, P. J., & Hall-McCorquodale, I. (1985). Mother-blaming in major clinical journals. *American Journal of Orthopsychiatry, 55*, 345–353.

Cloward, R. A., & Piven, F. F. (1979). Hidden protest: The channeling of female innovation and resistance. *Signs: Journal of Women in Culture and Society, 4*, 651–669.

Dew, M. A., Bromet, E. J., Brent, D., & Greenhouse, J. B. (1987). A quantitative literature review of the effectiveness of suicide prevention centers. *Journal of Consulting and Clinical Psychology, 55*, 239–244.

Dressler, D. M., Prusoff, B., Mark, H., & Shapiro, D. (1975). Clinician attitudes toward the suicide attempter. *Journal of Nervous and Mental Disease, 160,* 146–155.

Ellis, T. E. (1986). Toward a cognitive therapy for suicidal individuals. *Professional Psychology: Research and Practice, 17,* 125–130.

Farberow, N. L. (1968). Group psychotherapy with suicidal persons. In H. L. P. Resnik (Ed.), *Suicidal behaviors: Diagnosis and management* (pp. 328–340). Boston: Little Brown.

Fellner, C. H. (1961). Provocation of suicidal attempts. *Journal of Nervous and Mental Disease, 133,* 55–58.

Frederick, C. J., & Resnik, H. L. P. (1971). How suicidal behaviours are learned. *American Journal of Psychotherapy, 25,* 37–55.

Fremouw, W. J., de Perczel, M., & Ellis, T. E. (1990). *Suicide risk: Assessment and response guidelines.* New York: Pergamon Press.

Furst, S. S., & Ostow, M. (1979). The psychodynamics of suicide. In L. D. Hankoff & B. Einsidler (Eds.), *Suicide: Theory and clinical aspects* (pp. 165–178). Littleton, MA: PSG Publishing.

Goldblatt, M. J., & Schatzberg, A. F. (1990). Somatic treatment of the adult suicidal patient: A brief survey. In S. J. Blumenthal & D. J. Kupfer (Eds.), *Suicide over the life cycle: Risk factors, assessment, and treatment of suicidal patients* (pp. 425–440). Washington, DC: American Psychiatric Press.

Harris, J. R., & Myers, J. M. (1968). Hospital management of the suicidal patient. In H. L. P. Resnik (Ed.), *Suicidal behaviors: Diagnosis and management* (pp. 295–305). Boston: Little Brown.

Hawton, K., & Blackstock, E. (1976). General practice aspects of self-poisoning and self-injury. *Psychological Medicine, 6,* 571–575.

Hawton, K., Marsack, P., & Fagg, J. (1981). The attitudes of psychiatrists to deliberate self-poisoning: Comparison with physicians and nurses. *British Journal of Medical Psychology,* 54, 341–348.

Hawton, K., O'Grady, J., Osborn, M., & Cole, D. (1982). Adolescents who take overdoses: Their characteristics, problems and contact with helping agencies. *British Journal of Psychiatry, 140,* 118–123.

Hendin, H. (1951). Psychodynamic motivational factors in suicide. *Psychiatric Quarterly, 25,* 672–678.

Hendin, H. (1981). Psychotherapy and suicide. *American Journal of Psychotherapy,* 35, 469–480.

Heshusius, L. (1980). Female self-injury and suicide attempts: Culturally reinforced techniques in human relations. *Sex Roles, 6,* 843–857.

Hirsch, S. R., Walsh, C., & Draper, R. (1982). Parasuicide: A review of treatment interventions. *Journal of Affective Disorders, 4,* 299–311.

Hirsch, S. R., Walsh, C., & Draper, R. (1983). The concept and efficacy of the treatment of parasuicide. *British Journal of Clinical Pharmacology, 15,* 189S–194S.

Jack, R. L. (1992). *Women and attempted suicide.* Hillsdale, NJ: Erlbaum.

Jack, R. L., & Williams, J. M. (1991a). The role of attributions in self-poisoning. *British Journal of Clinical Psychology, 30,* 25–55.

Jack, R. L., & Williams, J. M. (1991b). Attribution and intervention in self-poisoning. *British Journal of Medical Psychology, 64,* 345–358.

Jacobson, N. S., Holtzworth-Munroe, A., & Schmaling, K. B. (1989). Marital therapy and spouse involvement in the treatment of depression, agoraphobia, and alcoholism. *Journal of Consulting and Clinical Psychology, 57*, 5–10.

Johnson, K. K. (1979). Durkheim revisited: "Why do women kill themselves?" *Suicide and Life-Threatening Behavior, 9*, 145–153.

Kaplan, A. G. (1987). Reflections on gender and psychotherapy. In M. Braude (Ed.) *Women, power and therapy: Issues for women* (pp. 11–24). New York: The Haworth Press.

Kaplan, A. G., & Klein, R. B. (1989). Women and suicide. In D. J. Jacobs & H. N. Brown (Eds.), *Suicide: Understanding and responding* (pp. 257–282). Madison, CT: International Universities Press.

Kaplan, H. I., & Sadock, B. J. (1988). *Synopsis of psychiatry*. Baltimore, MD: Williams & Wilkins.

Kaplan, M. (1983). A woman's view of DSM-III. *American Psychologist, 38*, 786–792.

Kiev, A. (1975). Psychotherapeutic strategies in the management of depressed and suicidal patients. *American Journal of Psychotherapy, 29*, 245–355.

Kirsch, N. L. (1982). Attempted suicide and restrictions in the eligibility to negotiate personal characteristics. *Advances in Descriptive Psychology, 3*, 249–274.

Lesse, S. (1975). The range of therapies in the treatment of severely depressed suicidal patients. *American Journal of Psychotherapy, 29*, 308 325.

Lester, D. (1989). The study of suicide from a feminist perspective. *Crisis, 11*, 38–43.

Liberman, R. P., & Eckman, T. (1981). Behavior therapy vs insight-oriented therapy for repeated suicide attempters. *Archives of General Psychiatry, 38*, 1126–1130.

Linehan, M. M. (1981). A social-behavioral analysis of suicide and parasuicide: Implications for clinical assessment and treatment. In J. F. Clarkin & H. I. Glazer (Eds.), *Depression: Behavioral and directive intervention strategies* (pp. 229–293). New York: Garland Press.

Linehan, M. M. (1987). Dialectical behavioral therapy: A cognitive behavioral approach to parasuicide. *Journal of Personality Disorders, 1*, 328–333.

Linehan, M. M., Armstrong, H. E., Suarez, A., Allmon, D., & Heard, H. L. (1991). Cognitive-behavioral treatment of chronically parasuicidal borderline patients. *Archives of General Psychiatry, 48*, 1060–1064.

Linehan, M. M., Camper, P., Chiles, J. A., Strosahl, K., & Shearin, E. (1987). Interpersonal problem solving and parasuicide. *Cognitive Therapy and Research, 11*, 1–12.

Maltsberger, J. T., & Buie, D. H. (1974). Countertransference hate in the treatment of suicidal patients. *Archives of General Psychiatry, 30*, 625–633.

Maltsberger, J. T., & Buie, D. H. (1989). Common errors in the management of suicidal patients. In D. J. Jacobs & H. N. Brown Eds.), *Suicide: Understanding and responding* (pp. 257–282). Madison, CT: International Universities Press.

McGrath, E., Keita, G. P., Strickland, B. R., & Russo, N. F. (1990). *Women and depression: Risk factors and treatment issues*. Washington, DC: American Psychological Association.

McIntosh, J. L. (1992). Older adults: The next suicide epidemic? *Suicide and Life-Threatening Behavior*, *22*, 322–332.

Miller, H. L., Coombs, D. W., Leeper, J. D., & Barton, S. N. (1984). An analysis on the effects of suicide prevention facilities on suicide rates in the United States. *American Journal of Public Health*, *74*, 340–343.

Mintz, R. S. (1961). Psychotherapy of the suicidal patient. In H. L. P. Resnik (Ed.), *Suicidal behaviors: Diagnosis and management* (pp. 271–296). Boston: Little Brown.

Moss, L. M., & Hamilton, D. M. (1956). Psychotherapy of the suicidal patient. *American Journal of Psychiatry*, *112*, 814–820.

Nidiffer, F. D. (1980). Combining cognitive and behavioral approaches to suicidal depression: A 42–month follow-up. *Psychological Reports*, *47*, 539–542.

Nolen-Hoeksema, S. (1987). Sex differences in unipolar depression: Evidence and theory. *Psychological Bulletin*, *101*, 259–282.

Novotny, P. (1972). Self-cutting. *Bulletin of the Menninger Clinic*, *36*, 505–514.

Olin, H. S. (1976). Psychotherapy of the chronically suicidal patient. *American Journal of Psychotherapy*, *30*, 570–575.

Patel, A. R. (1975). Attitudes towards self-poisoning. *British Medical Journal*, *2*, 426–430.

Ramon, S., Bancroft, J. H. J., & Skrimshire, A. M. (1975). Attitudes towards self-poisoning among physicians and nurses in a general hospital. *British Journal of Psychiatry*, *127*, 257–264.

Reid, W. H. (1989). *The treatment of psychiatric disorders: Revised for the DSM-III-R*. New York: Brunner/Mazel.

Richman, J. (1986). *Family therapy for suicidal people*. New York: Springer.

Richman, J., & Rosenbaum, M. (1970). A clinical study of the role of hostility and death wished by the family and society in suicidal attempts. *The Israel Annals of Psychiatry and Related Disciplines*, *8*, 213–231.

Rosenbaum, M., & Richman, J. (1970). Suicide: The role of hostility and death wishes from the family and significant others. *American Journal of Psychiatry*, *126*, 128–131.

Salkovskis, P. M., Atha, C., & Storer, D. (1990). Cognitive-behavioral problem solving in the treatment of patients who repeatedly attempt suicide: A controlled trial. *British Journal of Psychiatry*, *157*, 871–876.

Schotte, D. E., & Clum, G. A. (1987). Problem-solving skills in suicidal psychiatric patients. *Journal of Consulting and Clinical Psychology*, *55*, 49–54.

Schotte, D. E., Cools, J., & Payvar, S. (1990). Problem-solving deficits in suicidal patients: Trait vulnerability or state phenomenon? *Journal of Consulting and Clinical Psychology*, *58*, 562–564.

Schrut, A., & Michels, T. (1974). Suicidal divorced and discarded women. *Journal of the American Academy of Psychoanalysis*, *2*, 329–347.

Schwartz, D. A. (1979). The suicidal character. *Psychiatric Quarterly*, *51*, 64–70.

Schwartz, D. A., Flinn, D. E., & Slawson, P. F. (1974). Treatment of the suicidal character. *American Journal of Psychotherapy*, *28*, 194–207.

Sefa-Dedeh, A., & Canetto, S. S. (1992). Women, family and suicidal behavior in

Ghana. In U. W. Gielen, L. L. Adler, & N. Milgram (Eds.), *Psychology in international perspective* (pp. 299–309). Amsterdam: Swets & Zeitlinger.

Simpson, M. A. (1976). Self-mutilation and suicide. In E. S. Shneidman (Ed.), *Suicidology: Contemporary developments* (pp. 281–315). New York: Grune and Stratton.

Stillion, J. (1995). Through a glass darkly: Women and attitudes toward suicidal behavior. In S. S. Canetto & D. Lester (Eds.), *Women and suicidal behavior* (pp. 71–84). New York: Springer.

Tabachnick, N. (1961a). Interpersonal relations in suicidal attempts. *Archives of General Psychiatry, 4,* 16–21.

Tabachnick, N. (1961b). Countertransference crisis in suicidal attempts. *Archives of General Psychiatry, 4,* 64–70.

Tekavcic-Grad, O., Farberow, N. L., Zavasnik, A., Mocnik, M. & Korenjak, R. (1988). Comparison of the two telephone crisis lines in Los Angeles (USA) and in Ljubljana (Yugoslavia), *Crisis, 9,* 146–157.

Turner, R. J. (1980). The use of health services prior to non-fatal deliberate self-harm. In R. D. Farmer & S. R. Hirsch (Eds.), *The suicide syndrome* (pp. 173–186). Beckenham, Kent: Croom Helm.

Wolfersdorf, M., Blattner, J., Grober, M., Nelson, F., & Dalton-Taylor, B. (1989). Who calls? A comparison of callers of the telephone service at the Suicide Prevention Center, Los Angeles, CA, USA, and the callers of the "Telephonseelsorge," Ravensburg, FRG. *European Journal of Psychiatry, 3,* 33–48.

Wolk-Wasserman, D. (1985a). The intensive care unit and the suicide attempt patient. *Acta Psychiatrica Scandinavica, 71,* 581–595.

Wolk-Wasserman, D. (1985b). Suicidal communication of persons attempting suicide and responses of significant others. *Acta Psychiatrica Scandinavica, 73,* 481–499.

Zich, J. M. (1984). A reciprocal control approach to the treatment of repeated parasuicide. *Suicide and Life-Threatening Behavior, 14,* 36–51.

Zinberg, N. E. (1989). The threat of suicide in psychotherapy. In D. J. Jacobs & H. N. Brown (Eds.), *Suicide: Understanding and responding* (pp. 295–327). Madison, CT: International Universities Press.

19
Surviving the Suicidal Death of a Loved One: Women's Experience of Grief Integration

Lois Sapsford

Working as a suicide bereavement counselor, I found myself challenged by the stories of the women who attempted to unravel an experience of suicide in the family. I noticed a recurring incongruence between my clients' experiences and needs and the grief theory that served as my clinical framework. Clients provided feedback about the literature I had given them, indicating that it was somewhat helpful *but* that it did not fit their experience. In fact, it often angered them, eliciting accusations of "They obviously don't understand me."

Traditional theories of grief begin with the "acceptance of the death" stage and end with a final stage of "resolution," described as withdrawal of energy from the dead and re-investment in the living (Worden, 1982), acceptance (Kübler-Ross, 1969), reorganization (Bowlby, 1980), or resolution of grief (Rando, 1988). Without exception, the suicide bereavement literature approaches the phenomenon of grief based on these resolution models (Barrett, 1989; Hewett, 1980).

The suicide grief research literature has tended to focus on: (a) the immediate grief reactions, from 6 weeks after the suicide up to, and including, the first year of grief (Calhoun, Selby, & Faulstich, 1980; Demi, 1984; Shneidman, 1985; Solomon, 1981; Whitis, 1968; Wrobleski & McIntosh, 1987) and (b) suicide-related grief symptoms, as compared to nonsuicidedeath grief symptoms (Demi, 1978; Demi & Miles, 1988; Glick, Weiss & Parkes, 1974; Henslin, 1972; McIntosh & Kelly, 1988; Parkes, 1975; Shepherd & Barraclough, 1974; Sheskin & Wallace, 1976; Silverman, 1972).

The paucity of empirical and theoretical literature regarding the process and outcome of grief beyond the first year was recognized as an area requiring study at the 1989 American Association of Suicidology Annual Meeting. Panel members Dunne, Pfeffer, Farberow and Rudestam concluded that "the impact of loss upon all family members; the process and outcome of bereavement beyond the first year; and the impact on the family system required extensive future study" (Archibald, 1989, p. 9). What is the long-term experience of women's grief after the suicidal death of a family member?

THE STUDY

I chose a qualitative research design based on Glaser and Strauss' grounded theory methodology (Glaser, 1978; Glaser & Strauss, 1967). Chenitz and Swanson (1986) have defined grounded theory as: "a highly systematic research approach for the collection and analysis of qualitative data for the purpose of generating explanatory theory that furthers the understanding of social and psychological phenomena" (p. 3). Within the boundaries of grounded theory methodology, my task was to learn from women who had experienced a death by suicide in their family, and to develop a theoretical understanding of their grieving based solely on their accounts, leaving the aside traditional theories about grief. This methodology is in keeping with feminist principles (Miller, 1986).

The sample of four chosen for the study included women who had sought counseling after the suicide of someone in their family, as well as women who had had a close family member die by suicide, but who had not sought counseling to deal with this tragedy. All women had experienced the death by suicide of a close male family member (ranging from three to seventeen years prior).

Data were collected using an unstructured in-depth interview. I sought to focus on the respondent's own words (Chenitz & Swanson, 1986). Each respondent's interview was audiotaped and transcribed in full. Open-ended questions were preferred (e.g., "What has been your experience of grief after the suicide of your family member?") to avoid imposing a set framework upon women's experience (Suransky, 1982).

The constant comparative method of analysis as developed by Glaser and Strauss (1967) was used to analyze the data collected. Following this method, data collection and analysis occurred simultaneously, resulting in the generation of grounded theory. Theoretical sampling continued until the core categories were "saturated"; that is, "no new data and no additions are added to the category and one overriding core category can explain the relationship between all of the others" (Chenitz & Swanson, 1986, p. 8).

Qualitative research must be measured in terms of responsibility and credibility. Responsibility means that the researcher must be trustworthy enough to represent the participant's experience. Each piece of emerging theory was discussed with the participants in a group format, and confirmation by the participants was one criterion for judging the accuracy of my interpretations. One woman in my study cried as she read the first draft of the developing model, noting the impact of reading an accurate account of her experience and receiving validation of her experience by hearing others describing the same process.

Credibility in qualitative research requires answering the question, "If I apply this theory to a similar situation, will it work, that is, allow me to interpret, understand, and predict phenomena?" (Chenitz & Swanson, 1986, p. 13). On the basis of the information obtained in the interviews, a model of long-term grief in women survivors was developed.

THE STUDY'S PARTICIPANTS

Anna

Anna, a single, 30-year-old psychologist, was raised in a small Canadian prairie town in a family of five. Anna related that she was close to both her siblings as children. However, she was particularly close to "Ned," her now-deceased brother. In describing their relationship she stated: "We were always very close. We just liked one another's personalities—a real connection between the two of us."

Anna remembered experiencing a "sixth sense as to something being wrong" on the day her brother killed himself. She found herself avoiding answering her phone at work during that day. She stalled going home after work certain that the telephone was going to deliver a sad message. "I found myself becoming just more and more saddened—and defensive and wanting to protect myself and my time. Finally the news came (he killed himself) and . . . it was horrible!"

Betty

Betty, a 42-year-old journalist and single mother, described an estranged relationship with her parents. The lack of stability and consistent caring by her parents was the main reason she and her brother developed a strong relationship. "It was Bob and I against the world."

Betty clearly remembers receiving word of her brother's death by suicide while in Europe, where she had moved with her husband. "my husband, came home with the padre and said—(pause)—your brother's dead. It had happened 3 days prior, and my parents had already cremated him, and he was gone."

Betty tried escaping from her feelings. She became dependent on both prescription and street drugs. For 15 years after her brother's suicide she describes herself as "absolutely blocking it [the death by suicide]. I just wouldn't allow it in."

Sixteen years later, Betty "allowed" herself to face her grief. While searching for information about her brother's death, she recalls being told by professionals that her grief should not be as important or as real to her after sixteen years: "I was so angry at them. I thought—it's got nothing to do with whether it's been 16 years ago . . . 16 years ago . . . is just the date. It actually happened last month."

Connie

Connie, age 36, was employed as a secretary in a senior citizens' complex. She was single and lived alone. She introduced herself through a description of her family. "I have one brother left, but we're not even close; and I'm not my Dad's little baby anymore because he's not there and I . . . never was my Mom's little baby. She's my little baby, sort of."

Connie's brother, Mike, killed himself a couple of years after he had been diagnosed with diabetes. He had become very depressed and underwent a "whole personality change." Connie describes her relationship with Mike as "my closest family connection." Connie was informed of her brother Mike's death by suicide by her father: "and then I got a phone call from my father one day that Mike had shot himself in the middle of the night and it was—I guess—shock, you know, for the whole two weeks."

Connie recalled a conversation with her brother David just prior to David's own death by suicide, 7 years after Mike's death by suicide:

> We'd been talking about Mike committing suicide and David was saying that he was going to commit suicide . . . He said to me, nobody has any right to tell anybody else that they have to live and I said yes, I realize that, . . . like that couldn't happen twice, but it did.

Connie remembered her reaction after hearing about David's suicide. "It made me think of it more; for a while . . . I thought that maybe I had to, too, for some reason."

Debbie

Debbie, a 39-year-old widow of 3 years, and mother of two preteen daughters, related how she wanted to share her experience of her husband's suicide to help others deal with grief. She had a university degree and was employed as a hair stylist.

Debbie discussed the changes over time in her marriage from mutual caring to her assuming a caretaking role for her husband. Her husband had been hospitalized three times for severe depression. "I felt more like his mother, I didn't feel like a wife anymore."

Debbie told of an incident that occurred the night before her husband's death by suicide.

> Gary asked me to read to him, I just thought he really needs a mother right now, so we sat on the couch and he had his head on my lap and I read to him—that night Gary was up all night pacing and smoking.

He ended his life the next day right after Debbie had left the house to call the physician because of her growing concern for his physical and mental well-being. Debbie returned to their home to discover his body.

> I called his name and looked in the kitchen and bedroom and then I went downstairs. He was laying down on the floor and I thought his head was smashed in, I thought he smashed his head in with something—(cries)—and his eye was gone, you could see the brains—(cries)—there was no blood.—I ran outside and screamed for help!—(cries)—How can I tell my kids that their Dad is gone?

GRIEF INTEGRATION: A THEORETICAL MODEL

The model of grief integration is based on the stories narrated by the four women introduced above. Rather than seeing grief as leading to a finite "resolution," this model proposes that grief after suicide is a life-long process. The model also suggests that the stages of grief are experienced in a nonlinear fashion; each stage within a cycle can be repeated, bringing the griever to a new level of integration. According to the study's participants, grief involves "maintaining and re-creating the relationship" with the deceased. It is an emotional connection with the deceased that allows for an integration of the grief. A summary of the Grief Integration Model is presented in Table 19.1 and Figure 19.1.

Phase I: Grief Suppression

Some of the women discussed how their role as family caretaker led them to "push aside" their grief, in order to facilitate caring for the pain of others. Other women described denying the importance of the death by replacing

TABLE 19.1 Summary of the Grief Integration Model

Phase I—Grief Suppression

Characteristics:
Caretaking
Replacement
Running/escaping
Safety is a necessary precondition to movement into Phase II.

Phase II—Grief Emergence

Stage 1: Meaning Making
Focus: Outward/Suicide-Related
Characteristics:
Searching
Need for information
Spiritual questioning
Social stigma

Stage 2: Intense Grief
Focus: Inward/Suicide-Related
Characteristics:
Guilt
Anger
Sadness
Fear
Shame
Unpredictability
Preoccupation with the deceased
Physical health problems

Stage 3: Implications for the Self
Focus: Inward/Self-Related
Characteristics:
Abandonment
Identity loss
Connectedness
Dreams
Presence felt
Family shifts
Social expectations

Stage 4: Action in Relation
Focus: Outward/Self-In-Relation
Characteristics:
Completing picture of the deceased
Recreating existing relationships
Authenticity
Self-empathy
Permission

TABLE 19.1 Continued

Phase III – Grief Integration
Characteristics:
Grief residing with the survivor
Altered quality/frequency/duration of grief
Re-creation of relationship with deceased
Dreams as connection
Replacing the suicide as most important memory

the deceased with another person, and attempting to become a new person in a new relationship. Avoidance of grief was achieved by some women through alcohol, drugs, and multiple moves.

The women were able to move out of this phase when they felt safe enough to grieve. A critical condition of safety was defined by the research participants as a sense of control over their life and some sense of confidence in one's own and others' survival. This safety was often found in the family. If family support was unavailable, the women had to feel connected with a supportive social network before they could move on to the "emergence" phase.

Phase II: Grief Emergence

The "emergence" phase involved four interrelated stages.

Stage 1: Meaning Making

At the stage of meaning-making, women focused on the suicidal act. They remembered seeking information in order to "make sense" of the fact that someone very close to them had taken his own life. Their energy was directed outward. At this stage, many women engaged in spiritual questioning. This experience involved drawing upon and/or discarding spiritual beliefs.

Stage 2: Intense Grief

The "intense grief" stage involved examining one's own emotional response. For most women this stage was characterized by feelings of guilt, anger, sadness, fear, shame, unpredictability, idolization of, and pre-occupation with, the deceased, and physical health problems. It is during this stage that all the survivors reported being at the highest risk for suicidal behavior.

Betty described her feeling of being overwhelmed by emotions.

> There was a time when I could never stop crying, . . . I had nightmares, . . . and then I was getting caught up in the whole loneliness, you

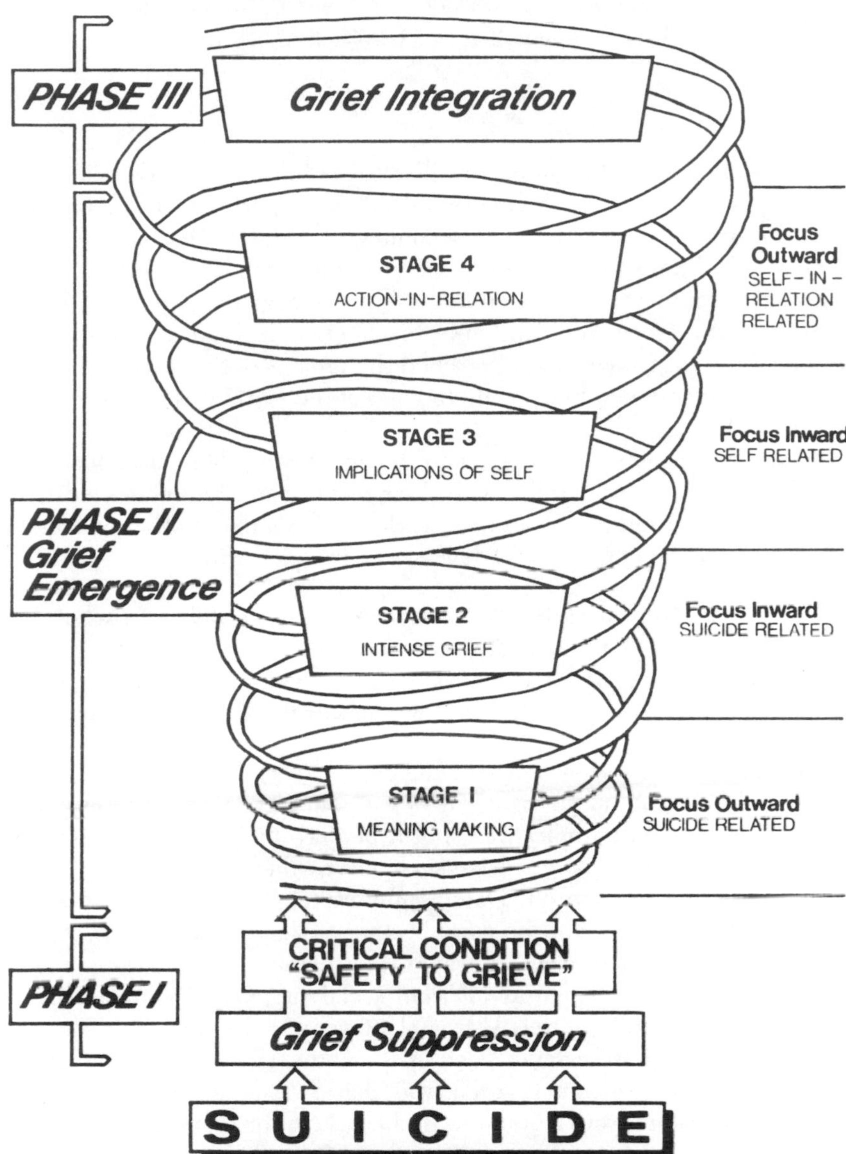

Figure 19.1. Grief Integration Model

> know, what he was feeling at that time and God—it must have been hell—I get scared of that [her own suicide] because . . . we look alike, we have a lot of character similarities . . . I isolated myself and I stopped growing.

Stage 3: Implications for the Self

Attention shifted from the suicide to the self. Many women described a feeling of abandonment and loss of identity. They reported focusing on the relationship with the deceased and becoming aware of a sense of connectedness. Many of the women also experienced a fear of identity-loss as they felt strongly identified with the relationship; all began wondering which personal qualities they would be able to maintain without a relationship with the deceased. One woman described the dreams of the deceased as "a comforting connection to him" while the rest of the world was telling her to move on.

At this stage many survivors acknowledged having thought about killing themselves as they struggled with their identity and the often conflicting message presented by their social world. For example, Betty described an overwhelming feeling of loss-of-self as she struggled with the loss.

> I think what happened was—I really had become invisible. I really didn't know who I was because [my brother] was . . . who I could check out who I was with. He made my identity. It was him I relied on. When he was gone, there was nobody—there was nobody there!

The attitude of family, friends, clinicians, and society at large were described similarly by all the survivors. They experienced being pushed to "let go of him," "get on with [their] life," "put it behind you," "finish your grieving and get on with it." Upon hearing such advice, they felt misunderstood, and angered. "It pisses me off. Damn right. What do you mean, let him go—shit. I can't let him go—he's my brother!" They responded to these pressures by cutting themselves off from these "helping" relationships.

Connie described being cut off from social supports due to people's "false expectations" for her grief. Also, as she turned to the clinical literature for support, she found the same "lack of . . . understanding . . . That grief book makes me sick. The one that tells you [that] . . . you're going to be mad for a month, and then you're going to be blah, blah for a month, and then it's going to be over."

Many survivors remembered a feeling of wanting others to hear how important it was for them to remember and maintain a connection with the deceased. Anna expressed this need in her comment, "Why aren't you able to hear my grief when my brother died?"

It seems that survivors moved into the new stage of grieving when they realized that they did not need to give up the personal qualities that had been developed in relationship with the deceased, and that they could maintain a connection with the deceased in a new way.

Stage 4: Action in Relation

During this stage, survivors typically engaged in various outward-oriented activities. They asked themselves: Who was he outside of his relationship with me? Completing the picture of the deceased allowed the survivor to begin establishing a different relationship with the deceased—to see him in a "different light."

Each of the survivors experienced new honesty about themselves and the relationships they chose to maintain, create, or terminate at this time. Anna described this honesty in the following manner: "There's some really good things that have happened with the family. We were always really close. But I think there's more acceptance of one another's differences, of our weaknesses."

She also talked about the importance of her friendships: "My friendships are very precious to me and I experience their meaning in a different way since my brother died. I pay more attention to people. I listen more. I take more of an interest."

Another common experience of survivors was that of permitting themselves to still feel sad. Anna described her sadness in the following words:

> I can't say . . . it's a constant state. It's more what I go through at points in time. The missing [him] is probably stronger with the passage of time, . . . But the missing him doesn't have to be the despairing kind of longing for him to be back like it was at the outset . . . What accompanies [missing him is] . . . more understanding of why he made the choice to kill himself and what he had to offer when he was here.

Acceptance of their own sadness, and the continued discussion of the deceased's influence in their lives, however, continued to be viewed by others as pathological. All women found ways to counteract this message. Some found the validation they sought within their new and stronger sense of identity. All recognized their need to listen first to their own experience. Betty described her desire to be connected with other suicide survivors as a way of adding more strength to her experience: Connie and Debbie both became involved in survivor support groups, and noted the benefit in having their continued connection to the deceased validated by other survivors.

Phase III: Grief Integration

The key characteristic of this phase was that grief was experienced as residing within the survivor. Connie described her thoughts about grief integration in the following manner: "I guess mine [grief] is sort of like . . . traveling with me, . . . and it will always be there. . . . like a circle around you." Connie's description of her grief "traveling with" her was interpreted as an indication that an integration process had taken place. She experienced a continued connection with her deceased brothers. "It's like it [grief] is a part of me. Everything is connected to me, everything that's ever happened is."

The circular and developmental nature of her grief is described in the following words: "I really think this [grief] could go on forever. . . . I don't believe that you resolve . . . a suicide, . . . that grief at all . . . I don't think I ever will. I think it goes through changes . . . daily."

Similarly, Anna discussed her grief as "residing with" her. "What's different is I don't feel the sense of horror. It doesn't feel so raw, . . . because I've lived with that . . . almost three years, so it . . . resides with me easier."

Many women also talked about a need to replace the suicidal act as the most important memory of the deceased. As a result of their obtaining a fuller picture of the deceased, they were able to integrate this picture into their grief; his qualities and strengths while alive replaced the suicidal death as the most prominent memory of him. "The most important thing in his life was art . . . and . . . art [has] become the most important memory [of him] rather than the suicide."

All the women in the study reported some continuing concerns about developing trusting relationships with men. Anna discussed not being able to trust her own judgement in choosing close relationships with men. "I lost some people I loved the most, and I'm not going to give that (trust) to anyone else."

DISCUSSION

According to Worden (1982), grieving ultimately requires an "emotional withdrawal from the deceased person so that this emotional energy can be reinvested in another relationship" (p. 15). This notion of withdrawal does not fit the experiences of the survivors interviewed in this study. Grief was described by them as a life-long process. Many saw the term "resolution" as inadequate to account for their experience. In Anna's word's, "to resolve [to me] means that something is terminated—and I think about him every single day, and every day in some way. And so that letting go, I'm not going to let go of the image." Rather than seeing grief as involving an emotional withdrawal, the women in my study talked about "maintaining and re-creating the relationship" with the deceased. This difference in terminology is not just a minor nuance in language. Rather, it refers to a different experience in the griever, with unique social and clinical implications.

The grief model that emerged from my study of bereavement is different from most stage models of bereavement. For example, in the most recent comprehensive work on suicide bereavement, *Life after suicide: The survivor's grief experience* (Barrett, 1989), the grief process is seen as a dual process of separation and reconstruction:

> Separation: Initially, then the function of grief is to help the survivor detach emotionally from the deceased. If detachment does not occur, the survivor will cling both emotionally and psychologically to the deceased.
>
> Recovery: the specific purpose of the reconstruction process is to re-direct the survivor's emotional investment away from the decedent and toward new relationships. (p. 19)

According to Barrett's (1989) model, "only after emotional detachment from the decedent is accomplished can the task of recovery from grief be earnestly pursued" (p. 106). According to the model I developed, integration (not recovery) and re-defining the relationship (not emotional detachment) are the key processes in grief work.

My grief integration model is consistent with the conclusions of a recent review of empirical evidence on suicide bereavement (Van Der Wal, 1990). According to Van Der Wal, death "only ends life; it does not end a relationship" (p. 158). She argues that available studies have not given "clear indications regarding the degree of integration. The lack of long-term research automatically results in a lack of information with regard to integration of the loss" (p. 158).

Thinking about grief in terms of integration rather than resolution is also consistent with theoretical developments in the literature on the psychology of women (Tavris, 1991). Until recently, women were understood largely in terms of what they were missing when measured against a male paradigm. One of the main premises of the emerging women's developmental theory is that "women's core self-structure, or their primary motivational thrust, concerns growth within relationship, or what we call the 'self-in-relation' (Kaplan, 1991, p. 3)." Within this framework, connection with others is a key component of psychological growth.

Within my grief model, women experience grief as growth within a relationship. Change in the relationship with the deceased parallel changes in the sense of self.

The grief integration model has several clinical applications. Counselors may consider encouraging their grieving clients to re-connect with the deceased, rather than prescribing the "letting go" or "resolution" of grief. It may also be useful to introduce clients to the grief integration model at time of initial contact as a way to stimulate discussion regarding the survivor's own experience of grief. The model should not be presented as the "normative truth." Each survivor's experience should help refine this emergent model.

EPILOGUE

Victoria Alexander (1987) described her changed sense of self following her mother's death by suicide:

> I am not the same person I was before my mother's death, not only because of her loss, but because suicide has become part of the vocabulary of my experience. It has a permanent place at the core of my life, and I am both more vulnerable and stronger for it. (p. 117)

Within the model of grief integration, grief "has a permanent place." In Connie's words, grief is never "resolved." Rather it becomes "a part" of the person.

Connie, killed herself a couple of years after the completion of this study. Like most people who kill themselves, she did not leave explanations of her act. Those of us who had been privileged to know her and learn from her will have to struggle through our own process of grief. As a researcher and therapist, I now find myself in the role of suicide survivor. As I remember Connie and reflect on those things I learned about myself and about her experience, I more fully understand the process of finding a place for that grief to be a part of who I am. I am beginning to understand Connie's words: "It's like grief is a part of me. Everything is connected to me, everything that's ever happened." My hope is that her death will remind us of the importance of furthering understanding of the experience of those who are left to grieve.

ACKNOWLEDGMENT

This chapter is dedicated to my co-researchers—Anna, Betty, Connie, and Debbie. Their courage in sharing their stories, their tears and their wisdom, creates the essence of this research.

REFERENCES

Alexander, V. (1987). Living through my mother's suicide, In E. Dunne, J. McIntosh, & K. Dunne-Maxim (Eds.), *Suicide and its aftermath* (pp. 109–117). New York: Norton.

Archibald, L. (1989, Summer). Suicide bereavement research. *NewsLink, 14*, p. 9.

Barrett, T. (1989). *Life after suicide: The survivor's grief experience*. Fargo, ND: Aftermath Research.

Bowlby, J. (1980). *Attachment and loss: Vol. III. Loss, sadness and depression*. New York: Basic Books.

Calhoun, L. G. Selby, J. W., & Faulstich, M. E. (1980). Reactions to the parents of

the child suicide: A study of social impressions. *Journal of Consulting and Clinical Psychology, 48*, 535–536.
Chenitz, W. C., & Swanson, J. M. (1986). *From practice to grounded theory*. Menlo Park, CA: Addison-Wesley.
Demi, A. M. (1978). Suicide and non-suicide survivors compared. *Community Nursing Research, 11*, 91–99.
Demi, A. S. (1984). Social adjustment of widows after a sudden death: Suicide and non-suicide survivors compared. *Death Education, 8*, 91–111.
Demi, A. S., & Miles, M. S. (1988). Suicide bereaved parents: Emotional distress and physical health problems. *Death Studies, 12*, 297–307.
Glaser, B. G. (1978). *Theoretical sensitivity*. Mill Valley, CA: Sociology Press.
Glaser, B. G., & Strauss, A. L. (1967). *The discovery of grounded theory*. Chicago: Aldine de Gruyter.
Glick, I., Weiss, R., & Parkes, C. (1974). *The first year of bereavement*. New York: Wiley.
Henslin, J. (1972). Strategies of adjustment: An ethnomethodological approach to the study of guilt and suicide. In A. C. Cain (Ed.), *Survivors of suicide* (pp. 215–227). Springfield, IL: Charles C. Thomas.
Hewett, J. H. (1980). *After suicide*. Philadelphia: Westminster Press.
Kaplan, A. G. (1991). The self-in-relation: Implications for depression in women. In J. Jordan, A. Kaplan, J. B. Miller, I. Stiver, & J. Surrey, *Women's growth in connection: Writings from the Stone Center* (pp. 206–222). New York: Guilford,
Kübler-Ross, E. (1969). *On death and dying*. New York: Macmillan.
McIntosh, J. L., & Kelly L. D. (1988). Survivors' reactions: Suicide vs. other causes. In D. Lester (Ed.), *Suicide '88* (pp. 89–90). Denver, CO: American Association of Suicidology.
Miller, J. B. (1986). *Toward a new psychology of women*. Boston: Beacon Press.
Parkes, C. M. (1975). Unexpected and untimely bereavement: A statistical study of young Boston widows and widowers. In B. Schoenberg (Ed.), *Bereavement: Psychosocial aspects* (pp. 119–138). New York: Columbia University Press.
Shepherd, D., & Barraclough, B. M. (1974). The aftermath of suicide. *British Medical Journal, 2*, 600–603.
Sheskin, A., & Wallace S. E. (1976). Differing bereavements: Suicide, natural, and accidental death. *Omega, 7*, 229–242.
Shneidman, E. S. (1985). Some thoughts on grief and mourning. *Suicide and Life Threatening Behavior, 15*, 51–55.
Silverman, P. R. (1972). Intervention with the widow of a suicide. In A. C. Cain (Ed.), *Survivors of suicide* (pp. 186–214). Springfield IL: Charles C. Thomas.
Solomon, M. I. (1981). Bereavement following suicide. *Psychiatric Nursing, 22*, 18–19.
Suransky, V. P. (1982). *The erosion of childhood*. Chicago: University of Chicago Press.
Tavris, C. (1991). The mismeasure of women: Paradoxes and perspectives in the study of gender. In J. P. Goodchilds (Ed.), *Psychological perspectives on human diversity in America* (pp. 87–136). Washington, DC: American Psychological Association.

Van Der Wal, J. (1990). The aftermath of suicide: A review of empirical evidence. *Omega, 20*, 149–171.

Whitis, P. R. (1968). The legacy of a child's suicide, *Family Process*, 7, 159–169.

Worden, W. J. (1982). *Grief counseling and grief therapy: A handbook for the mental health practitioner*, New York: Springer.

Wrobleski, A., & McIntosh, J. L. (1987). Problems of suicide survivors: A survey report. *Israel Journal of Psychiatry and Related Sciences, 24*, 137–142.

Index